CW00942963

Monastic Archaeology

Papers on the Study of Medieval Monasteries

Monastic Archaeology

Papers on the Study of Medieval Monasteries

Edited by

Graham Keevill, Mick Aston and Teresa Hall

Oxbow Books

Published by
Oxbow Books, Park End Place, Oxford OX1 1HN

© Oxbow Books and the individual authors, 2001

ISBN 1 84217 047 3

A CIP record for this book is available from the British Library

This book is available direct from

Oxbow Books, Park End Place, Oxford OX1 1HN
(Phone: 01865-241249; Fax: 01865-794449)

and

The David Brown Book Company
PO Box 511, Oakville, CT 06779, USA
(Phone: 860-945-9329; Fax: 860-945-9468)

or from our website

www.oxbowbooks.com

*Cover illustration: Trinity MS R.17.1 ff.284–5: Christ Church waterworks drawing
(reproduced by courtesy of the Master and Fellows of Trinity College Cambridge)*

Printed in Great Britain at
The Short Run Press
Exeter

Contents

1   Introduction: Past approaches to the archaeological study of monastic sites
    (Graham D Keevill) 1

2   Strategies for Future Research and Site Investigation *(J Patrick Greene)* 4

3   The Expansion of the Monastic and Religious Orders of Europe
    from the Eleventh Century *(Michael Aston)* 9

4   Living in a Vale of Tears: Cistercians and site management in France:
    Pontigny and Fontfroide *(Terryl N Kinder)* 37

5   Production and Consumption of Food and Drink in the Medieval Monastery
    (James Bond) 54

6   Monastic Water Management in Great Britain: A review *(James Bond)* 88

7   Pieces of Patterns – Archaeological Approaches to Monastic Sites in Oxfordshire
    (Graham D Keevill) 137

8   Romsey Abbey: Benedictine Nunnery and parish church *(Ian R Scott)* 150

9   The Planning and Development of a Carthusian Church – the example
    of St Anne's Charterhouse, Coventry *(Iain Soden)* 161

10 The Demolition and Conversion of former monastic buildings
    in post-dissolution Hertfordshire *(Nick Doggett)* 165

11 Fountains Abbey: archaeological research directed by conservation
    and presentation *(Glyn Coppack)* 175

12 The Hulton Abbey Project: research archaeology and public accountability
    (W Klemperer) 183

13 Education on Abbey Sites *(Liz Hollinshead)* 192

1   Introduction: Past approaches to the archaeological study of monastic sites

Graham D Keevill

The pioneering monastic studies of the late 19th century through to the 1930s perhaps inevitably placed an extremely strong emphasis on the elucidation of ground plans. Information on plan development was also desirable where possible (though interpretations made then are by no means unchallengeable because of the partial nature of the studies; see Coppack, this volume). The best analyses were often based on detailed site surveys allied to extensive documentary research, and some of the extraordinary ground plans (often covering very large surface areas in difficult terrain) stand as lasting testaments to the work of their producers. Sites were studied systematically, and the detailed descriptive reports which appeared virtually annually in the likes of *Archaeologia*, the *Antiquaries Journal* and the *Archaeological Journal* (to say nothing of county periodicals) graphically demonstrate the pioneering zeal and industry of St John Hope, Norman, Brakspear, Clapham, Peers and others. Nevertheless there are few of these surveys which can be taken entirely on trust today, especially where further work has since taken place.

It is not necessarily surprising that most of the surveyors began with a general notion of how monastic plans should look. There were, after all, Catholic monasteries in Britain and Europe to provide a living template, along with post-Dissolution surveys, descriptions and illustrations of many medieval houses. There were also a number of medieval depictions of monastic houses and their precincts to provide a contemporary witness (most notably the famous St Gall template of the 9th century, and the equally well-known late 12th-century plans of Christ Church Canterbury). The basic requirements of church and cloister with buildings ranged around them were fairly readily understood, but the best early surveys recognised that this was not a blueprint that all sites would

automatically conform to. The influence of local topography on the location of the cloister to the south or north of the church was easily recognisable, and the importance of water supplies was also clear. Detailed studies could take this further; at Worcester, for instance, the unusual location of the dorter and reredorter on the west side of the cloister was recognised as a pragmatic use of the location: the river Severn ran along this side of the abbey precinct (Brakspear 1916). An important series of papers also sought to examine the influence of different orders on the architecture and layout of monasteries (eg Clapham 1923; Graham and Clapham 1926), or specific aspects of monastic sites such as water supply (Micklethwaite 1893; Norman 1899; St John Hope 1902; Norman and Mann 1909), while others examined sites on a regional basis (eg Brakspear 1928).

Inevitably, however, the strength of emphasis on the plan tended to restrict the degree of attention to detail around and within the monastic buildings. Furthermore attention was so strongly focused on the church and cloister that the service ranges of the outer court and on occasion even such important inner areas as the infirmary cloister were often overlooked. There are exceptions, of course, such as St John Hope's survey of Hulne (St John Hope 1890), and Brakspear in particular was ahead of his time in this as in other areas of his work. The general attitude was clear, however, and continued largely unaltered into the 1950s, when the recognition of medieval archaeology brought with it a greater sensitivity to the overall monastic environment. Nevertheless a conscious and general shift of emphasis away from church and cloister towards the wider monastic landscape had to wait until much more recent times (see, for instance, virtually all of the papers in Gilchrist and Mytum 1989). The change was codified in the Society for Medieval Archaeology's submission of a framework of research priorities (SMA 1987, section I(c)ii) to English Heritage. Curiously the eventual English Heritage report (EH 1991) scarcely mentioned *any* aspect of monastic archaeology in its overview of priorities for the 1990s.

Ironically this wider approach to abbeys, though entirely justified in its own right, has deliberately drawn attention away from the church and cloister, the indisputable heart of monastic life. Relatively little attention has been paid to the spiritual and religious aspects of monasticism, perhaps in the belief that early studies of abbeys had already paid due heed to such topics. This would be erroneous, because most early work was aimed at elucidating the architectural development of the churches and determining the layout of the cloisters. All too often there was little (if any) thought of an archaeology of context, whether ceremonial or functional. Recent work at sites such as Bordesley Abbey (Hirst *et al* 1983), Norton Priory (Greene 1989), Sandwell Priory (Hodder 1991), the Coventry Charterhouse (Soden 1995 and this volume) and Hulton Abbey (Klemperer this volume) has shown the potential for archaeological study of ceremonial matters. Fergusson and Harrison's magisterial examination (1999) of Rievaulx Abbey, that great Yorkshire monument to the Cistercian movement, perhaps shows us the true potential of placing religion at the core of such studies. The archaeology of ritual need not stop at prehistoric sites, and this should be an essential element of monastic studies. We should be examining plans critically rather than relying on notions of what "is" typical.

The genesis of the Oxford conference on monastic archaeology

All of the above was relevant to my own work during the early 1990s, especially at Eynsham Abbey in Oxfordshire (this volume) where I was in charge of a major archaeological project on a Benedictine house with late Saxon origins. There were many opportunities to share information and ideas with colleagues, most notably at the *Medieval Europe 1992* conference in York. The idea for a conference dedicated to monastic archaeology grew out of such exchanges and the realisation that there was a great deal of new work being done which deserved a wider audience. This was true both of individual sites or projects and of more general thematic programmes. There was, of course, ample precedent for holding such reviews of work in progress, notably the conferences on rural and urban monasteries the proceedings of which were published in Gilchrist and Mytum 1989 and 1993 respectively. An approach to Oxford University's Department of Continuing

Education (OUDCE) late in 1993 to see whether they would be interested in hosting such a conference at Rewley House met with an enthusiastic response. A weekend towards the end of 1994 was duly booked. The task of preparing a draft list of speakers and topics was an interesting one in its own right, the difficulty being to keep the numbers of possible contributions down to a manageable number from OUDCE's point of view. It was gratifying to find that all of the speakers I had chosen were both interested in the idea and willing to contribute; just as remarkably they were all available on the weekend in question. The programme, therefore, came together very quickly and included such luminaries of modern archaeology as Mick Aston, Paul Bennett, Martin Biddle, James Bond, Glyn Coppack, Patrick Greene and Terryl Kinder along with a few names (including my own) which would doubtless have been less familiar to the typical mix of professional colleagues and well-informed amateurs (in the best possible sense of the word) which typifies conferences at Rewley House. The conference itself was immensely enjoyable, even for me given my duties as organiser and host on OUDCE's behalf.

Even at the early planning stage, meanwhile, publication of the proceedings had been very much in my mind. There was a conscious degree to which I wanted to emulate the efforts of Gilchrist and Mytum in disseminating the results of the earlier conferences, not only because this would spread the information further than is possible at a single event but also, to be honest, for the (hopefully) impressive entry it would make on my own bibliography! To be fair to myself the former was always far more important to me than the latter. To this end I approached David Brown of Oxbow Books to see whether he would be interested in including the book in his burgeoning Oxbow Monographs series, and once again the response was encouragingly enthusiastic. I therefore made the intention for publication clear to all contributors from the beginning, mindful of the very considerable commitments they would all have already, and several made it clear that those commitments would preclude them from putting forward a text for the final volume. This was fully understandable, and sufficient numbers were prepared to work up their presentations to provide the momentum for taking the idea of publication forward to actuality. Nevertheless I felt that some additional papers would be valuable, and to this end I approached a number of people who I had not been able to include as speakers at the conference itself because of the pressure on numbers already referred to, but whose projects were nevertheless both of great interest and very germane to the overall scope of the report as it continued to take shape.

Throughout 1995 and into 1996, therefore, I was in regular contact with all the likely contributors and draft papers began to come in from quite early on in the former year. Having been the original organiser it seemed sensible that I should edit the proceedings, although given the very high standard of the work coming in this was not as onerous a task as it could have been. Even so a lot of work was done at this stage and there was a considerable amount of discussion with authors about the general sweep and/or fine details of their texts, and the choice of illustrations. There were still a number of outstanding contributions, however, and perhaps unwisely I decided to wait for these; I still had it in mind to submit the complete text to David Brown later in 1996, and the book was duly mentioned in the introduction to one of David's catalogues.

During 1996, however, I embarked on what was to become the most rewarding project of my professional archaeological career to date, in the moat at the Tower of London. Unfortunately the sheer commitment in time required by this work (I was in London virtually daily for almost three years) left me no opportunity to pursue the monastic publication during the day, and my family took complete precedence over what was left of my time (if Prime Ministers can do it, why not archaeologists?). Gradually I began to feel that the book might not come to press, even though it was tantalisingly close to completion and despite occasional prompting from some of my senior contributors (especially Mick Aston). I did not give up hope completely, not least because the book would still be a valuable contribution to its subject.

Fortunately the project was rescued when Mick Aston and his assistant Teresa Hall offered to take on the task of completing the editorial tasks in 1999. David Brown confirmed that he was still interested in publishing the book, and work progressed through into 2000. The eventual appearance of the monograph is a testament to Mick and Teresa's efforts and commitment, as well as to those of all the individual contributors. Val Lamb at Oxbow books did a remarkable job in bringing the text to final publication. I am delighted to be able to offer, at last, my heartfelt thanks to them all – as well as extending my apologies for the late arrival of the fruits of their labours. I hope everyone will agree that it was worth waiting for.

Bibliography

Brakspear H 1916, On the dorter range at Worcester, *Archaeologia* 67, 241–56

Brakspear H 1928, Excavations at some Wiltshire monasteries, *Archaeologia* 77

Clapham A 1923, The architecture of the order of Premonstratensians, with special reference to their buildings in England, *Archaeologia* 73, 117–46

EH (English Heritage) 1991, *Exploring Our Past: strategies for the archaeology of England*

Fergusson P and Harrison S 1999, *Rievaulx Abbey: Community, Architecture and Memory*, Yale University Press

Gilchrist R and Mytum H (eds) 1989, *The Archaeology of Rural Monasteries*, BAR 203

Gilchrist R and Mytum H (eds) 1993, *Advances in Monastic Archaeology*, BAR 227

Graham R and Clapham A 1926, The Order of Grandmont and its houses in England, *Archaeologia* 75, 159–210

Greene J P 1989, *Norton Priory: the archaeology of a medieval religious house*, Cambridge University Press

Hirst S M, Walsh D A and Wright S M 1983, *Bordesley Abbey II*, BAR 111

Hodder M A 1991, *Excavations at Sandwell Priory and Hall 1982–88*, South Staffordshire Archaeological and Historical Society Transactions 31

Micklethwaite J 1893, On a filtering system of the 14th century at Westminster Abbey, *Archaeologia* 53, 161–70

Norman P 1899, On a conduit head in Queen Square, Bloomsbury, *Archaeologia* 56, 251–66

Norman P and Mann E A 1909, On the White Conduit, Chapel Street, Bloomsbury, and its connexion with the Grey Friars' water system, *Archaeologia* 61, 347–56

St John Hope W H 1890, On the Whitefriars or Carmelites of Hulne, Northumberland, *Arch J* 47, 105–29

St John Hope W H 1902, The London Charterhouse and its water supply, *Archaeologia* 58, 293–312

SMA 1987, Archaeology and the Middle Ages: recommendations by the Society for Medieval Archaeology to the Historic Buildings and Monuments Commission for England, *Medieval Archaeology* 31, 1–12

Soden I 1995, *Excavations at St Anne's Charterhouse, Coventry, 1968-87*, Coventry Museums & Galleries

2 Strategies for Future Research and Site Investigation

J Patrick Greene

The advent of the National Lottery, and the National Heritage Memorial Fund's estimated income of £150 million a year from its proceeds, provides a challenging context in which to consider future research and investigation strategies for monastic archaeology. New funds could provide excellent opportunities to proceed with research projects that, for lack of resources, have been intriguing to contemplate but impossible to implement. The NHMF guidelines certainly encompass such possibilities, 'The fund will support research and recording projects which are related to a heritage asset. They should relate to a particular building, site or collections and be aimed either at preserving evidence of something under threat or at gathering information necessary for the better care and management of the asset concerned' (NHMF Lottery Guidelines). Ancient monuments, historic buildings and their contents and settings, landscapes and museum collections are all eligible, and thus most of the research projects that are mentioned in this paper could qualify. However, it must be emphasised that there are also many projects that do not require large resources of money (although they may be demanding in terms of time) and which can continue to be pursued by monastic archaeologists, professional and amateur, resulting in the steady accretion of knowledge about individual sites, orders or monastic practices.

This paper concentrates largely on post-Conquest topics as aspects of the archaeology of Saxon monasteries are discussed elsewhere in this volume. However, the first topic addresses the transformation of Saxon to Norman monasteries.

Refounded Saxon monasteries

The testimony of the archaeological record is capable of being particularly vivid at times of rapid and dramatic social and political change. The Norman Conquest had the greatest impact on monasticism in Britain until the Dissolution. Recent work at Canterbury, St Albans and Eynsham has resulted in the discovery of the remains of Saxon buildings on sites that were refounded as Norman monasteries. The massive and extensive nature of masonry foundations at Canterbury and St Albans in particular has shown the large scale of the pre-Conquest establishments, but also the thoroughness with which the Norman abbots of the refounded abbeys set about the total replacement of existing buildings, however grand. There is clearly a potential for many further discoveries of a similar nature on sites of refounded monasteries.

The original layout of monasteries

With few exceptions monasteries existed for several centuries and underwent modifications as a result of wealth (expansion), poverty (contraction), civil disorder, warfare and fire (destruction and rebuilding), changes of liturgical practice, structural failure, and the effects of the Dissolution. Detecting the earliest arrangements can be very difficult without large-scale excavation, as at Norton (Greene 1989a), or where circumstances have conspired to keep the buildings largely in their original form (as with the church at Portchester). It is in the *early* arrangements, however, that schemes of design are likely to be found, as has been revealed by careful measurement at Norton and Bordesley (Hirst, Walsh and Wright 1983). Subsequent additions and modifications are likely to be more pragmatic in design than the original scheme, in which it may be possible to detect the presence of a 'master plan' for the individual monastery, or possibly for groups of monasteries of equivalent size and date. Much more could be learnt about the transmission of ideas of planning, layout and measurement by comparative studies of early monastic plans, particularly those that fall into a specific group such as twelfth century simple cruciform churches. That such may exist even in the midst of the grandest monastic remains has been dramatically demonstrated at Fountains Abbey (Coppack 1994).

The excavation of an early, temporary site

Many monasteries suffered a false start due to factors as various as poor water supply, flooding, a change of mind by the donor of the land, or of the brethren themselves, or even the famous case of the confusion caused by the bells of Rievaulx Abbey and Byland Abbey on their adjacent sites in Ryedale. Fifty Augustinian and Cistercian houses moved site (Robinson 1980; Donkin 1978). It follows that there is the opportunity to select such a site with a known history and likelihood of good preservation for a large-scale excavation. The short occupation would result in simple stratigraphy enabling extensive examination to take place, relatively quickly. It should be possible to reveal three aspects of the early stages of a monastery:

a) Temporary timber buildings for the brethren to live and worship in, as have been discovered at Fountains, Norton, Sandwell and a few other sites. The opportunity to uncover a complete suite of such buildings would amplify greatly the excavated evidence and documentary accounts of the early years at Fountains, Meaux and Kirkstall for example.

b) The layout and construction techniques of masonry buildings. If the site chosen had been occupied for, say, two decades, substantial progress is likely to have been made with the construction of the church and the layout of the claustral buildings. Excavation would provide a valuable picture of a stage in development that is obscured on sites where subsequent occupation, rebuildings, and burials in the church have complicated the archaeological record.

c) The short duration of occupation would provide a usefully restricted chronological context for artefacts, contributing to studies of material culture.

A linked investigation: Britain, France, Ireland

It would be possible to select pairs of sites for intensive investigation in France and Britain, and Britain and Ireland where a number of shared characteristics existed – for example the date of foundation, the order, the founder, the size, the presence of standing remains and earthwork features. It might be possible to detect a common approach to design in the foundation period, but equally revealing would be the ways in which the subsequent history of the houses diverged or paralleled each other. There would be possibilities of extending such a transnational study to other countries. Funding through European Union programmes concerned with the Common European Cultural Inheritance could be explored.

Recording of standing buildings

There is no doubt that monastic remains are suffering accelerated deterioration as a result of aerial pollution, especially particulate emissions from vehicles and the chemical effects of acid rain. There is a need to raise public awareness of this damage, as well as recording deteriorating remains for posterity. Projects such as that carried out by the Lancaster University Archaeological Unit at Furness Abbey provide a model for such studies, but recording can take place at a number of levels including those within reach of the amateur archaeologist. The structures of standing, occupied buildings can also provide considerable information from, for example, the study of their timber roof structures as at Ely, Lincoln and Canterbury. Much can also be learnt about techniques of construction of masonry buildings from traces such as marking-out lines, and the outline of mouldings as recently discovered at Guisborough where masons had used the flat surface of paving to design the nave arcade.

Monastic cloisters

Whilst there is a powerful argument for concentrating future excavations of monastic sites away from the main claustral buildings, a surprisingly neglected subject for study is the cloister itself which would certainly repay detailed examination. There are several possible avenues of research:

a) The structure of early cloister walk arcades. The revelation of the complex triple-shafted trefoil headed arcade at Norton, the traceried, glazed cloister at Bordesley, and the recently discovered twin-shafted cloister arcade at Haverfordwest demonstrate the exciting possibilities that exist. Whilst it might be imagined that to recover such designs would be impossible, experience has shown that fragments of open cloister arcades were frequently built into the foundations of their fenestrated successors and can be recovered by excavation. The quality of stonework, especially the embellishment with foliage and figures in West Country style at Norton and Haverford-west, demonstrates the high level of investment that monasteries with limited resources were prepared to apply to the cloister.

b)   The cloister garden. Surprisingly little is known about the layout and use of cloister gardens – were they grassed, planted with herbs or other useful plants, or decorative shrubs and trees? The use of techniques of garden excavation and pollen analysis developed at sites such as Fish-bourne Roman Palace, and more recent gardens such as Kirby Hall and Hampton Court (Dix 1994) could be applied to monastic sites.

c)   Drainage of the cloister. Considerable quantities of water drained from the roofs of the church and claustral ranges into the cloister; little is known about how it was removed (soakaways, drains, or used as part of the monastery's water supply). At Norton it was carried in a drain beneath the west range, and in the final remodel-ling of the cloister a drain around the perimeter of the cloister became a 'water feature'. In addition to rain, water was then brought by pipe into a monastic cloister for distribution from a cistern, for use in a cloister lavatorium. This too had to be removed.

d)   The position of the cloister. The association of cloisters placed to the north of the church with the cult of the Virgin has been suggested for nunneries (Gilchrist 1989). Irish friaries usually have the cloister to the north. These are both worthy of study using international comparisons.

Monastic precincts and properties

Attention has rightly been given in recent years to the precincts and estates of monasteries, but much remains to be done. Sites where the claustral build-ings have been investigated and which have full documentation provide the best opportunities as the surroundings can then be related to the monastic core within a historical framework. Thus sites such as Fountains and Rievaulx have proved particularly interesting, and yet even at Fountains the functions of up to forty buildings lying to the south of the River Skell in the outer courtyard are unknown (Coppack 1994). Structures such as bridges, mills, spring houses, barns, smithies, dovecotes etc can be studied with resulting information about the monastic economy. Earthwork surveys, and aerial photography such as the revealing study of Norfolk houses such as Shouldham and West Dereham demonstrates the extensive nature of precincts and estates, and often impressive measures taken for

water management. Another worthwhile study is that of precinct boundaries which are capable of being traced through standing walls, earthworks, charters and field names. The features of monastic estates, including granges, widen the study still further; the earthworks and structures of a site such as Monknash Grange in South Glamorgan show what can be located (Williams 1990); the study of the field boundaries at Roystone Grange in Derby-shire shows how the landscape of this grange of Garendon Abbey has evolved (Hodges 1991). A final topic offered for study is that of extractive industries – quarries, mines, sandpits, clay digging and peat exploitation on monastic estates. International comparisons can be particularly revealing (Pressouyre 1994).

Artefact studies

The collections of museums, compounds at ancient monuments, and standing buildings themselves have many classes of artefacts whose study can enhance the knowledge of monasteries and monastic life. Some studies have been assisted by results of recent excavations, most notably the casting of bells for monastic churches, and the techniques and trade of tile manufacture (Lillich 1993). An excellent study of a class of artefact closely associated with monasteries is that of the pilgrim badges in the Salisbury and South Wiltshire Museum which provides a model of how insights into belief, iconography, social mobility and techniques of production can be obtained (Spencer 1990). The study of loose moulded stones from excavations on sites which are apparently well-known can reveal aspects of the demolished struc-tures that have never been suspected. The study of marking out lines on individual moulded stones can show how the mason has measured and shaped them, and tool-marks can reveal the tools used. The comparison of mouldings from different buildings, as well as masons marks, still have enormous potential for the investigation of comparative dating, the movements of craftsmen, and the size of labour forces (despite being studied for a century and a half – the use of computers to process the complex and voluminous material has the potential to revolu-tionise these studies).

Anatomical studies and burial practices

Despite the number of excavations of monastic churches and graveyards there is still a paucity of reports on anatomical research and burial practices. Very big, well-excavated samples such as the 1600 skeletons from Whithorn (Hill 1991) and skeletons from St Gregory's Priory in Canterbury provide excellent opportunities for demographic and health studies, with the information made much more useful still by comparison with other regions (and countries) and chronologically. There needs to be a clear distinction drawn between the different groups likely to be buried on a monastic site – the inmates themselves, benefactor families, lay servants, and possibly inhabitants of the demesne estate.

Environmental studies

The wealth of information produced by the study of environmental remains shows this to be one of the most productive areas for expanding knowledge of monastic life and practices. Analysis of faunal remains, especially animal and bird bones, shells, fish bones and scales etc has revealed much about monastic diet, butchery practices etc. Vegetable remains, in the form of grains, seeds, pollen etc have likewise elucidated diet, the flora of monastic precincts and medicinal practices. The assessment of locations where such material is likely to be found should be part of any excavation strategy for an individual site. Drains, moats, fishponds and rubbish pits have high potential for preserved organic materials.

The Dissolution

Most sites with standing masonry are capable of being studied in terms of how monastic buildings were damaged or converted to new uses at the time of the Dissolution or thereafter, but surprisingly little research has been published. The combination of structural studies, sometimes excavation and always documentary, cartographic and pictorial research can provide valuable information into one of the most fundamental transformations that society in Britain has undergone (albeit more gradual in Scotland and Ireland, but nonetheless far reaching). Standing buildings themselves usually represent the point at which systematic demolition and casual 'quarrying' stopped, and thus can provide copious information on the process of destruction.

The interpretation of monastic sites

Research is invaluable for interpretation in three major aspects:

a) Good interpretation has as a prerequisite high quality research, or what is presented to visitors is misleading, or stereotyped, or bland, or all three (Greene 1989b; 1992).

b) The requirement of authoritative presentation

can stimulate research. For example, the preparation of a model of a monastic site requires the synthesis of information from a breadth of sources with the discipline of presenting it in three-dimensional form. The recreation of the chapter house entrance at St Mary's Abbey, York, by the Yorkshire Museum is the result of innovative research into twelfth-century architectural details, and into contemporary materials used in the reconstructed portal and flanking windows.

c) There is a need for evaluation of visitors' responses to the interpretation of monastic sites to improve the quality of presentation and publications.

Conclusion

Despite a century and a half of research into medieval monasticism, the field for further investigation remains very extensive. The potential scope is widening as innovative techniques of investigation and recording, and novel research methodologies such as spatial analysis are applied to the vast subject of monasteries. The international nature of monasticism makes it particularly appropriate for collaborative research on a European scale. A sense of urgency is generated by the knowledge that standing monastic sites are vulnerable to increasingly intensive land use. The need to interpret monasticism to a public interested in the past yet often with little contact with religious observance is particularly challenging, requiring evaluation into methods of interpretation.

Bibliography

Coppack G 1994, *Fountains Abbey*, London, Batsford/ English Heritage.

Dix B 1994, 'Garden archaeology at Kirby Hall and Hampton Court', *Current Archaeology* 140, 292–9.

Donkin R A 1978, *The Cistercians: Studies in the Medieval Geography of England and Wales*, Toronto.

Gilchrist R 1989, 'The archaeology of English medieval nunneries: a research design' in Gilchrist and Mytum, 251–60.

Gilchist R and Mytum H (eds) 1989, *The Archaeology of Rural Monasteries*, British Archaeological Reports British Series 203.

Greene J P 1989a, *Norton Priory; the Archaeology of a Medieval Religious House*, Cambridge University Press.

Greene J P 1989b, 'Methods of interpretation of monastic sites' in Gilchrist and Mytum 1989, 313–25.

Greene J P 1992, *Medieval Monasteries*, Leicester University Press (paperback 1994).

Hill P H 1991, *Whithorn 3: Excavations at Whithorn Priory 1988–90*, Whithorn Trust.

Hirst S M Walsh D A and Wright S M 1983, *Bordesley Abbey II*, Oxford, British Archaeological Reports III.

Hodges R 1991, *Wall-to-Wall History: the story of Roystone Grange*, London, Duckworth.

Lillich M D, 1993, *Studies in Cistercian Art and Architecture 4*, Cistercian Publications.

Pressouyre L (ed), 1994, *L'Espace Cistercien, Comite des Travaux Historiques et Scientifiques*, Memoires de la Section d'Archaeologie et d'Histoire de l'Art No 5, Paris

Robinson D M 1980, *The Geography of Augustinian Settlement in England and Wales*, Oxford, British Archaeological Reports.

Spencer B 1990, *Salisbury and South Wiltshire Museum Medieval Catalogue: Part 2, Pilgrim Souvenirs and Secular Badges*, Salisbury.

Williams D H 1990, *Atlas of Cistercian Lands in Wales*, Cardiff, University of Wales Press.

3 The Expansion of the Monastic and Religious Orders in Europe from the Eleventh Century

Michael Aston

Summary

The massive expansion in the number of monasteries, particularly in the twelfth and thirteenth centuries, is partly a reflection of the development of many new orders, or congregations, of monastic and religious communities in the eleventh, twelfth and thirteenth centuries. This was a Europe-wide phenomenon reflecting developing religious activities – not only of monks, nuns and canons, but also of hermits, friars or mendicants and military groups, including hospitallers. This article considers the problems of identifying the various congregations, finding out about their origins and development, and particularly their geographical spread. A great deal of further research is needed before the full impact of monastic and religious orders on medieval Europe can be fully appreciated. Here, all that is attempted is a 'broad-brush' survey, which it is hoped will stimulate other researchers, with a greater knowledge of a particular order, to fill in the details. If this article promotes further debate and research, it will have achieved its objective.

Introduction

We are fortunate in the British Isles in having the series of massive and comprehensive volumes by the late Dom David Knowles, and others, to provide a gazetteer of the former medieval monastic and religious houses. For any establishment we can generally easily ascertain its order, foundation date, founder, brief history, assessed income and date of dissolution. It is impossible to understand the development of monasticism in this country without this basic information. Yet most of the influences for this development, with the single exception of the Gilbertines (and possibly the Bonshommes and the Order of St Thomas of Acre), came not from this country but from Europe, and in particular from Burgundy in France. Britain was merely one part of Europe; monasticism was pan-European on a scale that makes the European Union seem insignificant – all the monastic communities in the west, for example, were united in one sense, in that they all used the same language, Latin.

It is impossible, therefore, to understand the development of monasticism and the vast increase in the number of religious establishments between 1066 and 1350 without reference to European developments. European monastic contact was probably responsible for the spread of many of the developments not only in religious matters, but possibly also in farming, engineering and related ideas over much of Europe, though this remains as yet unproven. To understand Britain we need to know what was happening in Europe, though in this article consideration will be given mainly to those orders which had an influence in Britain.

As we shall see, it proves extremely difficult to define the exact number of separate orders that came into existence in the early middle ages. Here, reference is made to over ninety, and no doubt more will emerge, especially where there was little influence on Britain, and particularly from the Catholic countries of Eastern Europe, about which much less has been written in English and much less generally is known in the west.

A further problem is the great variety in the types of order. Strictly speaking, monastic orders were those with enclosed monks or nuns, though as time went on groups of lay brothers or sisters were formed in some orders. There were also, from the late eleventh century, increasing numbers of groups of canons, not entirely enclosed, relating closely to local communities and usually ordained as priests. From the twelfth century onwards, numerous orders of armed monks were formed (seemingly a contradiction in terms) – knights and hospitallers who defended pilgrims, looked after travellers and fought non-Christians (though not exclusively) in the Holy Land, Spain and Eastern Europe. In the thirteenth century the preaching and teaching mendicant (begging) orders were developed, spreading widely and achieving great success, often against developing heresies, and in the developing universities of Western Europe at Paris, Bologna, Montpellier and Oxford.

At all times groups of hermits living ascetic lives, attempting to follow the example of the Desert Fathers and a strict interpretation of the Rule of St Benedict, gave rise to new orders. Similarly, hospitaller orders looking after the sick, including lepers, the poor, old, infirm and so on developed at all times.

Between the tenth and sixteenth centuries (see Table 3.1) over ninety separate orders were developed in Europe, despite an attempt at the Fourth Lateran Council in 1215 to prevent the generation of new groups, "lest too great a variety of religious [orders] create confusion in the church of God" (King 1999, 235; Morris 1989, 448).

Table 3.1 *The number of new orders between the 10th and 16th centuries.*

Period	Number of new orders
10th century	2
11th century	12
12th century	29
13th century	30
14th century	8
15th century	4
16th century	8
TOTAL	93

(At least – this is a very rough figure, see Table 3.2 at end of paper)

Given that some orders changed their complexion over time, there were at least twenty groups of monks and hermits (Cistercians, Carthusians, Tironensians, and so on), twenty-seven military orders (Templars and Hospitallers, but also many others), seventeen orders of friars, sixteen major groups of canons and ten hospital orders.

The expansion of monastic and religious orders

At the moment it is very difficult to discuss the expansion of most of the orders across Europe in any detailed or meaningful way, as the basic research has not been done. In order to demonstrate expansion (and contraction) it is necessary to know of all the houses of an order (not only as communities but also

the various sites they have occupied), their foundation dates and circumstances, and something of their history. While we might know roughly how many houses formerly existed for a particular order – such as over 2000 dependencies of Cluny, or the thirty priories of Val de Choux (the Valliscaulians) – it is usually not very easy to locate these or find their foundation dates (or sometimes even their names). As yet there is no equivalent of the Knowles (and his co-workers) volumes, which exist for various parts of Britain, for any other part of Europe; Cottineau (1939, 1970) is useful, but full of errors and not indexed beyond the alphabetical list of houses. It does not include friaries or houses of the military orders.

For some orders the situation is different and there have been recent significant advances. Perhaps the most studied order is that of the Cistercians. Not only is there an atlas of houses (Van der Meer 1965), there are numerous articles with elaborate diagrams of filiation of houses and chronological developments (eg Donkin 1978 and others) and volumes on individual countries and regions (see, eg: Williams 1984 and 1990 on Wales; Stalley 1987 on Ireland; McGuire 1982 on Denmark; and France 1992 on Scandinavia). Particularly useful recent volumes are *L'Espace Cistercien* (Pressouyre 1994 and Kinder 1998). Surprisingly, despite Donkin (1978) and Norton and Park (1986), there were until recently no comparable volumes on the Cistercians for England and Wales, or Britain as a whole (but see Fergusson 1984). Now, however, following the nine hundredth anniversary in 1998 there is Coppack 1998, Robinson 1998 and Williams 1998.

It is thus not difficult to find out about Cistercian monasteries in almost any country in Europe. The same could not be said of other orders until recently. There have, however, recently been detailed studies of the Grandmontines (Hutchison 1989), the Premonstratensians (Bond 1993) and the Carthusians (Aston 1993), in which each order's houses are mapped in Europe and some indication given of foundation dates, rate of growth and density in particular areas. For Britain, similar research exists for the Gilbertines (Graham 1901 and Golding 1995), Trinitarians (Gray 1993), Augustinians (Robinson 1980) and friars (Butler 1984 and 1987 and Lawrence 1994).

It will only be possible in this article, therefore, to indicate the major periods of foundation of orders, the different types and other characteristics, and (where available) their distribution. Specific information, which can be used to indicate the definite existence of a group as a separate order, includes recognition by the papacy and the date of the first general chapter. In the final section a case study of north-east England shows what will be possible in understanding the impact of monasticism in a region when we have more ordered data.

Hermits and their successors

Following the disruption of the Vikings in Europe in the ninth century, there was much refurbishment and refoundation of monasteries in the tenth century. At that time, and until the late eleventh century, many monasteries in the west followed the Rule of St Benedict, all were autonomous and each was occupied by monks or nuns. They were not thought of as 'Benedictine' – this idea only developed in the thirteenth century after the Fourth Lateran Council of 1215 – and there were few 'families' of monasteries.

The first groups of filiated houses followed the new foundations and refoundations of the tenth century. In particular, the foundation of Cluny in Burgundy in 909 marked a turning point. This was founded by William of Aquitaine and staffed with monks from the sixth-century Irish foundation of Beaume Lès Messiers (near Lons le Saunier, Burgundy). In the tenth and eleventh centuries Cluny founded and refounded a large number of houses in western Europe – in all, it was said to have had a 'family' of 2000 priories and dependencies (Evans 1938).

Other refounded houses included Gorze in Lorraine, where Adalbero I of Metz gave the ruined monastery in 933 to archdeacon Einold of Toul and John of Gorze to found an austere community. Together with the monasteries at St Evre in Toul and St Maximin in Trier, the group followed the 'reform' of Gorze, with numerous houses adopting the customs of Gorze. Eventually, 170 monasteries were involved in the reform, especially a number in Germany beyond the influence of Cluny. It was never as centralized as Cluny, but thirty-one houses were attached to Gorze as its priories.

Other, similar 'Benedictine' groups continued to emerge. As a foretaste of what was to come, La Chaise Dieu was founded in 1043 by Robert de Turlande with a group of hermits seeking a more austere life than was available in the chapter of the Benedictine monastery of St Julian at nearby Brioude. From its remote upland site in the Auvergne, La Chaise Dieu produced many saintly abbots and engaged the interest of numerous popes, reaching the height of its influence in the period 1250–1300. For much of the time it was second only to Cluny as head of a congregation of three hundred abbeys and priories in France, Spain and Italy.

Nearby, also in the Auvergne, Le Monastier sur Gazeille was refounded in the tenth century. Named after the seventh-century St Chaffre, the Chaffriennes of Le Monastier had 235 dependencies in 1179, mainly in the volcanic uplands of the south-west Massif Central in France, including such picturesque sites as Thines and Chamalières (Figs 3.1 & 3.2).

These, however, were not the most significant developments in terms of European monasticism. In the eleventh century the desire for solitude, isolation and a return to a more austere, severe or ascetic lifestyle led to groups of hermits retreating into marshes, forests and mountains; from these small beginnings grew the greatest orders of the middle ages.

We can see the beginnings in Italy, although there may have been many more undocumented (and therefore unknown) instances of groups of hermits in other parts of Europe. In 1015 St Romuald (†1027) founded a hermitage with a group of hermits on land granted by Count Maldoli, hence 'Campus Maldoli'. The site at Camaldoli is high in the Appenine mountains and consisted of two parts: a communal monastery, with separate hermit cells above it for those who aspired to be like the Desert Fathers; eventually it influenced over a hundred monasteries, along with Fonte Avellana, another hermitage.

A similar foundation was Vallombrosa, also high in the mountains. This was founded in *c*1039 by the Florentine John Gualbert (†1073). Here, lay brothers were instituted in a separate monastery, providing the model for the organization of several later orders.

Chronologically, the next group was the Grandmontines, founded as a group of hermits at Muret, near Limoges in France, by Stephen in 1076. On his death in 1124 the community moved to Grandmont. The order was very severe, with hermits living communally in great poverty and the monasteries run by lay brothers. The houses are very small; most were in France, particularly in the west, but there were two in Spain and three in England (Fig 3.3) (Hutchison 1989).

Of the early hermit groups, the Carthusians were perhaps the most successful. In 1084 a small group of monks retreated with Bruno into the wilderness of the Chartreuse near Grenoble in the French Alps. Before the original site was destroyed by an avalanche in 1132, the basic arrangement of cells around a large cloister for the monks (or fathers), with a separate lower house (called a 'correrie') for lay brothers (cf the Vallombrosians), had been established. The full extent of the order, around three hundred sites in total, covered most of Europe, from Ireland and Portugal in the west to Belorussia and former Yugoslavia in the east, with a northern foundation in Sweden and a failed site in Denmark (Fig 3.4) (Aston 1993). Further research is needed into the length of occupation and the dates of abandonment of most sites.

The Cistercians also began as a group of hermits. The original group was established by Robert, a disaffected Benedictine from Molesme in Burgundy,

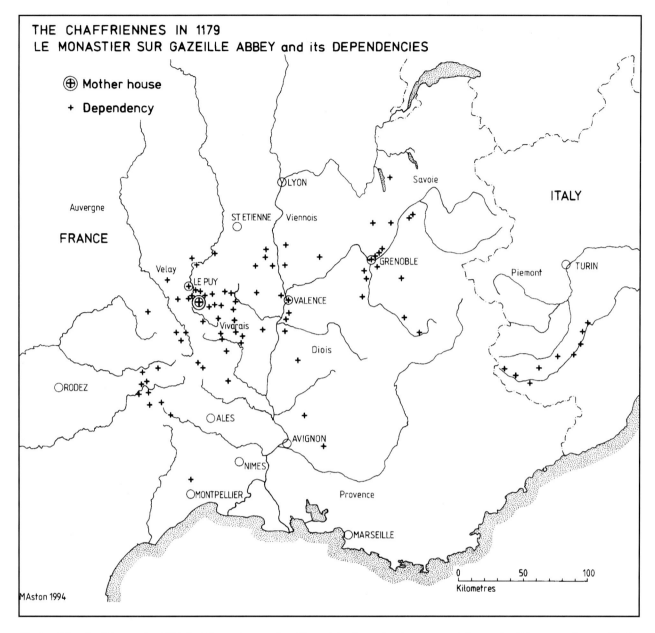

Fig 3.1 *The Chaffriennes in 1179: Le Monastier sur Gazeille and its dependencies – map of the south of France and part of Italy, showing main houses.*

in a marshy area ('cisterna') near Nuits St George in the forests of Burgundy in 1098. As with the other groups mentioned so far, there was no intention on the part of the founder to establish a new order. Indeed, a return to a more literal interpretation of the Rule of St Benedict was the motivation, away from the rest of society in isolated, or 'desert' conditions. Robert went on to Tonnerre and it was left to his followers, in particular Stephen Harding (an English Benedictine from Sherborne in Dorset), to develop the Cîteaux community. Lay brothers were established within the monastery, manual labour reinstated as part of the monastic day, and eventually granges, or individual outlying farms, were set up to

exploit directly the land acquired by the monks. Daughter houses of Cîteaux were founded in 1113 at La Ferté, 1114 at Pontigny, and 1115 at Clairvaux and Morimond, and this established the pattern of mother/daughter affiliation, which provided a powerful bond in the Cistercian 'family tree', enabling reinforcement of discipline in the order. The institution of an annual General Chapter at Cîteaux of all abbots also strengthened this process. The group was recognized as a separate order of Benedictines in 1119, to distinguish them from the existing Benedictine and Cluniac groups, and their expansion was prodigious. Between 1098 and 1124 twenty-six houses were built; between 1125 and 1151 a further 307 were

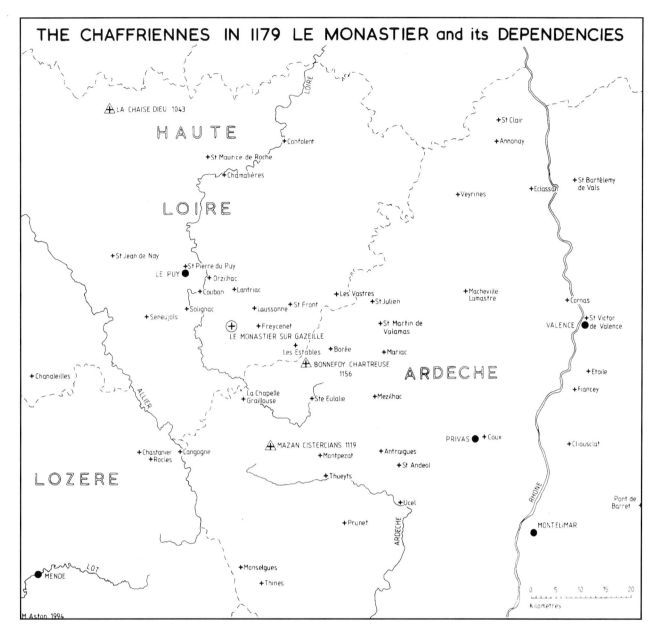

Fig 3.2 *The Chaffriennes in 1179: Le Monastier sur Gazeille and its dependencies – map of the central estates and dependencies around the mother house.*

established. Much of this expansion occurred during the lifetime of the charismatic St Bernard of Clairvaux (*c*1090–1153). Despite attempts in 1152 to restrict the growth of the order, a further 195 houses had been established by 1200. Over ninety per cent of the approximately 740 Cistercian houses founded between 1098 and 1675 were in existence by 1300 (Donkin 1978).

Since each new community was an offshoot (or daughter) of an existing monastery, it is easily possible to trace lines of affiliation through the five original houses and their offshoots: Cîteaux (109 houses), La Ferté (16 houses), Pontigny (43 houses), Clairvaux (356 houses) and Morimond (214 houses).

In this way we can also see areas of influence in Europe with, for example, Morimond's influence spreading down into Spain and Italy and across to eastern Europe, while the British Isles were mainly influenced by Cîteaux and especially Clairvaux (Figs 3.5 & 3.6). The order was widespread (Fig 3.7), more so than the Carthusians, and only really equalled by the Premonstratensian canons: from Ireland and Portugal in the west, through many Mediterranean islands (Majorca, Sardinia, Sicily and Cyprus), to Norway, Sweden (France 1992), Estonia and Latvia in the north, and Greece (Panagopoulos 1979), Turkey and Palestine in the east. Dates of foundation, and hence rate of spread over Europe and the

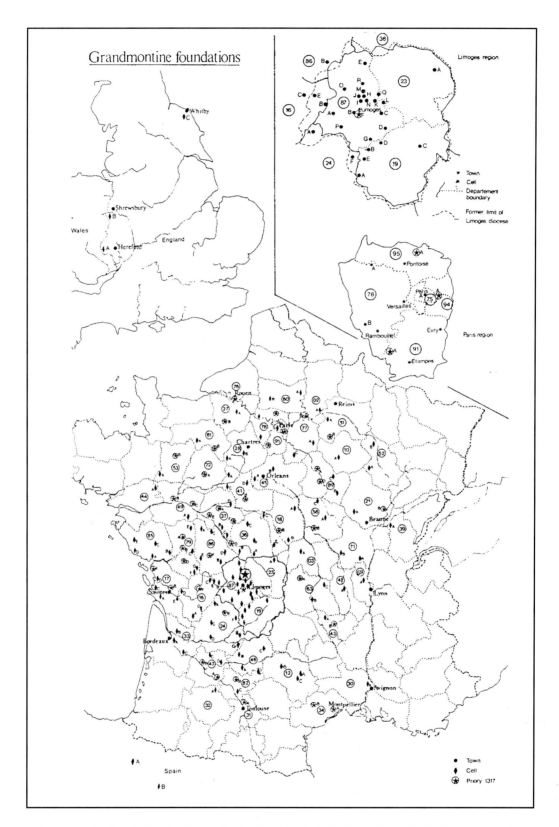

Fig 3.3 *Grandmontine foundations in France, England and Spain (after Hutchinson 1989). Reproduced with permission.*

Fig 3.4 Carthusian foundations in Europe and their provinces (after Aston 1993).

near East, have been mapped by Donkin (1978). What we know of the chronological and geographical spread of the Cistercians should serve as the model for all other orders.

These hermit groups may be the best known, certainly in Britain where they all had affiliated foundations. All through the middle ages numerous other groups and hermits continued to emerge, and their followers were often organized into new, separate orders.

One example is the Valliscaulians. Towards the end of the twelfth century Viard, a lay brother of the Carthusian priory of Loubigny or Lugny in the diocese of Langres in Burgundy, was permitted to live as a hermit in a cave in a wood at Val de Choux. Odo III, Duke of Burgundy, in fulfillment of a vow

built a monastery on the site of the hermitage and in 1193 Viard became prior and formed rules for the new foundation, drawn partly from the Cistercian and Carthusian observances. The order of the 'Brethren of the Cabbage Valley' was confirmed by Pope Innocent III on 12 February 1205. Eventually there were said to be thirty dependent houses, but the names of only twenty are known – seventeen of these were in France, the principal at Val Croissant in the diocese of Autun, and there were three in Scotland (Ardchattan, Beauly and Pluscarden); there were probably houses in Germany, too.

This cameo of the development of the Valliscaulians is typical of the development of monasteries, orders and their expansion – a hermit, an isolated hermitage, patron, building of an abbey,

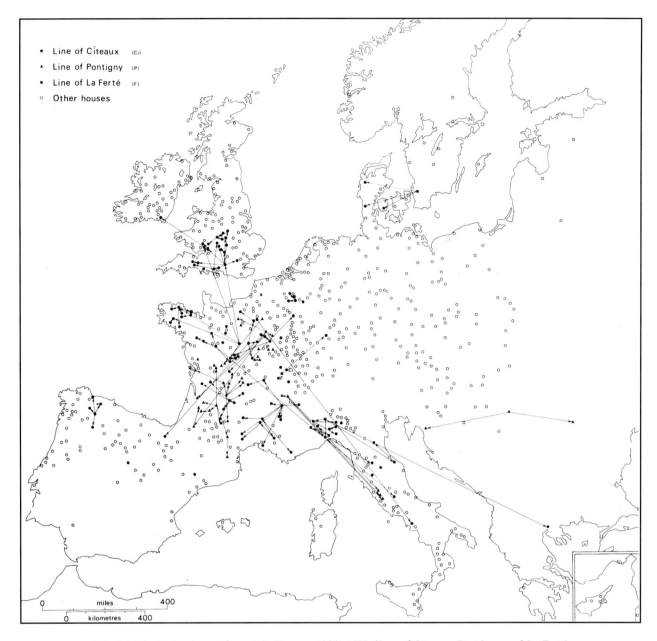

Fig 3.5 *The Cistercian settlement in Europe, 1098–1675: lines of Cîteaux, Pontigny and La Ferté*
(after Fig 3, Donkin 1978). Reproduced with permission.

recognition by the papacy, establishment of a separate order with its own customs, expansion into neighbouring lands.

The same course can be seen with the hermit St Stephen at Aubazine (or Obazine, in Correze, France), though a separate order was never established. Stephen initially applied to ally his monasteries with the Carthusians, but following their rejection he took his monks and houses into the Cistercian order. Similarly, Vitalis founded a hermitage at Savigny in 1105 in the forest on the border between Normandy and Brittany (eventually there were thirty-two affiliated Savignac houses in France, England, Wales and Scotland). Tiron, founded by

Bernard in the forest of Perche, by 1191 had nine abbeys in France, seven in Scotland (Cowan and Easson 1976: Arbroath, Fyvie, Kelso, Kilwinning, Lesmahagaw, Lindores and Selkirk), one in Wales, and around a hundred dependent priories.

Even after new types of religious orders had been developed (friars and fighting monks, for example), hermits still provided the focus for new orders. The Celestines – the hermits of St Damian or the hermits of Morone – were founded by Peter of Morone, later Pope Celestine V, after 1235 when he spent years as a hermit on Monte Morone. In 1264 the order was approved by Pope Urban IV and in the early fifteenth century it had 150 monasteries, though there

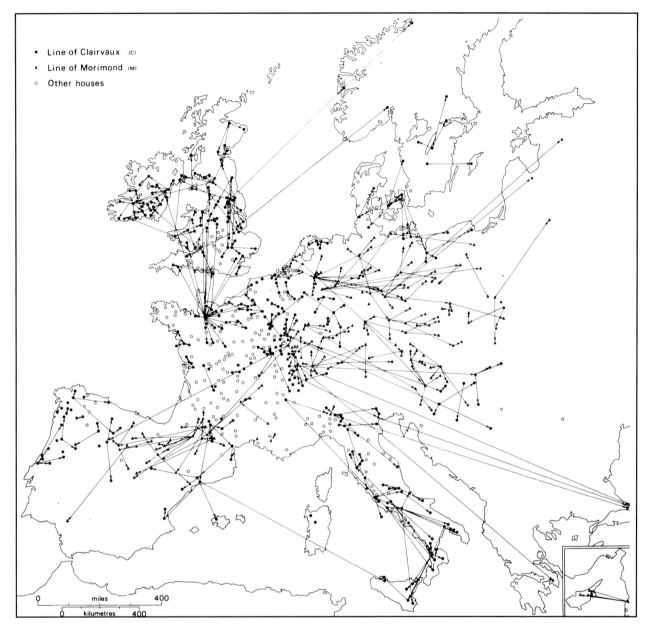

Fig 3.6 *The Cistercian settlement in Europe, 1098-1675: lines of Clairvaux and Morimond (after Fig 4, Donkin 1978). Reproduced with permission.*

were none in Britain, despite Henry V's intention to found one at Sheen by Richmond, Surrey in the early fifteenth century.

The Servites began in similar fashion in 1233, with St Bonfilius and his merchant companions leaving Florence to live as hermits on Monte Senario. In 1244–5 the first steps were taken towards founding an order; in 1249 the hermits were under papal protection and in 1256 the order was constituted. By 1300 there were three provinces of Tuscany, Umbria and Romagna, with forty priories. The order still exists and the brethren are generally considered to be friars.

Similarly, St Silvester Guzzolini in 1227 renounced his benefice and became a hermit on Monte Fano near Fabriano (Italy), building a monastery in 1231 and founding the so-called 'blue' or Silvestrine Benedictines. In 1247 the order was approved by Pope Innocent IV, and on the death of Silvester in 1267 the Sylvestrines had eleven monasteries. The Olivetans began in similar fashion: in 1313 Bernard of Tolomei with some followers withdrew to Accona and founded a monastery at Mount Olivet. In 1344 the Olivetan congregation was approved by Clement VI and despite coming into existence in a period of decline in monasticism, there were fifty Olivetan monasteries by around 1400.

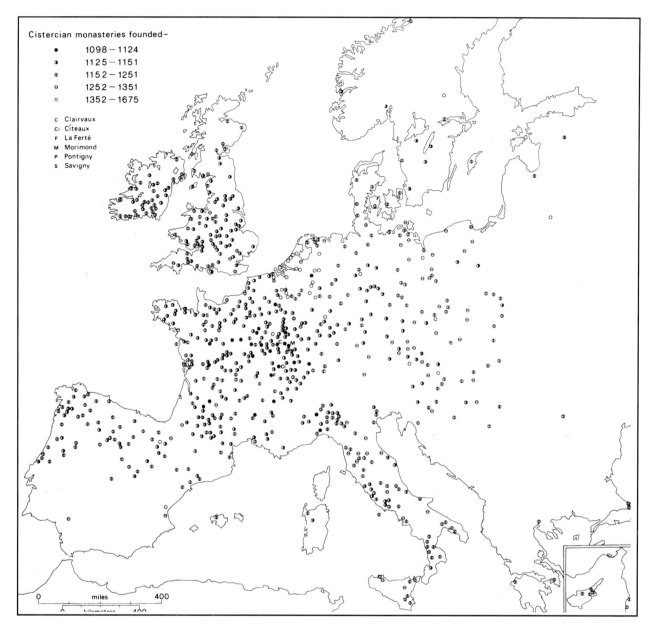

Cistercian monasteries founded–

- •   1098 – 1124
- ◑   1125 – 1151
- ◍   1152 – 1251
- ◒   1252 – 1351
- ○   1352 – 1675

c   Clairvaux
c₁ Cîteaux
F   La Ferté
M   Morimond
P   Pontigny
S   Savigny

Fig 3.7 *The Cistercian settlement in Europe, 1098-1675 (after Fig 1, Donkin 1978). Reproduced with permission.*

Finally, as is clear from the above examples, orders changed over time, beginning with groups of hermits and ending as 'normal' monasteries. The Paulists (also the Hermits of St Paul) are a good example of this, originating as a religious order of priests and brothers in 1250 with the union of two monasteries in Hungary – Patach, founded in 1215 by Bishop Bartholomew of Pecs, and Pisilia, established by blessed Eusebius Esztergom. The order received papal approval in 1308, adopted a strict observance of the Rule of St Augustine, and spread widely in Hungary, Austria, Germany, Sweden, Italy, Prussia, Lithuania and Poland. In 1420 Mendo Gomez introduced the hermits into Portugal and William Callier brought them into France, where

they were called the Brothers of Death. The order was contemplative until the sixteenth century. Thereafter, its members were involved in parochial, educational and charitable work.

The Canons

The canons as religious groups developed from the middle of the eleventh century, when it was felt that clergy serving cathedrals and churches should follow a monastic regime and live in common, following similar vows. The movement to reform clergy began in Italy and southern France at such centres as San Frediano in Lucca and San Lorenzo of

Ulcio near Turin, and St Ruf on the outskirts of Avignon in France. At the 1059 Lateran Synod, Hildebrand (the future Pope Gregory VII who gave his name to the Gregorian Reform of the late eleventh/early twelfth century (Morris 1989)) saw the advantage of canons following a regular life and the Synod gave its approval. These canons followed the rule of St Augustine of Hippo (Lawless 1987) and the movement spread to England around 1100 (Dickinson 1950). Under Henry I (1100–35) many houses were founded, or existing institutions re-developed as Augustinian priories; by 1300 about 206 houses had been founded in England and Wales (Robinson 1980).

There were a number of separate groups of canons and it is useful to consider them as discrete congregations; in the past they have tended to be considered as one, which masks their important individual characteristics (contra Knowles and Hadcock 1971).

The Order of the Holy Sepulchre of Jerusalem was developed with regular canons instituted at the mother house of St Sepulchre in Jerusalem in 1114 (Dickinson 1950), while the Order of Arrouaise was begun around 1090 by Cono and two other hermits at St Nicholas, near Bapaume in northern France. The Arrouaisians followed a severe, contemplative regime and made little headway until the period of Abbot Gervase (1121–47), when Cistercian observances were adopted and general chapters instituted (1121).

The Order of St Victor of Paris (the Victorines) was founded in 1108 by Abelard's teacher, William of Champeaux, who, with a few companions, retired to live as canons in an old hermitage of St Victor outside Paris (Dickinson 1950). An abbey was developed, an order founded and a general chapter instituted (before 1139). The order was closely associated with the development of the University of Paris and produced an important group of medieval writers. They had their own General Chapter for about a hundred years before losing their distinctive character and becoming indistinguishable from other Augustinians.

Other than the Augustinians, the most famous group of medieval canons, and those that had the widest geographical spread and longest chronological development, were the Premonstratensians. The development of the order founded by Norbert (†1134) in 1120, the mother houses, the spread of Premonstratensian abbeys all over Europe – there were eventually over 700 sites, though the maximum number occupied at any one time never exceeded 500 – has all been thoroughly discussed and mapped by Bond (1993) (Fig 3.8).

The Premonstratensians spread from Ireland and Portugal in the west, through the Mediterranean with houses on Majorca, Sicily and Cyprus, to the east with monasteries in Palestine, Greece and Constantinople. In Eastern Europe there were large numbers, including some in the Baltic states, Hungary and Poland. There were relatively few in the Scandinavian countries.

By contrast, the houses of the only English medieval order – the Gilbertines – were restricted in distribution to England, and then mainly in the east, especially Lincolnshire. Founded in 1131 at Sempringham in Lincolnshire by Gilbert (†1189), initially for women, the order developed with mixed houses of nuns, lay sisters, canons and lay brothers (Elkins 1988). Later, only houses for canons were established (Graham 1901 and Golding 1995).

Other groups of canons include the Order of Santa Cruz, otherwise known as the Canons Regular of the Holy Cross of Coimbra, founded in 1131 by Tello, archdeacon of the cathedral of Coimbra in Portugal, which owed much to the Order of St Ruf and spread widely through Spain and Portugal with nineteen monasteries.

Somewhat later was the Congregation of Windesheim in the Netherlands. This developed from a religious society of mainly document copiers and printers, the Brethren of the Common Life, under the mystic Gerard Groote (1340–84), who lived in a house at Deventer. In 1384 at the death of Groote, Florent Radewijns took over and more houses were built in cities in the Netherlands and Germany. As early as 1387 the Deventer Brethren had founded a monastery at Windesheim (near Zwolle) with canons regular of St Augustine. In 1393 the congregation of houses was established with three Dutch monasteries; in 1402 the order was confirmed by the pope and general chapters instituted. By 1430 there were forty-five monasteries and by 1500 there were ninety-seven; decline later resulted in thirty-two monasteries in 1728.

In the fifteenth century the Congregation of the Lateran was begun at Fregionaria, near Lucca, under Bartholomew of Rome. It was confirmed by Pope Eugene IV in 1421 and the brethren were given charge of the Lateran Basilica, but they were replaced by secular canons in 1471.

It is frequently not easy to sort out a particular order; it may prove difficult to disentangle its origins from later arrangements, and changes in its development, or different emphases in various geographical areas, may make a difficult problem of definition impossible. A good example seems to be the group known in England as the Crutched Friars. These seem to have been founded before the main friar groups of the Dominicans, Franciscans and so on, and to have been still in existence after 1274, when other groups like the Friars of the Sack and the Pied Friars had been dissolved.

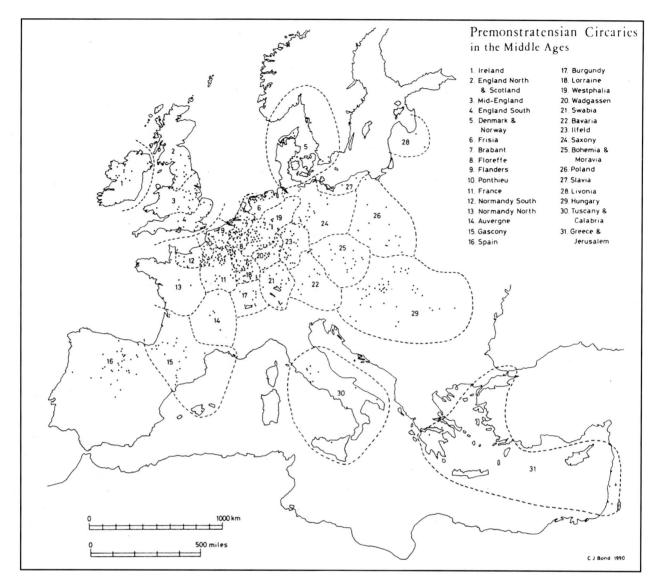

Fig 3.8 Premonstratensian foundations in Europe, with their circaries (after Fig 19.1, Bond 1993). Reproduced with permission.

The answer may possibly be that they were, in fact, part of a widespread order of canons called the Fratres Cruciferi, or Brethren of the Holy Cross (also called the Croziers). These may have begun in Italy under the former crusader Cletus of Bologna, who founded a community of canons under the rule of St Augustine known as *cruciferi* or *cruciati*. They received approval from Pope Alexander III in 1169 and at its greatest extent the congregation had five provinces (Bologna, Venice, Rome, Milan and Naples) with two hundred houses. They ran a number of hospitals and were called the Augustinian Hospitallers. It is probable that they had houses in Ireland (Gwynn and Hadcock 1970, 209). In 1591 the Italian group received the privileges of the mendicant orders but the order was suppressed by Pope Alexander VII in 1656. The Flemish branch (the Order of the Holy Cross, Crozier Fathers), to which the English houses

are usually assigned (Knowles and Hadcock 1971, 208), was founded at Clarlieu, near Huy in Belgium, by Theodore of Celles (1166–1236) in 1210. The Croziers spread rapidly in the thirteenth century through Belgium, Holland, France, Germany and England – where they arrived at Whaplode in Lincolnshire after 1244. They were recognized by the pope in 1248, when there were five houses in existence (including the one in England). Later they held hospitals in Ospringe, Reigate and Colchester. They were not affected by the 1274 decision at the Council of Lyons to restrict the entry of new friars to the mendicant orders, indicating that they were not friars. There may, however, be little or no connection between the houses of northern and southern Europe, the only link being the common name, which may be causing confusion.

The northern group was refounded with new

vigour after 1410, with a number of new houses in the Low Countries, especially St Agatha and Uden in the Netherlands. In 1840 a modern period of revival began. Here was an order with many strands to its development, including canons, 'friars', and hospitals. It seems at least possible that many other otherwise inexplicable groups, such as the Bethlehemites, the Bohemian Order of the Cross with a Red Star, the Fratri de Ordine Martyrum (Polish branch) and numerous hospitals, all belonged to this order of Crozier Fathers (Knowles and Hadcock 1971, 209).

The military orders

In Britain, scholars of monasticism and the religious orders are generally familiar with the Knights Templar and the Knights Hospitaller. While these are the most famous and influential of the groups of fighting monks in the middle ages, however, they are merely two of a very large group of military orders founded in the twelfth and thirteenth centuries (Seward 1995). Even earlier there were secular confraternities where groups of nobles swore oaths to religious houses to protect them and their pilgrims; included in these were groups at Liège and Grande-Sauve in France (Forey 1992). The military orders originated at the time of the Crusades, when it was necessary to take and then hold the holy places in Palestine and defend pilgrims visiting such sites. Their role was to provide armed escorts for pilgrims and to guard the holy places. When necessary they were expected to fight Muslim armies threatening to retake land in Palestine, Syria and elsewhere. As such, their centre of operations was in the east, although they had houses – preceptories and commanderies – all over Europe which acted as recruitment centres, local bases and centres for collecting money from estates and benefactors.

The earliest group was probably the Knights of the Holy Sepulchre 'founded' by Godfrey of Bouillon (c1067–1100) in 1099 after the First Crusade had secured Jerusalem and he had been made the first crusader ruler. He established a confraternity of pilgrims who had been to Jerusalem and been knighted. In a changed form the order is still in existence.

However, it was the twelfth century that saw the major development in military orders, with at least ten groups being developed. Most significant were the Knights Hospitaller (also known as the Knights of St John of Jerusalem, the Knights of Malta – the Sovereign Order of the Hospital of St John of Jerusalem, then of Rhodes, then of Malta), which began in the early 1100s, was formed into an order in 1113 and transformed into a military order by the

1130s. Even before 1113 a group had been founded to look after the hospice and hospital in Jerusalem, with a church which was dedicated to St John the Baptist; this hospital was in use 1108–87. After the fall of Acre in 1291, the Order evacuated to Limassol in Cyprus. Friction with the Lusignan kings of Cyprus resulted in a further move to Rhodes in 1307–9. When this was taken by Suleiman the Magnificent in 1522/3, the Holy Roman Emperor Charles V ceded Malta to them, which they held until Napoleon's capture of the island in 1798. The Order was re-established as a charitable religious institution after the fall of Napoleon, but it had lost its base in Malta, which had been ceded to Britain. It established a new headquarters in Rome in 1878 and continues as an aristocratic religious and hospitaller organization with branches throughout the world, including several protestant countries. The English order was recognized by royal charter in 1888 and is best known for its secular philanthropic activities through the St John Ambulance Brigade (Sire, 1994).

The Templars (also known as the Order of the Temple, Poor Fellow Soldiers of Christ and the Temple of Solomon, Poor Brothers of the Temple, Knights Templar) were founded in 1118 by a Burgundian knight, Hugh de Payns, and a knight from the north of France, Godfrey of St Omer, for the protection of pilgrims to the Holy Land. In the thirteenth century it became 'one of the most powerful monastic orders in Christendom' (Barber 1994). Baldwin II (d1131), king of Jerusalem, gave over to the Knights, as a base, part of his palace, which it was believed was part of the temple of Solomon (subsequently the al-Aqsa mosque), and in 1128 Bernard of Clairvaux, the most famous early Cistercian, wrote them a rule – 'De Laude Novae Militae' (Upton-Ward 1992).

It was not long before the idea of other groups was developed, both as hospital orders (see below) and also as orders to fight the infidel (and heretics) in other parts of Europe. In the Iberian peninsula Christians were pushing back the Moors (Muslims) all through the middle ages. Much of the fighting was undertaken by military orders, using castle-monasteries behind the frontier and away from the conflicts.

Of prime importance was the Order of Calatrava, the Spanish military and religious order of the reconquest. This was founded in January 1158 by king Sancho III of Castile, who ceded the fortress of Calatrava, in the modern province of Ciudad Real, to Raymond, abbot of the Cistercian monastery of Fitero, "to defend against the pagans, the enemies of the cross of Christ". Many soldiers took the monastic habit and the order was formed; in 1187 the order was affiliated to Morimond, one of the original Cistercian abbeys. In 1195 Calatrava was lost to the

Muslims, a serious blow to the order, and its headquarters were moved to Salvatierra; this was also lost in 1211. In 1212 Calatrava was recovered and the Muslims were defeated at Las Navas de Tolosa, and by 1221 the order had moved to new headquarters at Calatrava La Nueva castle. The Knights of Alcantara (formerly Knights of San Julian del Pereiro) may have originated in 1156, but the first evidence of the order comes in 1175 with a charter of Ferdinand II of Leon to a community at Pereiro, on the borders of Leon (Spain) and Portugal. In 1187 the order, which was attached to the Cistercians, was affiliated to Calatrava (along with Aviz – see below) and transferred to the castle at Trujillo, which was captured by the Muslims in 1195. In 1218 Calatrava ceded the fortress of Alcantara to the Knights of San Julian and it was henceforth known as the Order of Alcantara.

The wealthiest of all these Iberian military orders was Santiago (also Knights of St James, Order of Caceres, Order of Ucles). This was established at Caceres (in the province of Extremadura in Spain, then belonging to the joint kingdom of Leon and Castile) in 1170 by Pedro Fernandes and his companions, and king Ferdinand II of Leon, realising the value of such an order, ceded Caceres to them. In 1171 the order was put under the protection of St James of Compostella and by 1184 the order held property in Portugal, Castile and Aragon in Spain, England and Carinthia. In 1176 the order was recognized by Pope Alexander III and an annual general chapter instituted. Ucles was the main base in the kingdom of Castile, so the order is sometimes called the Order of Ucles.

The Portuguese military order of Aviz (or Evora) began with the capture of the fortress of Evora (in the province of Alemtejo) from the Moors in 1166. In 1176 the king ceded certain properties to the master and knights of Evora to follow the Rule of St Benedict, but it is not clear if it was independent or a branch of the Calatrava order. In 1201, however, Pope Innocent III granted the privileges of Calatrava to the knights of Evora; it became the Order of Aviz in 1211, when Alfonso II donated the fortress of Aviz and the headquarters were moved there. The Order of Aviz was also affiliated to Morimond.

The third greatest military order in Europe was, without doubt, the Teutonic Knights; they lead us from the Holy Land to fighting non-Christians in Eastern Europe. The order, Domus S Mariae Theutonicarum in Jerusalem, emerged from a field hospital founded by merchants of Lubeck and Bremen in the camp at Acre in 1190. It was approved by Pope Clement III in 1191 and converted to a religious order of knighthood in 1198. In 1199 Pope Innocent III gave the order the Rule of the Knights Templar and the first master was the Rhenish knight,

Herman Walpot of Bassenheim. In 1191 the headquarters were at Montfort, near Acre in Palestine; this was later moved to Venice and then in 1309 to Marienburg (now Malbork, near Danzig (Gdansk) in Poland). From here the order was in a good position to attack the pagans of Eastern Europe.

This task was also undertaken by a further group of orders of knights whose activities were entirely confined to the Baltic states – the Knights of the Sword (also Brothers of the Sword, Livonian Knights), founded in 1201 by Bishop Albert I of Riga, with the help of Abbot Theodoric of Riga (Forey 1992). The order was confirmed by Pope Innocent III in 1204 and it was to follow the Rule of the Templars; its purpose was to convert the heathen Esths and Livs of Livonia. They merged with the Teutonic Knights in 1237, although retaining some separate identity because of the geographical separation of their territories from the Prussian lands of the Teutonic Knights, as the war continued with pagans in Poland, Lithuania and Russia, and were dissolved in 1561 when Livonia became part of Lithuania.

A less successful group were the Knights of Dobrin, founded in 1228 when Bruno and fourteen knights were invested in an order at the castle of Dobrin (now Dobrzyn, west of Warsaw in Poland), following the style of the Knights of the Sword of Livonia, of whom they may have been former members. In 1235 they merged with the Teutonic Knights, although there were said to be still ten knights in a breakaway group based at Drohiczyn until they were extinguished by the pagans in 1240.

Rather less well-known, at least in Western Europe, is the Polish military Order of the Holy Cross with the Red Heart. This was a military order organized in 1250, with its headquarters at Cracow (now Krakow, in Poland). It developed particularly in the sixteenth century, spreading into Poland, Lithuania and Bohemia.

Two other orders need to be mentioned in connection with these crusading activities – the Order of the Trinitarians, and the Mercedarians. The former was founded by the Provençal St John de Matha (1160–1213) and possibly St Felix of Valois (1127–1212) at Cerfroid (Cerfroy), near Château-Thierry in Aisne, France, in 1197 and was approved in 1198. Although Cerfroid remained the motherhouse, a more famous centre was St Mathurin in Paris – hence the Mathurins, an alternative name. The order was founded to support poor pilgrims and travellers, but principally for the redemption or ransom of captives in the hands of infidels, either by providing money or by substituting themselves as captives. Their houses in north-west Europe were centres of recruitment and collecting points for funds, but there were some hospitals for the treatment of captives and others. By the middle of the thirteenth century the Trinitarians possessed more than a hundred houses across Europe, grouped into provinces (Lawrence 1994). After the fall of Jerusalem they became like Augustinian canons, taking over some of the property of the Augustinian canons of the Holy Sepulchre.

The Mercedarians (also known as the Order of Our Lady of Mercy, the Knights of St Eulalie, the Order of the Blessed Virgin Mary for the Ransom of Captives) performed a similar role in the wars in Spain against the Muslims. The order was founded in 1218 by St Peter Nolasco (*c*1189–1258) and James I (1208–76), King of Aragon 1213–76. In the presence of St Raymond of Pennafort, Peter and thirteen noblemen donned habits and took vows in Barcelona cathedral. A fourth vow (after poverty, chastity and obedience) was to provide hostages for the captives of the Moors in Spain and Peter was also concerned to relieve the suffering of Christian slaves among the Moors as well. The order was approved in 1235.

These orders, and of course the Hospitallers, had a strong hospital element, even though they were military in character. Other orders, as we shall see, existed specifically for medical reasons.

The hospital orders

There were large numbers of hospitals in the middle ages. The term covered both those establishments that looked after the sick and old, as well as those which were in effect hostels for travellers and pilgrims. Many were attached to Benedictine or Augustinian religious houses and run by the staff in them; some were attached to nunneries. Fontevrault, founded around 1100 by Robert of Arbrissel in the Loire Valley, France, had nuns and canons, but there were also several hospitals within the precinct – for lepers and old people.

There were also several orders founded specifically to run hospitals. We have seen how the Knights Hospitaller ran the hospital in Jerusalem and, as well as being a military order, provided hostels for pilgrims and travellers. The Antonines (also called the Canons Regular of St Anthony of Vienne and the Antonines of the Latin Rite) in effect founded the modern concept of hospitals. In 1070–4 Jocelyn, the local lord of part of the Dauphine in eastern France, brought back a supposed relic of St Anthony (*c*250–356: the first hermit and arguably the founder of monasticism) from pilgrimage. The pope ordered the creation of a Benedictine priory to look after the relics in 1088. By 1095 the saint and the relics were already being sought out by sufferers of St Anthony's fire, or ergotism, a particularly unpleasant disease caused by eating diseased rye (ergot of rye), so Gaston de la Valloire founded the Frères de l'Aumone (Brothers

of the Almonry) to look after sufferers. The village in effect became a hospital next to the priory. It was only in 1297, however, that an autonomous order was created when Pope Boniface VIII placed the brothers under the Rule of St Augustine; the abbey created was to be under direct control of the Holy See. Based on this centralized establishment, rather like Cluny, the order went on to develop over 1300 other hospitals dependent on forty-three principal preceptories (Fig 3.9). 'Collectors' gathered money for the order; we hear of this in London in 1225, but much of the money went into building a more elaborate church and other buildings back at St Antoine. In 1774, long after the decline of ergotism, and with the development of other provisions for the sick and the poor, the order was dissolved and the assets attached to the Order of Malta (Hospitallers). The Antonines had a house in London, St Anthony's in Threadneedle Street (Graham 1927), and another in Scotland at Leith (Cowan and Easson 1976).

Of even greater significance seems to have been the Order of the Holy Spirit, an order of hospitallers founded *c*1180 in France by Guy de Montpellier. With the patronage of Pope Innocent III and later popes, this order rapidly became the vehicle for a Europe-wide comprehensive social programme that lasted for more than five hundred years.

Before 1198 the main centre of the order was the Hospital of the Holy Spirit at Montpellier in southern France. It already had eight affiliated houses, including two in Rome, and was clearly medically very progressive; in 1198 Pope Innocent III recommended the order to all bishops. Guy was in Rome in 1204, when the Hospital of the Holy Spirit of Saxia was given to the order. By 1208 the order was organized with brothers and sisters following the same rule and looking after the sick, indigent, orphans, foundlings, unmarried mothers, the aged, insane and homeless. Laymen were enrolled into a Confraternity of the Holy Spirit – they provided money and so many days service. There is clear documentary evidence of at least 1,240 affiliated houses in Europe, though there were probably many more.

Although its early growth and expansion was over by 1444, it was refounded in 1477 and survived until suppressed by Pope Pius IX in 1847. During the middle ages "the Order of the Holy Spirit and its affiliates embodied the spirit of Christian mercy on a vaster scale and with more creative adaptability than anything hitherto seen in Christendom. From the beginning it courageously enlisted women religious as infirmarians; it maintained an incorruptible policy of gratuitous service; it spurred medical progress by its schools of anatomy, surgery, and pharmaceutics; it introduced an elaborate program of music therapy not only for mental

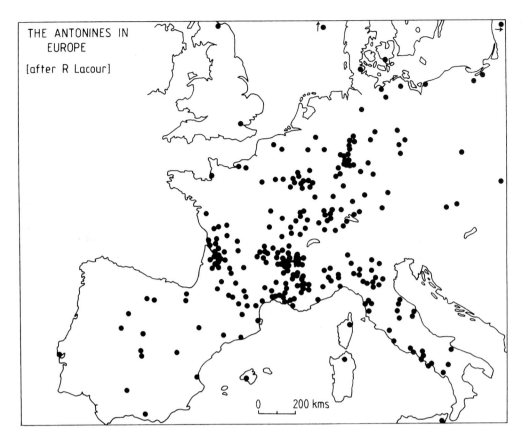

Fig 3.9 *Main houses of the Order of the Antonines in Europe.*

patients but for all, including infants at feeding time. As an organization it passed from history, but as the spirit of humility serving Christ in the sick and poor it passed over into younger orders and lives on to this day" (Hug 1967, 104).

Rather less well known in the west was the Bohemian Military Order of the Cross with a Red Star, which began in 1233 when Princess Agnes of Bohemia gave the brethren the church of St Peter and the hospital of St Francis in Prague, and was formalized in 1237 with the approval by Pope Gregory IX of the congregation under the Rule of St Augustine. In 1250 the papacy allowed the brothers to wear a black habit with a red Maltese cross with a six-point star. Although claiming to be a military order, a claim justified in the Hussite wars and the Thirty Years War, it was in effect a hospital order; from the house in Breslau in Silesia (now Wroclaw in Poland) the brothers established numerous hospitals. Despite general reform of the order in the seventeenth century and suppression of the Silesian house in 1810 by Prussia, the order still exists in the Czech Republic, with its headquarters in Prague.

No doubt other hospital groups existed. In England the Bethlehemites ran a mental hospital in London by 1247; Matthew Paris mentions this as the Hospital of St Mary of Bethlehem in 1257. In 1547 it

was still a royal establishment for lunatics – Bedlam. A few similar houses, though whether of the same order is not clear (they were probably Croziers), existed in Scotland, Pavia in Italy, and Clamecy in Nievre, France.

Mendicant orders

Following the development of hermit groups, canons and military orders, the final great development of religious orders within the medieval church was that of the friars. There were numerous orders of these (we probably have not yet isolated all the separate groups) and they had a wide variety of origins, from preachers and teachers to hermits. As mendicants, they lacked corporate possessions, usually not even owning their own monasteries (which belonged to sympathetic laymen), and they enjoyed great mobility, moving about preaching and teaching and not being confined to any one single monastery.

The earliest friars were founded by St Dominic to preach against the Cathars and the Albigensian Heresy in southern France, but the Black Friars, Dominicans or Preachers, as they were known, were not formally organized into an order until 1216. St Francis of Assisi founded and organized his poor men between 1208 and 1217, though as the Grey Friars, Franciscans or Minors they did not become an approved order until 1223. Both of these orders became very important, attracting thousands of recruits and establishing hundreds of houses all over western Europe. The other two main orders of friars began as disparate groups of hermits and were only formalized later on. The Carmelites, or White Friars, began in the Holy Land as hermits and were introduced into western Europe as conditions became difficult in the east; they were recognized as an order in 1226. The Augustinian or Austin Friars also began as hermits and absorbed other groups, such as the Boniti – they were recognized as an order by 1256.

These four orders were the only ones to survive a decree of the Second Council of Lyons under Pope Gregory X, issued on 17 July 1274. Other groups, such as the Mercedarians (founded 1235) and the Servites (founded 1256), as we have seen, were able to survive by changing their form; others, such as the Order of the Holy Cross, though called the Crutched Friars in England, were in effect an order of canons regular known as the Crozier Fathers (Knowles and Hadcock 1971; Gwynn and Hadcock 1970). The Friars of the Sack, founded 1251, and the Friars of the Blessed Mary (also Friars of St Mary de Areno, Fratres de Pica) or Pied Friars, founded 1257, gradually disappeared as older members died off and no new recruits were allowed. However, even after 1274 groups of friars were still constituted into new orders, such as the Minim Friars founded in 1435.

The Friars of the Sack (also Brothers of Penance of Jesus Christ or de Sacco) had sixteen houses in England and one in Dublin, Ireland (Chettle 1945). They originated just before 1250 in Provence, through a Franciscan novice who had been expelled; they followed the Rule of St Augustine and were based on the Dominicans. In 1251 a general chapter was held at Marseilles with representatives of twelve houses, all in the south of France, including Montpellier.

Although some Friars of the Sack joined the Austin Friars when their order was definitively established in 1256, the order continued to expand into Italy, Spain (with Zaragoza in 1263), Flanders (Liège, 1265) and Germany. It remained mainly centred in France, with important houses in Paris, Poitiers and Caen. By 1274 they had around a hundred communities scattered across the cities of Europe, with houses in the university cities of Paris, Bologna, Oxford, Montpellier and Cologne to educate their preachers (Lawrence 1994).

After 1274 some houses collapsed quickly. Villefranche (diocese of Elne) was empty by 1279; all the French houses had gone by 1304. Some went to the Austin Friars – Acre in 1290, Paris in 1293 and

Reims, Orléans and Tournai by 1320 – and the house at Parma was given to the Servites. Other houses were sold off: the Aragonese houses in the diocese of Valencia in Spain, Bologna in 1285 and Venice in 1288. The house at Majorca held on until 1300.

There were numerous other groups of so-called friars, which contemporaries, as well as later historians, have found very confusing. We know of, for example, the Friars de Ordine Martyrium, some of whom were a Polish congregation of Crutched Friars; and the Italian Cruciati (another Brethren of the Cross), approved by Pope Alexander III in 1169, and which at its greatest extent had two hundred houses in five provinces in Italy – Bologna, Venice, Rome, Milan and Naples (Knowles and Hadcock 1971 and Knowles 1948 says these were the Italian branch of the Crutched Friars and that both of these groups were part of the Crozier Fathers and hence canons (see above), but this sounds unlikely). There were also the Williamites (or Williamite Friars), who seem to have been not really an order, but followers of William of St Amour (1200–72) and who c1250 were adversaries of both the Dominicans and the Franciscans in the University of Paris. They were disbanded in 1274 (Lawrence 1994).

Future research

There has been no discussion in this article of many other groups of religious persons, such as the Waldenses (Fraternity of the Poor Men of Lyons), Beguines and Beghards, Humiliati (Poor Lombards), Poor Catholics of Dunandus, Apostolici, Fraticelli, Brothers and Sisters of the Free Spirit, or the Boniti. Most of these were never formalized, remaining as largely disorganized groups of poor people; some had elements of what was considered heresy, although others were recognized and even supported by various popes. More research is needed before they are excluded from or included in the main discussion of this article; few, if any, had any impact in Britain. Nor has much been said of the many confraternities which preceded, or developed alongside, the main orders, or of the nuns or groups of lay people forming the second and third orders of some groups. Nor has it been possible to discuss such groups as the Bonshommes of Ashridge and Edington, who seem unrelated to other groups also called Bonshommes (including Grandmontines, Minims and Friars of the Sack) (see Chambers 1979).

It is nevertheless clear that there is a very large number of fully recognized new orders of monastic and religious communities in the middle ages. For most we do not have a complete list of their houses, with foundation dates, length of occupation and brief histories. This makes it very difficult to demonstrate the impact of the foundation of monastic and religious houses in any particular area, the relationship between houses of different orders and with the local lay population. Without these basic data, in the form of a "Knowles and Hadcock" set of gazetteers, the real impact of monasticism will remain elusive and the interrelationships in society and the landscape obscure.

Case study – North-Eastern England: Yorkshire, Lincolnshire and Nottinghamshire

To show what is possible in Britain from the information available, we can look at one example where there is adequate information about a variety of monasteries, of different orders, foundation dates and types.

Parts of north-eastern England had been rich in monastic institutions in the period before the eleventh century. In Northumbria large numbers of sites were established in the seventh and eighth century, only to be extinguished by Viking attacks in the ninth century. By the year 1000, monasticism was effectively dead in this region – only Crowland, of the ancient Benedictine houses, survived (as a refoundation in 971).

With the available data we can chart the monastic settlement of the area. Excluding friaries and military houses, there are approximately 137 houses considered in this region (Fig 3.10); minor and temporary sites are overlooked.

There are various religious groups represented in these three counties in the middle ages; it will serve as an example of which there must be many parallels in Europe. Benedictines (both monks and nuns) are there, of course: at least fourteen houses for men and ten for women. These include houses like Lastingham and York St Marys, Bardney, Whitby and Selby, as well as lesser known houses such as the nunneries at York Clementhorpe and Nun Monkton. There were also Cluniac houses at Pontefract, Lenton and Monk Bretton.

The Cistercians had many houses and it is well known how great their impact was here, with such famous sites as Rievaulx, Fountains and Kirkstall. There were many more, however, and with several communities relocating on occasions, numerous sites are represented. There were also many houses of nuns claiming to be Cistercians – at least nineteen houses in this area.

Other new orders are well in evidence, particularly in Lincolnshire. There, the Premonstratensians were first established at Newsham in 1143. Twelve other houses of this order were founded before 1200. The Gilbertines originated in this region, so not surprisingly they are well represented here –

Sempringham (founded in 1139) was followed by six other mixed houses of nuns and canons, including the well-known house at Watton in Yorkshire, and several houses of canons alone. There was also one Grandmontine house, several (late) Carthusian monasteries and a Trinitarian house. Augustinian canons were well represented in the region from the early twelfth century, with such houses as Bolton, Bridlington, Guisborough, Kirkham, Thornholme, Worksop and Newstead. They had thirty-one houses/sites in all.

The dates of most of these foundations are reasonably well documented and most are undisputed, as there are good accounts of their origins in documents. It is thus possible for us to chart with reasonable accuracy the number of sites in use at any particular time, and to ascertain the rate of increase and the slowing down of foundation later on (Fig 3.11).

Thus, from the one house in existence in the pre-1000 period (Crowland), and the one pre-1066 Norman Conquest house (Spalding), there is a considerable increase in the period up to 1100. In that period a further ten houses were established, all Benedictine except for the Cluniac house at Pontefract (c1090). Some were refoundations – Whitby (1077), Bardsey (1087) – but most were new sites, some destined to be of great significance, such as Selby Abbey (1069–70). Yet this was still a very thin cover over such a vast area.

As with many other parts of Europe, the situation was to be changed beyond all recognition in the twelfth century (Fig 3.12). No less than 114 monasteries were established between 1100 and 1200, slightly more in the first half of the century than the second (63/51), representing something like 76 percent of the total monasteries founded in this area in five hundred years. As we have seen, many of these represented the impact of the new orders.

Although in the period 1100–50 there were still Benedictine and Cluniac houses being founded (eight Benedictine houses – four for men and four for women – and one Cluniac house at Lenton) and in the period 1150–1200 a further Benedictine monastery, eight Benedictine nunneries and a house each for Cluniac monks and nuns (making twenty houses, or 21 percent of the century's total, in all), most new monasteries were of the new orders.

Between 1100–50 the Augustinian canons occupied nineteen sites, followed by one further site by 1200. The Cistercians occupied fifteen sites by 1150 and a further five by 1200, but this includes a lot of moves. Eight and eleven Cistercian nunneries were established between 1100–50 and 1150–1200 respectively. Three Premonstratensian abbeys were founded by 1150, and a further ten by 1200. There were seven Gilbertine houses of nuns and canons by

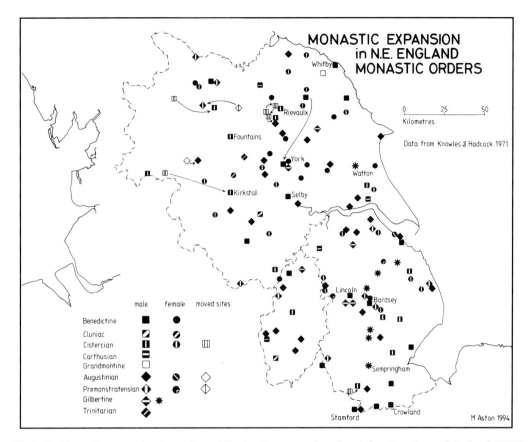

Fig 3.10 Monastic expansion in north-east England – monastic orders (after Knowles and Hadcock 1971).

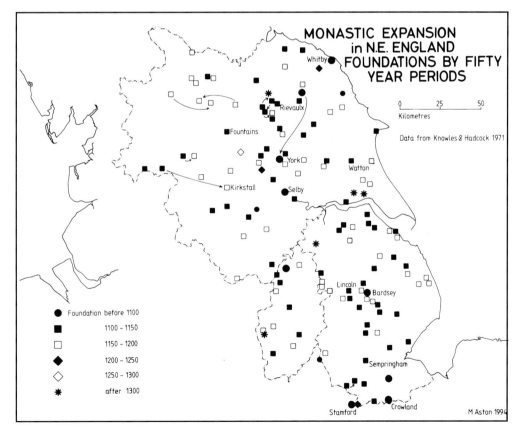

Fig 3.11 Monastic expansion in north-east England, pre 1000 to 1400.

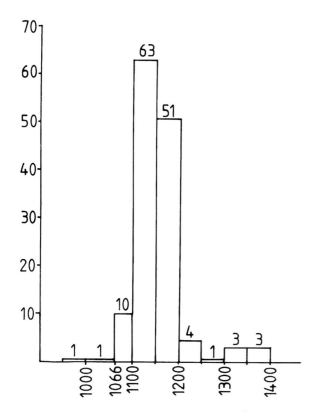

Fig 3.12 Monastic expansion in north-east England – founda-tions by fifty-year periods (after Knowles and Hadcock 1971).

1150, and one house of canons alone; by 1200 three more houses of canons had been founded.

By 1200 one might expect that saturation point had been reached – were there any other baronial families who had not yet founded monasteries, was there any more surplus land to provide the endowment estates of new sites? The rate of foundation of monasteries falls off dramatically, with only five in the century to 1300, and six in the period to 1400. Who were these latecomers? Interestingly, while further houses of Augustinian canons are stationed at Newstead (Lincs) and elsewhere, it particularly includes a Grandmontine house (Grosmont, 1204), a Trinitarian house (Knaresborough, 1252) and the arrival of the Carthusians, arguably the most ascetic and well respected of the severe groups of hermits of the middle ages, whose popularity never really waned, but who nevertheless never had the great impact of the more obvious orders. In this region are some of the most interesting Carthusian foundations – Beauvale (1343), Hull (1377), Axholme (1397–8) and particularly Mount Grace (1398).

While we might marvel at the number of houses eventually established in these three counties, and be impressed by the rate of foundation and the variety of establishments, this is not the reason for including this example here. Indeed, the above discussion poses all sorts of further questions. Why

was the rate so impressive, where did the financial and other resources come from in such a short length of time, who staffed all of these new establishments? It must have had an enormous impact on local communities. Answering these questions (and others) is the real reason for gathering and assessing these data and is why we need comparable information for all of Europe.

The main point is that for Britain and Ireland it is possible to discuss these problems and questions, because the data are already assembled, for England in successive volumes of the Victoria County History for many counties, the Ordnance Survey Monastic Britain maps (now sadly out of print), but mainly of course in the volumes by Knowles and Hadcock (1971), Cowan and Easson (1976) for Scotland, and Gwynn and Hadcock (1970) for Ireland. The basic data are already in existence for the British Isles.

Conclusions

A full discussion of the expansion of monastic orders in Europe from the eleventh century onwards, therefore, is hampered by a number of problems. The first task is to define the number of orders in existence in the middle ages in Europe. An attempt has been made here (see appendix), but it is clear that this is incomplete and that there are a number of problems of definition to be sorted out. Secondly, the number of individual sites established for each of these orders needs to be ascertained on a country by country, region by region approach. Dates of foundation, founders, movement of sites and brief histories all need to be refined – Cottineau (1939) provides a beginning, but with computerised data-bases much more ordering and analysis of data is now possible. There is no doubt in this author's mind that all of this information is readily available in the archaeological records and archives of various countries, regions and departments/counties. But it is not generally available to researchers with a Europe-wide view. What is needed is the equivalent of 'Knowles and Hadcock' for each country or region.

Only when this has been undertaken can the full impact of monasticism in Europe begin to be dis-cussed. What is possible has been indicated by the single example of north-east England, relying on simple, readily available data of order, foundation date and location. Such information is needed over Europe as a whole.

As this English example demonstrated, only when the basic data are made available can real discussion be undertaken on the expansion and impact of the monastic and religious orders in Europe. Much more significantly, however, when such basic data have been co-ordinated it will be possible to examine the much wider and more important and interesting questions about monasticism in Europe in the middle ages – how many orders were there, what was their impact overall or on specific areas, what was the role of patrons in particular geographical areas or with particular orders? What was the impact of the many monasteries founded in one area – on each other and on local communities? Did monastic ownership affect farming, industry, commercial activities and so on? Such questions are at the heart of the study of medieval Europe from an archaeological and historical point of view. With the modern development of Europe as a wider social, political and economic unit in our own time, it is an appropriate and optimum moment for such studies. There is much to be done.

Acknowledgements

It will be clear to anyone reading this account that I owe a great debt to the compilers of the entries in both the original and the New Catholic Encyclopedia. This cornucopia of information formed the basis for much of the discussion and gazetteer presented here.

I would like to thank Carinne Allinson for her careful work on preparing the text and Father Daniel Rees for access to the superb library of Downside Abbey, Somerset. Joseph Bettey, James Bond, Andrew Davison, Father Philip Jebb and David Robinson read and commented on earlier drafts of the text; James Bond and David Robinson made available their extensive knowledge of various aspects of monasticism and saved me from numerous errors. I am very grateful to them. Any remaining errors and misunderstandings are, of course, my own.

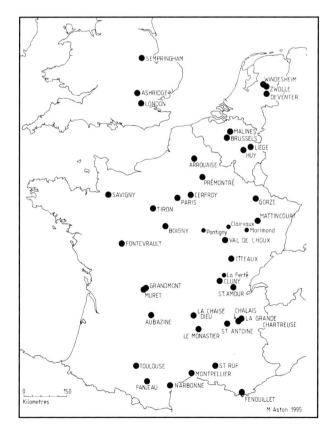

Fig 3.13 Mother houses of monastic and religious orders in France, England, Belgium and the Netherlands.

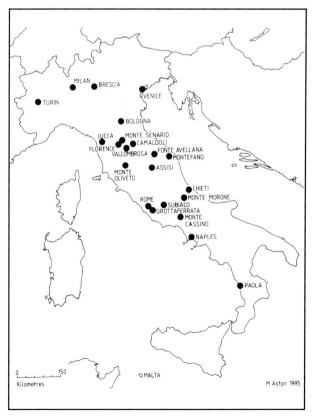

Fig 3.14 Mother houses of monastic and religious orders in Italy.

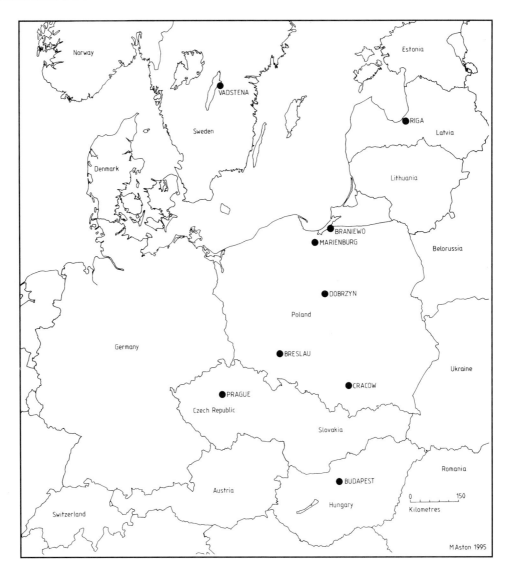

Fig 3.15 *Mother houses of monastic and religious orders in eastern and northern Europe.*

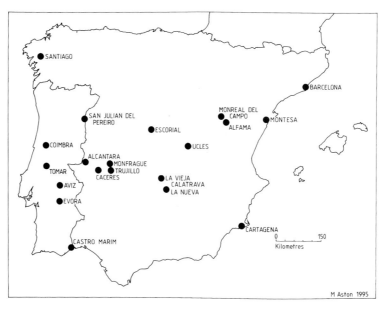

Fig 3.16 *Mother houses of monastic and religious orders in Spain and Portugal.*

Table 3.2 New Monastic and Religious Orders in Europe
(900–1600)

The following abbreviations are used in the table:

O: Order; C: Congregation (eg: 1095/1301 indicates that the group started in 1095, but did not become an order until 1301)

Mon: Monks; Her: Hermits; Can: Canons; Fr: Friars; Mil: Military; Hos: Hospitallers; N/C: Nuns/Canons; Tea: Teaching Order (eg: Mil/Hos indicates the order was a military hospital order; Her-Mon indicates the order began as hermits and later became monks)

Ben: Rule of St Benedict; Aug: Rule of St Augustine; Bas: Rule of St Basil; Ad: Adopted (followed by date); Tem: Rule prepared by Bernard of Clairvaux for the Knights Templar in 1128: 'De Laude Novae Militae'

Cist: Cistercians (Cistercian observances when in 'Rule' column); Cal: Calatrava (indicates customs of Calatrava were followed when in 'Rule' column); Cart: Carthusians (Carthusian customs when in 'Rule' column)

D: Dissolved; S: Supressed; A: Affiliated; (may be followed by the relevant dates); E: Still in existence

[1] Assets attached to the Order of Malta (Hospitallers).
[2] In 1490 united with Knights of Malta, except for Lazarites in France.
[3] Secularized and dissolved in the 19th century. Nuns of Calatrava continue in one convent in Madrid.
[4] Now an honorary society of noblemen.
[5] Except for small group, who became Knights of Monfrague.
[6] Secularized at the Reformation. Dissolver 1805 by Napoleon.
[7] From Order of Mountjoy.
[8] Merged with Teutonic Knights in 1237, but because of territorial holdings tended to maintain a separate geographical identity.
[9] The Knights of Dobrin merged with the Teutonic Knights in 1235, except for a small group who refused to accept the merger and lived on under Duke Conrad's protection at Drohizyn until c.1240, when their master was captured by the pagans.
[10] 1262 attempts to amalgamate with Abbey of Feuillant (Cist). E1267/68. Gone by c.1280.
[11] Continued in Lithuania to early 19th century.
[12] Constitution modelled on that of the Franciscans.
[13] One community survived in Marseilles to 1316.
[14] Only Uden Netherlands remains.
[15] United in 1399/1400 to Knights of Montesa by Pope Benedict XIII, at the request of King Martin of Aragon.
[16] Replaced by seculars in 1471.
[17] After separation of Franciscans into two groups – the Observants and Conventuals – by Pope Leo X in 1517, the Coventuals in France and Belgium were known as the Cordeliers.
[18] From Observants.

Date of Foundation	Name of Order	Type	Founder	Headquarters/ Mother House	Date of Papal Approval	Date of First General Chapter	Rule Followed	Present State
TENTH CENTURY								
909	[CLUNY/CLUNIAC]	Mon	Duke William the Pious of Aquitaine & St Berno of Baumes Les Messieurs	Cluny			Ben	D1789
933	[GORZE]	Mon	Adalbero I of Metz, Einold of Toul & John of Gorze	Gorze			Ben	D1789
ELEVENTH CENTURY								
by 1005	[GROTTA FERRATA]	Her	St Nilus	[Grotta Ferrata]			?Bas	E
1015	CAMALDOLI/ CAMALDOLESE	Her	St Romuald	Camaldoli		(C13th) Padua, 1239	Ben	E
1039	VALLOMBROSA/ VALLOMBROSANS	Her	St John Gualbert (Gualberto)	Vallombrosa (near Fiesole)			Ben	E
1039	ST RUF	Can		St Ruf, Avignon			Aug	D
1043	CHAISE DIEU	Mon	St Robert of Turlande (or Chaise Dieu)	Chaise Dieu				D
1059/63	CANONS REGULAR OF ST AUGUSTINE/BLACK CANONS	Can	[Pope Gregory VII]	San Frediano at Lucca & San Lorenzo of Ulcio near Turin, & St Ruf, Avignon	1059/63	1215	Aug	E
1076 (Muret) [1124 to Grandmont]	GRANDMONTINES/ BONSHOMMES	Her/Mon	St Stephen of Muret	Muret, then Grandmont			Aug, to Ben, to Rule of Grandmont	SI772
1084	CARTHUSIANS	Her	St Bruno	La Grande Chartreuse	1142?		Ben	E
1090	ARROUAISIANS/ORDER OF ARROUAISE	Can	Cono & two hermits	St Nicholas, Arrouaise		1121	Aug Influenced by Cist (ad 1121)	
1095 [01301]	ANTONINES/ANTONIANS/ CANONS REGULAR OF ST ANTHONY OF VIENNE/ANTONINE HOSPITALLERS	Hos-Can (1301 on)	Gaston de Dauphine & his son Guerin	St Antoine en Viennois	1297		Aug (ad 1247)	D1774[1]
1098	CISTERCIANS/WHITE MONKS	Her-Mon	St Robert of Molesme	Citeaux	1119?		Ben	E
1099	KNIGHTS OF THE HOLY SEPULCHRE	Mil	Godfrey of Bouillon	[Holy Sepulchre, Jerusalem]				E
TWELFTH CENTURY								
1100	FONTEVRAULT	N/C	St Robert of Arbrissel	Fontevrault				D
1104 X 1134	ORDER OF MONREAL DEL CAMPO	Mil	King Alfonso I of Aragon	Monreal del Campo			Tem	Abortive
c1108	CALESIANS	Her	?	Chalais, near Grenoble				A-Cart 1303
1108	VICTORINES/ORDER OF ST VICTOR OF PARIS	Can	William of Champeaux	St Victor, Paris			Aug	D
1108/9 or 1114	TIRONENSIANS/ TIRONIANS	Her-Mon	St Bernard of Abbeville or Tiron	Nogent (1109–14) Tiron (1114 on)			Ben	D

Date of Foundation	Name of Order	Type	Founder	Headquarters/ Mother House	Date of Papal Approval	Date of First General Chapter	Rule Followed	Present State
1105 (hermitage) 1112-15 (abbey)	SAVIGNAC/GREY MONKS	Her-Mon	St Vitalis de Mortain	Savigny	1119	1122-39	Ben	Cist 1147
c1070/80	HOSPITAL OF ST JOHN OF JERUSALEM	Hos-Can (1301 on)	Merchants of Amalfi	Dependency of the abbey of St Mary			Ben	
1113 or by 1108	KNIGHTS HOSPITALLER/KNIGHTS OF ST JOHN OF JERUSALEM/KNIGHTS OF RHODES/KNIGHTS OR MALTA	Hos-Mil from 1136	Gerard	St John the Baptist, Jerusalem (1070-1187) Tyre, then Acre (1188-1291) Limassol, Cyprus (1291-1307) Rhodes (1307-1522) Malta (1530-1798)		1113	Hos	E (St Johns) Secularized †1798
1114	CANONS REGULAR OF THE HOLY SEPULCHRE OF JERUSALEM	Can		Holy Sepulchre, Jerusalem			Aug	D?
1118/19 or about 1120	KNIGHTS TEMPLAR/POOR FELLOW SOLDIERS OF CHRIST AND THE TEMPLE OF SOLOMON/POOR BROTHERS OF THE TEMPLE	Mil	Hugh de Payns & Godfrey of St Omer	The Temple of Solomon (later al Aqsa mosque, Jerusalem (1118-87) Tyre, then Acre (1187-1291) Limassol, Cyprus (1291-1312)			Tem	S1312
1120	PREMONSTRATENSIANS/ NORBERTINES/WHITE CANONS	Can	St Norbert of Xanten	Prémontré	1125	1128	Aug	E
1130	[AUBAZINE/OBAZINE]	Her-Mon	St Stephen of Muret	Aubazine/Obazine				D
1131	GILBERTINES	N/C	St Gilbert of Sempringham			1147	Aug (Canons) Ben (Sisters) Cist (Lay brothers)	D by 1539
1131/2	ORDER OF SANTA CRUZ/ORDER OF COIMBRA/PORTUGUESE CANONS REGULAR OF THE HOLY CROSS OF COIMBRA	Can	Tello	Coimbra, Portugal	1135		Customs of St Ruf	S1833
1120? (first mentioned 1142)	ORDER OF ST LAZARUS/HOSPITALLERS OF ST LAZARUS OF JERUSALEM	Hos-Mil by 1244?		Boigny, by Orléans, France (after 1291)			Aug	A1490[2] S1847
1145 or c1180	ORDER OF THE HOLY SPIRIT	Hos	Guy of Montpellier	Hospital of Holy Spirit, Montpellier before 1198 Holy Spirit in Saxia, Rome (1204 on)	1198			
1158	ORDER OF CALATRAVA	Mil	King Sancho III of Castile & Abbot of Fitero?	Calatrava (Castile, Spain) (1158-95) Salvatierra (1195-1211) Calatrava la Nueva (c1220 on)	1164 & 1187		Ben (Cist)	[3]
1156-76	KNIGHTS OF SAN JULIAN DEL PEREIRO/KNIGHTS OF TRUJILLO/KNIGHTS OF ALCANTARA (Later ORDER OF ALCANTARA)	Mil	Suero of Salamanca or Gomez of San Julian	Pereiro, Leon, Trujillo (1187-95) Alcantara (1218) Spain	Time of Alexander III		Ben (Cist)	A-Cal[4]
by 1169	CRUCIATI or CRUCIFERI	Can	Cletus of Bologna	Bologna	1169		Aug	S1656
1170	ORDER OF SANTIAGO/KNIGHTS OF ST JAMES, SANTIAGO DE COMPOSTELLA/ORDER OF CACERES/ORDER OF UCLES	Mil	Pedro Fernandez (a Leonese nobleman) & his companions	Caceres (1170-4) Ucles (1174 on) (Leon, Spain)	1175 (Alexander III)	1175	Aug	D early 19th cent by Napoleon
1173	ORDER OF MOUNTJOY (MONTEGAUDIO?)	Mil	Roderick, former count of Sarria (formerly of Order of Santiago) & Companions	Aragon, Spain			Ben (Cist)	A-Tem 1196[5]

Date of Foundation	Name of Order	Type	Founder	Headquarters/ Mother House	Date of Papal Approval	Date of First General Chapter	Rule Followed	Present State
by 1176	ORDER OF EVORA/ORDER OF AVIZ	Mil		Evora (1176-1211) Aviz (1211)	1201		Ben	A-Cal
by 1179	CHAFFRIENNES	Mon	[St Chaffre]	Le Monastier sur Gazeille				D
pre 1190 [Mil 1198]	ORDER OF THE TEUTONIC KNIGHTS/ORDER OF ST MARY OF THE GERMANS	Hos-Mil (1190s)	Merchants of Lubeck & Bremen	Montfort (Acre), (1190-1291), then Venice (1291-1309), then Marienburg (1309 on)	1191 (Clement III) 1199 (Innocent III)		Tem	[6]
1190s	ORDER OF ST THOMAS OF ACRE	Can/Mil Canons again by late C14th	Community of canons re-organized as military order by Peter des Roches Bishop of Winchester 1227	Hospital of St Thomas, Acre (to 1291) Cyprus (1291 to late C14th) London (late C14th on)			Aug	
1193	VALLISCAULIANS/ BRETHREN OF THE CABBAGE VALLEY	Her-Mon	Viard & Otto III, Duke of Burgundy	Val de Choux			Cart & Cist	A-Cist 1764, D1789
1196	ORDER OF MONFRAGUE (MONTEGAUDIO?)	Mil[7]	Remainder of Knights of Mountjoy led by Roderick Gonzalez who refused to accept amalgamation with Templars in 1196	Monfrague				A-Cal 1221
by 1197	WILLIAMITES	Mon & Nuns	William of Vercelli		1197		Ben	D?
1197	TRINITARIANS/ MATHURINS/RED FRIARS	Can/Hos	St John de Matha & 'St Felix of Valois'	Cerfroid (or Cerfroy) (St Mathurin, Paris second most important house)	1198		Aug (Customs St Victor)	D?
THIRTEENTH CENTURY								
*c*1200	ORDER OF SAN JORGE DE ALFAMA	Mil	Pedro II of Aragon	Alfama, Aragon				A-1400 Montesa
1201/1202	KNIGHTS OF THE SWORD (OF LIVONIA)/BROTHERS OF THE SWORD/LIVONIAN KNIGHTS/MILITIA OF CHRIST OF LIVONIA/ORDER OF THE SWORD BRETHREN	Mil	Bishop Albert I of Riga (= Albert of Buxhorden) & Abbot Theodoric (or Theodorick) of Riga	Riga	1204 (Innocent III)		Tem	A-1237[8] Teutonic Knights D1561
1207-10	FRANCISCANS/GREY FRIARS/MINORS	Fr	St Francis	Porzioncola chapel, Assissi	1210, 1223	1260	Franciscan	E
1212	MINORESSES/POOR CLARES	Fr (sisters)	St Clare	St Damiano, Assisi (1212-1257), Santa Chiara, Assisi (1257 on)			Franciscan	E
1210/11	CROZIERS/CROZIER FATHERS/CANONS REGULAR OF THE HOLY CROSS/ORDER OF THE HOLY CROSS	Can	Theodore of Celles, Canon of Liège	Charlieu/Huy (Belgium)	1247	1248	Aug (Domincan)	E
1216	DOMINICANS/BLACK FRIARS/PREACHERS	Fr	St Dominic	Toulouse, Prouille, Fanjeau	1216	1243	Aug	E
1218/35	MERCEDARIANS/ORDER OF OUR LADY OF MERCY/KNIGHTS OF ST EULALIE/ORDER OF THE BLESSED VIRGIN MARY FOR THE RANSOM OF CAPTIVES	Mil Can?	St Peter Nolasco & James I, King of Aragon	Barcelona	1235			
*c*1221	MILITIA OF THE FAITH OF JESUS CHRIST	Mil	?Amury of Montfort	South of France	Time of Honorius III		Tem	
1226 or 1242	CARMELITES/WHITE FRIARS	Her-Fr	St Simon Stock (1247-68) Transformed hermits to order of friars	Originally on Mount Carmel				E
by 1227	ORDER OF ST THOMAS OF ACRE	Hos-Mil	Peter de Roches, Bishop of Winchester		Time of Gregory IX (1227-41)			
by 1228	KNIGHTS OF DOBRIN/ ORDER OF DOBRIN	Mil	Bishop Christian of Prussia & Duke Conrad of Masovia (Polish)	Dobri(n) or Dobrzn	1228 (by Gregory IX)		Tem? Modelled on Knights of Sword of Livonia	Merged 1235[9]

Date of Foundation	Name of Order	Type	Founder	Headquarters/ Mother House	Date of Papal Approval	Date of First General Chapter	Rule Followed	Present State
1231	ORDER OF THE SWORD or OF THE FAITH AND PEACE	Mil	Amanieu (Archbishop of Auch from 1226)	West of Toulouse	Gregory IX			[10]
1233	KNIGHTS OF THE BOHEMIAN MILITARY ORDER OF THE CROSS WITH A RED STAR	Hos/Mil	Princess Agnes of Bohemia	Church of St Peter & Hospital of St Francis Seraphinus Prague	1237		Aug	E
1233	SERVITES/ORDER OF FRIAR SERVANTS OF ST MARY	Fr	Buonfiglio Monaldi (St Bonfilius) & companions	Cafaggio/Florence & Monte Senario	1249/56			E
1247	BETHELEHEMITIES	Hos	??Part of Order of Cross with a Red Star??	London, Hospital of St Mary of Bethlehem				E?
1227/47	SYLVESTRINES/BLUE or SYLVESTRINE BENEDICTINES	Her-Mon	St Silvester Guzzolini	Monte Fano	1247		Ben	E
1211	CRUTCHED FRIARS/ORDER OF THE HOLY CROSS (see CROZIER FATHERS, 1210/11)	Fr?						
by c1250	WILLIAMITES/WILLIAMITE FRIARS	Fr	William of St Amour (1200-72)	?St Amour, Jura, France?				D1274
1250	ORDER OF THE HOLY CROSS WITH THE RED HEART	Mil		Cracow				[11]
1250	PAULISTS/HERMITS OF ST PAUL/ORDER OF ST PAUL THE FIRST HERMIT (BROTHERS OF DEATH)	Her?-Can?	?Bishop Bartholomew of Pecs & Eusebius of Esztergom	Abbeys of Patach & Pisilia in Hungary	1308		Aug	E
Pre 1250, 1251 or 1255	FRIARS OF THE SACK/BROTHERS OF PENITENCE OF JESUS CHRIST/SACCATI/ BONSHOMMES	Fr		Fenouillet by Hyères, Provence	1251, 1255	1251	Aug[12]	S1274[13]
Earlier than 1256	AUSTIN FRIARS/AUGUSTINIAN FRIARS/HERMIT FRIARS OF ST AUGUSTINE	Her Fr from 1256					Aug	
1257	FRIARS OF THE BLESSED MARY/PIED FRIARS/FRIARS OF DOMINA?	Fr						S1274
c1256	CELESTINES/HERMITS OF ST DAMIAN/HERMITS OF MORONE	Her/Fr	Pietro di Morone, subsequ Pope Clement V (but not pope when he founded the order)	Monte Morone	1264		Ben	E
by 1256-7	FRIARS OF ORDINE MARTYRUM (see CROZIER FATHERS)	Fr? or Can		Poland				See CROZIER FATHERS
c1264	URBANISTS/URBANIST POOR CLARES [Reformed Poor Clares – Franciscans]	Nuns	Pope Urban IV (wrote rule)					
by c1265/1266	ORDER OF THE BLESSED VIRGIN MARY [FRATRES GAUDENIES – 'Jovial Brothers']	Mil	Loderingo degli Andalo (Bologna) & Catalano di Guido	Italy	1261 by Urban IV			Gone by 1270s?
1270s	ORDER OF SANTA MARIA DEL ESPANA	Mil (esp at sea)		HQ at Cartagena (Castile, Spain)				A-1280 Santiago
1283	BONSHOMMES	Can?	Edmund, Earl of Cornwall	Ashridge				D1539
1294/c1308	POOR HERMITS OF THE LORD CELESTINE/FRANCISCANS OF NARBONNE		Macerata/ Liberto	From Celestines From 1308 at Narbonne			Ben	Died out early 14th cent
FOURTEENTH CENTURY								
1307	ORDER OF SAO TIAGO		From Portuguese Templars & Santiago					
1317	ORDER OF CHRIST/ORDER OF KNIGHTS OF CHRIST	Mil	King Dinis of Portugal from Portuguese Templars & Santiago	Initially Castro Marino, subsequently Thomar (1357 on)	John XXII 1319	1321	Cal	
1313	OLIVETANS	Her-Mon	Bernard Tolomei (1272-1348)	Monte Oliveto	1319/44		Ben	E?

Date of Foundation	Name of Order	Type	Founder	Headquarters/ Mother House	Date of Papal Approval	Date of First General Chapter	Rule Followed	Present State
1318/19	KNIGHTS OF MONTESA/(MILITARY) ORDER OF OUR LADY OF MONTESA	Mil	From Mercedarians Pope John XXII at request of King James II of Aragon	Montesa (near Tativa)			Cal	A-Cal 1321. Intro Cist. D19th cent
1344 (O1370)	BRIDGETTINES/ORDER OF THE MOST HOLY SAVIOUR	N/C	St Bridget of Sweden (1304-73)	Vadstena	1370			E
1370	ORDER OF ST JEROME/JERONIMITES/ HIERONYMITES/ LOS JERONIMOS/ BRETHREN OF GOODWILL	Her	Pedro Fernandez Pecha (†1374)	(Italy) Subsequently El Escorial, Spain	1373		Aug	S1835 in Spain
1384/1386-7/(C1393)	WINDESHEIM CANONS/CONGREGATION OF WINDESHEIM	Can	Gerard Groote, Florent Radewijns & followers	1387 mother house founded at Windesheim	1402		Aug	[14]
by 1363	ORDER OF SAN JORGE DE ALFAMA/ST GEORGE OF ALFAMA	Mil			1363			[15]
FIFTEENTH CENTURY								
1406	COLETTINES/COLETTINE POOR CLARES [Reformed Poor Clares – Franciscans]	Nuns	St Colette of Corbie (†1447)	Ghent, Belgium (1442)				
by 1421	CONGREGATION OF THE LATERAN	Can	Pope Eugene IV	Lateran Basilica, Rome	1421			[16]
c1435	MINIMS/HERMITS OF ST FRANCIS OF ASSISI/BONSHOMMES	Her-Fr	St Francis of Paola (1416-1507)	Paola, Calabria	1435 1474 (Sixtus IV)			E
1349/50-1460	CELLITES/ALEDIAN BROTHERS/ CONGREGATION OF CELLITES/ [POOR BROTHERS/BREAD BROTHERS/CELLITE BROTHERS]	Hos	Tobias?	Malines (Mechelen, Belgium)	1460		Aug	E
SIXTEENTH CENTURY								
post 1515	ALCANTARINES (Reformed Franciscans)	Fr	St Peter Gravito of Alcantara (1499-1562)	Pedrosa in Extredadura				E?
1517	CORDELIERS[17]							
1518/1528 (O1563)	ORDER OF SOMASCHA	Hos	St Jerome Emiliani (1481-1537)	St Rose, Venice? Somascha	1540		Aug	E
1524	THEATINES (after Caraffa was Bishop of Chieti – ie Theate in Latin, hence Theatines)	Reg Clerics	St Cajetan (†1547) & his companions, Gian Pietro Caraffa (later Pope Paul IV), Bonifacio de Colli & Paolo Ghislevi	Rome (1524-7), then Naples (from 1527)				E
1525	CAPUCHINS/ORDER OF FRIARS MINOR CAPUCHIN	Fr[18]	Br Matteo de Bascio (†1552)		1536	1529	Franciscan	E
1530	BARNABITES/REGULAR CLERICS OF ST PAUL	Tea Clerks	St Anthony Zaccaria (†1539), Ven James Morriga, Ven Bartholomew Ferrari	St Barnabas, Milan	1533	1579		E
1534	SOCIETY OF JESUS/JESUITS	Missionary Priests	St Ignatius Loyola (†1556)		1540			E
1535	COMPANY OF ST URSULA/INSTITUTE OF ST URSULA/URSULINES/ ORDER OF ST URSULA	Tea Clerks	St Angela de Merici (1474-1540)	Brescia, Italy	1544 (Paul III 1612 (Paul V)			E
1537	HOSPITALLERS OF ST JOHN OF GOD	Hos	St John of God (†1550)		1572		Aug	E

Bibliography

Aston M A 1993, 'The Development of the Carthusian Order in Europe and Britain: a preliminary survey' in Carver M (ed), *In Search of Cult: Archaeological Investigations in Honour of Philip Rahtz*, The Boydell Press, Woodbridge, pp 139–51

Barber M 1994, *The New Knighthood: A History of the Order of the Temple*, Cambridge University Press

Bond C J 1993, 'The Premonstratensian Order: a preliminary survey of its growth and distribution in Medieval Europe' in Carver M (ed), *In Search of Cult: Archaeological Investigations in Honour of Philip Rahtz*, The Boydell Press, Woodbridge, pp 153–85

Butler L 1984, 'The Houses of the Mendicant Orders in Britain: Recent Archaeological Work' in Addyman P V and Black V E (eds), *Archaeological Papers from York presented to M W Barley*, York Archaeological Trust, pp 123–36

Butler L 1987, 'Medieval Urban Religious Houses' in Schofield J and Leech R (eds), *Urban Archaeology in Britain*, Council for British Archaeology Research Report 61, pp 167–176

Chambers G E, 1979, *The Bonshommes of the Order of St Augustine at Ashridge and Edington*, 2nd edition, Edington

Chettle H F 1945, 'The Friars of the Sack in England', *Downside Review* LXIII, pp 239–51

Coppack G 1998, *The White Monks; the Cistercians in Britain 1128–1540* Tempus, Stroud

Cottineau L H 1939, 1970, *Repertoire Topo-Bibliographique des Abbayes et Prieures* (3 vols), Protat Freres, Macon

Cowan I B and Easson D E 1976, *Medieval Religious Houses Scotland*, Longmans, London

Dickinson J C 1950, *The Origins of the Austin Canons and their Introduction into England*, SPCK, London

Donkin R A 1978, *The Cistercians: Studies in the Geography of Medieval England and Wales*, Pontifical Institute of Medieval Studies, Toronto (Studies and Texts No 38)

Elkins S K, 1988, *Holy Women of Twelfth-Century England*, University of North Carolina Press

Evans J 1938, *The Romanesque Architecture of the Order of Cluny*, Cambridge University Press

Fergusson P 1984, *The Architecture of Solitude*, Princeton

Forey A 1992, *The Military Orders, from the Twelfth to the Early Fourteenth Centuries*, Macmillan, London

France J 1992, *The Cistercians in Scandinavia*, Cistercian Studies Series 131, Cistercian Publications Inc, Kalamazoo, Michigan

Golding B 1995, *Gilbert of Sempringham and the Gilbertine Order c1130–c1300*, Clarendon Press, Oxford

Graham R 1901, *St Gilbert of Sempringham and the Gilbertines, A History of the only English Monastic Order*, Elliot Stock, London

Graham R 1927, 'The Order of St Antoine de Viennois and its English Commandery, St Anthony's, Threadneedle Street', *Archaeological Journal* 84, pp 341–406

Gray M 1993, *The Trinitarian Order in England: Excavations at Thelsford Priory*, L Watts and P Rahtz (eds), Tempus

Reparatum, British Archaeological Reports British Series, 226

Gwyn A and Hadcock R N 1970, *Medieval Religious Houses, Ireland*, 2nd edn 1988, Irish Academic Press, Dublin

Hug P L 1967, Order of the Holy Spirit in *New Catholic Encyclopaedia* Vol 7, McGraw-Hill, pp 103–4

Hutchison C A 1989, *The Hermit Monks of Grandmont*, Cistercian Studies Series 118, Cistercian Publications Inc, Kalamazoo, Michigan

Kinder T 1999, *L'Europe Cistercien* Zodiaque

King P 1999, *Western Monasticism: A History of the Monastic Movement in the Latin Church*, Cistercian Publications Inc, Kalamazoo, Michigan

Knowles D and Hadcock R N, 1971, *Medieval Religious Houses England and Wales*, Longman, London

Knowles D 1948, *The Religious Orders in England* Vol 1, Cambridge

Lawless G 1987, *Augustine of Hippo and his Monastic Rule*, Clarendon Press, Oxford

Lawrence C H 1994, *The Friars: The Impact of the Early Mendicant Movement on Western Society*, Longman, London

McGuire B P 1982, *The Cistercians in Denmark*, Cistercian Studies No 35, Kalamazoo, Michigan

Morris C 1989, *The Papal Monarchy: The Western Church from 1050 to 1250*, Clarendon Press, Oxford

Norton C and Park D (eds) 1986, *Cistercian Art and Architecture in the British Isles*, Cambridge University Press

Panagopolous B K 1979, *Cistercian and Mendicant Monasteries in Medieval Greece*, University of Chicago Press

Pressouyre L (ed) 1994, *L'Espace Cistercien*, Comite des Travaux Historiques *et Scientifiques*, Memoires de la Section d'Archaeologie et d'Histoire de l'Art No 5, Paris

Riley-Smith J (ed) 1991, *The Atlas of the Crusades*, Times Books, Swanston, London

Robinson D (ed) 1998, *The Cistercian Abbeys of Britain*, Batsford, London

Robinson D M 1980, *The Geography of Augustinian Settlement*, British Archaeological Reports, British Series, 80

Fr Sebastian, (nd), *The Capucins*, J S Burns & Sons, Glasgow

Seward D, 1995, *The Monks of War; the Military Religious Orders*, Penguin

Sire H J A, 1994, *The Knights of Malta*, Yale University Press, New Haven and London

Stalley R 1987, *The Cistercian Monasteries of Ireland, An Account of the History, Art and Architecture of the White Monks in Ireland from 1142 to 1540*, Yale University Press, London

Upton-Ward J M 1992, *The Rule of the Templars*, Boydell Press, Woodbridge

Van Der Meer F 1965, *Atlas de L'Ordre Cistercien*, Elsevier, Amsterdam/Brussels

Williams D H 1984, *The Welsh Cistercians*, Caldy Island, Tenby

Williams D H 1990, *Atlas of Cistercian Lands in Wales*, University of Wales Press, Cardiff

Williams D H 1998, *The Cistercians in the Early Middle Ages*, Gracewing, Leominster

4   Living in a Vale of Tears.
Cistercians and site management in France:
Pontigny and Fontfroide*

Terryl N Kinder

Introduction

Cistercian architecture has been the object of enquiry for so long that one might well ask what more there is to say.[1] So much has been written about the architecture, particularly of the claustral buildings, that a popular belief has arisen that the plan of a Cistercian abbey is wholly predictable and can be reconstituted after finding a portion of one or two walls. But were these abbeys exactly alike, there would obviously be no need for further archaeological investigation. In fact, no two identical abbeys have yet been found, although a general layout of the buildings around the cloister may be anticipated to some extent, at least in men's abbeys.[2] Good excavations show that there is tremendous variety in site planning and construction. The scale of the buildings depended upon the size and wealth of the community, and every monastery was subject to decisions based on topography, availability of materials, and regional economy and industry, among other variables. The history of the region – local tradition, revolutions, religious reform (Protestant or Catholic), favour or disfavour of the ruler toward the Order – also affected the evolution of individual abbeys. Wealth or impoverishment in later centuries – from war, pestilence, famine, political manipulation – as well as the quality of management also determined expansion, transformation, or demolition of the early buildings. Recent research concerning the role of water systems, location of buildings beyond the cloister ranges – such as infirmary and noviciate, gatehouse and guest quarters – plus a host of domestic and industrial buildings, not to mention land and resource management, are influencing how we think about Cistercian abbeys.[3]

Parallel to the continuing archaeological investigation of sites, there has also been exploration into the economic and legal history of individual monasteries, publication of sermons, chronicles and other literary works by Cistercian authors, inventories of Cistercian libraries, studies including codicological and artistic aspects of books, as well as an (overdue) investigation into the many aspects of women's abbeys. New research also includes the structures which served the domestic, utilitarian, industrial and agricultural aspects of monastic life, both inside the precinct wall and beyond it; the best of these studies expand to include the constitution, construction, management and evolution of the grange estates, with their forests, mines, quarries, fishponds and other elements.[4] This work, it is hoped, will encourage a fuller evaluation of the history of Cistercian material culture than has hitherto been provided by the over-simplified concept of "ideals vs. realities". This view, which has dominated research for the past few decades, was essentially the result of an attempt at creating Cistercian history from the literary sources – especially the prohibitions ferreted from the *Statuta* – rather than from the all-embracing evidence of the Cistercian life which presents a rather more complex and nuanced picture.[5] The corpus of information continues to expand in virtually every field and direction. The danger is that as each discipline refines or revolutionises itself, it incorporates into new thinking the premises of outdated work in other fields. Interdisciplinary exchange is thus essential.

Another aspect of this question is of a more material nature (if not frankly monetary and therefore frequently political), and touches the buildings themselves. Hundreds of thousands of tourists visit Cistercian sites in France each year. One might well ask why these abbeys continue to attract attention? There are several reasons. First, the centralised organisation of the Cistercian Order and its enormous success have left hundreds of abbeys with a certain coherent resemblance, which provides thematic continuity to visitors. Cistercians went to every corner of the mediaeval world – beyond the borders of modern Europe – in the one hundred or so years (*c*1120–1220) after the establishment of the first five houses.[6] This expansion occurred at the precise moment when the gothic architectural style emerged and was in a state of fervent experimentation. Secondly, since they are located in the countryside, Cistercian sites have fared better than multiply-reconstructed urban foundations, and have distinct pastoral appeal in our largely urban culture. Thirdly, the buildings were well built and the sites admirably tamed and organised, and they are still inspiring, even as ruins. The monks took the new "French style" everywhere they went – at least for the first generation of building – and this clean style with its clear lines, fresh open spaces, and repeated forms is very appealing to modern taste. Fourthly, what we now call "aesthetics" was rather a part of the spirituality of the Middle Ages – and spirituality was expressed in one's daily actions – but these concepts have been separated out and compartmentalised in contemporary secularised culture.[7] The buildings and sites maintain this spiritual after-life (promoted under other names), even when monks are gone and vaults are down, precisely because of their deep appeal to the human psyche. In addition, an on-going monastic tradition can help our interpretation of historic buildings, and the fact that the Cistercian Order still exists gives continuity to this splendid patrimony, even if few contemporary monasteries are located at historic sites.

While Cistercian architecture *per se* is not the topic of this paper, a few observations may help clarify other issues (Figs 4.1–4.4). The churches are usually discussed in terms of their simplicity, harmonious proportions and lack of ornament, and they are frequently compared – usually to the disadvantage of the monastic buildings – to contemporary cathedral projects, which are described as more daring, innovative and fundamentally interesting. To do this, however, is to miss the point. A cathedral is the chief ecclesiastical building of the diocese, a powerful politico-religious statement in stone, and its function is quite different from that of an abbey, especially a Cistercian abbey. The latter is basically a self-sufficient village for monks and its church a place of prayer and liturgical celebration for them. To understand a monastic church, one must understand the life led in a monastery and the reasons why a man or woman would chose such a life. A glance through the pages of the *Rule* of Saint Benedict shows the orientation – to prayer, worship, quietude, stability, manual labour – a *mode d'emploi* for living a celibate Christian life in community, albeit with an intensely interiorised component. Nothing is said about architecture. How, then, did Cistercians come to create an identifiable style? Or did they?

The beginnings of an answer may be found in the *Rule* – that is to say, in western monastic life itself.[8] In trying to understand Cistercian architecture, it is useful to remember that Cistercians lived, following the *Rule*, essentially in silence. It was a life turned inward, a life of liturgical devotion, meditation and manual labour. The harmony, simplicity and tranquillity so frequently evoked to describe the architecture are a reflection of the human goals that the monastic life strove to achieve – inner harmony, inner simplicity, inner peace. This lifestyle (in modern parlance) – this spirituality (in medieval) – is reflected in the walls themselves. The buildings could be described in the first instance as being a shell around monastic life – that is, protecting it from the elements. At the same time, the walls are also, of course, something else. They are a mirror of that life, and they are an ideal surrounding; the walls, in their simplicity, reflect the goal of monastic life, thereby encouraging its progress; the built environment assists, reflects and encourages the direction intended by monastic vows.[9] In 1943 Winston Churchill said "we shape our buildings, and afterward our buildings shape us",[10] but he could well have been citing Cistercian construction of some 800 years earlier.

Cistercian architecture and its decor have behind their design one common element, albeit manifested in many ways according to location, size, type of stone, and so forth. That element is the focusing of the attention inwardly, to provide a harmonious and positive ambience for prayer. Coloured window glass and narrative capitals were forbidden in Cistercian abbeys – not for dislike of art or beauty – but because colour and narrative attract the eye and engage the mind in linear thinking, and linear thinking is not the primary intention of Cistercian life. Cistercians sought an ambience that favoured an interiorising experience, reaching toward God via silent prayer, and this objective is not facilitated by saints' lives in red and blue dancing in the light. Colour pulls the attention outward; it has an exteriorising effect. Saturated colour can bring feelings of excitement, glory, exaltation, even frenzy. Cistercian churches may occasionally be large and use the latest construction technology, but they are deliberately unadorned, the colour is white or neutral, the decoration is minimal; "spectacular" is not an adjective one would normally use to describe them. The animation is provided by the light – as it moves from east to west through the building in the course of a day, from low along the horizon to high in the sky from winter to summer, from sharply contrasting shadow and light to diffuse outlines according to the weather. It is a slow rhythm, and this very slowness – playing along the clean lines of the architecture – can assist a person seeking it to achieve an inner harmony. The source of "Cistercian

Fig 4.1 *Le Thoronet (Var), interior of the abbey church, north aisle, west bay*

Fig 4.2 *Noirlac (Cher), nave of the abbey church*

Fig 4.3 *La Rieunette (Aude), nave and sanctuary of the abbey church.*

Fig 4.4 *Noirlac (Cher), refectory.*

style" then, is in Cistercian life itself. The rest is details. They are fascinating details – involving origins and influences and many technical questions – but erudite obsession must not be permitted to obscure the point. The spiritual and the material were not separate in the medieval period.

The two abbeys discussed below illustrate work at two very different sites, similar only in that they belonged to the Cistercian order, and were located in valleys. Management decisions involved in creating a suitable environment for monastic life were highly practical, for life in a valley carried the most basic of practical consequences. The several moves that some communities made before settling in a permanent location were often related to water (or lack of it) and its management. Water allows life, and monastic water sources had to be wisely chosen and the systems kept in good repair – cleaned out, diverted, augmented when the supply lessened. A great deal of work has been done recently on hydraulic management of riverine sites by Cistercians, pointing to the fact that their vision of the importance of water power put them in the forefront of hydraulic technology in the Middle Ages.[11]

Pontigny

Pontigny, second daughter of Cîteaux, was founded in 1114 at the site of a *métairie* in the gently sloping valley of the Serein River, which in the Middle Ages marked the frontier between Burgundy and Champagne (Fig 4.5). Here already is a source of potential conflict, as the respective counts on either side of the river were avowed enemies. By establishing an abbey in this area, a political no-man's-land became, among other things, a buffer zone. Donations and

vocations abounded, and Pontigny was destined to become the head of a modest filiation of forty-four abbeys in France, Italy, and Hungary. The original parcel of land was in the territory of Guillaume II, Count of Nevers, Auxerre, and Tonnerre, but construction of this huge abbey – undertaken in the late 1130s and terminated toward mid-century – had as patron his old enemy, the Count of Champagne, Thibaud II.[12]

Today all that is visible of that building campaign is the church and the lay brothers' building. The church shows something of the scale of the abbey, with a total length of 117 metres, including the ambulatory and radiating chapels which replaced the more modest square apse toward the end of the twelfth century.[13] Even in its original mid-twelfth-century form, the church reflected the Cistercians' openness to new technology; when the transepts were up and foundations were being laid westward into the nave, the project was radically changed and the nave covered with ribbed vaults, the first in Burgundy, and with flying buttresses along the north flank.[14]

In order to establish the required self-sufficiency, the Cistercians developed an economic system whereby they owned and worked granges (farms) located around the abbey, sometimes dozens of kilometres – or even further – away.[15] Lay brothers, or *conversi*, manned the granges, returning to the abbey on Sundays and feast days. The monks also performed manual labour, but in areas closer to the abbey, since the *Rule* did not permit them to spend the night outside the monastic compound. Their offices, too, were shortened during haying season and the harvest.

As anyone who has tried to pin down historic evolution from these documents knows, it is often

Fig 4.5 *Pontigny (Yonne), aerial view from the southwest.*

very difficult to determine what criteria were used
to identify a property as a grange, since the way in
which the land holdings are described varies from
document to document. Pontigny owned at least one
grange as early as 1120; by 1156, eleven *grangia* were
named among other land holdings.[16] In 1166, a rather
more detailed document mentions no fewer than
twenty-six properties, although, confusingly, only
two of these are specifically called *grangia*; the rest
being lands, vineyards, fields, woods, or *quicquid
juris habetis....*[17] Since these were working farms they
no doubt evolved constantly, and it is impossible to
know what type of agriculture was predominant at
what grange at any given date unless a document
mentions it, nor how many buildings existed, nor of
what type they were.

From 1120 to the Revolution, Pontigny's properties continued to evolve, reflecting the economy of
each period. The lack of sufficient lay brothers after
the thirteenth century created a shortage of man-
power, and granges further afield were leased out or
eventually sold, some becoming the nuclei of towns.
Of the eleven in operation in 1156, six are still working
farms, and all six have historic buildings. None are
classified as historic sites, however, and an autoroute
project recently threatened three of them.[18]

One example may suffice: Villiers-la-Grange,
located 35 kilometres south-east of the abbey, is first
mentioned in connection with Pontigny in the mid-
1140's. Although the land was probably already being
cultivated (the site dates back to Merovingian times),
the Cistercian occupation of Villiers gave a considerable boost to its development. The property was
consolidated and prospered within a short time,
despite conflicts with a neighbouring Cistercian
grange (belonging to another abbey) and with a
powerful neighbour of Benedictine persuasion. It later
succumbed to the ravages of the Hundred Years'
War and was leased out to seculars toward the end of
the fifteenth century, with subsequent complaints by
the renters of banditry (by anyone passing by) and
excessive taxation (by the King). The site was
abandoned for a time, then re-inhabited before the
Revolution. These vicissitudes – which occurred of
course to a greater or lesser extent everywhere – are
mentioned especially to throw into relief the exceptional nature of the preserved structures. One building
now serving as a barn was probably built as a
combination dormitory-kitchen-workroom for the lay
brothers in the later twelfth or early thirteenth
centuries. Two stories in height and measuring 20.7
by 9.9 metres, the construction is of outstanding
quality despite the modern transformation of inner
volumes and wall openings (Fig 4.6). In 1729 the
building, then inhabited by a ploughman, had a
surrounding wall with its own gatehouse, setting it
apart from the rest of the village which itself was

Fig 4.6 Villiers-la-Grange (Yonne), east face of barn.

surrounded by a precinct wall. Slightly to the east is
a small chapel dedicated to Saint Edmund of
Abingdon,[19] which was enlarged when the grange
was leased out, but which retains its essentially
romanesque character and continues as parish church
for the handful of families who inhabit Villiers today.
The *pièce de résistance* is the survival of a large cistern
between the chapel and the lay brothers' building,
measuring 8 by 16.12 metres. This spectacular
structure was conceived as two parallel naves, each
covered with a barrel vault and separated by an arcade
of ten arches resting on nine chamfered rectangular
shafts (Fig 4.7). Fields and vineyards lay beyond the
walls of this grange-cum-village, yet even here traces
of monastic habitation remain. Numerous boundary
stones engraved with a crozier between the letters S
and E – for Saint Edmund of Pontigny – are still
present at corners of the irregularly-shaped fields; a
map of 1782 describes the surveying done at that
time and allows restitution of the form of these land
parcels, which no doubt echo medieval field patterns.[20]
Here the Cistercian imprint remains in the land itself.

Despite having founded numerous granges in the
surrounding countryside, the monks lived at Pontigny for over twenty years before beginning permanent construction at the abbey itself. Nothing is
known of the primitive buildings, but there is no
mention of change of site; Pontigny appears to be

Fig 4.7 Villiers-la-Grange, arcade of cistern.

one monastery where the original land donation and early accretions were sufficiently manageable that the community did not have to move. The first busy settlement decades would have given the founders ample occasion to observe the flood and drought patterns (and discuss them with neighbours), devise the best use of the land, and reflect upon the siting of future abbey buildings. Meanwhile, they built a dam two kilometres east of the site of the future cloister to create a millstream just under three kilometres in length, with a usable drop of 5.5 metres (Fig 4.8). This canal runs westward inside the precinct wall of the abbey, and the medieval mill was located along or just outside the western wall; the building itself was rebuilt *c*1685 and still exists.[21] A fulling mill was added to the abbey's industries in the mid-eighteenth century (it survives as a restaurant), and another earlier mill – perhaps for a forge – was located further downstream.

Pontigny Abbey is located south of the river, and the church was built upslope on the highest ground. The cloister was thus laid out to the north, toward the

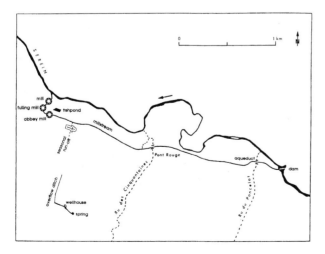

Fig 4.8 Pontigny, south river bank drainage and millrace management, with location of spring

river and canal. The refectory at Pontigny is not perpendicular to the cloister – as it frequently is in Cistercian abbeys – but parallel to it, probably because the claustral complex was laid out and built before perpendicularly placed refectories became common Cistercian abbeys, and also because the location of the millstream reduced the amount of available building space. In fact, one proof that the water system existed before construction of the abbey is that the cloister is not square or rectangular, but trapezial (Fig 4.9). The millstream cuts through the property at a slight angle, and the claustral buildings (refectory, kitchens, warming room) were laid out to the north, as close as they dared go to its edge. The eastern wing of the cloister does, however, traverse the millstream; sacristy and chapter are in their usual location, and monks' workroom (with a winepress) is on the other side of this canal. The dormitory ran the length of this wing on the upper floor, and the monks' latrines were no doubt located over the stream at dormitory level, such as one may still see at the Cistercian abbeys of Royaumont and Maubuisson (Val d'Oise) or Zwettl in Austria. A sluice-gate system could then divert this water to the fishpond to nourish the aquatic plants. No traces of the lay brothers' latrines have been found, but an intriguing passage in a 1241 account of one of Saint Edmund's miracles gives a graphic description of an unknown part of the medieval abbey, the guesthouse sewers. According to this document, a sick man in the pauper's infirmary fell into the latrine and, delirious with fever, made his way through deep, smelly, narrow, stone-vaulted, tortuous passages in cold rushing water until he was found the next morning outside a postern gate, still in the water but cured of his fever.[22] Alas, the location of the medieval gatehouse, guest quarters, infirmary and all such "inter-phase" buildings has not been identified, but this latrine – and any other – would have been built over a fast-moving stream.[23] It is clear that before construction could take place these water systems had to be laid out and built.[24] What can we know of them today?

The terrain south of the Serein River where Pontigny was built consists of clay. Its excellent quality was no doubt recognised in the Middle Ages and it is still used for the manufacture of high-quality tiles and bricks.[25] The natural drainage of the slope therefore had to be taken into consideration when building the millrace (Fig 4.8). To the east, where the canal runs through the fields, two aqueducts allow seasonal run-off to pass underneath the race and empty into the river. A third such natural run-off is located underneath the church, and it was accommodated by means of a stone drain transecting the nave and aisles near the point where they join the transept, continuing under the cloister and emptying into the millrace.

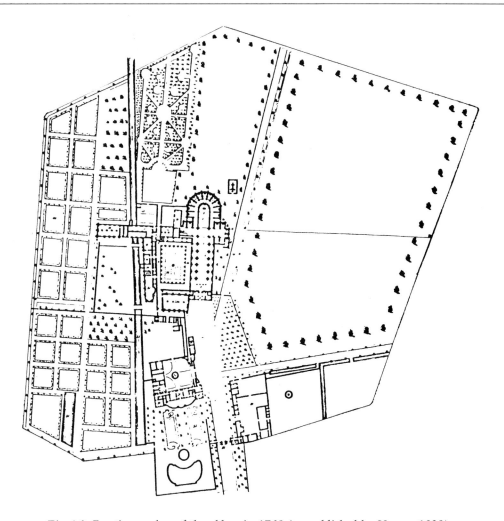

Fig 4.9 *Pontigny, plan of the abbey in 1760 (as published by Henry, 1839).*

So far we have discussed the management of pluvial drainage in clayey soil, and the construction of a millrace for industrial purposes although it was also used for sewage removal. A third system involved bringing a supply of pure water into the cloister. A few elements of this system still exist, while traces of others may be tracked in the land-scape and pieced together with the help of oral accounts.

To begin with the end of the line, two famous stone basins still adorn the gardens at Pontigny, neither now in its original location (Fig 4.10). Each was cut from a single block of limestone, quarried some 50 kilometres south-east of Pontigny between Massangis and Montbard.[26] The two are nearly identical in form: a slightly pitched basin pierced with two central holes for incoming (and continu-ing) pure water, and with exit holes at regularly spaced intervals around the periphery. The exterior edge is finished with a torus between cavets and a large roll moulding at the bottom, a common twelfth-century profile. The smaller of the two vessels measures 3.40 metres in diameter and has 31

regularly spaced holes, no doubt once fitted with lead spouts, which would have allowed water to run out of the basin into the waiting hands of 31 monks at the same time. The larger fountain is 4.32 metres in diameter with 40 peripheral orifices, several of which still retain traces of lead spigots.

The presence of two fountains is somewhat problematic. Their size and weight (the smaller weighs six metric tonnes) discourage speculation that they were superposed. More likely, one served the monks and the other the lay brothers. Their original location is not known – by the eighteenth century both had been moved – but it is probably safe to imagine that one was in a fountain-house in the cloister, opposite the monks' refectory, such as one finds at many Cistercian sites (Fig 4.15).

To end with the beginning of the line, one might then ask about the source of the water – and fortunately some interesting traces remain. Evidence suggests that there were two springs or wells, one of which still exists approximately 800 metres uphill to the south.[27] It is 4.16 metres in depth and 1.98 metres in diameter; the lower courses are of large (36 x 36

Fig 4.10 *Pontigny, smaller basin, now in garden of lay brothers' building.*

cm) curved ashlar blocks, of the same pure-white limestone as the church, with a layer of clay tile between each stone. The upper part of the well is of rubble construction, closed with a beehive vault. The western side of the well has a round-arched opening, also of white ashlar, which is now sealed off. Some twenty years ago the owner of the property blocked off this aperture to what he called the "souterrain", a tunnel he described as being nearly high enough for a man stand in it. According to a plan of 1856, this was the entrance to one "voûte de la fontaine" (elsewhere referred to as a cistern), measuring about 20 metres in length and connecting the well to a "maisonnette" (wellhouse).[28]

To the existing well, the nearly forgotten plan, and the oral tradition, can be added the disappearing traces in the landscape. Until only a few years ago, a pond about 350 metres north-east of this area, in the direction of the abbey, served as an overflow. The former name of the nearest street was "Rue aux Canes", in honour of the ducks who are reported by village elders to have marched there every evening after spending the day on the lower millstream. The 1856 plan also shows a ditch, labelled as communal property and serving as an overflow. Portions of this ditch are still visible behind back gardens, but they are only identifiable as such when placed in a much larger context that includes, effectively, this entire hydraulic system. Examination of the land register (*cadastre*) reveals that this ditch represented a property limit pre-dating the present main highway, which is a post-medieval creation cutting through medieval land parcels without respect for their shape or orientation.

The crowning element to this fascinating detec-tive story – and the one that allows a link to the two stone fountains – is an aerial photograph taken during the drought of 1991. On this photo, repro-duced here in an interpretative drawing for clarity, two fine lines can be seen coming from the hill to the south and leading toward a square in the field between the well and the abbey, about 30 metres from the church (Fig 4.11). Two other lines leave the opposite side of the square and diverge, one toward the church and the other toward the lay brothers' building. This square likely represents the outer walls of a filtering tank (the cover has probably caved in), where water from at least two springs was directed, filtered, and redistributed to two different places within the abbey – and one is strongly tempted to suggest the two fountains.

There are numerous reasons for supposing that these fountain basins were sculpted at the same time the church and cloister were built, the well was dug, and the filtering system created. A source of pure water was a daily necessity, and by definition would have had to come from the south (uphill), thus having to pass beneath the church in order to reach the cloister. The church and lay brothers' building were, by analysis of their construction, built very rapidly, and there is every reason to believe that the other two wings of the cloister went up during the same campaign. It is therefore also likely that the fountain-house was part of this project from the beginning, and that pipes were laid before construction of the church, or at least the nave. In addition, the limestone from which the fountains were made is the same stone used for the lower portions of the nave and transepts of the church (*c*1137–1150), the period when the monks were using this quarry.

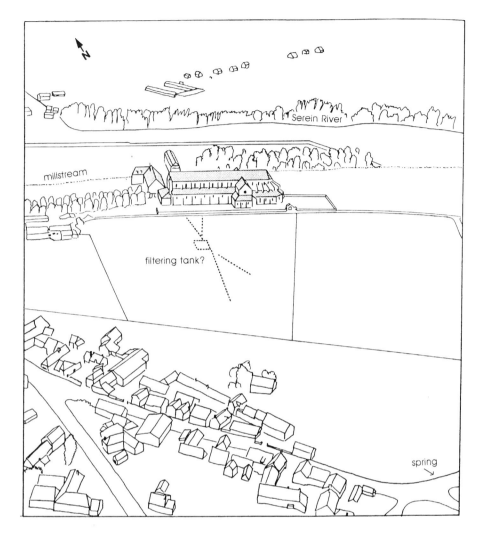

Fig 4.11 *Pontigny, interpretation of an aerial photograph of 1991, showing field traces of possible filtering tank (drawing by E Yeni from a photo by D N Bell).*

In this fashion, the monks of Pontigny diverted, tapped and arranged the available water for industrial, domestic and hygienic use. Several of the systems still function, and each is partially visible when the landscape is attentively studied, even though numerous traces have been lost in the course of the last generation. Most certainly further site work will disclose other segments of what must have been an extensive underground system of a very early date in Pontigny's history.

Fontfroide

The abbey of Fontfroide has quite a different story to tell. The site, in the foothills of the Pyrénées in southern France, is rocky and mountainous, what one would be tempted to call a "typically Cistercian" valley (Fig 4.12). It comes as a surprise to learn that it was founded in 1093 as a Benedictine monastery, and became

attached to the Cistercian order in 1145.[29] The abbey's prosperity is evident from this time, the count of Toulouse and viscount of Béziers being among the many benefactors from all strata of society. Four years after becoming Cistercian, Fontfroide founded the abbey of Poblet at the request of the count of Barcelona, and later established two more houses for men and two for women, besides acquiring an immense domain itself in the form of granges, vineyards and other properties.[30] Although the sequence has never been adequately established, their style suggests that permanent abbey buildings were erected at Fontfroide during the later twelfth and thirteenth centuries, using the handsome local sandstone.

Despite being able to boast of an abbot who became pope,[31] the community at Fontfroide had lived through many difficulties by the fourteenth century and a glance at the history provokes wonder at how monastic life survived until the Revolution. Prominent problems included involvement in the papal

Fig 4.12 *Fontfroide (Aude), view from the east.*

schism (unfortunately the wrong side; the antipope was in nearby Avignon), two sequestrations of property by the Holy See, devastation of lands and buildings during the Hundred Years' War, and imposition of the commendatory system from 1476 until the Revolution. Yet a neo-classical face-lift on several buildings, plus the creation of gracious courtyards, portals and terraced gardens, bespeak of a campaign to build and to modernise in the seventeenth or eighteenth centuries. Precisely when the community would have had the money or the will for such work is unclear, reminding us of the eloquence of architecture even when written records are silent. The medieval buildings, with these modifications, continued to serve the Cistercians until their expulsion in 1791.

As the abbey buildings and immediate grounds did not tempt a bidder at the reserve price representing low market value, Fontfroide was not sold in the wake of the Revolution. The church was stripped of its best furnishings by the bishop of Carcassonne, who then offered the remains to regional priests needing to refurbish their churches. The city of Narbonne retained possession of the abbey, and use was found for it as an almshouse. The land, however, proved too poor and dry to provide sufficient revenue for this institution, and the municipal authorities – eyeing cash value in current romantic taste – hatched the idea of mining the cloister. Marble shafts and columns were sold to a count in Lyon in 1830.[32] In 1833 the monastery and its surrounding land were bought by the Baron Bourlet de Saint-Aubin, under whose aegis – and the assistance of the celebrated architect and restorer, E. Viollet-le-Duc – the church and chapter were classified as historic monuments.

The Baron paid for many repairs himself, including removal of a large quantity of silt from the church and cloister in 1839, after a storm which brought nine feet of water into the abbey. According to the terms set for state assistance to the restoration – that the abbey not be put to any use that was out of its character – Fontfroide was re-sold to a second community of Cistercian monks in 1858. They lived within its walls until the definitive separation of church and French state in 1901. The abbey then narrowly escaped purchase by the American sculptor, George Grey Barnard, whose collection of medieval antiquities now forms an important part of The Cloisters Collection in New York; it was acquired by a local family in 1908 and remains in the possession of their heirs. The architectural ensemble of Fontfroide has never been the object of a detailed scholarly examination.

Those who conceived the construction of Fontfroide Abbey were certainly aware that building at the confluence of two valleys is a perilous endeavour. Soil is generally poor and stony here, and rainfall erratic; when it rains, downpours can be torrential. The site is bordered on three sides by a stream bed, dry now most of the year but roaring during rains (Fig 4.13). Three major forest fires in the past thirty years have resulted in near-complete deforestation, changes in vegetation, and a vastly diminished quantity of water; the stream now runs only after several days of heavy rain. In the Middle Ages latrines were built over it (one survives) and it was most likely harnessed for industrial use; this torrent constitutes what we shall call here the "external" water system.[33]

There is no constant water table in this region; rainwater infiltrates the rock and replenishes the

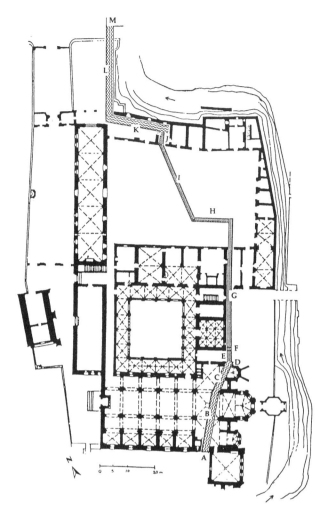

Fig 4.13 Fontfroide, plan of the site. A–M indicate changes in section of the underground channel.

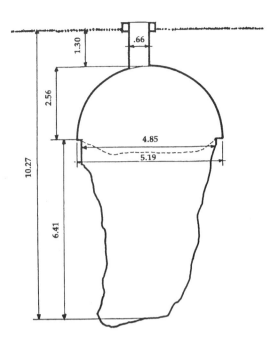

Fig 4.14 Fontfroide, section of water reservoir under north courtyard (Cl Orrit 1993).

Fig 4.15 Valmagne (Herault), cloister fountain-house.

perched water tables in the surrounding hills. Saliant bedrock was used as lower wall surface in several buildings, and water begins leaching from the rock soon after rain begins. This circumstance was used to good advantage in the outer courtyard to the north, where a natural fissure in the bedrock – over 5 metres in diameter and dropping to 10 meters – was covered with a barrel vault to create a water reservoir (Fig 4.14). After pumping it empty to examine the crevice for man-made conduits (there are none), the reservoir remained dry for three weeks until a heavy rainfall; in 48 hours it had re-filled to the previous level of some 5 metres of water.

Water was no doubt brought inside the abbey via another system, whose details are only partly known. It was piped from (at least) two springs located in the garrigues to the south; both are still in use. In a Cistercian abbey, water was brought into the fountain-house in the cloister, opposite the refectory, such as the one still standing at nearby Valmagne Abbey (Herault) (Fig 4.15). This structure – along with the kitchen and warming room – was

probably located along the north side of the cloister at Fontfroide, but the entire north wing was re-modelled during the neo-classical period. As a result, precise location of the medieval refectory is no longer known.[34]

It is possible that the same water problems plaguing the abbey of Fontfroide today were a source of constant work and worry in earlier centuries. One unresolved situation is the current lack of proper drainage in the cloister, where 1328 square metres of

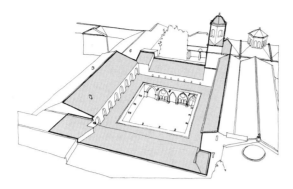

Fig 4.16 Fontfroide cloister. Shaded areas represent 1328m² of roof surface draining into the cloister (R Martin, ACMH).

roof water stagnate in the garth until seeping gradually eastward toward the chapter house and eventually the stream (Fig 4.16). This is perhaps not a new problem. A document of 1727 describes the collecting together of relics for safe-keeping "because of flooding", while mentioning that the chapter room was in good condition but unusable because of the scorpions.[35] Dampness in the cloister may also explain why book cupboards were being moved around as early as the mid-thirteenth century.[36] Where was this water destined to go in earlier centuries?

One possibility is a tunnel approximately 165 metres in length which traverses the site from south to north (Fig 4.13). It begins under the south transept of the church as a channel 1.55 metres in width with a slightly pointed barrel vault, and changes direction or vaulting type (or both) more than a dozen times, narrowing at one point to 55 cm in width. Anomalies in construction make its operation unclear. It was perhaps not intended from the beginning to run the full extent of the site in the present manner, but its original ingresses and egresses are not now visible, and silt has accumulated in varying quantities – up to a metre in places where it could be verified – creating different interior levels. The presumed source of the flow preceding the channel along the south side of the church is also undefined, and may already have been cut off by medieval re-building. All along this channel one can read the history of Fontfroide's construction and reconstruction in the changing masonry, dimensions, mortar and types of vaulting, but until it is cleared of silt, a full assessment cannot be made.

Back in the cloister, the rains continue, particularly via the downspouts which are part of a system created by Viollet-le-Duc to protect the outer walls of the galleries from ruin, but which may have replicated an earlier (medieval?) system for projecting water beyond the walls of the cloister.[37] Destination of the water once it left the roof and walls does not appear to have been of concern in the nineteenth

century, although it was likely a serious consideration of the medieval inhabitants.

Taking up nearly the entire width of the cloister garth at its western end is a barrel-vaulted cistern, with a single transverse arch across the centre (Fig 4.17). It is entirely built of large blocks of local sandstone, and measures 18.80 metres in length by 5.50 metres in width at the south end, 5.80 metres at the north end. The crest of the vault lies 0.78 metres below current ground level; interior depth is 2.62 metres from crest to floor at the south end, 2.87 metres at the north end. There are two square (modern) entrances, one over each of the two sections, that would have served as well to protect the vault from overflow.

Apparently long in disuse, the cistern contains approximately 70 cm of silt, about one-third of which was removed in 1993 to reveal a thick coat of water-proofing mortar covering the floor and walls. Directly below the northern entrance, a "basin" – 54 cm in diameter and 35 cm deep, carved from a single piece of sandstone – is sunk seamlessly into the floor. It was perhaps intended as a pump base or dipping basin, since the cistern is wider and lower at this (north) end.

Fig 4.17 Fontfroide, cloister cistern.

The original system for channelling water into the cistern may have proved insufficient and appears to have been replaced by a second; portions of both were found on excavation in 1994 (Fig 4.18). When the cistern was built, three terra cotta conduits were set at irregular intervals into the crest of the southern half of the vault. These conduits are square on the outside with a round interior diameter of 7 cm. A circular lip projected above the extrados of the vault (A), presumably for attachment to a channelling system, while a "bed" of broken tile and stone imbedded in clay led from the south-west corner of the cloister toward the conduit (B). This probably once held a drainage pipe or trough, positioned to receive roofwater from a corner gutterspout.

That this system wore out – or proved insufficient – is suggested by the presence of a second system.

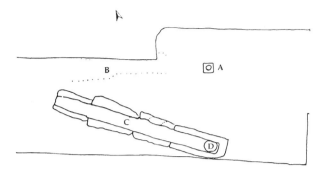

Fig 4.18 Fontfroide, trench in southwestern angle of the cloister revealing extrados of the cistern with drainage systems. A, terracotta pipe. B, path of stones and broken tiles. C, stone trough in four sections. D, hole in vault crest.

What was once a stone trough now has four remaining (of a probable five) sections running diagonally from the same (south-west) corner toward the outer wall of the cloister (C). The terminal stone has an opening 15 cm in diameter which is roughly aligned with a hole pierced in the vault crest (D). That this represents work executed after construction of the cistern itself is suggested by the somewhat ragged nature of the hole, located in the southern extremity of the vault crest where it abuts the foundation of the cloister wall, and also by the fact that the terminal stone was wedged in place using terra cotta fragments from the lip of the earlier conduit. Could this cistern have been the medieval storage tank for roof water? It seems likely, although the precise way in which water was channelled – and from which roofs – is not yet entirely clear.[38]

Despite their distinct functions, the various water systems at Fontfroide do seem to flow together in unexpected ways. As mentioned above, a fountain-house located in the cloister normally brought spring water inside the abbey for cooking, washing and liturgical needs. This structure is lacking at Fontfroide today, but the 1727 document leaves no doubt about its existence, as well as its deteriorated condition. An estimate for work in that year stated that the pipeline for water coming from the spring to the fountain needed to be replaced, and that the basin of the fountain and the arcading of the fountain-house also

had to be repaired.[39] That this work was never done is implied in a document of 49 years later; in 1776 a man was paid to demolish the fountain.[40]

A new chapter in the life of this fountain may have opened in July 1993 when some of the silt was removed from the cloister cistern. Among the many stone fragments found in this dense deposit were two curved and polished pieces of white marble,[41] measuring 103 x 50 and 95 x 37 cm respectively (Fig 4.19). Both are 23.5 cm in greatest thickness, and have a flat bottom with an upper surface that tapers toward the lip. The top and bottom are roughly finished, while the moulding of the outer lip is finely chiselled and polished. Holes were made at intervals of 35 cm – probably for lead fittings – by piercing the lip in two directions: from the lip horizontally inward and from the top diagonally downward.

These fragments are very possibly remains from the cloister fountain. They do not seem to have been part of a water-holding basin, such as the two from Pontigny, but belonged rather to a kind of "overshot" system. Water might have cascaded from an upper level, fallen onto the concave upper surface (of which these marble fragments are portions), and descended both via the pierced holes – fitted with lead spigots to project the water toward the user – and in a curtain over the edges to a catch-basin below.

An unexpected clue to the reconstitution of this fountain was found in the archives. Fontfroide was granted its coat-of-arms from the armorial deputies of the King on 14 June 1697, and the document itself bears the motif of a two-tiered fountain with an octagonal collecting basin at ground level, water spilling graciously against a handsome azure sky (Fig 4.20).[42] While one must allow for a certain artistic

Fig 4.19 Fontfroide, marble fragments (of fountain?) found in cistern, with profile.

Fig 4.20 *Fontfroide, coat-of-arms, 1697*
(Arch dép Aude, H.458)

license, it is doubtful that a water-fountain would have been used as the emblem of the abbey without a living likeness, not to mention the wordplay on its evocative name. The coat-of-arms was issued in 1697, thirty years before the 1727 document describing needed repairs; the fountain could still have been functioning. The profile of the marble fragments is roughly comparable that of the central portion of the heraldic fountain: an "overshot" system with a convex edge, including the narrow basin-like dip toward the centre seen on the fragments.

The continuing story of water in Fontfroide's cloister could be summarised as follows. By 1776 the fountain – and most likely the incoming pipeline – were beyond repair and the fountain was demolished, several large marble pieces being pushed into the nearby cistern. The position of the fragments – imbedded vertically in the silt – suggests that the cistern had not been in use for some time, nor was it considered a viable receptacle by Viollet-le-Duc in the 1830's. Debris found in the upper layers of silt confirm this hypothesis. It can therefore safely be said that the cistern has been an object of curiosity but not used (except as a garbage pit) for the past several centuries.

The fragmentary nature of Fontfroide's classification as a historic monument – virtually room by room since 1840 and as yet incomplete – does not bode well, either for the repair or the understanding of its hydraulic systems, which need to be seen in a fuller geological, architectural and archaeological context. It is hoped that its operation will be understood, and perhaps in part reconstituted, through future study and excavation.

Conclusion

If modern-day pilgrims flock to these abbeys for their beauty and tranquillity, then appreciation for the way of life that created them can only be heightened by learning that "behind the scenes", both in space and in time, there lurked every

problem that can befall a property owner in any period. Hydraulic systems are just one such aspect – invisible (when functioning properly) but essential. Cistercian sites, as we have seen, were developed pragmatically, but pragmatism can have other aspects besides the hard financial edge that is usually the prime measure of efficiency today.

Yet the anachronisms encountered on a daily basis by the guardians of any historic monument reflect the often stupefying problem of reconciling a building from another era and quite different use to current norms, laws, and customs.[43] Visitors expect, for example, well-functioning toilet facilities before almost anything else; while monastic latrines fascinate visitors, few would find it comfortable to use them, not to mention the sanitation and safety laws that would prevent it. Another example is electricity. Fire exits, emergency generators, smoke detectors, and the like are obligatory in buildings receiving large groups of people, and all pose haunting problems to those concerned with the aesthetic result.[44] A further problem owners must face is crowd security; the widespread threat of terrorist attacks in autumn 1995 obliged the guardians of Fontfroide to hire bomb specialists for a *Monuments historiques* open-door weekend. Other questions are environmental. The Pontigny town council voted in 1995 to purchase the upstream portion of the former millstream from the then owner(s), who did not clean their sections of the canal or maintain the aqueducts. This type of action is to be commended – particularly as benefit to tourists is not obvious – and it will doubtless result in better maintenance and functioning of the water-course and an assured supply of water in the canal.

Restoration decisions can also be a source of constant torment; visiting Cistercian sites in England, in France, in Germany, in Poland, in Spain (to cite only a few countries), one has ample opportunity to see generational, as well as national, variations in taste. If the public likes to see a clean and tidy building, should the architect scrape off the old pigment, match the colour, and re-paint, as is frequently done? Or should old paint be left for future study, when as-yet-uninvented technology may permit the detection and interpretation of unseen elements that can answer questions we have not yet thought to ask? Often ephemeral traces are reminders of how monastic habitation has left its imprint in the land, in choice of location, on the walls, and ultimately in the way thinking evolved and decisions were made and implemented centuries before.[45]

These examples are no more than different aspects of the same two questions, namely: how can the past serve the present and the future, and how can buildings made for small groups of monks in the Middle Ages be democratised for tourism today, and still retain the integrity necessary for study after a century or two of increasingly hard wear? With the development of tourism as one of the few growing industries in a stagnating economy, it is to be hoped that intelligent decisions will be made for the long-term conservation of sites as well as for short-term economic gain, and that scholars and archaeologists will find a way to share their passion and their information with those who influence public opinion and maintain these historic places.

Notes

* I am indebted to Graham Keevill and David Bell for their helpful suggestions in the preparation of this paper. Illustrations are by the author unless otherwise stated. This article was written in 1995, before the 1998 nonacentenary of the foundation of Cîteaux Abbey and the abundant literature produced for this event. Relevant notes have been updated.

1 Early efforts to amass comparative information on the architecture of Cistercian abbeys were, for example, Henri d'Arbois de Jubainville, *Études sur l'état intérieur des abbayes cisterciennes* (Paris, 1858); Edmund Sharpe, *The Architecture of the Cistercians*, 2 vols (London, 1874–1876); Georg Dehio and Gustav von Bezold, *Die Kirchliche Baukunst des Abendlandes*, 2 vols. (Stuttgart, 1884–1901), especially vol I, p 517–537, "Die Kirchen der Cistercienser-ordens". While innumerable monographs have since been written, the monumental effort at synthesis by Marcel Aubert and the Marquise de Maillé, *L'architecture cistercienne en France*, 2 vols (Paris, 1942; 2nd edn 1947) has taken on a canonical aspect and continues to be cited authoritatively in France despite the appearance of more modern studies of individual abbeys. M.-Anselme Dimier, *Recueil des plans d'églises cisterciennes*, 2 vols (Paris and Grignan, 1949; plus a two-volume supplement in 1967) remains a useful starting-point for church plans and bibliography. Dimier planned a third series but did not live to see its completion; his intellectual heirs have agreed that plans should now also include claustral and other buildings, but whether such an ambitious – and daunting – project will be realised remains an open question.

2 Few women's houses have been studied with the interest or depth of men's abbeys, excepting those with royal connections – such as Maubuisson, Lys or Las Huelgas – which should not be taken as the norm. One exemplary exception is Bernadette Barrière's work on Coyroux (most recently, "The Cistercian Convent of Coyroux in the Twelfth and Thirteenth Centuries", *Gesta*, vol 31/2 (1992), 76–82). See, for example, Michel Desmarchelier, "L'Architecture des églises de moniales cisterciennes, essai de classement des différents types de plans"; *Mélanges à la mémoire du Père Anselme Dimier*, B Chauvin, ed, vol III:5 (Arbois [France], 1982), 79–121; John A Nichols, "Medieval English Cistercian Nunneries: Their Art and Physical Remains", *Mélanges Dimier*, III:5, 151–176; Marie-Élisabeth Montulet-Henneau, *Les Cisterciennes du pays Mosan. Moniales et vie contemplative à l'époque moderne* (Bruxelles-Paris-Rome, Institut Historique Bele de Rome, 1990); *idem*,

Filles de Cîteau au pays mosan (Huy [Belgium], 1990); Roberta Gilchrist, *Gender and Material Culture. The archaeology of religious women* (London/New York, 1994); *Hidden Springs*, I–II, John A. Nichols & Lilian Shank, eds. (Kalamazoo, Michigan, 1995); and the acts of the symposium on Cistercian nuns held at Royaumont in 1998, *Cîteaux et les femmes* (Grâne [France], in press).

3 Much more attention has been paid in recent years to the context of these monastic settlements, such as the exemplary study of the granges of Chaalis Abbey by François Blary (*Le Domaine de Chaalis: XIIᵉ – XIVᵉ siècles*, Paris, Éditions du Comité des Travaux Historiques et Scientifiques, 1989), and the entire issue of the *Cahiers de la Ligue Urbaine et Rurale* dedicated to Cistercian grange sites (no 109, Paris, 1990). For land management and outbuildings, see *L'espace cistercien* (Paris, Éditions du Comité des Travaux Historique et Scientifiques, 1994) and volume 5 of *Studies in Cistercian Art and Architecture* (M P Lillich, ed, vol 5, Kalamazoo, Michigan, 1998); on water management, the acts of the 1992 colloquium sponsored by the Foundation Royaumont, *L'Hydraulique monastique* (A Bonis & M Wabont, eds, Grâne [France], 1996), and the acts of the 1993 symposium sponsored by the Fundação Oriente in Arràbida, Portugal, *Hidráulica Monástica Medieval e Moderna* (*Actas do Simpósio Internacional, Convento da Arrábida, 15–17 November 1993)*, Lisbon, 1996).

4 An attempt was made to encourage this line of reflection by holding an international colloquium, *L'espace cistercien*, at Fontfroide Abbey in 1993; acts were published under the same title (see n 3). Three exemplary studies have recently appeared: *Pour une histoire monumentale de l'abbaye de Cîteaux, 1098–1998*, Martine Plouvier & Alain Saint-Denis, eds, (co-edition *Cîteaux, Comm. cist.* [series *Studia et Documenta*: 8], Acey, France and the Association Bourguignonne des Sociétés Savantes, Dijon, 1998); Peter Fergusson & Stuart Harrison, *Rievaulx Abbey: Community, Architecture, Memory* (Yale University Press, New Haven & London, 1999); Thomas Coomans, *L'abbaye de Villers: Construction, configuration et signification d'une abbaye cistercienne gothique*, (co-edition Éditions Racine, Brussels and *Cîteaux, Comm. cist.* [series *Studia et Documenta*: 11] Brecht [Belgium], 2000).

5 The *Statuta* are essentially the result of discussions at General Chapter of situations existing within specific abbeys, and they need to be interpreted with caution. Often problems were discussed, whereas non-problematic situations were not, and a problem within one abbey should not be extrapolated as existing everywhere. See Chrysogonus Waddell, "The Cistercian Institutions and their Early Evolution", *L'Espace cistercien*, 27–38. Waddell is curently preparing a new edition of the 12th c *Statuta*, to be published by *Cîteaux, Comm. cist.* (series *Studia et Documenta*). For other early Cistercian documents, see his *Narrative and Legislative Texts from Early Cîteaux. An Edition, Translation and Commentary* (*Cîteaux, Comm. cist.* [series *Studia et Documenta*: 9] Brecht, Belgium, 1999), as well as his critical review (in *Cîteaux, Comm. cist.*, v 51 [2000] p 299–386) of Constance H Berman's recent book *The Cistercian Evolution: The Invention of a Religious Order in*

Twelfth-Century Europe (Philadelphia, 2000), the radical-appearing premises of which are unfortunately based on misinterpretations of the manuscript evidence.

6 Cîteaux 1098, La Ferté-sur-Grosne 1113, Pontigny 1114, Clairvaux and Morimond 1115.

7 See David N Bell, "Is There Such a Thing as 'Cistercian Spirituality'?", *Cistercian Studies Quarterly*, v 34.4 (1999), 455–471. While anti-clericalism is not uncommon in France, there is more of a widespread indifference to the subject of religion, perhaps due in part to the strict separation of church and state early in the 20th century and to the fact that religion may therefore not be taught in schools. This determination for secularity in French culture has by now become rather an act of faith, and can, unfortunately, be taken to extremes. (For example, I was told not to discuss religion in a course destined for tour guides in former Cistercian abbeys, so fearful were the organisers that such information would be used to proselytise or otherwise impinge upon the participants' right to a neutral [read: religion-free] ambience.) As a result, much of the visiting public now has no real idea what a monastery was or why it existed.

8 The ideas concerning architectural context mentioned here have since been treated more fully, especially in *L'Europe cistercienne* (Zodiaque Press, La Pierre-qui-Vire, 1997, 1999²), to appear in English as *Cistercian Europe, Architecture of Contemplation* in summer 2001 (William B. Eerdmans Publishers, Grand Rapids, Michigan), and also in *Architecture of Solitude* (David Heald & Terryl N Kinder, Abrams, New York, 2000).

9 An interesting example of this phenomenon is the return of monks to Sénanque in 1858; they were not Cistercian when they arrived, but by living in the 12th monastery they were "converted" to the Cistercian order.

10 In addressing the question of how the destroyed parliament should be rebuilt, Churchill claimed that evolution of the British government was a function of the space in which it developed, and changing the space would change the government in ways unintended (Oct 28, 1943).

11 Paul Benoît and Monique Wabont, "Mittelalterliche Wasserversorgung in Frankreich. Eine Fallstudie: Die Zisterzienser", *Die Wasserversorgung im Mittelalter*, (Geschichte der Wasserversorgung, Band 4) Mainz, 1991, 185–226; see also n 3 for acts of recent colloquia. Paul Benoît's students at the University of Paris-I Sorbonne have collected a substantial amount of data on water systems in Cistercian sites in northern France.

12 Terryl N Kinder, "Toward Dating Construction of the Abbey Church of Pontigny", *Journal of the British Archaeological Association*, v 145 (1992), 77–88.

13 Terryl N Kinder, "The Original Chevet of Pontigny's Church", *Studies in Cistercian Art and Architecture*, II (M P Lillich, ed), (Kalamazoo, Michigan 1984), 30–38 & figs 1–15 (p 257ff).

14 See my *L'Europe cistercienne*, chapter "Technique et innovation", esp. p 222.

15 The word *grangia* in Cistercian terms carries two meanings – the land itself, and the buildings erected on the site, particularly barns. The classic study is by Colin Platt, *The Monastic Grange in Medieval England* (London/Melbourne/Toronto, 1969). For a recent study of many

aspects of Cistercian granges and their management, see *L'espace cistercien, passim*.

16 For a summary of these possessions, see Terryl N Kinder, "Les granges de l'abbaye de Pontigny", *Cahiers de la Ligue Urbaine et Rurale*, 109 (Paris, 1990), 33–39.

17 Bull issued by Pope Alexander III; published by V B Henry, *Histoire de l'abbaye de Pontigny* (Auxerre/Avallon, 1839), 335–339.

18 Terryl N Kinder, "Pontigny et ses domaines: Richesse et précarité d'un patrimoine encore agricole", *L'Espace cistercien* (Paris, 1994), 441–450; and in reply, Pascale de Maulmin, "Pontigny et ses domaines: Les problèmes concrets de la protection" (same volume), 451–453.

19 St Edmund died nearby and was buried at Pontigny in 1240 and canonised in 1246, becoming – along with the Virgin Mary – patron saint of the abbey.

20 For a fuller study of this fascinating site, see Terryl N Kinder, "As Above, So Below. Architecture and Archaeology at Villiers-la-Grange of Pontigny," *The Joy of Learning & the Love of God. Essays in Honor of Jean Leclercq*, E Rozanne Elder, ed, (Cistercian Studies Series: 160, Kalamazoo, MI/Spencer, MA, 1995), 157–177; *idem*, "Villiers-la-Grange", *Dossiers d'Archéologie*, n° 234 (June–Jul 1998), 104–105.

21 Archives départementales de l'Yonne, Auxerre, H 1432.

22 Bibliothèque municipale, Auxerre, ms 123, fo. 121ᵛ, col. b. I am greatly indebted to Jean-Luc Benoit for pointing out this fascinating passage.

23 Description here rules out the river, but not the millrace, which exits the abbey proper on the western side of the precinct wall where the current (post-medieval) entrance is located, perhaps on medieval foundations?

24 For a more detailed account of Pontigny's hydraulic systems, see "Aménagement d'une vallée de larmes: les Cisterciens et l'eau à Pontigny", *L'Hydraulique monastique* (as in note 3), 383–395.

25 Terryl N Kinder, "Clay and what they did with it: Medieval Tiles and Bricks at Pontigny", *Studies in Cistercian Art and Architecture*, M P Lillich, ed, (Kalamazoo, Michigan, 1993), 15–44 & figs 1–30 (p 198–221). An abridged version appeared as "Briques et carreaux de pavement : un artisanat médiéval à Pontigny?", *Bulletin de la Société nationale des Antiquaires de France*, (Paris, 1992), 123–137.

26 I am indebted to Annie Blanc, of the Centre de Recherches sur les Monuments Historiques, Paris, for her invaluable help in tracing the quarries used to build the abbey and its fountains and other elements; for a summary, see Annie Blanc, "Les pierres de l'abbaye de Pontigny: Recherche des carrières d'origine", *Les Cisterciens dans l'Yonne* (T N Kinder, ed, Les Amis de Pontigny, Pontigny, 1999), 97–98.

27 It is interesting to note that water from this well is particularly reputed for its softness, in contrast to the very hard water from other springs in the vicinity.

28 I would like to thank M. Jean Aléonard, former mayor of Pontigny, for having shown me his copy of this plan, and also for confirming the existence of the "maisonnette", which he remembers. His description recalls similar structures at Clairvaux and at Royaumont, where the wellhouse was built into the hill to protect the spring.

29 E Cauvet, *Étude historique sur Fontfroide, abbaye de l'ordre*

de Cîteaux, située dans le diocèse & la vicomté de Narbonne (de 1093 à 1790), (Montpellier/Paris, 1875), 177–186.

30 F. Grèzes-Rueff, "L'abbaye de Fontfroide et son domaine foncier aux XIIᵉ–XIIIᵉ siècles, *Annales du Midi*, t. 89, 1977, 253–280.

31 Jacques Fournier, elected to the Holy See in 1334 as Benedict XII.

32 H Cau with O-H Viala, "L'affaire des colonnettes disparues", *Oculus. Bulletin de l'Association pour l'animation culturelle de l'abbaye d Fontfroide*, no 3, 1991, 9–12. These supports were identified and repatriated in 1994 and installed in the south gallery of the cloister.

33 For a detailed examination of this site, see my article "The Archaeology of Water at the Cistercian Abbey of Fontfroide (Aude)", *Hidráulica Monástica Medieval e Moderna* (as in note 3); a briefer version appeared as "Les installations hydrauliques dans l'ancienne abbaye cistercienne de Fontfroide (Aude)", in the *Bulletin de la Société nationale des Antiquaires de France*, (Paris 1995), 107–115; and a somewhat popularised version as "L'archéologie et l'eau à Fontfroide. Vivre dans une vallée de larmes", in *Oculus. Bulletin de la S.C.I. et de l'Association des Amis de l'Abbaye de Fontfroide*, nᵒ 9 (May 1996), 10–16. The conclusions drawn there are the result of my excavations in 1993 ("Ancienne abbaye de Fontfroide", *Bilan scientifique 1993: Direction Régionale des Affaires Culturelles, Service Régional de l'Archéologie, Languedoc-Roussillon* [Montpellier 1994], 50–51) and 1994 (Fouilles à l'abbaye de Fontfroide", *Bilan scientifique 1994: Direction Régionale des Affaires Culturelles, Service Régional de l'Archéologie, Languedoc-Roussillon* [Montpellier 1995], 69–70).

34 Excavations in 1995 in the north-east quadrant of the cloister revealed at least three water systems, although none point conclusively to the fountain house. Excavations are planned over the next several years to try to discern water supply and evacuation systems over the centuries in this cloister.

35 Archives départementales, Aude, H.610. Scorpions live in hot climates but seek cool damp areas, and had evidently displaced the monks in the early eighteenth century.

36 David N Bell, "*Fons sapientiae*: A Study of the Book Collection of the Abbey of Fontfroide from the Twelfth Century to the Sixteenth", *Cîteaux: Commentarii cistercienses*, t. 46, 1995, p 88, n 26.

37 Traces of previous downspouts are visible in the corners, but the combination of many rebuildings and the friable nature of the sandstone do not allow reliable dating of these elements.

38 According to the owners, in the past 30 years there have been two days (1977, 1989) when the quantity of rain in 24 hours equalled or exceeded the capacity of the cistern, if the roof run-off had been as it is today (Fig 4.16), and all 1328 m² had been channelled into the cistern. In both cases this one storm provided approximately one-third of the annual rainfall for that year. Such a storm would obviously have caused a flood in the cloister once the cistern overflowed, but perhaps in the Middle Ages that was considered sufficient. For today's purposes, the fact that there *can* be a flood has caused the cistern to be condemned as

inadequate and an overflow must also be dug.

39 "...relever toute la canonade ou tuyaux depuis la source de ladit fontaine jusqu'à l'entrée de la maison..."; "...reparer toutes les arcades de la fontaine qui est vis à vis le refectoir et qui fournit à toute la maison, et en refaire le bassin tout à neuf...". Archives départementales, Aude, H.610.

40 Archives départementales, Aude, H.210.

41 White marble was not infrequently used in this region for decorative purposes; Fontfroide's cloister and chapter room have marble capitals and shafts, and documents speak of numerous marble ornaments in the church.

42 Archives départementales, Aude, H.458. This motif appears on other official abbey documents, including wax seals and book stamps, the latter believed by David N Bell to date from the 17th century ("*Fons Sapientiae...*", p 100, with illustration).

43 For monuments that are *classés* (the highest level of protection, which is the status of large portions of Pontigny and Fontfroide), decisions regarding major maintenance projects must have the administrative authorisation of the *Conservateur Régional des Monuments Historiques*, who would usually consult the *Architecte en Chef des Monuments Historiques* for major work needed, or the *Agence des Bâtiments de France* for smaller problems including maintenance. Once the administrative accord is granted, decisions – such as choice of supplier for materials and labour – are made by the *maître d'ouvrage*, who is usually the owner, whether private individuals (such as at Fontfroide) or the mayor and town council for communal property (Pontigny). *Maîtres d'ouvrage* – particularly those who may not have experience in managing an ancient monument – are strongly urged to hire an architect who is well-versed in historic buildings to oversee such work, but the advantage that would be gained is rarely seen as justifying the extra expense.

44 In the case of Pontigny, the church was originally wired in the late 1920s and 1930s, and in order to avoid the additional cost and time that a study was thought to entail, the earlier wiring was re-done in identical fashion in 1995, without the benefit of more subtle illumination than bare bulbs hanging from the vaults. Black cables, grey protection tubing and black attachment collars (the only materials said to be available by the local electrical company hired to do the work) were eventually reconciled with the creamy white limestone by means of matching paint (not included in the original budget), since the alternative would have been to gouge channels in the twelfth-century walls, an idea rejected by the *Agence des Bâtiments de France*. Nevertheless, in the course of work, holes were drilled in medieval ashlar blocks and electrical wires stapled to the visible surface of the 12th century *charpente* over the vaults; workmen were later required to rip out the wiring and find another solution, plugging the holes they had made.

45 Changes in stone colour and texture are what allowed me to determine the disposition of Pontigny's original choir (see n 13). Had the stones in question been lower they would probably have been painted; had the restoration been modern, they would have been replaced.

5   Production and Consumption of Food and Drink in the Medieval Monastery

James Bond

Introduction

Any human society has certain basic requirements of food, drink, shelter and clothing, and directs part of its energy towards securing those necessities. Medieval monastic communities developed somewhat specialised requirements for buildings, clothing and diet as a symbol of their separateness from the secular world. The distinctive patterns of production and consumption which resulted can be reconstructed, at least in part, from both documentary and archaeological sources. This paper will explore some of the evidence for the monastic production and consumption of food and drink.

The Monastic Diet

The Rule of St Benedict, the most influential document in western monasticism, laid down certain strictures on food. The times of the main meal and of supper were to vary according to the season (*Rule*, Ch 41). For the main meal a choice of two cooked dishes was to be provided, with a further option of fruit or vegetables when available. A pound of bread each day was to serve both for dinner and supper. The Rule insisted upon abstinence from the flesh of four-footed animals (Ch 39). An exception was made for the sick, however, who were allowed to eat meat to restore their strength (Ch 36). Instructions on drink are a little more ambivalent, a *hemina* (half-pint) of wine daily for each monk being suggested, with encouragement to greater abstinence, but also with latitude for increasing the allowance when circumstances of work or summer heat required it (Ch 40). Special austerity was urged in Lent, though no precise requirements were spelled out (Ch 49). The general tenor of the Benedictine Rule was the avoidance of gluttony and drunkenness (cf *Luke*, xxi, 34).

The observance of the Rule became modified in due course by custom (Knowles 1963, 456–465). Within the Cluniac régime a more generous allowance of food and drink was permitted on the grounds that the demanding cycle of sung services could not otherwise be maintained. By the twelfth century small extra dishes known as pittances were served in the refectory several days a week, with additional allowances for servers, readers and others with special responsibilities. Furthermore, the abbot was by then tending to eat apart from his monks, regularly entertaining guests with a more lavish table, at which meat began to appear. In due course meat-eating was adopted by the whole community. The statutes of the Cistercians sought a return to the strict vegetarian diet (Knowles 1963, 641–2), but they too eventually succumbed to meat-eating, and by the fifteenth century retained little of their earlier frugality.

Other monastic orders varied in their attitudes to diet. The Carthusians followed a strict régime consisting of slender allowances of fish, cheese, eggs and vegetables, with only bread and water on Fridays (three days a week in Lent). Canons following the Augustinian Rule generally enjoyed a more varied range of food and drink; nonetheless, some reformed orders of canons influenced by the Cistercian ideal, including the Arrouaisians and Premonstratensians, initially elected for strict vegetarianism. The Grandmontine custumal permitted no meat even in the infirmary, and forbade the enlivening of fish, eggs, cheese and vegetable dishes with spices or sauces (Hutchison 1989, 115–6). The Trinitarians fasted four days a week from mid-September to Easter, but allowed themselves meat on certain Sundays (Gray 1993, 11). Even the Knights Templar, whose active military role precluded a diet of extreme austerity, were allowed meat only three times a week by their earliest rule (Upton-Ward 1992, 26).

However, some relaxation in dietary restrictions is evident in most orders in later centuries.

The Exploitation of Monastic Estates

Embedded within the Benedictine Rule there is an assumption that the monastery should be self-sufficient, drawing upon the resources of its own estates for all its needs. A feature of many old Benedictine estates is the way in which they spanned different types of countryside, the extensive arable lands around the home manors being complemented by pastoral and woodland properties, often at a greater distance. This provided opportunities for early experiments with regional agricultural special-isation, exemplified by Abingdon Abbey's dairy farms in the Ock valley, or Pershore Abbey's sheep farms on the Cotswolds (Bond 1979, 63; Smith 1939). The Cistercians were able to develop even more specialised economies in wool and hide production on some of their granges (Donkin 1978, 67–102) which cannot be pursued here.

The manner of estate exploitation changed during the Middle Ages. Many of the greater Benedictine houses such as Glastonbury, Worcester, Canterbury, Ely and Ramsey had sufficient landed endowments to develop a food-farm system, whereby each manor was responsible for supplying produce to maintain the community for two or three weeks each year (Smith 1943, 128–132; Miller 1951, 36–41; Neilson 1898, 18–21; Raftis 1957, 10–12). However, the practical difficulties surrounding the direct exploita-tion of extensive, scattered demesnes meant that by the eleventh century the land was regularly farmed out, with renders in kind gradually being super-seded by fixed cash rents (Knowles 1963, 441–4). Costs of transport from distant manors made it more economical to sell that produce and to purchase from markets nearer at hand, and the food-farm system slowly gave way to a practice of leasing most of the estates and buying in supplies.

During the late twelfth and early thirteenth centuries population growth resulted in rising prices and a rapidly-expanding market, making direct management of agricultural resources more attrac-tive. Many monastic houses took their demesnes back in hand, and this period marks the zenith of Benedictine high farming. Abbots and priors like Michael Amesbury (1235–52) and John Taunton (1274–90) at Glastonbury, Henry Eastry at Christ Church, Canterbury (1285–1331), John Brookhamp-ton (1282–1316) at Evesham and Geoffrey Crowland (1299–1320) at Peterborough increased their demesnes by purchase, improved their productivity through assarting, drainage and reclamation works, and achieved considerable profits (Smith 1943, 132–

45, 150–65, 172–89; 1947, 109–116; Knowles 1979, i, 42–54). However, conditions began to change again in the fourteenth century through demographic collapse, rising labour costs and other factors. Once again it became more advantageous for the abbey to lease out its demesnes to lay tenants, rather than to continue farming itself (Dobson 1973, 272–5). By the Dissolution many abbeys retained only a single home farm and isolated country residences, all other property being leased. Even then, however, rents were as likely to be paid in grain, meat and hay as in cash, so the original basis of the estate organisation might not wholly be lost.

The periods at which these changes occurred varied considerably: Worcester Priory was selling most of its demesne crops and buying in supplies from the market by the 1290s (*Worc.Compot.*, 8–32). Permanent leasing of whole demesnes did not begin on the Canterbury estates before the 1370s (Smith 1943, 192–4), while Abingdon and Tavistock per-sisted with direct exploitation well into the fifteenth century (Bond 1979, 60; Finberg 1969, 242–3). In some cases there were temporary reversals of the process, as at Westminster, where the abbey re-sumed using its own demesne produce for a time in the fourteenth century (Harvey 1977, 134–40). Idiosyncratic local decisions often ignored general economic trends, and it would be futile to expect perfect conformity with any preconceived models.

Archaeological and Documentary Sources

Any attempt to investigate monastic production and consumption faces many difficulties. Neither archae-ological nor archival research can provide a complete picture and both have inherent limitations. In general, written sources still offer a much fuller impression than the evidence from excavation. However, the use of monastic documents for purposes of historical reconstruction is far from straightforward. Erratic survival of records means that written evidence for the internal economy of many houses is entirely lacking. Few classes of documents span the entire monastic period. Account rolls, where they survive, provide direct evidence for purchases and sales; but they occur most frequently during the later thirteenth and fourteenth centuries, when demesne production was contracting. Internal administration was not standardised; while the cellarer, kitchener, pittancer, granger and gardener were the obedientiaries most likely to be concerned with food supply, their precise responsibilities varied from house to house and from period to period. Records of transactions involving any particular commodity may be scattered through several different sets of accounts. Most monastic houses had to feed guests and lay servants as well as the monastic community itself, and accounts do not always identify the destination of the purchases.

Records of production from the demesne manors are likely to be fuller than records of production within the precinct, although surpluses from the latter were sometimes sold. Variable accounting procedures and local and temporal variations in units of measurement often make it difficult to extract any data which have much statistical validity. Records of production, however oblique and imperfect, survive more fully than records of consumption. Indeed, direct and detailed written evidence for what was eaten is relatively rare. Chapter 36 of the Benedictine Rule requires that the brethren eat in silence while listening to a reading, and if they require anything during the meal, then 'let the thing be asked for by means of some sign rather than by speech'. Many abbeys improvised elaborate systems of sign language for this purpose, and a mid-eleventh-century key from Christ Church, Canterbury, includes signs for boiled vegetables, raw vegetables, leeks, pottage, pepper, beans, peas, apple, pear, plums, cherries, sloes, bread, cheese, butter, milk, eggs, honey, fish, wine, ale and herbal drink (*Mon.Ind.*, 32–7). The two part-years for which records survive of the monks' diet at St Swithun's Priory, Winchester, covering the periods 1 November 1492 to 1 June 1493 and 12 December 1514 to 19 September 1515, stand almost alone as a record of day-by-day consumption, detailing the entrée and main course at dinner, supper, pittances and special allowances for the servers; and even these records identify only cash purchases, omitting home-produced items such as bread, cheese, vegetables and ale (*Winch.Compot.*, 306–362). For Westminster Abbey the kitchener's day-books, recording the main items of cooked food served at dinner and supper, survive for about a dozen years between 1495 and 1525; they have been studied, but not fully published (Harvey 1993, 34–71). There is also a surviving fragment of the abbot's kitchen records at Peterborough which details daily consumption at the abbot's hall and at his Eyebury manor by the abbot, his staff and servants, horses and dogs, running from 29 December 1370 to Easter 1371; this does note the number of loaves from the bakehouse and other items from store, purchases being recorded only where supplies on hand were lacking (*Pet.Accts.*, 56–83). Cellarers' accounts sometimes provide week-by-week records of purchases which can give some idea of variations in consumption through the year (eg *Durh.Accts.*, *Wilt.Accts.*).

Archaeology can sometimes detect evidence at the production stage, but can more readily identify buildings and equipment concerned with the storage and processing of food (Fig 5.1). It is better able to identify consumption waste, through the evidence of kitchen-middens or sewage deposits. Unfortunately, however, major stratified concentrations of domestic refuse are rarely found in monastic houses, since kitchen waste was often recycled to provide compost for the gardens. Moreover, monasteries were particularly efficient in their methods of sewage removal, so the opportunity to study faecal deposits is even more limited. Small quantities of food debris may survive in kitchens, refectories or drains, but even where chance food residues are found it can be difficult to determine their origin and representativeness, eg whether they represent a single meal or an accumulation over a long period. Nevertheless, evidence from St Alban's Abbey, as yet unpublished, may demonstrate the potential of middens for illuminating long-term changes in monastic diet.[1] Nunneries may have a special potential in this respect, since the stricter enclosure of the sisters may have resulted in less efficient clearance of domestic waste, while sanitation was often less sophisticated, relying more on simple garderobes. The Benedictine nunnery of Polsloe in Devon has produced over 10,000 animal bones from the early sixteenth century, far in excess of the totals from most male houses, while latrine deposits from Denny in Cambridgeshire, dating from the period when the site was occupied as a Franciscan nunnery, produced remains of elderberry, blackberry, figs and grapes (Gilchrist 1994, 87–9, 113–5, 125–6).

The archaeological evidence suffers greatly through bias in survival and bias in recovery. The extent to which plant and animal remains survive is largely determined by soil conditions, while the material can easily be lost without adequate sieving and recovery techniques. Survival and recovery are inevitably skewed towards larger bones and plant remains preserved in waterlogged conditions, mineralised, dessicated or carbonised. Different methodologies employed by archaeozoologists to determine the relative proportions of species represented in bone assemblages can render comparison between sites difficult. It remains virtually impossible from archaeological evidence to estimate the *scale* of production or consumption over any given time-span.

Both documentary and archaeological approaches share a common difficulty, that whereas it may be feasible to prove presence, it is impossible to prove absence. The production or consumption of any given commodity may leave some clues, but negative evidence cannot prove that a particular food was not consumed. Documentary evidence is, on the whole, still likely to give a more reliable measure of the quantities and proportions of foodstuffs produced or consumed. However, archaeology continues to expand its range of techniques, and can be expected to add much more to our knowledge in future. The

Production and Comsumption of Food and Drink in the Medieval Monastery

RESOURCES	FORM OF EXPLOITATION	RAW MATERIAL PRODUCT	STORAGE / HOUSING	PROCESSING	FOOD PRODUCT	PLACE OF CONSUMPTION	DISPOSAL OF SURPLUS & WASTE
Cultivated Land	Arable Fields	Wheat, Maslin, Barley, Dredge, Oats, Rye, Peas, Beans	Barn, Granary	Mill, Malting kiln, Bakehouse, Brewhouse	Bread, Ale	Monks'/Canons' Refectory, Lay Brothers' Refectory	WASTE, Plant Remains
	Garden	Leeks, Onions, Garlic, Coleworts, Mustard, Culinary herbs		Drying kiln, Monks' Kitchen	Pottage		
			Beehives		Honey, Mead		
	Orchard	Apples, Pears, Plums, Cherries, Hazelnuts, Walnuts	Apple-house	Cider-mill	Cider		
					Oil		
	Vineyard	Grapes		Wine-press	Wine, Verjuice		
	Pasture	Cattle	Cowhouse, Byre, Vaccary	Dairy, Slaughter-house; Infirmary Kitchen, Abbot's Kitchen	Beef, Veal, Milk, Butter, Cheese	Infirmary, Misericord	Animal Bones
		Sheep	Sheepcote, Bercary	Dairy, Meat Kitchen	Mutton, Lamb, Milk, Cheese		Middens
	Farmyard	Poultry	Henhouse, Goosehouse		Hens, Chickens &c., Geese, Ducks, Eggs		
		Pigeons	Dovecote		Squabs		Sewage
Uncultivated Land	Park	Fallow Deer			Venison	Abbot's/Prior's Dwelling	
	Warren	Hare, Rabbit, Wildfowl			Partridge, Pheasant	Guesthouse	
	Wood-Pasture	Pigs, Wild fruits, nuts, Mushrooms	Pigstyes		Pork, Sucking Pig	Corrodians' Quarters	
Sea	Marine & Estuarine Fisheries	Herring, Cod, Ling, Plaice, Sole &c., Sturgeon &c., Shellfish	Fish Stores	Drying Rack, Smoking-house	Dried fish (Stockfish), Smoked (Red) fish, Pickled (Green) fish		Fish Bones
Fresh Water	River Fisheries	Eels, Roach, Perch					
	Fishponds	Bream, Pike, Carp					
	Heronries, Swanneries	Waterfowl					
Purchases (only imports listed)		Wine, Figs, Raisins, Almonds, Rice, Sugar, Spices, Olive Oil					SURPLUS, Sales at Market
Donations in kind							Alms

Fig 5.1   Resources, products and consumption on monastic estates, and their archaeological manifestation (C J Bond)

two disciplines are complementary, and both are essential if we are to hope to approach a true understanding of medieval monastic production and consumption. The discussion which follows aims merely to explore the potential, using a sample of the published evidence, as a step on the road towards the more comprehensive balanced synthesis which is needed.

Cereal Production and Use

Wheat and barley provided the two main staples of the medieval diet, bread and ale, but other cereal crops were also important. The four custodies of Christ Church, Canterbury, in south-east England in 1322 included 2,677 acres under wheat, 2,385 acres under oats, 1,434 acres under barley and 367 acres under rye (Smith 1943, 141). Records of the quantities of grain threshed from four of the granges of Sibton Abbey in 1365, 1366 and 1367 amount to an average of 223 quarters of wheat, 214 qrs of barley, 204 qrs of oats and 18 qrs of rye per annum (*Sibton Doc.*, 32). Obviously the proportions of different crops will vary, both according to location and year by year.

Most monastic estates operated some sort of mixed economy, but clearly old-established houses in the south and midlands stood a better chance of acquiring extensive endowments of good-quality arable land than later foundations in the north and west. Many of the older Benedictine houses were situated in fertile countryside, and houses like Battle and Canterbury successfully increased the yields from their estates by marling and manuring (Smith 1943, 135–9; Brandon 1972, 419–20; Mate 1985, 22–31). Tavistock, less fortunately located, made considerable efforts to improve its stony, phosphate-deficient lands through the application of farmyard manure and sea-sand and the practice of beat-burning (Finberg 1969, 86–115). Other forms of improvement can also be observed during the high farming period. During the thirteenth century Battle Abbey was using legumes in rotation to eliminate fallow on its Sussex coastal manors, where between one-third and half of the arable acreage bore a continuous sequence of crops (Brandon 1972, 406). Some of the Ramsey Abbey demesnes similarly reveal an increase in the amounts of corn sown after 1320 accompanied by the increasing use of legumes (Raftis 1957, 161). Benedictine houses were also involved in the extension of cultivation: at Bury St Edmunds, for example, Abbot Samson 'cleared many lands and brought them back into cultivation' (*Chron.Brakelond*, 28). The Cistercians and several other later orders were even more actively involved in assarting and bringing new land into cultivation,

developing a different system of consolidated estates directly cultivated from granges (Bishop 1936; Donkin 1978, 51–67; Williams, 1984, ii, 197–308). On Cistercian estates too there are records of marling, manuring and liming (Donkin 1978, 66; Williams 1984, 285).

It was obviously advantageous to concentrate the main arable production reasonably close to the house, and lack of suitable land nearby may have led to the migration of more than one community. In bad seasons even well-endowed houses might be forced to look beyond their own estates for their supplies: in the famine year of 1189, for example, the Cistercians of Margam were forced to buy corn both in Bristol and in Ireland, and the Abbot of Neath similarly was buying corn in England in 1234 (Donkin 1978, 143–4; Williams 1984, ii, 284, 315). Some Cistercian and Premonstratensian houses in the north-west of England – Furness, Holm Cultram, Cockersand – regularly imported grain from Ireland (O'Neil 1987, 21). A few houses like Malton Priory elected to concentrate on pastoral farming and buy in most of their grain.

Crop yields naturally varied greatly according to weather and soil conditions. Average sowings were of the order of 2–3 bushels per acre, and it was suggested by the author of one late thirteenth-century treatise that barley ought to yield eightfold, rye sevenfold, maslin, dredge, beans and peas sixfold, wheat fivefold and oats fourfold (*Husb.*, 418–9). While these figures might be expected to be ideal attainments, in practice on well-managed demesnes they were sometimes exceeded. On Tavistock Abbey's manor of Hurdwick for the period 1412–1537 yields of wheat averaged 5.8:1, rye yields averaged 8.5:1, large oats 4.2:1 and small oats 5.7:1; the wheat yield amounted to 11.73 bushels per acre (Finberg 1969, 110–13). By contrast yields on the Canterbury estates seem surprisingly low, averaging only 3 or 3.5:1 for wheat (Smith 1943, 135). Several abbeys used a significantly higher sowing rate on their home demesnes than on their more distant properties. Christ Church, Canterbury, for example, sowed wheat at 3–4 bushels per acre, barley at 5–6 bushels per acre and oats at 4–6 bushels per acre in Kent, compared with 2.5, 3.5–4 and 2.5–3 bushels per acre respectively elsewhere (Mate 1985, 25). Battle Abbey similarly employed a much higher seeding rate in Sussex and Kent than on its distant estates in the Thames valley (Brandon 1972, 408).

Whether demesne cereal produce went directly towards the sustenance of the community or was regarded as a cash crop varied from house to house and from period to period (Fig 5.2). An absentee owner like the Abbey of Bec naturally found it more convenient to sell the grain from its English estates. In 1288–9 sales of corn from fifteen Bec manors

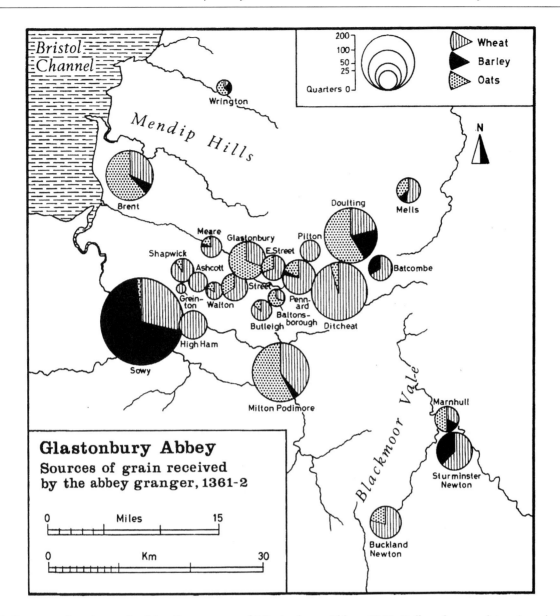

Fig 5.2 Sources of grain received by the granger of Glastonbury Abbey, 1361–2 (based upon data given by Keil, 1962); the grain received at the abbey clearly does not reflect the total production of the abbey's demesnes (C J Bond)

brought in over £275; wheat and barley were the principal cash crops, oats and mixed corn being grown primarily for fodder and for the use of the monastic servants (Morgan 1968, 46, 50–51). By contrast at Bolton Priory in the early fourteenth century there seems to have been no great impulse to sell surplus corn from the demesnes, and almost all of the production was consumed by the canons themselves (Kershaw 1973, 147–8). At Oseney too most grain was consumed on the abbey manors or sent in to the conventual granary, and only limited surpluses, unpredictable from year to year, reached the market (Postles 1979). In 1398–9 Selby Abbey purchased 84 qrs of wheat and 140 qrs 1 bushel of oats, but also arranged for the transport of 160 qrs of wheat, 60 qrs of barley and dredge and 110 qrs of

oats from its own estates at Stallingborough, Garthorpe, Eastoft and Carlton (*Selby Accts.*, 71–2).

Direct archaeological evidence for cereal cultivation may survive in the form of carbonised or waterlogged grains. Wheat, barley, oats and rye have all been recorded from the Bordesley Abbey mill site (Carruthers 1993, 204–212).

The storage and processing of cereal grains

Barns for storing unthreshed grain are the most impressive relics of the monastic economy to survive in the landscape, and represent the principal tangible manifestation of medieval cereal production in the high farming period. On the Evesham estates Abbot Randulph built five new barns which were

Fig 5.3 *The monastic barn at Middle Littleton, Worcestershire (photo C J Bond)*

'much better ones than had been there before', while Abbot John Brookhampton built no less than 'eight magnificent barns' of which only that at Middle Littleton survives (Fig 5.3; see Bond 1973, 13–19). Similar works were undertaken by Abbot John Taunton and Abbot Walter Monington on the Glastonbury estates, and the vital role of such buildings is underlined in many other chronicles.

Monastic barns vary considerably in size. Three distinct groups have been defined (Fig 5.4): large barns, those in excess of 40 m x 9 m; medium barns, between 25 m and 40 m in length and 8–9 m wide; and small barns, less than 25 m x 8 m. Within the group of 'large' barns there is a case for recognising an extra-large category: those more than 70 m long (Cholsey, Abbotsbury) or more than 15 m wide (Beaulieu St Leonards). This variety must surely imply different functions or forms of estate organisation. Large barns may reflect a policy of centralised storage of all grain from numerous manors. Medium barns sometimes represent the storage of produce from a single manor. Small barns may be tithe barns, or may be intended specifically for the storage of either wheat or barley, or may represent the storage of grain destined for the support of a particular obedientiar's office. Unfortunately, even for medium-sized barns serving a single manor, there is no easy equation between barn capacity and arable demesne acreage. Barns were clearly used for storing more than just cereal crops on occasions, while the way in which the crop was harvested and stored could make an enormous difference to the space required (Bond and Weller 1991). Occasionally the quantities of grain stored are recorded: on the estates of Merevale Abbey in 1538, for example, the home barns at Merevale housed 80 qrs of wheat and 60 qrs of barley, maslin and rye, while 20 qrs of wheat, 4 qrs of rye and 12 qrs of peas were stored at Newhouse Grange (Watkins 1994, 101). Many individual monastic barns have been the subject of detailed architectural studies, but there have been relatively few attempts to understand how they were used within the cycle of production and consumption, or to relate them to the estates to which they belonged: a recent survey of Cistercian barns (Holdsworth 1994) has pointed out the limitations in our present knowledge.

Granaries for the storage of threshed grain less frequently survive, although at least one medieval example remains on Shaftesbury Abbey's grange at Bradford-on-Avon. Others have been excavated, along with corn-drying kilns, at Thornholme, Mount Grace and at the Templars' preceptory at South Witham (Coppack 1989, 207; 1990, 109, 118–120; Selkirk 1968). The Dissolution survey of Rievaulx shows that there the former lay brothers' dormitory had been converted to a granary (Coppack 1994, 424). Water-mills and wind-mills were a vital element in the processing of grain. The high farming period is reflected by the construction of many new mills: Abbot John Brookhampton, for example, built no less than sixteen new watermills and several windmills on the Evesham estates (*Eves.Chron.*, 288; Bond 1973, 38–9), while Abbot Michael Amesbury is also credited with sixteen new mills on the Glastonbury estates (Smith 1947, 114). Some monastic water-mills survive in whole or in part, but few have been excavated, and their place in the monastic economy still awaits more detailed study (cf Bond 1989, 102–4; 1993, 72–3; 1994a; and this volume).

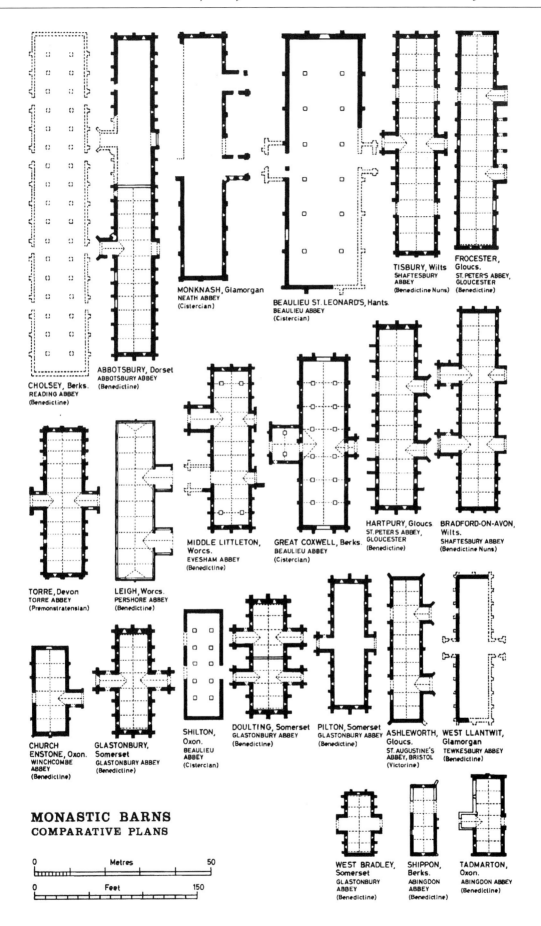

Fig 5.4 *Comparative plans of monastic barns; the wide range of sizes clearly reflects the different ways of organising the storage of cereal products from the estates (C J Bond)*

Bread

The Benedictine Rule allowed 1 lb of bread a day to each monk; on days when supper was served, one-third of that allowance was to be kept back for the later meal. By the late Middle Ages this allowance was often exceeded: at Westminster each monk's daily conventual loaf seems to have weighed about 2 lb after baking (Harvey 1993, 59). Canons seem to have eaten rather more. The Victorine canons of St Augustine's in Bristol were allowed 10½ loaves a week (about 3½ lb of bread a day), the prior and sub-prior an extra half-loaf, and the novices and *conversi* seven loaves each (*Brist.Compot.*, 132–5). Kershaw (1973, 132) estimates that the Augustinians of Bolton each ate about 2½ lb of bread a day, representing an annual consumption of 2.5 qrs of corn per head.

Some concern for quality is frequently evident. The granger's account at Glastonbury shows that *cural*, inferior wheat, was mainly consumed on the manors rather than sent in to the abbey, and was often used in the payment of hired labourers; in 1361–2, 701 of the 1,086 qrs of wheat received by the granger from 24 different manors went to the abbey's baker for making *wastell*, the highest quality bread made from the best flour (Keil 1962, 87–9). Several grades of bread can be recognised: the finest white bread (*panis albus* or *panis domenicus*) eaten by the abbot and his visitors and given to the sick and to monks recuperating from being bled; the ordinary brown bread (*panis bissus*); and a coarser bread which could be given in extra quantities when hard physical work was needed (cf. Knowles 1963, 641). The Beaulieu bakehouse account mentions (in addition to the regular *panis conventualis*) *panis hospitum* for the guesthouse, *panis clermatin*, sifted bread, and *panis familie*, bread made from the flour of rye, barley, beans and peas and intended for the paid staff (*Beaul.Accts.*, 289–304).

Some idea of the scale of production and consumption can be seen from monastic accounts. At Peterborough we have for just over two months in 1370–1 a daily record of the number of loaves of white and brown bread received from the bakehouse by the abbot's household, the number consumed and the number left over (*Pet.Accts.*, 56–83). At Wilton Abbey 2–3 qrs of corn were used to make bread for the whole community every week (*Wilt. Accts.*, 148–56). The lay brothers of Beaulieu were allowed 430 loaves a year at 20 loaves per bushel in 1269–70, implying a per capita annual consumption of just over 2 qrs 5 bushels (*Beaul.Accts.*, 291). At Bolton Priory the consumption of wheat between 1296 and 1319 generally varied between 208 and 352 qrs; in the famine year of 1316–17 only just over 185 qrs were available, and this had to be supplemented

by 33 qrs 7 bushels of maslin and 4 qrs 3 bushels of rye. For the coarser bread over the same period an average of 120–170 qrs of grain was used, rising to over 208 qrs in a good harvest year but down to 87 qrs in 1316–17. Oatmeal formed a significant component of this bread in the earlier years, but was rarely used after 1302, whereas the proportion of wheat increased to a quarter or a third (Kershaw 1973, 144–5). Between 1302 and 1315 an annual average of 286 qrs of wheat and 140 qrs of mixed grain was consumed there by a community of about 170 (ibid, 132–3, 144–5). At Selby Abbey in 1413–14 283½ qrs of grain were baked into bread; allowing 2½ qrs per person per year, this implies a community numbering some 113 persons (*Selby Accts.*, 130 fn5,6). The Selby granger's account of 1404–5 accounts for 412 qrs of wheat from various sources, of which a little over 316 qrs were delivered to the baker to make bread for the monks and corrodians; 3 qrs 3 bushels was baked into fine white bread for the abbot and his visitors; and 7 qrs 4.5 bushels went to the kitchener for pastry (ibid, 141–4).

Monastic bakehouses have, as yet, received little systematic study. There was a bakehouse attached to the early thirteenth-century guesthouse of Kirk-stall Abbey, which was enlarged and altered later in the century, and then demolished in the fifteenth century (Wrathmell 1987, 12–17). At Thornholme Priory what may have been the original guesthouse near the precinct entrance was converted to a bakehouse in the early thirteenth century by the insertion of a small oven into a mural fireplace in the east wall, which was later reconstructed as larger sub-circular bread oven; the whole building was then dismantled at the end of the fourteenth century (Coppack 1989, 191–200). Other examples have been excavated at Mount Grace, Bradwell Abbey and Grove Priory (Coppack 1990, 107–8).

Ale

Ale was consumed in impressive quantities in English monasteries. In many houses little other drink was available and, being boiled and containing preservatives, it was much safer than water. The monks of Abingdon in the middle of the thirteenth century claimed that Abbot Aethelwold had permitted them each 3 gallons a day (*Ab.Chron.*, i, 346–7, ii, 278–9), while at Eynsham in 1284 the recently-retired abbot had a corrody of 4 gallons a day (Bond 1993, 69). By comparison the weekly allowances at St Augustine's Abbey in Bristol of 12 gallons of good ale to the prior and sub-prior, 10 gallons to each canon and 6 gallons to the novices and *conversi* seem quite modest (*Brist.Compot.*, 136–7). Various Cistercian regulations were aimed at curbing the excessive consumption of ale during the twelfth century, especially amongst the lay brothers on the granges (Knowles 1963, 656–7). At Beaulieu Abbey the monks were allocated a gallon of ale a day within the precinct, increased to two gallons when away from the abbey on community business. Corrodians also regularly received a gallon a day, with allowances of a further gallon for their servant. Servants and grooms of the abbey were allowed two-thirds of a gallon of mixed ale. The lay brothers received a daily allowance of half a gallon of second-quality ale (Kershaw 1973, 133).

Ale in these quantities could represent a considerable demand upon any abbey's agricultural resources. The treasurer's accounts at Abingdon record the assignment of 110 qrs and 111 qrs of first-grade malt and 173 qrs and 272 qrs of second-grade malt to the cellarer for brewing for internal consumption in 1375–6 and 1383–4 respectively (*Ab. Accts.*, 23, 42). An acre of land could be expected to yield about 6 bushels of wheat or 7 bushels of barley a year in the Middle Ages, and one bushel of unmalted barley might yield about 18–20 gallons of ale. Even at the rate of consumption of one gallon per monk per day, this still represents 20 bushels of barley a year; so the production of ale required around 2–3 acres of land for every member of the community. Many houses like Bristol St Augustine's, Merevale Abbey and Bicester Priory regularly bought in ale, since production from their own brewhouse was insufficient for their needs (*Brist. Compot.*, 120–3, 136–7; Watkins 1994, 99; Blomfield 1884). Barley was the preferred cereal for malting, but where this was in short supply wheat or oats could be used. At Glastonbury in 1361–2 malting accounted for 416 qrs of barley, 384 qrs of oats, 369 qrs of wheat and 145 qrs of dredge (a mix of oats and barley) (Keil 1962, 90). At Ramsey dredge was generally used for malting up to about 1350, but more barley was grown when legumes came into the regular rotation, and barley then superseded dredge for malting (Raftis 1957, 179). Much of the malt used at Bolton Priory came from oats. Oats suffer a loss of up to 25% on malting, so the yields of malt were considerably less than the quantity of oats handed to the maltster. At Bolton Priory between 1296 and 1319 an average of 856 qrs of corn was malted each year, but there were considerable variations from year to year; in the famine year of 1316–17 only 286 qrs of malt were produced. Between 1304 and 1315 an average of 832 qrs of malt was brewed into ale, all of which appears to have been consumed within the abbey by the canons, along with the corrodians and servants. One quarter of malt could be expected to produce about 60 gallons of ale, so the cellarer of Bolton was supplied with around 50,000 gallons a year, allowing nearly a gallon a day for each member of the community

(Kershaw 1973, 133). In 1404–5 the Selby Abbey granger accounted for 501 qrs 4 bushels of barley from various abbey properties, of which 431 qrs were used in brewing, and 651 qrs 4 bushels of dredge, of which 543 qrs 4 bushels went for brewing (*Selby Accts.*, 145–6). The total quantity of malt accounted for by the granger that year amounted to 992 quarters; of this, 752 quarters was used for brewing ale for the monks and corrodians, the rest remaining in store, given away or lost in winnowing and storage (ibid, 130, 145–6). In 1413–14 714 qrs of malt were used for brewing, suggesting a production of 42,840 gallons, which would again allow each member of the community around a gallon a day (ibid, 130, fn 5).

Many of the records speak of several different strengths and grades of ale. Ale brewed only with grain is thick and sticky, and a variety of herbs and spices were added to clarify, flavour and preserve it. A fifteenth-century dietary from Muchelney Abbey mentions sage, rosemary and rowan for this purpose (*Much. Mem.*, 14).

Buildings connected with malting and brewing existed on many monastic sites, but relatively few have been examined. Harold Brakspear's work at Waverley identified a brewhouse south of the guesthall (Brakspear 1905). Glyn Coppack's excavations in the south-west corner of the outer court at Thornholme revealed evidence for the conversion of the steward's hall to a brewhouse in the early thirteenth century. The brewhouse was subsequently enlarged, but then in the late fourteenth century was partly demolished and rebuilt to house a malt kiln (Coppack 1989, 203–7). The brewhouse at Nuneaton Priory contained a small vat in a circular projection at the corner of the building, possibly for steeping barley before it was spread out to germinate (Andrews *et al* 1981, 61, 64–5). Possible brewhouses have also been identified at Tintern (Courtney 1989, 106), Waltham (Musty 1978), St Neot's (*Medieval Archaeol* 9, (1965) 179–80) and in the Templars' preceptory at South Witham (Selkirk 1968, 237).

Other cereal crops

Oats mainly provided fodder for horses, but were also used to feed poultry and other livestock, while in times of shortage they could be used for malting or converted to meal or flour used in gruel, pottage or porridge. In 1404–5 the granger of Sibton Abbey accounted for 507 qrs of oats from the abbey estates, of which 24 qrs was used for oatmeal pottage, 232 qrs fed to horses, dogs, swans and other birds, 180 qrs mixed with barley and dredge for malt, and 10 qrs lost by desiccation or eaten by rats and mice (*Sibton Doc.*, 147). Oats were a particularly important crop in the colder, wetter areas of Wales, the north and the west, and several different varieties can be distinguished in the records (Williams 1984, ii, 285; Finberg 1969, 95–7; Keil 1962, 86–7). At Bolton priory over 100 qrs of oats were used for pottage in 1296–7 and 1297–8, but by 1300–1 only 62 qrs were used in this way; clearly bread was preferred when it was available (Kershaw 1973, 145–6). The granger of Glastonbury in 1361–2 accounted for 579 qrs of oats received from eighteen manors, of which more than half was malted and most of the remainder used as fodder, while 145 qrs of dredge were used entirely for malting (Keil 1962, 87–8).

Oats were also grown in other parts of England, particularly on marginal land. They represented the principal crop on the Beaulieu estates in 1269–70, accounting for 44% of the total arable production (*Beaul.Accts.*, 25–6). On the Canterbury estates they comprised 29% of the total arable acreage in 1322, but in the custody containing the manors around Romney Marsh the proportion rose to 40% (Smith 1943, 140–1). On some of the marginal fen-edge manors of Ramsey Abbey oats represented 50% of all corn production in the middle of the thirteenth century, though fifty years later they had almost disappeared from the rotation as the abbot turned large acreages over to sheep pasture (Raftis 1957, 161–3). They were also a not insignificant crop on the Oseney estates in the south midlands, though yields there were indifferent and the abbey often had to buy in supplies (Postles 1979, 31).

Rye was grown in many parts of England, particularly in areas of light soils, but it was the least important of the four main cereals. On Tavistock Abbey's manor of Hurdwick a rough average of 20 acres was under rye each year, and in 1524 19 acres of rye there yielded 39 qrs 6 bushels (Finberg 1969, 98–103). In 1404–5 the granger of Selby Abbey received 38 qrs 2 bushels of rye and 2 qrs 4 bushels of maslin, a mixed crop of wheat and rye (*Selby Accts.*, 144). Rye accounted for only 3% of the arable acreage on the Beaulieu estates in 1269–70, and only at the distant Coxwell grange did it total over 100 acres (*Beaul.Accts.*, 25). Similarly only 4% of the total arable acreage on the Canterbury estates was under rye in 1322, though the proportion was greater on the Essex manors (over 200 acres, comprising 11 per cent; Smith 1943, 140–1). Rye was also grown in limited quantities on Abingdon Abbey's Vale of White Horse estates (*Ab.Accts.*, 6–7, 10, 59, 65, 82) and on Oseney's properties in east Oxfordshire and the Cotswolds (Postles 1979, 34, 36). Buckwheat makes an occasional appearance as an introduction from Asia in the early sixteenth century, but its cultivation was never extensive or important.

Other field crops

Broad beans, peas and other legumes were grown as a field crop in many parts of England, and were used both as fodder and for human consumption. Pulses were an important ingredient in pottage, one of the staples of the medieval diet. On the Canterbury estates peas were usually sown at a rate of 5 bushels per acre, beans and vetches at 4 bushels per acre; together legumes accounted for 18% of the total sown acreage of the abbey demesnes in 1322, rising to 28% in East Kent (Smith 1943, 134, 139–41). Beaulieu Abbey received a total of 218 qrs of vetch, 127 qrs of peas and 97 qrs of beans from ten of its New Forest granges in 1269–70, and further purchases by the granarian indicate that this was not sufficient to meet the need (*Beaul.Accts.*, 25–6). In three years, 1365–7 inclusive, Sibton Abbey received an average of 137 qrs of peas per annum from four of its granges (*Sibton Doc.*, 32). The granger of Glastonbury in 1361–2 accounted for a little over 79 qrs of beans and peas from various of the abbey's Somerset estates, but this was a trifling amount compared with the huge quantities of cereals handled (Keil 1962, 88). Merevale occasionally sold surplus legumes from its fields, but most of its produce seems to have been for internal consumption: 28 qrs were threshed in 1499 (Watkins 1994, 95). A similar picture emerges on the English estates of the Norman abbey of Bec (Morgan 1968, 50, 52). Only small quantities of peas and beans were bought at Wilton, while legumes hardly figure at all in the Tavistock accounts (*Wilt.Accts.*; Finberg 1969, 100).

Purchases of beans and peas are regularly recorded in the Battle cellarer's accounts, for sowing (*Batt.Accts.*, 117, 130, 140, 144), for consumption by the community (ibid, 115, 120, 128, 134) or to feed the sucking pigs (ibid, 44). Both green and white peas were used in soup, especially in Lent (ibid, 59, 63, 98, 102, 111, 149). In 1439–40 the land assigned to the cellarer yielded 3 qrs 4 bushels of peas, of which 2 bushels was kept for seed while the remainder used in the household (ibid, 126). In 1465–6 the crop sown the previous year produced 1 qr 2 bushels of peas, a further 1 qr 1 bushel was received from the bailiff of Wye, and 2 bushels were bought for seed; of this 1 qr 7 bushels were consumed within the household and 6 bushels sown on a 3–acre plot (ibid, 145).

While peas and beans were often dried for keeping through the year, no specialised type of building for their storage can be recognised, and they were clearly sometimes stored along with cereals in barns (Bond and Weller 1991, 85). Moreover, pulses are elusive in the environmental record, being rarely preserved by waterlogging. Their contribution to the monastic diet could hardly be assessed if we were dependent solely upon the archaeological evidence.

Garden Crops

Gardens were a feature of monastic precincts from earliest times. The famous plan made in the early ninth century for Gosbert, Abbot of St Gall in Switzerland, depicts a kitchen garden with eighteen beds of named culinary vegetables, a physic garden with sixteen beds of named medicinal herbs and an orchard and shrubbery in the cemetery with nine different kinds of fruit and four varieties of nut trees (Horn and Born 1979; Harvey 1981, 32–4). Kitchen gardens, infirmary gardens and ornamental grounds are all authenticated from English records in the later Middle Ages, while gardens played a particularly central role in houses of the Carthusian order. The aesthetic purposes and medicinal products of monastic gardens cannot be pursued here.

Produce from the kitchen garden which went directly to the table would often escape notice in the accounting procedure, so it is easy to underestimate the importance of garden vegetables in the monastic diet. In fact, pottage was a standard hot dish for all classes of medieval society. At Westminster it normally made up the first dish at every dinner, though by the late Middle Ages it had declined in popularity as beef increasingly took its place (Harvey 1993, 43). Special varieties of pottage called *sew* and *caudle* were eaten at Winchester on 40 out of the 206 days recorded in 1492–3, but regular pottage is probably not recorded (*Winch.Compot.*, 307–362). The Durham accounts mention peas as a constituent of pottage (*Durh.Accts.*, i, 6). Oatmeal, colewort, leeks, or broad beans provided other basic ingredients, boiled up in stock, and sometimes enriched with onions, shallots, garlic, parsley or other herbs (Harvey 1984). The fifteenth-century Muchelney dietary mentions sage, borage, langue-de-boeuf (a culinary variety of bugloss), parsley, marigold, rosemary, thyme, hyssop, summer savory and Good King Henry as flavourings for pottage (*Much.Mem.*, 14–16). Other green herbs and seasonings were eaten raw. Spiced vegetables appeared at Winchester, but only at the Christmas and Easter feasts (*Winch. Compot.*, 314, 324, 332, 345). The Westminster evidence suggests that green vegetables had been more readily available there in the early Middle Ages, but contributed relatively little to the diet by about 1500 (Harvey 1993, 60).

Monastic gardens could cover considerable acreages, though not all of the land was necessarily cultivated. Material from a well in the garden of the London Greyfriars suggested a varied habitat including grassland, scrub and water-filled ditches or ponds (Armitage and West 1985). At Glastonbury there were at least two separate gardens within the precinct in addition to an orchard and vineyard, but parts of both gardens were under grass in 1333–4, being grazed by sheep or horses or mown for hay (Keil 1959–60). Similarly at Battle, where there are mentions of three separate gardens, both the infirmarer's and the cellarer's gardens included some pasture (*Batt.Accts.*, 51, 57). The infirmary garden at Westminster also sometimes produced a crop of hay (Harvey 1992, 98).

Not all of the cultivated ground was given up to garden vegetables: in some cases parts of gardens were used as orchard, or for industrial crops like hemp, flax, madder or bedstraw. However, the Glastonbury gardens in 1333–4 produced a range of pot vegetables, including 3 qrs of onions, 2000 heads of garlic sent to the abbey kitchen, 6000 heads of garlic sent to the larderer with a further 3000 heads kept back for seed, and also quantities of leeks and beans (Keil 1959–60). The precinct of St Augustine's Abbey at Bristol similarly included at least four gardens, producing onions, garlic, leeks, herbs, saffron, filberts, grapes, plums and warden pears, as well as lavender and teasles (*Brist.Compot.*, 140–1, 202–3, 220–4). The cellarer of Battle regularly bought seedlings of leeks and onions for planting in the garden (*Batt.Accts.*, 42, 53, 102, 111, 136). The keeper of the curtilage at Beaulieu, who looked after several small gardens which were apparently interspersed among the outer precinct buildings and workshops, employed five men and produced cereals and vegetables for pottage; but leeks and beans were the only vegetables recorded as yielding sufficient surpluses to be sold (*Beaul.Accts.*, 192–4). Sales of surpluses from the garden of Norwich Priory in 1340 produced 1s 3d for beans, 1s 1d for herbs, 11d for garlic and 13s 4½d for apples and pears (Harvey 1984, 95). Beans, coleworts and leeks are mentioned along with hemp and flax in a description of the Eynsham Abbey garden in about 1360 (*Eynsham Cart.*, ii, 37).

Broad beans and peas were grown mainly as a field crop, to be dried for keeping through the year or used as fodder; but by the thirteenth century there are some indications that they were beginning to appear as garden crops to be eaten green. In 1283 half a bushel of peas was bought for planting in the garden of the Winchester priory manor of Michelmersh (Harvey 1984, 95). Green peas of an early ripening variety called 'hastyngez' were grown in the great garden of St Augustine's Abbey, Bristol, in 1491–2 and 1511–12, along with beans (*Brist.Compot.*, 220–1). Green peas also figure in the Durham accounts (*Durh.Accts.* i, 70).

Unimproved colewort, from which the leaves were plucked when required, was sown several times a year in order to ensure a constant supply. Improved varieties of cabbage were beginning to appear by the fourteenth century: the Selby Abbey kitchener made small purchases of cabbages in 1416–17 (*Selby Accts.*, 167).

At least three varieties of mustard were known in the Middle Ages, of which the black mustard (*brassica nigra*) was the most widely cultivated. The early tender leaves were used as spring greens, the seed-leaves were used as a salad ingredient, and the seed itself was ground in small querns for use as a condiment. At Battle in 1512–13 the cellarer recorded the purchase of 3 bushels of mustard seed and 1½ pipes of vinegar for making mustard (*Batt.Accts.*, 160). Mustard was one of the most consistent items consumed at St Swithun's, Winchester, appearing on the table on 132 out of the 206 days recorded in 1492–3 (*Winch.Compot.*, 307–362). In February 1499 15 'potts' of mustard were bought for £1 in Coventry for use at Merevale Abbey (Watkins 1994, 99). The Selby kitchen accounts record the expenditure of 4s 9d on 2 bushels and 3 pecks of mustard seed in addition to 16d for a man from York to repair the grinding stones of the mustard mill (*Selby Accts.*, 167). A mustard mill also occurs in the 1308 survey of the Templars' camera at Strood (Rigold 1965, 89). This equipment has yet to be recognised archae-ologically.

Root and tuber crops made little significant contribution to the diet in England before the end of the Middle Ages, but there is an unusually early reference to skirrets sold from the Abbot of West-minster's private garden at Eye manor in 1275–6; while in 1327 beet seed was bought for the same garden (Harvey 1992, 105). Soft fruits were collected from the wild but there is little evidence for their cultivation; on one occasion a dish of strawberries was bought in Coventry for Merevale Abbey (Watkins 1994, 99). Mushrooms were also collected from the wild: they were eaten at Winchester on 48 out of the 206 days for which records survive in 1492–3, especially in Lent (*Winch.Compot.*, 307–362). Although herbs were widely used for flavouring, mentions in monastic accounts are not common. Parsley was used at Durham (*Durh.Accts.*, iii, 610). Experiments with more exotic crops such as saffron were carried out after the fourteenth century. Prior More of Worcester managed to obtain 3½ oz of saffron from his garden at Worcester and 2¼ oz from his manor at Grimley in 1519, but his own gardens could not satisfy his needs, and in 1532 we find him buying 1 lb of saffron in Hereford (*Jnl.Pr.More*, 118, 181, 218, 357). It was an uncertain crop in the English climate, and very laborious to harvest, and most of the saffron used in medieval English kitchens was imported. Perhaps the fullest monastic list of garden herbs comes from a record of purchases of seed for

the Abbot of Westminster's private garden at Eye in 1327, which included borage, chervil, coriander, cress, fennel, hyssop, langue-de-boeuf, parsley and savory as well as other vegetables (Harvey 1992, 105, 107–112). Bay and rosemary were grown at the London Charterhouse, many plants being taken thence for the royal garden at Chelsea after the Dissolution (ibid, 106).

The archaeological evidence for the produce of monastic gardens remains very limited. A few gardens likely to have been involved in vegetable production have been excavated, notably at Mount Grace, where unfortunately the nature of the subsoil did not favour the preservation of plant seeds or pollen. Peas, beans and lentils were recovered from the Abingdon grange of Dean Court, and lentils have also been recorded from Hyde Abbey (Moffett 1994, 404). The waterlogged fills of two fifteenth-century drains at the Oxford Blackfriars have provided in addition to various fruit and nut remains evidence of mustard and marigold (Robin-son 1985). Seeds of fennel, which may have been for culinary or medicinal use, have also been recorded at Dean Court (Moffett 1994, 404). Certain veget-ables like brassicas have been particularly elusive in the archaeological record, though historical sources show that they were eaten; however, research led by Dr Richard Evershed in the School of Chemistry at Bristol University has recently devised a technique of recovering lipids from the fabric of cooking pots, including waxes from leafy plants, and this offers a new method of identifying their consumption.

To what extent monastic kitchen-gardens suc-ceeded in supplying the need for vegetables and potherbs is difficult to assess. Obviously the yields varied from season to season, and gardener's accounts never survive in a sufficiently continuous run to monitor the effects of changes in cultivation policy. Kitchener's accounts sometimes record purchases to make up shortfalls in production, along with occasional sales of surpluses. In the late thirteenth and early fourteenth century the bursar at Durham was purchasing herbs like fennel and saffron (*Durh. Accts.*, ii, 494–5, 503, 511). At Abingdon the kitchener was having to buy in garlic and onions at a cost of 12s before 1377, along with other more exotic crops; but in 1440–1 8s was received from sales of onions from the garden (*Ab.Accts.*, 38, 119). The Sibton Abbey kitchener spent 1s 3d on onions, garlic and mustard in 1363–4 (*Sibton Doc.*, 119), while the Selby kitchener spent 5s 4½d on cabbages and leeks, 3s on onions and 12d on garlic in 1416–17 (*Selby Accts.*, 167–8). The kitchener of Bristol and the cellarer of Battle both made regular purchases of mustard (*Brist.Compot.*, 144–5; *Batt.Accts.*, 59, 63, 69, 71, 74, 77). Prior More of Worcester bought 3 bunches of onions for 7d in 1525 (*Jnl.Pr.More*, 225).

Fruit and Cider Production

Orchards were a feature of monastic estates in many parts of England, particularly in the south and west. The gardener's accounts of Abingdon Abbey on several occasions record expenses incurred in collecting fruit and income from sales of apples and warden pears (*Ab.Accts.*, 53, 55, 76, 129). The Glastonbury gardener's account of 1333–4 records a total of over 100 qrs of apples being sent in to the abbey from seven different manors (Keil 1959–60, 99–100). Abbot Selwood of Glastonbury planted a new orchard over three acres in extent at East Brent with finest-quality apples and pears (Harvey 1981, 136). Apples and pears were sold from the Westminster infirmarer's garden on many occasions through the fourteenth century (Harvey 1992, 104–5).

Cider-making may have been introduced into England from Normandy in the twelfth century, and by the fifteenth century special varieties of cider apple had been evolved. However, it remains difficult to estimate what proportion of the apples and pears were eaten directly and what proportion converted to cider or perry. It was estimated around 1300 that 10 qrs of apples and pears ought to yield one tun of cider (*Husb.*, 429). The orchard account of Beaulieu Abbey records the production of 18 tuns of cider in 1269–70 and the sale of 10 tuns (*Beaul.Accts.*, 273–9), and there were also sales of one or two tuns from the gardens of several of the granges (ibid, 114, 120, 140, 157, 170). The cellarer's orchard at Battle regularly produced a surplus of several tuns of cider for sale, up to 10 tuns sold for 22s 4d in 1438–9, though in that year the costs of making making five tuns of cider amounted to 8s 5d (*Batt. Accts.*, 119, 121–3). Apples were occasionally bought in, for example 4½ bushels purchased in 1320–1, and these may have been eating varieties (ibid, 53). The produce of Glastonbury Abbey's orchards at Sowy all seems to have been made into cider on the spot in 1333–4 rather than sent in to the abbey (Keil 1959–60, 99–100). Similarly in 1340 the entire crop of apples from the Westminster infirmarer's garden went for cider (Harvey 1992, 104–5).

The production of cider required specialised buildings, equipment and storage vessels. There was an apple-house at Durham in 1484–5, and another at Abingdon just after the Dissolution (*Durh.Accts.*, i, 98; P.R.O., L.R.2/189, fo. 211ᵛ). A cider mill is mentioned in the Battle cellarer's accounts on several occasions: in 1438–9 4s 3d was received for the use of the mill by outsiders, in 1440–41 3s 4d was paid for two spindles made for the mill, and in 1512–13 8d was spent on repairs and 6d for a lock and key for its door (*Batt.Accts.*, 119, 130, 157–8). Cider-making equipment is also mentioned in the inventory of the gardener's store at Abingdon (*Ab.Accts.*,

57–8). Barrels for the storage of cider were often purchased: 15 empty tuns bought at Beaulieu Abbey in 1269–70, four at Worcester Priory in 1294–5 (*Beaul.Accts.*, 238; *Worc.Compot.*, 30). The Abingdon gardener's account of 1388–9 records payments of 3s 4d for two tuns and 3s for making cider, while 13s 4d was received from sales (*Ab.Accts.*, 53, 55). Buildings and equipment of this nature have not yet been recognised archaeologically on any monastic site, except possibly at Fountains.[2]

Other fruit receives occasional mention. A custumary of Westminster compiled in about 1270 required the gardener to supply particular fruit during Lent and at certain feasts, including apples, pears, cherries, plums and medlars (Harvey 1981, 78; 1992, 105). Abbot John Islip of Westminster was supplied with apples, warden pears and quinces for his own use early in 1510 and strawberries in June and July (Harvey 1993, 61). In 1412–13 the expenses of Denny Abbey included a purchase of what may be quinces (*coton*) (Poster and Sherlock 1987, 81–2).

There is some archaeological evidence for fruit consumption. Two fragments of apple core were found on the kitchen floor at the Abingdon grange of Dean Court (Moffett 1994, 404). Pips and seeds of orchard and soft fruits sometimes survive in refuse and sewage deposits: material from a drain and culvert at the Oxford Blackfriars revealed the consumption of a considerable range of fruits, including apple, pear, plum, sweet cherry, raspberry, alpine strawberry, grape and fig (Robinson 1985, 200–1). Excavation at the Bordesley mill produced one bullace stone, and indications that sloe, elderberry, blackberry, raspberry and strawberry may have been collected from the wild as food plants (Carruthers 1993). Wild blackberry or raspberry is also represented at Dean Court (Moffett 1994, 399, 405).

Nuts

Hazel and walnut trees often seem to have been grown in monastic orchards. The gardener's accounts at Abingdon record expenses for collecting nuts from the orchard and income from sales of filberts (*Ab.Accts.*, 53, 55, 76, 129). John Harvey has noted some evidence for nut plantations on the estates of St Swithun's Priory, Winchester: in 1260–1 19 qrs of nuts were planted on newly-assarted ground at Alton Priors, and at Silkstead in 1276 a bushel of nuts was planted out in the wood of Beauforest (Harvey 1981, 13, 16). Hazel was present in the Westminster infirmarer's garden, but not walnut (Harvey 1992). Purchases of nuts regularly appear in the Battle cellarer's accounts (*Batt.Accts.*, 44, 47, 50, 52, 59, 71). Hazel and walnut are represented in the drain and culvert deposits of the Oxford Blackfriars (Robinson 1985, 200–1), while hazel occurs alone at Dean Court (Moffett 1994, 399, 405).

Almond is frequently mentioned in written sources (see further below) and one almond endocarp has been recovered from the Oxford Blackfriars (Robinson 1985, 200–1). Although the almond is a native of the eastern Mediterranean and was cultivated mainly in southern Europe, it is capable of growing and fruiting in Britain. However, there is so far no direct evidence for its cultivation here in the Middle Ages, and it was probably imported.

Vineyards and Wine Consumption

Wine was expensive in England before the Norman Conquest, and its consumption was limited to days of special privilege, or *caritates*. However, increasing imports from northern France and the Rhineland, together with the spread of vineyards in England, resulted in a considerable increase in wine consumption in the early twelfth century. This was given even greater momentum by Henry Plantagenet's acquisition of Gascony and the rich vineyards of the Garonne through his marriage with Eleanor of Aquitaine in 1152. At Battle Abbot Walter de Lucy (1139–71) left a *caritas* of white wine for the entire community annually on the anniversary of his death, 'and the measure of wine for each brother should not be less than a gallon' (*Batt.Chron.*, 252–3). At Abingdon at least 76 feasts in the year were celebrated with wine, though the regulations there limited each individual to one-sixth or one-twelfth of a pint (*Ab.Chron.*, i, 346–7, ii, 312, 314–7). At Westminster Gascon wine was served to the monks in place of ale on about a hundred feast days and anniversaries each year, the allowance sometimes being as much as a quart each (Harvey 1993, 44, 58). Despite the efforts of some reformers, such as Abbot John at St Albans (1195–1214), wine could appear at the table with both dinner and supper a couple of times a week (Knowles 1963, 464–5). Elsewhere, however, as at Winchester, refectory customs seem to indicate that wine was normally reserved for the abbot or prior, for special dignitaries and guests, for celebration of the mass, and major festive occasions (*Winch.Compot.*, 59).

Bede mentions vineyards growing in many places in England in the early eighth century, and vineyards had certainly begun to appear on monastic estates by the tenth century: one example at Panborough (Fig 5.5) was acquired by Glastonbury Abbey in 956 (Hudson and Neale 1983), while another at *Waecet* (probably Watchfield in the Vale of White Horse rather than, as usually stated, Watchet in Somerset, despite difficulties with the

Fig 5.5 Aerial view of the vineyard at Panborough, Somerset (photo M Aston)

form of the place-name) was acquired by Abingdon Abbey in 962 (*Ab.Chron.*, i, 321). There appears to have been a considerable expansion in vine cultivation after the Norman Conquest. Abbot Walter planted a new vineyard at Hampton near Evesham Abbey in 1084 (*Eves.Chron.*, 97; Bond 1973, 43–4). Vineyards are recorded in 45 locations in the Domesday survey, although no more than a dozen of these were monastic property. Glastonbury, Muchelney, Evesham, Canterbury and Ely were amongst the owners, the last-named being the most northerly listed. They were usually only two or three acres in extent.

Expansion continued during the twelfth century. A new vineyard at Peterborough is attributed to Abbot Martin of Bec (1132–55) (*E.H.D.*, ii, 211). William of Malmesbury praised the vineyards of the Vale of Gloucester which, he says, produced wine 'little inferior to the French in sweetness'; he also describes the vineyard at Thorney in the Fens, 'with the vines trained high upon poles' (*Gesta Pont.*, 292, 326). Worcester priory had vineyards on its estates at Broadwas, Doddenham, Fladbury, Grimley,

Hallow, Ripple and Westbury in 1240 (*Worc.Reg.*, 21, 32, 34, 43, 47, 51, 110). Where there was no main vineyard, vines could still be grown in odd corners within the precinct; this appears to have been the case at Beaulieu, where the forester's account records the production of 775 vine stakes, of which only 375 were used in the abbey itself (*Beaul.Accts.*, 40, 200–1). Even the Scottish border abbeys of Melrose and Jedburgh had a few vines planted in sheltered corners against orchard walls (Cox 1935, 11, 18).

English vineyards made a significant contribution to the provision of wine in the twelfth and early thirteenth centuries, but by the end of the thirteenth century they were clearly in decline. Climatic deterioration – harder winters, late spring and early autumn frosts, dull wet summers – and increased imports of better-quality French wines clearly had much to do with this. The increased costs of labour after the Black Death in many cases proved the final blow. The former vineyard of Battle Abbey was already producing only hay by 1275 (*Batt.Accts.*, 43, 46, 48), later being cultivated for oats and peas (ibid, 51, 68, 71, 76, 80, 89, 112, 126, 145). Two-thirds of Glastonbury Abbey's vineyard at Meare had been converted to arable land and one third to meadow by 1355 (B.L. Egerton MS 3321, f.71b–72).[3] The Canterbury vineyard seems to have been abandoned around 1350 (Seward 1979, 134). The Abingdon vineyard shows decreasing production between 1369 and 1412, and may have been abandoned entirely by 1450, though the name continued in use (*Ab.Accts.*, 17, 52–5, 75, xxxv). At Peterborough labourers were still being hired to stake the vines and weed the vineyard in 1404–5 (*Pet.Accts.*, 122–3). At Ely, while the vineyard was still maintained in 1469, little wine had been produced over the previous century and a half. Despite the difficulties some monastic vineyards did survive to the Dissolution: a terrier of Barking Abbey in 1540 mentions a fenced vineyard of five acres, well-stored with vines (Barty-King 1977, 62), while Richard Layton, one of Cromwell's visitors, reported that the sub-prior of Warden had been apprehended in the vineyard there with a whore (Seward 1979, 135).

Even where home-grown grapes did not ripen sufficiently to be used for wine, they were still valuable for verjuice, a kind of sharp fermented vinegar used in cooking and pickling. The entire crop at Abingdon was retained in the infirmary in the bad season of 1412–13 for making verjuice (*Ab.Accts.*, 75). Must, newly-pressed grape juice not yet fermented or incompletely fermented, was provided for the Abbot of Battle and the guests there in 1278–9, and in 1319–20 Battle's manor of Wye provided 22 gallons of must (*Batt.Accts.*, 44, 49). Grapes could also have been eaten as fresh fruit,

though there appears to be little record of this. Other grape products such as raisins and currants were imported from southern Europe (see further below).

The sites of some monastic vineyards can be located with some confidence from later maps and field-names (eg Hudson and Neale 1983; Bond 1973, 43–4). Wine-making equipment has not yet been recognised archaeologically from any English monastic site. Grape pips have been found in Saxon deposits at Cathedral Green, Winchester. Charred grape pips have come from a fourteenth-century context at the Abingdon grange at Dean Court (Moffett 1994, 404).

Accounts frequently record purchases of wine. Early imports were mainly from Burgundy and northern France through the port of Rouen, but after the Angevin acquisition of Gascony Bordeaux became a much more important source of supply. Beaulieu Abbey was bringing in wine from Gascony by its own ship (*Beaul.Accts.*, 170–1), while Quarr was chartering its ships to Southampton merchants for the same purpose (Hockey 1970, 131–3). At Battle red and white wine was being purchased in London, Winchelsea, Hastings, Sandwich and Canterbury in considerable quantities, for the abbot, for guests, for monks who had been bled, and for treats (*Batt.Accts.*, 49); purchases in London included in 1369–70 one roundell (about 18½ gallons) of white wine from Rennes (ibid, 62). Purchases at Bolton Priory averaged 500–750 gallons a year, rising in 1308–9 to over 2000 gallons (Kershaw 1973, 148–9). In 1333–4 St Swithun's priory at Winchester spent over £92 on wine, including 76 casks of red and two pipes of white, though some of this may have been intended for resale (*Winch.Compot.*, 228). The bursar of Selby in 1398–9 records the abbot's chamberlain being sent to Hull and York to buy a total of over 2,400 gallons of imported red and white wine for the abbot and for the entertainment of guests (*Selby Accts.*, 65, 67, 72–3). The bursar of Durham spent nearly £56 on red and white wine from merchants in Newcastle-upon-Tyne in 1422–3 (Dobson 1973, 261). Merevale Abbey bought 6 gallons of red wine from a Coventry merchant for the feast of Christmas, 1498, and the following February purchased six more gallons of red wine (Watkins 1994, 99).

In addition to ordinary red and white wines from France, stronger, sweeter and more expensive wines were sometimes imported from greater distances. The fifteenth-century Muchelney dietary recommends for special occasions malmsey in the morning and rumney in the evening (*Much.Mem.*, 14–16). Malmsey was originally made in Crete and the Aegean and took its name from Monemvasia on the Morea whence it was exported, though by the fifteenth century supplies in western Europe were increasingly coming from the Portugese colony of

Madeira. One pipe of malmsey appears among the cellarer of Battle's purchases in London in 1371–2; it cost 116s 8d (*Batt.Accts.*, 66), while among the purchases of the abbot's receiver at Peterborough in 1404–5 were 1¼ gallons of malmsey from Lynn (*Pet.Accts.*, 118). Rumney was another sweet wine originally from Rumania and Greece. The bursar of Durham was unable to obtain rumney locally, and was bringing it up from London (Dobson 1973, 265). The cellarer of Battle bought three barrels of rumney in 1412–13, while six gallons of rumney were purchased for Merevale Abbey in February 1499 (*Batt.Accts.*, 105; Watkins, 1994, 99). The cellarer of Battle also bought a barrel of osey, a sweet Alsatian wine, in 1369–70, and bought another tun of osey at Canterbury in 1385–6 for £8 (*Batt.Accts.*, 62, 81). Bastard, a sweet red or white Spanish wine, was bought for Battle in 1412–13 and for Durham in 1464–5 (Batt.Accts., 105; Durh.Accts., iii, 640). Prior More of Worcester bought a quart of sack, a strong dry white wine from Spain or the Canary Islands for 4d in 1518 (this is the first known record of its consumption in England), and also drank osey, malmsey and rumney (*Jnl.Pr.More*, 8, 74, 76, 81).

Honey and Mead

Honey was important as a sweetening agent before imported sugar became available, and bee-keeping is well authenticated from the documentary record. At Beaulieu Abbey in 1269–70 at least a dozen of the workshop departments had their own beehives, producing over 60 gallons of honey, of which half was sold (*Beaul.Accts.*, 175, 177, 184, 193, 194); honey was also produced on many of the granges (ibid, 73, 83, 97, 124, 135; see also Vernon 1979). Elsewhere it was bought in: the kitchener of Selby Abbey purchased over 20 gallons of honey in 1416–17, all of which was consumed within the abbey by the community and its visitors (*Selby Accts.*, 164). At Battle it was reported in 1359–60 that less had been spent on honey that year since *ysopatum*, presumably some sort of herbal brew made from hyssop and sweetened with honey, was not served to the convent as it used to be (*Batt.Accts.*, 59).

Before the Norman Conquest mead made from honey often seems to have been drunk on feast days instead of ale: it is mentioned in the Abingdon dietary and in the Waltham Abbey statutes (Knowles 1963, 464–5). After the twelfth century the production of mead generally seems to have been eclipsed by the readier availability of wine, though at Battle the cellarer still paid 19s 6d for mead in 1278–9 (*Batt.Accts.*, 44).

There is some archaeological evidence for bee-keeping. The head of a worker honey-bee has been

identified at the Oxford Blackfriars (Robinson 1985, 197). Eva Crane mentions bee boles at eleven monastic sites in England and nine in Scotland. Bee boles are notoriously difficult to date, since they show no chronological evolution in form, and it is doubtful whether all those now existing on monastic sites are in fact medieval; but those at Buckfast Abbey are suggested to be twelfth century and those at Pluscarden Abbey thirteenth century (Crane 1983, 121–2, 132–4).

Imported Fruits, Herbs and Spices

Some of the other commodities consumed within the monastery could never be produced on any English monastic estate and had to be imported. Usually the cellarer would attend fairs to acquire the more exotic goods: purchases for Bolton Priory, for example, included rice, sugar, raisins, almonds, figs, pepper, saffron, cumin, mace and cloves, mainly from St Botolph's Fair at Boston (Kershaw 1973, 151).

Figs and raisins appeared occasionally on the table, particularly in winter and during Lent. At Winchester in 1492–3 figs appeared on four days and raisins on three days in Lent, in each case on a Friday. Figs will ripen in favourable conditions in parts of southern England, but most were imported dried. The Durham accounts distinguish between figs of Malaga and figs of Seville (*Dur.Accts.*, ii, 510). Figs were expensive, though visibly cheaper by the later Middle Ages as more were imported. In 1334–5 the kitchen expenses at Winchester included 41s 6d spent on 3 *copulis* (1 *copula* = c 60–75 lbs) of figs and raisins (*Winch.Compot.*, 229). The Sibton kitchener in 1363–4 spent 12s on 1 copula of figs and raisins (*Sibton Doc.*, 119). In 1398 the bursar of Selby spent 8s on 1 *copula* of figs and raisins, while in 1416–17 the Selby kitchener spent 13d on 13lb of figs and a further 15s on 1 *secta* of figs and raisins purchased in Hull (*Selby Accts.*, 67, 164). In 1412–13 the accounts of Abingdon Abbey record 4s spent on figs because the tree in the garden had not fruited that year, and a further 6s on the purchase of 1 *copula* of figs in London (*Ab.Accts.*, 76). At Peterborough the abbot's receiver's account of 1404–5 records expenditure of 14d on figs and raisins, while the sacrist spent 15s on the same fruit for Lent around 1515 (*Pet.Accts.*, 117–8, 205). Fig pips are frequently found in medieval cesspits. Currants were also imported: at Winchester in 1334–5 10 lbs of currants were bought for 20d (*Winch.Compot.*, 235), and at Abingdon in 1356–7 the infirmarer bought 1 lb of currants (*Ab.Accts.*, 14). Dates, along with figs and raisins, appear fairly regularly amongst the purchases of the Battle Abbey cellarers: 1 lb of dates cost 20s 10d in 1371–2, and in 1407–8 and 1409–10 dates were bought with other exotic fruits, nuts and spices in London (*Batt.Accts.*, 47, 50, 59, 62, 66, 71, 76, 97, 101). Abbot John Islip of Westminster managed to acquire oranges on three or four occasions during the first four months of 1510, but these were a rare luxury (Harvey 1993, 61).

Almonds had long been grown in southern Europe. Some varieties will fruit adequately in southern England, but there is little evidence for their widespread cultivation here before the early sixteenth century, and most almonds seem to have been imported. Almonds were used in various ways: whole, blanched and fried, scattered over pottages; pounded to serve as a thickening agent in morterelles (see further below); or in the form of milk of almonds used in cooking and as a substitute for cow's milk on fasting days. Milk of almonds appears on three days at Winchester in 1492–3, including one Friday in December and one day in Lent, while a substantial purchase of almonds is recorded in the Winchester receiver's account of 1334–5, including 714 lbs (51 qrs) bought at St Giles's Fair, the rest from a Lombard spice merchant (*Winch.Compot.*, 234, 311, 317, 322). The pittancer's accounts at Abingdon include 4s 6d for purchase of almonds in 1322–3 (*Ab.Accts.*, 3). The Sibton kitchen accounts record a total of 16s 6d on 62 lbs of almonds in 1363–4 (*Sibton Doc.*, 119). The abbot's receiver of Peterborough paid 17s for 100 lbs of almonds in 1404–5 (*Pet.Accts.*, 117–8). The Selby kitchener spent 10s 8d on four dozen [?lbs of] almonds bought at York, 12s on a further four dozen [?lbs], and 7d on 2 lbs of almonds on three separate occasions in 1416–17, all used in the victuals of the abbot and convent and visitors (*Selby Accts.*, 164, 192).

Rice cultivation had been introduced into Spain and Sicily by the Arabs, and by the fifteenth century it was grown on the plains of Lombardy. It was being imported into England by the thirteenth century, and was expensive enough normally to figure in the spice section of accounts. Purchases for the Durham larder included 204 lbs of rice in 1309–10 and 173 lbs in 1311–12 (*Durh.Accts.*, i, 8, 9). In 1334–5 the receiver's roll at Winchester records a much more substantial purchase of over 200 qrs of rice; it appears there as an entrée on seven days out of the 206 recorded in 1492–3, including four successive Fridays in Lent (*Winch.Compot.*, 234, 311, 317, 321–3). The Selby kitchener purchased 113½ lbs of rice in 1416–17 at a cost of 11s 9½d, all of which was consumed by the community and its guests (*Selby Accts.*, 164, 192). Rice was sometimes an ingredient in morterelles or mortrews, mixed with breadcrumbs, ground almonds, milk and fish, pork or chicken pounded to pulp in a mortar and then braised; these provided an occasional entrée or pittance at Winchester (*Winch.Compot.*, 317, 326, 329).

Sugar cane cultivation had also been introduced into southern Spain and Sicily by the Arabs, but was there on its margins, requiring a warmer climate. By the thirteenth century it was grown successfully on Cyprus, and the Knights Hospitaller built a sugar refinery there at Kolossi in the fourteenth century. It too was initially very expensive and was treated as a spice for accounting purposes, but by the fourteenth century had become much more widely available and much cheaper. In 1334–5 106 lbs of Cyprus sugar bought for Winchester Priory cost £6 7s 9d, while Cyprus sugar frequently figures in the Durham accounts (*Winch.Compot.*, 234; *Durh.Accts.*, i, 11, 13, 16, 21, 36, 37; ii, 518, 566). Moroccan sugar was also used at Durham (*Durh.Accts.*, i, 8, 9, 15, 16, 36; ii, 495, 503, 510). Various monastic accounts mention special kinds of sugar: *albissime* or *blanch*, white sugar (*Ab.Accts.*, 14; *Durh.Accts.*, iii, 608); de *skaffatyne*, *caffatyn*, kitchen sugar (*Durh.Accts.*, ii, 547, 549, 551; *Winch.Compot.*, 235); *fracte*, broken sugar (*Ab.Accts.*, 14); *in plateis*, candied sugar, melted and then poured out over a slab dusted with rice flour and flavoured with rose or violet (*Durh.Accts.*, i, 125, 272; ii, 289, 290, 291, 295, 521, 555, 659; iii, 695; *Winch.Compot.*, 235); and *roset*, red-coloured and rose-flavoured (*Durh.Accts.*, ii, 566; *Winch.Compot.*, 235).

Cooking oil could be extracted from linseed, rape, hempseed, walnuts or hazelnuts; one medieval English record estimates that one quarter of nuts ought to yield four gallons of oil, a ratio of 16:1 (*Husb.*, 428–9, 452n.22). However, most of the oil used for cooking was olive oil, probably imported from Spain. One gallon (*lagena*) of olive oil used by the infirmarer at Abingdon in 1356–7 cost 16d (*Ab.Accts.*, 14); two gallons for the kitchen at Sibton in 1363–4 cost 2s 8d (*Sibton Doc.*, 119); one barrel for the abbot's kitchen at Selby in 1398–9 cost 8s. (*Selby Accts.*, 67). In 1334–5 the kitchen expenses at Winchester included 41s 6d spent on 49 gallons of oil, while at Peterborough in 1404–5 16s 2d was spent on a little over 10 gallons, but in neither case is the type of oil specified (*Winch.Compot.*, 229; *Pet.Accts.*, 117–8).

Unless they are listed in kitchener's accounts, it is not always easy to distinguish spices used in the kitchen for flavouring from those intended for medicinal purposes in the infirmary, since many culinary spices were also believed to have a medicinal virtue. There are also some problems with the correct identification of spices listed in some records. Nevertheless, it is clear that fairly exotic ingredients were available. Pepper was imported from south-east Asia via the spice roads and the Italian ports of Venice and Genoa, and was widely used, though it remained relatively expensive. Selby Abbey bought some of its pepper from spicers in

York and London, and a total of 19 lbs of pepper bought for the kitchen in 1416–17 cost 35s (*Selby Accts.*, 163–4). The abbot's receiver of Peterborough accounted for 40 lbs of pepper bought at Stourbridge Fair in 1404–5 for 53s 4d (*Pet.Accts.*, 118).

Cumin, imported from the Mediterranean, figures in the kitchen accounts of Selby Abbey and the cellarer's accounts of Battle and Durham (*Selby Accts.*, 164, 192; *Batt.Accts.*, 45, 47, 55, 59, 62, 69; *Durh.Accts.*, i, 5; ii, 30). Anise, or sweet cumin, was purchased at Peterborough in 1404–5, and also regularly appears in the Durham accounts (*Pet. Accts.*, 117–8; *Durh.Accts.*, ii, 286, 295, 494, 495, 503, 527; iii, 637, 643, 659 etc). At Peterborough two purchases of cinnamon, totalling 12 lbs, were accounted for by the abbot's receiver in 1404–5; this must be cassia or 'Chinese cinnamon', a native of Burma which came into medieval Europe along the Asian spice routes, rather than true cinnamon, which remained unknown to Europeans before the Portuguese and Dutch settlement of Ceylon. Cloves, coriander, galingale, mace, cardamom and licquorice 'for the abbot' all appear in the same account, though none of them in quantities larger than a couple of pounds (*Pet.Accts.*, 117–8). Ginger was another native of the far east which came into medieval Europe along the spice routes to Arabia. Green ginger was bought at Hull for the use of the abbot of Selby in 1398–9 (*Selby Accts.*, 1988, 65), while the Peterborough account records purchases of 12 lbs of ginger and 1 lb of green ginger, for a total cost of £1 4s 7d (*Pet.Accts.*, 117–8); 20s was spent on ginger at Denny Abbey in 1412–13 (Poster and Sherlock 1987, 81–2). Three pounds of Saunders, a red food dye and flavouring derived from Indian sandalwood, was bought in small quantities of 1–3 lb at Battle in 1351–2 and 1440–1, at Peterborough in 1404–5, and at Selby in 1416–17 (*Batt.Accts.*, 55, 128; *Pet.Accts.*, 117–8; *Selby Accts.*, 164, 192); it was also used regularly at Durham (*Durh.Accts.*, i, 16, 17, 32, 33, 35 etc).

The most expensive of all spices was saffron, costing 12s–15s per lb: up to a quarter of a million flowers were needed to produce 1 lb of spice. Despite this it was quite widely used. Saffron was regularly purchased by the cellarer of Battle in London and Canterbury, usually in quantities of between 1 lb and 5 lb, though in 1319–20 13 lb was bought relatively cheaply for 39s 11d (*Batt.Accts.*, 42, 45, 50 etc). It also regularly appeared at Durham (*Durh.Accts.*, i, 2, 5, 8, 9, 11 etc). The kitchener at Abingdon spent 40s on saffron in one year, at Peterborough the total purchase of 3 lbs of saffron in 1404–5 amounted to £3 4s 8d, and at Denny in 1412–13 half a pound of saffron cost 5s 2d (*Ab.Accts.*, 38; *Pet.Accts.*, 117–8; Poster and Sherlock 1987, 81–2). As we have seen, saffron could be grown in Britain, but most of it was imported from Spain, France and Italy. A few of the other plants mentioned above, including anise (a native of the eastern Mediterranean), could also have been grown in monastic gardens in Britain, though there seems little evidence that they were cultivated.

There was also a long tradition of importing drug ingredients. An Anglo-Saxon leech book probably originally compiled at Winchester around the end of the ninth century, subsequently in the library of Glastonbury Abbey, lists an astonishing range of physic plants not only from southern Europe, Africa and the near East, but from as far away as India, Indonesia and China. The author has drawn extensively, but not unselectively, from a variety of classical and early European sources: it is noticeable that perishable fruits and herbs which could not have survived the journey to Britain have generally been omitted (Cameron 1990). Infirmary accounts for Abingdon Abbey in 1356–7 include the purchase of a number of exotic ingredients, not all of which can be identified securely, but which include ginger, galingale, licquorice, anise, caraway, nutmeg, mace, cloves, cumin, turmeric, cubebs (a variety of vine pepper), Chinese cinnamon or cassia, senna pods and tamarind (*Ab.Accts.*, 14). However, the medicinal uses of herbs and spices in the infirmary cannot be considered in depth here.

Fish

Fish played a major part in the monastic diet in England from the seventh century to the Dissolution, and a variety of sources was exploited to ensure a reliable supply. Monastic fisheries have been discussed at some length elsewhere (Bond 1988), and there is little point in repeating that information here. In some respects, however, perspectives have changed since the preparation of that article (cf Currie 1989), and a brief reconsideration of some of the evidence may be useful.

Numerous records underline the importance of fish. At Christ Church, Canterbury the *ferculum*, or dish for one monk, was calculated at one plaice, two soles, four herrings or eight mackerel in about 1300 (Smith 1943, 42). At Westminster fish was normally consumed at dinner on about 215 days each year, the allowance per head being about 1.25–2 lbs (Harvey 1993, 46, 51). The cellarer's accounts of Durham priory mention no less than 65 different kinds of marine life used for food (*Durh Accts.*, i, xxxiv). At Bolton Priory an average of £20 per annum was spent on fish between 1287 and 1305, around two-thirds of the total kitchen expenses; over the next ten years this increased to £36 per annum (Kershaw 1973, 151–2). The Sibton kitchen accounts of 1363–4 similarly highlight the large quantities of fish consumed in the refectory, recording a total expenditure of £13 15s 8d on fish, compared with £2 6s 7d on eggs and dairy produce and £1 18s 3d on meat (*Sibton Doc.*, 119). At St Swithun's Priory, Winchester, between November 1st 1492 and June 1st 1493 fish appeared as the main course of the main meal on 139 out of the 206 days, ie 67% of the total. As late as 1514–15 fish constituted the main course on 59% of the 278 days for which information is available (*Winch.Compot.*, 306–62).

It is evident that sea fish were far more important in the monastic diet than freshwater fish. Some houses appear to have had their own ships and coastal depots, but many more purchased their fish at the ports. Smoked, dried or pickled herring commonly formed the bulk of purchases, but varieties of cod, haddock and other fish also appear. The cellarer of Durham Priory purchased 20 lasts of herring in 1307–8, costing over £51, a last being a boatload or twelve barrels; this would imply between 200,000 and 264,000 fish (*Durham Accts.*, i, 2). The Winchester kitchen bill of 1334–5 mentions 42,000 red and 11,300 white herrings and quantities of salt salmon, cod, ling, hake, mackerel and conger bought at Portsmouth and Southampton (*Winch.Compot.*, 229). In 1416–17 Selby Abbey purchased a total of 38,520 red herrings and 1,440 white herrings in York, along with smaller quantities of salt ling, dried fish and salmon, almost all of which were consumed within the abbey by the community and its guests (*Selby Accts.*, 161–3, 189–91). Sturgeon, a particularly expensive luxury fish, appeared only on the abbot's table at Selby (ibid, 67). At Westminster about 50% of the sea fish consumed was salted, smoked, dried or pickled, with cod becoming significantly more popular in the later Middle Ages than the cheaper herring; cockles and mussels were sometimes served at supper; while luxury fish such as turbot, thornback ray, sole and conger eel appeared at the abbot's table and on feast days (Harvey 1993, 46–9). Consumption was not confined to houses within easy reach of the coast: sea fish were being marketed deep into the midlands by the thirteenth century (cf Bond 1988, 77).

The evidence from excavations is more limited, mainly because of the fragility of fish bones, which are more vulnerable to mechanical and chemical damage than mammal or bird bones, and the lack of adequate recovery methods employing wet sieving on many earlier excavations (Jones 1989). The variable survival of bone and cartilage may contribute a significant bias to the proportions of particular species identified, with hard-boned species such as conger perhaps looming larger in the archaeological record than they did in the medieval diet (Jones 1976). Nonetheless, what evidence is available further underlines the import-

ance of sea fish in the diet, even in inland houses. At the Austin Friars in Leicester freshwater fish bones were conspicuously absent from the kitchen midden, whereas cod, haddock, ling and plaice were represented in quantity (Thawley 1981, 173–4). At the Oxford Blackfriars herring were the dominant species in a large assemblage of fish-bones, followed by cod, and haddock; in all, five deep-water marine and four inshore species and three migratory species were represented, while freshwater fish were represented only by small quantities of the unpalatable chub and the meagre gudgeon (Wilkinson 1985, 292–3). The limited quantity of fish bones from the Dean Court grange of Abingdon Abbey was dominated by herring, and it is evident that marine fish were consumed there from the mid-thirteenth century onwards, though there was also some evidence of eel, pike and roach (Jones A K G 1994). The record of fish remains from the drain of Sawley Abbey is also dominated by marine species (Jones 1989, 176). Twelfth-century kitchen refuse deposits from the misericord sub-vault at Westminster have yielded at least 20 varieties of fish, of which cod, herring, haddock, whiting and plaice or flounder predominated; apart from eels, freshwater fish were again poorly represented (Jones 1976). Rare luxury items such as sturgeon, John Dory and turbot appear in small quantities at several of these sites. Disconcertingly, marine fish bone deposits have even come from the excavation of freshwater fishponds at Taunton Priory and Southwick Priory, evidently representing the disposal of waste material (Wheeler 1984; Currie 1991).

Freshwater fish could be obtained from lakes, marshlands, river fisheries and artificial fishponds. The abbeys of Peterborough, Ely, Ramsey, Thorney and Bury St Edmunds all had fisheries in the Fens, yielding enormous quantities of eels; Glastonbury, Muchelney and Athelney had similar resources in the Somerset Levels (Bond 1988, 79–83). The Thames, Severn, Trent and other rivers were punctuated with weirs containing basketwork fishtraps, many of which were in monastic ownership (ibid, 84–92). In 1416–17, in addition to the large quantities of sea fish mentioned above, the monks of Selby consumed a total of 1,221 eels, 12 pike, 67 pickerel, and 4,400 roach and perch from their Crowle and Selby fisheries (*Selby Accts.*, 189–91). Pike and fresh salmon were eaten at Westminster on feast days, and dace and roach were served frequently through the winter, though making up no more than 8% of the overall weight of fish consumed (Harvey 1993, 48–9).

Fishponds, intended for the storage and breeding of bream and pike, along with other fish like perch, roach and tench, were clearly the subject of considerable investment on many houses from the twelfth century onwards (Bond 1988, 92–104). Carp were not introduced into England until the late fifteenth century, and make only a limited appearance in monastic ponds. The journal of Prior More of Worcester contains many valuable details of the management and stocking of four groups of ponds on the Worcester priory estates just before the Dissolution (*Jnl.Pr.More*).

The remains of fishponds can be very impressive in terms of both size and complexity: many precincts included six, seven or more ponds, covering up to 6–7 ha. There may have been even larger ponds on the outlying estates: Currie (1988, 267) quotes *c* 52 ha for a pond belonging to St Swithun's Priory, Winchester, at Fleet (Hants), while by the early fourteenth century the monks of Byland may have operated up to a dozen ponds inside and outside the precinct, totalling up to 60 ha (McDonnell 1981, 24–7, 30–3; Hoffman 1994, 405). However, the temptation to deduce from this that the more extensive and elaborate ponds were commercially orientated, producing a surplus for market, receives scant encouragement from the documents (Currie 1989, 151–2). While occasional records of sales from ponds have long been known, for example at Abingdon in 1388–9 and 1412–13 (*Ab.Accts.*, 52, 74), these now seem to be exceptional. Caution is also needed in the interpretation of complex pond sites such as Titchfield (Hants) and Old Warden (Beds), where the monastic premises were converted to domestic use immediately after the Dissolution, a process which might result in the modification or extension of the ponds for aesthetic as well as practical purposes.

Despite the attention given to their construction, Currie has argued that medieval fishponds were not very intensively managed, and their overall yield was therefore low. A couple of instances are known where fish were fed in monastic ponds, at Abingdon in 1322–3 and at Peterborough in 1416–17, the latter being a purchase of two sticks of small eels to feed the pike (*Ab.Accts.*, 3; *Pet.Accts.*, 24). However, these too now seem to be exceptional. Currie has suggested that, without supplementary feeding, a pond one hectare in extent could support about 227 kg (500 lbs) of bream; but since these take about five years to reach edible size, it could produce only about 45 kg (100 lbs) per annum. Assuming 175 fish days per year at which each monk would receive a minimum of 170 g (6 oz), equivalent to 227 g (8 oz) unprepared weight per day, he calculates that a small house of ten brethren would need to find 385 kg (754 lbs) of fish a year, which would require 8.5 ha of ponds. A large house of 40 brethren would require 36.5 ha (Currie, 1988, 1989). The feeding of monastic servants, corrodians and guests would also need to be taken into account. It should be remembered that some houses had large ponds on their estates and granges in addition to those in the precinct, and were also able to draw upon river fisheries. Nonetheless, probably only a small minority of English houses can have come anywhere near self-sufficiency in fish production.

Fishponds tended to be emptied, cleaned out and refilled at regular intervals during their period of use (Bond 1988, 95), and perhaps because of this the few excavations of monastic examples have not generally produced much evidence for the fish stored within them. One notable exception is Owston Abbey, where scales and pharyngeal teeth of perch, bream, roach and pike were recovered, together with the less edible rudd and chub (Shackley *et al* 1988).

Fishponds were sometimes accompanied by buildings containing smoking or drying furnaces, serving as fish stores, providing storage for nets, basketwork traps and other equipment, or providing accommodation for the fishermen. The sole survivor of this type of building is the fish-house at Meare (Fig 5.6) built by Abbot Adam Sodbury of Glastonbury (Gray 1926). Other examples are documented elsewhere. Various repairs to a fishhouse in Durham are recorded, including the fitting of a glass window in 1490–1, while in 1456–7 12 stockfish and 20 'dogdrave' (apparently some kind of cod) were in store there (*Durh.Accts.*, i, 36, 96, 100; iii, 636). At least three buildings of this type have been excavated: at Washford in Warwickshire where the Knights Templar had a fishery (excavated by Margaret Gray; for a summary see Bond 1988, 103); at Cams Head in North Yorkshire, which belonged to Byland Abbey (Kemp 1984); and at Titchfield Abbey (Currie 1988, 286). Earthwork and field-name evidence suggests that further examples await discovery.

Excavation at Abingdon Abbey's Dean Court grange revealed two stone-lined tanks built within the kitchen in the late fourteenth century, apparently for the temporary storage of fish prior to cooking (Allen *et al* 1994, 289–301). A parallel for this feature may be provided by a survey of the palace of the Bishops of Bath and Wells at Wookey in 1552, which lists in the yard outside the kitchens '2 stone trowes for to kepe and water fyshe in yt' (Hasler and Luker 1993, 115).

Freshwater fish purchased in the market were expensive, because they were less readily available: in the fifteenth century a mature pike might cost 1s-3s, a bream or tench 5d or 6d, compared with a farthing for a herring or a halfpenny for a plaice or flounder (Dyer 1988). Their role in the monastic economy was evidently a special one, restricted to feast days and occasions when important visitors were entertained, rather than providing a staple element in the diet.

Fig 5.6 *The fish house at Meare, Somerset (photo C J Bond)*

Birds

Poultry

The flesh of birds did not come within the scope of St Benedict's prohibition, and was regarded as legitimate fare at Monte Cassino at least by 800 (Knowles 1963, 458, fn 2). There is plentiful evidence for the consumption of domestic fowl in English monasteries from the thirteenth century to the Dissolution. Geese, pullets and other poultry were purchased for the infirmary at Beaulieu in 1269–70, though the number is not stated (*Beaul.Accts.*, 255). From 1275 onwards the cellarer of Battle was making regular purchases of geese, cocks, capons, hens, chickens and ducks; again, quantities are often not stated, but the 1351–2 account records the purchase of 172 geese and 268 capons (*Batt.Accts.*, 56). Chickens were bought in some quantity for the nuns of Wilton in 1299; geese, also bought in, were eaten more rarely, while capons were normally provided from the abbey's own stock (*Wilt.Accts.*, 147–56). Sixty-two geese, 91 hens and 26 chickens were consumed at Bolton Priory in 1309–10 (Kershaw 1973, 153). The abbot of Peterborough and his servants consumed 96 hens, 70 capons, one gander and 32 geese between late December 1371 and the beginning of the following Lent (*Pet.Accts.*, 56–83). At Selby Abbey the bursar's account of 1398–9 records the purchase of 55 capons for the abbot; while the kitchener's account of 1416–17 records the receipt of 36 geese, 36 capons, 181 cocks and hens and 24 chickens from gifts and rents, most of which were consumed within the abbey (*Selby Accts.*, 67, 185–7). The kitchen accounts of Sibton Abbey in 1508–9 record the purchase of 26 geese, 51 goslings, 48 capons, 45 hens and 117 pullets (*Sibton Doc.*, 143). At Battle in 1512–13 13 goslings from the abbey's own stock were consumed in the refectory, but 25 geese and small birds, 122 capons, 28 cocks and hens and 709 pullets were bought in (*Batt.Accts.*, 160–1).

The Durham cellarers' rolls mention several buildings connected with rearing fowl. The goose-house was paved with flags in 1474–5, the walls of the capon-house were pointed in 1502–3 and the hen-house was boarded in 1512–13 (*Durh.Accts.*, i, 95, 102, 105–6). Clearly these were more than just ephemeral structures, but buildings of this type have yet to be identified archaeologically.

Goose and domestic fowl bones have been recorded from Norton Priory, the Oxford Blackfriars and the Leicester Austin Friars (Greene 1992, 151–2; Thawley 1981, 173; Harman 1988, 190–2). At Oxford goose was relatively much more common in the mid to late thirteenth century rubbish deposits than in the later scullery deposits.

The peacock, a native of India, may have been introduced into Britain during the Roman period, and had certainly appeared before the Norman Conquest. Some monastic houses may have kept them purely for ornament, but they may also have been destined for the table: in royal and aristocratic circles peacocks dressed in full plumage occasionally provided a centrepiece at great feasts, though the mature birds tend to be tough to eat. Thirteen peacocks were consumed along with other fowl during the feast to celebrate the installation of a new abbess, Emma la Blounde, at Wilton in 1299 (*Wilt. Accts.*, 153–6), while the granger's account of Selby abbey in 1404–5 mentions an allowance of oats and chaff for the peacocks (*Selby Accts.*, 147, 149). Prior More of Worcester had peacocks in his park at Hallow and on his manor of Grimley: in 1530 he was supplied with six from Grimley (*Jnl.Pr.More*, 289, 324).

Pigeons

Dovecotes are a common feature of monastic estates. The main product of the dovecote was the squab, the young bird taken before it learned to fly at about four weeks, which provided about 1 lb of tender meat. At one time it was widely believed that the function of dovecotes was to provide a supply of fresh meat through the winter months after the autumn slaughter of sheep and cattle. It has recently been shown that this view was misconceived, not only because the purchase and storage of fodder made it possible to maintain some supply of fresh beef and mutton through the winter, but also because pigeons themselves do not breed between October and March (McCann 1991). The cellarer's rolls of Durham priory frequently mention pigeon between 1307 and 1416, with some quantities being eaten in September and October, but they never appeared on the table through the winter months (*Durh.Accts.*, i, 1–112). The incomplete cellarer's roll from Wilton Abbey for 1299 records the consumption of 310 pigeons between late July and late September, of which 232 were from store and 78 bought in (*Wilt.Accts.*, 151–6). The cellarer of Battle made regular payments for pigeons, and on two occasions the quantities bought from Alciston manor are recorded: 700 in 1378–9, and 794 pairs in 1395–6 (*Batt.Accts.*, 74, 92). At Selby in 1416–17 a total of 731 pigeons from four different localities were consumed within the abbey (*Selby Accts.*, 187). In 1528 Prior More of Worcester had 160 pairs of pigeons from his dovecotes at Battenhall and Crowle (*Jnl. Pr.More*, 289).

The repair with lime of a dovecote in the West Orchard at Durham is mentioned in 1344, 1485–6 and 1502–3 (*Durh.Accts.*, i, 40, 98, 102). At least ten dovecotes are documented on the Evesham Abbey properties, and several of these survive, varying in size from 200 up to 900 nestholes (Bond 1973, 20–29).

Wildfowl

The fifteenth-century dietary from Muchelney Abbey mentions pheasant, partridge and quail in addition to domestic poultry, but excludes birds that dwell in water (*Much.Mem.*, 14–16). The common pheasant, a native of the Caucasus region, was introduced into England around the time of the Norman Conquest,

and nominally the earliest records are all from monastic sources. Rations at Waltham Abbey in 1058–9 were said to include one pheasant as the equivalent of a brace of partridges or a dozen blackbirds, though the document containing this information dates from the 1170s. In 1098 the Bishop of Rochester assigned to the monks of Rochester 16 pheasants, along with 30 geese and 300 fowl from four separate manors, and two years later the Abbot of Malmesbury claimed a right to hunt pheasants (Lever 1979, 335–6). None of these early records is contemporary, and they must be treated with some caution. A more reliably authentic reference occurs in the bursar's roll of Durham Priory in the time of Edward I, recording the purchase of 26 partridges and one pheasant (*Durh.Accts.*, ii, 498).

At the feast for the installation of the new abbess at Wilton in 1299, which went on for several days, 16 swans, 13 partridges and an unspecified quantity of larks were eaten, along with domestic fowl (*Wilt.Accts.*, 153–6). The cellarer of Battle bought 12 swans in 1395–6 and 12 cygnets in 1399–1400, and partridge appears once in the accounts, along with more regular purchases of domestic fowl (*Batt. Accts.*, 47, 92, 94). The Selby kitchener recorded the receipt of 71 ducks, 18 partridges and two pheasants in 1416–17, all consumed within the abbey; also 33 herons, of which 24 were eaten and the remainder sent as gifts to the Archibishop of York; also 27 swans and cygnets from Crowle and Selby dam, of which eight were consumed in the abbey, ten given away and nine died from disease (*Selby Accts.*,183–5).

It is likely that the choice poultry and wildfowl, recorded in quantities too small to supply the entire community, was destined for the abbot's table. The accounts of the abbot's kitchen at Peterborough record the consumption of ten cygnets, 54 ducks, 135 teal, three woodcock, 13 partridges and 16 fieldfares and the purchase of two wild geese between the end of December 1370 and the beginning of Lent the following year (*Pet.Accts.*, 56–70).

The archaeological evidence for the consumption of miscellaneous wildfowl remains very limited, though mallard, teal and woodcock have been reported from Norton Priory, while duck, moorhen and woodcock were represented in very small quantities at the Oxford Blackfriars (Greene 1992, 151–2; Harman 1985, 190–2).

Eggs

Eggs were used in considerable quantities. At Westminster over a period of 32 weeks in 1491–2 some 82,000 eggs were purchased, and the average daily consumption outside Lent was five eggs per person (Harvey 1993, 61). While Beaulieu Abbey kept

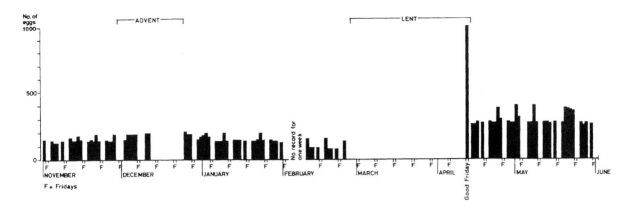

Fig 5.7 *The pattern of consumption of eggs at St Swithun's priory, Winchester, in 1492–3 shows that the fast days and seasons were still generally respected; the higher consumption at Easter probably reflects the greater laying capacity of hens in the spring and summer*

some poultry, the 17,017 eggs which the sub-cellarer provided as pittances in 1269–70 were all purchased (*Beaul.Accts.*, 309). At Wilton Abbey in 1299 some 200–300 eggs were bought for consumption every week (*Wilt.Accts.*, 147–55). The Battle cellarer's accounts record a regular and substantial expenditure upon eggs; the numbers are not recorded in the earlier rolls, but by the mid-fifteenth century some considerable totals were appearing - 42,000 in 1442–3, 47,300 in 1435–6, 48,475 in 1440–1, the prices of which were still some way short of the highest payment recorded earlier (*Batt.Accts.*, 115, 128, 134). The Sibton kitchen accounts of 1363–4 record the purchase of 4,170 eggs in 1363–4, while 1,605 eggs were supplied to the abbot in 1508–9 (*Sibton Doc.*, 119, 143). At Selby Abbey 2,760 eggs were received as rents and tithes in 1416–17, of which 2240 were eaten in the abbey, 120 given away to defray the costs of collection and 400 thrown away because they had gone bad (*Selby Accts.*, 187–8). The Winchester rolls of 1492–3 record the regular appearance of eggs in the priory refectory (Fig 5.7). Through much of the winter about 700 eggs were eaten each week, while weekly consumption through the summer (when the hens were laying better) averaged around 1400; however, they disappear entirely from the menu during the later part of Advent and the whole of Lent (*Winch.Compot.*, 307–329). At Peterborough over 1500 eggs were consumed by the abbot's household alone between the end of December and the beginning of Lent (*Pet.Accts.*, 56–83). Eggs were never normally eaten on Fridays or Saturdays, although 1000 eggs were provided for Good Friday at Winchester.

Eggs or egg yolks were used in a number of the dishes which served as occasional entrées or pittances at Winchester in 1492–3, particularly from Easter Sunday through into May. These included *jusshelle*, a broth or pottage of strained eggs,

breadcrumbs and meat, flavoured with saffron; *flavons* or *flawns*, a kind of cheesecake which included eggs, sugar and saffron baked in a pastry crust (also recorded at Battle and Durham); and *letlory*, milk heated with eggs and saffron and curdled into a custard (*Winch. Compot.*, 324–9). Three supper dishes also eaten occasionally at Winchester fall into the same category: *caudle*, a stiff pottage or purée made from egg yolks mixed with breadcrumbs and spices and heated with ale or wine; *tansy*, a sort of omelette flavoured with tansy leaves, eaten only in late April and early May; and *crispa* or crêpes made from the whites of eggs with milk, flour, salt and sugar (*Winch.Compot.*, 318–9, 326–8). At Westminster a rich cheese flan was consumed on Rogation days, while *dowcet*, a custard of cream, milk, eggs, sugar and currants, was enjoyed at supper on great feast days (Harvey 1993, 61). The archaeological record hardly reflects this element in the diet, though some eggshells have been recorded from the Oxford Blackfriars (Lambrick 1985, 206).

Meat Production and Consumption

In general the Benedictine prohibition against eating the flesh of four-footed beasts seems to have been observed at least until the eleventh century, and it was endorsed by the *Regularis Concordia* and by Lanfranc's statutes. There are occasional hints of backsliding, for example at the Old Minster at Winchester, where the first Norman prior successfully weaned the monks off meat by having the cook prepare exquisite dishes of fish (*Ann.Mon.* ii sa 1082; for other examples see Knowles 1963, 459), but there are no indications of widespread flouting of the Rule. However, the seeds of compromise were already present. Meat had always been permitted to the sick, but at St Alban's Abbot Paul (1077–93) found himself obliged to prohibit the extension of this privilege to monks who had been bled (*Chron. Maj.*, i, 59). The one surviving infirmarian's account roll from Peterborough shows regular purchases of beef, mutton, pork, veal, geese, capons, hens and pullets in 1379–80 (*Pet.Accts.*, 46–8). The entertainment of guests provided another loophole, and we find the cellarer of Battle buying six ox carcasses in 1275 in preparation for an expected visit from the king, while in 1319–20 beef was bought to await the arrival of the bishop (*Batt.Accts.*, 41, 48). Lard, offal and entrails, together with salted or pre-cooked meat, had generally come to be regarded as legitimate fare for the whole community by the twelfth century, though the resistance against fresh roast meat remained (Harvey 1993, 40, 56).

By 1333–4 the meat bill at St Swithun's, Winchester, amounted to over £104, and the community of a little over 60 monks with their servants and guests were consuming around two carcasses a day (*Winch. Compot.*, 229). The monks of Battle were allowed meat at the main meal three days a week outside the fast seasons, and the cellarer there regularly records the purchase of beef, veal, mutton, lamb and pork (*Batt.Accts.*, 18). Finally in 1336 a bull of Pope Benedict XII legitimised the status quo, permitting meat to Benedictine monks four days a week, though no more than half the community was to be allowed this indulgence on any given day. Wednesdays, Fridays and Saturdays, Advent and the period between Septuagesima and Easter were to remain meatless (Knowles 1979, ii, 4), though in practice the latter period of abstinence normally seems to have begun on Ash Wednesday at the beginning of Lent.

There remained considerable unease about the consumption of meat in the refectory. Consequently from the thirteenth century a number of monasteries built a second dining-hall known as the misericord, often between the infirmary and refectory, where meat could be eaten with a clear conscience. Examples are known not only at Benedictine houses such as Westminster, Tavistock and Canterbury, but also at Cistercian Waverley, Kirkstall and Fountains. Infirmary kitchens already equipped to cook meat might now also serve the misericord; or, as at Byland (Fig 5.8) and Kirkstall in the fifteenth century, a new meat kitchen might be built (Moorhouse & Wrathmell 1987, 33–39). One consequence of the increasing importance of meat in the diet might be the reduction in importance of the refectory itself, and its partial adaptation for other purposes.

Farm livestock: cattle, sheep and pigs

Many Benedictine abbeys had considerable flocks of sheep and herds of cattle on their outlying manors. The Huntingdonshire manors of Ramsey Abbey had relatively small herds of cattle, rarely more than a couple of dozen each, and these can have made only a limited contribution to the monastic table (Raftis 1957, 137–40). The stock culled here were probably often worn-out plough oxen and milk cattle no longer fit for lactation. Sheep were kept in considerably greater numbers, but mainly for their wool (ibid, 144–52). Extensive woodlands on the Ramsey manors provided pannage for pigs, and flitches of

Fig 5.8 The meat kitchen at Byland Abbey, North Yorkshire (photo C J Bond)

bacon were provided to the abbey as food rents from an early date, while fifteen or twenty hogs were regularly sent to market from each manor (ibid, 141–4). Peterborough also stands out as a producer of pigs, with several of the abbey's manors containing a hundred swine or more (Biddick 1984).

However, it was often more convenient to purchase meat at local markets rather than drive stock in from distant manors. At Wilton during the four summer months of 1299 beef was eaten almost daily except for fast days, all of it bought in. Much smaller quantities of veal, mutton and pork were purchased; only bacon was regularly supplied from store (*Wilt.Accts.*). In 1351–2 the meat consumed at Battle Abbey included 172 wethers, 11 calves and 17 lambs acquired from the abbey's manors, but a further 252 wethers, 54 calves and 12 lambs had been bought in the neighbourhood (*Batt.Accts.*, 56). In 1512–13 324 sucking pigs were bought, only 13 being provided from the cellarer's own office (ibid, 160).

Purchases made by monastic cellarers to supply the kitchens give some idea of the scale of consumption. At Battle 34 oxen, 3 bulls and 19 cows, 500 sheep and 88 lambs were bought for meat, plus an unspecified quantity of pork, sucking pig and veal, in 1395–6. In 1400–1 purchases included 54 beef carcasses and 610 wethers and ewes; and in 1402–3, 63 beef carcasses and 735 sheep (*Batt.Accts.*, 18n, 92). At Selby Abbey the purchases of the extern cellarer at Pontefract and Doncaster markets in 1413–14 included 51 bullocks (including three for fattening for Easter) and 70 sheep. Twenty of the bullocks and 69 sheep were sent on to the kitchener. However, this particular year was uncharacteristic, since the obedientiaries' offices were undergoing reorganisation, and the figures quoted above must represent a small proportion of the abbey's total consumption (*Selby Accts.*, 116–7, 127–8). In 1416–17 the kitchener himself provided fourteen complete carcasses and 2½ shoulders of ox, 49 cows, 15 bullocks and one heifer; 383 complete sheep carcasses with one quarter and 2½ shoulders of sheep and 66 lambs with two quarters and one shoulder; and 76 pigs, 3 boar, and 75 piglets. All this was for consumption by the abbot, convent and visitors (ibid, 160, 179–82, 183). In 1479–80 the extern cellarer delivered 500 sheep and 38¼ pigs to the kitchener; in 1478–9 the total was 765 sheep and 59½ pigs (ibid, 117, n 7).

Sheep and cattle played a major part in the Cistercian economy, particularly between the late twelfth and late fourteenth centuries; however, much of their production was geared towards the marketing of wool and hides, which cannot be examined here. In their attempt to return to a literal interpretation of the Benedictine Rule, the Cistercians were initially strict upon matters of diet. The Beaulieu accounts of 1269–70 suggest that meat-eating was still then restricted to the two infirmaries. Pigs were bred and fattened on several of the granges, while at the abbey piggery itself six boars and 14 sows were kept and 178 piglets born during the year; most of these were sold, but 26 went to the monastic infirmary larder (*Beaul.Accts.*, 182–4). Forty-five pigs were consumed in the monks' infirmary that year, along with 2½ carcasses of cattle, five sheep and quantities of offal (ibid, 255). The larder accounts (which are, in effect, the records of the slaughterhouse) list the carcasses of four oxen, seven cattle, two bullocks, 336 sheep, and one salt pig. Three of the oxen, two cattle and five of the sheep were destined for the monastic infirmary, but half of one cow and 20 sheep carcasses were kept back as a pittance for the beginning of Lent; much of the remainder went to the secular infirmary (ibid, 186–7).

Later records show how the Cistercians too in due course compromised. The kitchen accounts of Sibton Abbey record 38s 3d spent on beef, veal and pork already in 1363–4, though this was still a very small sum compared with the expenditure on fish. By 1508–9 meat made up a far higher proportion of kitchen purchases, and included two bulls, four oxen, 36 cattle and calves and 64 sheep for slaughter for the abbot's table, also two boar, six bacon hogs, seven pigs and 47 piglets (*Sibton Doc.*, 119, 143). Merevale Abbey had its own kitchen, dairy and store herds, but bought in calves for veal – sixteen calves were bought in a period of just over six weeks in May and early June 1498, while a further 37 heifers, steers and kine had gone to the kitchen by 23rd November. In the same year 57 sheep were taken from the flock of 474 at Pinwall Grange for slaughter, but the abbey was also purchasing sheep and lambs for food from outsiders (Watkins 1994, 96).

Canons following the Augustinian Rule always had fewer inhibitions about meat-eating. Beef, veal, mutton and pork were all purchased by the kitchener at Bristol (*Brist.Accts.*, 144–5). The larder accounts of Bolton priory from 1304–5 to 1318–19 record a considerable consumption of beef, mutton and pork. The number of beasts slaughtered varied considerably from year to year: for example, 295 sheep were killed in the first famine year of 1315–16, compared with only 23 in 1304–5, while 183 pigs were killed in 1306–7, compared with 31 in 1313–14. The canons supplemented the supplies of meat from their own flocks and herds by regular purchases, particularly of beef. Between 1287 and 1305 an average £10 a year was spent on meat, representing about one third of the total expenditure of the kitchen, and by 1315–19 average annual purchases of £28 on meat slightly exceeded the expenditure on fish for the first time (Kershaw 1973, 152–4).

It is difficult to gauge the quantities of meat eaten. By about 1500 it appears that each monk at West-

minster could expect to eat flesh meat in the misericord on about 75 days through the year, the average
daily allowance of meat being a little under 2 lbs.
Mutton accounted for 46% of the total weight of flesh
meat served as main dishes, beef 24%, pork 14% and
veal 11.5 %, but there was some seasonal variation.
Pork was never eaten between Easter and mid-
September, whereas lamb appeared mainly in late
spring and early summer, and veal particularly
between April and August (Harvey 1993, 51–56). At
St Swithun's, Winchester, meat appeared regularly
in the refectory in 1492–3. Out of the 206 days for
which records survive, beef occurred on 74 days
with an alternative of mutton on 71 days and pork
on three days in November when mutton was not
available. However the prohibition of meat continued to be respected on Fridays and throughout
Lent (*Winch.Compot.*, 307–329). From the figures
available Kitchin calculates a daily intake of 1½ lbs
of meat per monk. Unless this allowance was
intended also to serve dependents, this would
suggest an average individual consumption at
Winchester of around 280–300 lbs a year. Tackling
the problem from another angle, Kershaw has
estimated that the yields of edible meat in the
Middle Ages would be of the order of 250 lbs per
head of cattle, 50 lbs for pig and 25 lbs for sheep. On
this basis he calculates the average annual individual
consumption of meat at Bolton priory as of the order
of 160 lb (Kershaw 1973, 158).

The Winchester records underline the variety of
meat dishes prepared, suggesting that little was
wasted. A small sum of 2s 10d was paid to a woman
who prepared the intestines of pigs and other
animals slaughtered within the priory (*Winch.
Compot.*, 229), presumably for sausages and haggis
(by contrast entrails of stock at Battle seem generally
to have been sold on). *Tucket*, apparently some kind
of haggis, appeared at Winchester in 1492–3 as an
entrée on ten days in November and three days early
in May. *Batir*, a sort of meat pudding, appeared first
on Easter Sunday, and then more or less regularly
every Sunday, Monday, Tuesday and Thursday until
the end of June, when the record ceases. Delicacies
like calves feet and *sowse* (pickled pigs' feet and ears)
were reserved for the ministrants (*Winch.Compot.*,
307–329). Tripe from store was provided for supper
on Christmas Day, 1514 and on at least a dozen other
days through the following year outside Lent,
particularly on Sundays (ibid, 332, 335, 338, 345–6,
350–1, 353–5, 357–9, 361–2). The Battle cellarer's
account of 1512–13 records the purchase of tucket,
entrails and animal tongues for consumption in the
refectory (*Batt.Accts.*, 160). At Westminster the
summer menu included *charlet*, made from chopped
pork, veal or bacon, eggs and milk; while *umbles*,
sheep's entrails mixed with breadcrumbs and spices

and cooked in ale, were commonly eaten in winter
(Harvey 1993, 58, 62).

Vaccaries with byres and bercaries with sheepcotes are frequently mentioned in written sources,
but archaeological evidence for the housing of farm
livestock remains relatively limited. One excavated
thirteenth-century vaccary on Dean Moor, Dartmoor,
belonging to Buckfast Abbey, included a dwelling
and large byre flanking a central enclosed yard, with
further stock enclosures (Fox 1958). Some animal
housing of fifteenth-century date, perhaps for plough
oxen, has been excavated at Waltham Abbey
(Huggins 1972, 64–73, 78–9), and cowsheds were
amongst the preceptory buildings at South Witham
(Selkirk 1968, 237). A possible byre in the outer court
at Fountains has been identified by survey (Coppack
1994, 418). Sheepcotes were usually long narrow
buildings (one example belonging to Battle Abbey
measured 100 feet by 14 feet) on stone sill walls,
sufficiently distinctive to be recognisable as earthworks. However, a sheepcote probably belonging to
Bolton Priory excavated on Malham Moor was only
48 feet by 18 feet internally (Raistrick and Holmes
1962, 23). Little is known of the housing of pigs, either
from documentary or from archaeological evidence.
Beaulieu Abbey's pigs were regularly fed with
malting dregs, kitchen swill and granary rejects,
which surely implies some form of sty. The Durham
cellarer's accounts mention at least two swinehouses
and sties, and at Battle a pigsty was thatched with
broom in 1478–9 (*Beaul. Accts.*, 182–4; *Durh Accts*, i,
93, 100–1, 103; *Batt. Accts.*, 149). Two possible pigstyes
were among the buildings excavated at South Witham
(Selkirk 1968, 237).

The archaeological evidence for meat consumption rests mainly upon the animal bone content of
middens. However, there are many problems in the
interpretation of such evidence from limited
samples. Patterns of rubbish removal and disposal
may distort the sample, and material from the
monastic kitchen may become intermingled with
refuse from elsewhere.

Exceptionally at Kirkstall Abbey an extensive
dump of food refuse, including the bones of some
5000 animals, was found immediately west and
south of the meat kitchen. This included 90% ox or
cow, only 5% sheep and 3% pig. Clearly here beef
greatly outweighed the consumption of other meat.
The cattle and sheep bones were mostly from mature
animals, the ox bones in particular from beasts of 5
to 10 years, underlining the suggestion that only
oxen too old for ploughing could be spared for the
table. Most parts of the skeleton were represented,
and most bones had been chopped, suggesting
stewing rather than roasting, an appropriate treatment for old, tough meat (Ryder 1959; Moorhouse
and Wrathmell 1987, 152).

In the later monastic periods at Norton priory, cattle accounted for 30% of the bones of the three main farm livestock species, representing about 68% of the meat eaten. However, by contrast with Kirkstall, the evidence here suggests a more discriminating diet. Although the cattle were mostly killed at four years or over, there was little evidence of arthritis to suggest the culling and consumption of worn-out draught beasts, and there was a predominance of choice shoulder, foreleg, rump and hind-leg cuts. 47% of the bones were of sheep, mostly slaughtered at two or three years, again displaying a preference for legs of mutton; and 23% were pig, mostly under two years old or sucking pig (Greene 1992, 151).

At the Cistercian abbey of Bordesley cattle again represented the dominant species from the bone evidence from the mill site, followed by pig, whereas the proportion of sheep bones was unusually low, perhaps reflecting the unsuitability of the locality for sheep farming. The period of occupation of the mill, from the late twelfth to the early fifteenth century, was one when most of the abbey's lands were still directly farmed, so we are more likely to be seeing here the products of the precinct and granges than meat purchased in the market. However, the distance of the mill from the main claustral buildings means that the evidence here is more likely to reflect the diet of monastic employees and servants than of the monks themselves; the better joints of meat were conspicuously lacking (Lovett 1993, 231–5).

Perhaps surprisingly, in urban friaries the bone evidence points to the purchase of live beasts or whole carcasses rather than select joints. At the Oxford Blackfriars cattle and sheep, mostly mature animals of at least three or four years of age, made up 47% and 43% of the bone sample from the mid to late thirteenth century, with beef clearly making up a much larger proportion of the meat consumed, and a significantly higher proportion than in the tenements of the town itself. Pig bones represented only 9% of the bones, and pork clearly made up a relatively small part of the diet (Harman 1985, 190–2; Lambrick 1985, 205). Cattle were also predominant at the Austin Friars in Leicester and at the London Greyfriars, followed by sheep and pig (Thawley 1981, 173–4; Armitage and West 1985).

In addition to bone evidence, equipment associated specifically with the cooking of meat may be found. Reassessment of the earlier excavations at Kirkstall Abbey has led to the recognition of concentrations of dripping pans (long, narrow, shallow-sided trays with handles on one of the long sides, used beneath a spit to collect juices from cooking meat) around the kitchens and infirmary where they were likely to have been used (Moorhouse and Wrathmell 1987, 107–8).

Dairy produce

Milk from both cattle and sheep was available through the summer, but milking of sheep normally stopped around Lammastide in August, and lactation of cattle generally declined between September and December. Milk became very expensive through the winter. It is of some interest to find quantities of milk (3 quarts, 3 gallons and 2 gallons) being supplied to the abbot of Peterborough from Boroughbury on three Wednesdays in January, but there is then no further record until the account ends in Easter 1371 (*Pet.Accts.*, 58, 59, 63). At St Swithun's Priory, Winchester, milk from the priory's own farm at Priors Barton appears as an entrée on two days in May 1492 (*Winch.Compot.*, 328).

Butter was used as an alternative to animal fat or imported oil in frying, but had to be heavily salted for keeping. Most of the butter produced on Tavistock Abbey's three principal dairies was sold, including the entire 20 stone recorded from Werrington in 1386; some was given to officials and labourers as part of their remuneration, but relatively little was consumed within the abbey itself, and that exclusively from the nearest dairy at Hurdwick (Finberg 1969, 141–3). Purchases of butter costing 1d-3d are recorded for the household of the abbot of Peterborough every Wednesday from the commencement of the roll in December 1370 up to the beginning of Lent (*Pet.Accts.*, 58, 59, 61, 63, 65, 67, 69).

Cheese was the most effective way of utilising milk for longer-term storage through the winter after lactation ceased in December. At Westminster, except during Lent and on Fridays, cheese consumption averaged at least 2.5 oz per head per day (Harvey 1993, 62). Considerable cheese production is documented on the Tavistock estate, the Werrington dairy achieving 142 stone in the glut year of 1386. Again the greater proportion was sold, but in most years between five and 20 stone was delivered to the abbey for internal consumption, the Hurdwick dairy being the principal supplier (Finberg 1969, 139–141). By contrast on the Ramsey estates cheese production from the small fenland herds was limited and little surplus was available for sale; nor does milk from the much more numerous fenland sheep ever appear to have been used for cheese here (Raftis 1957, 137).

Five of Beaulieu's granges were sending butter and cheese to the sub-cellarer in 1269–70 (*Beaul. Accts.*, 312). The Sibton Abbey kitchener spent 22s 8d on cheese and 3s 1d on butter and milk in 1363–4 (*Sibton Doc.*, 119). Selby Abbey's dairy at Stainer produced 173 gallons of milk and 7½ stone of cheese in 1416–17, all consumed within the abbey (*Selby Accts.*, 191). Separate dairy accounts began at Sibton Abbey in 1507: by 1513 production amounted to 86 weys of cheese, 357½ gallons of butter, 35 gallons of milk and 21 gallons of cream from 140 cows (*Sibton Doc.*, 37–9, 141–2).

Yields per head of cattle seem very variable. One thirteenth-century source estimates that one cow should produce sufficient milk for 98 lbs of cheese and 14 lbs of butter (*Husb.*, 431). These totals were exceeded at Sibton, where average annual production from 1507–1514 was of the order of 0.61 weys (around 157 lbs) of cheese and 3.1 gallons (21.7 lbs) of butter per cow (*Sibton Doc.*, 37–8). By contrast, annual production at the Tavistock dairies seems to have averaged around 32 lbs of cheese and 4½ lbs of butter per cow (Finberg 1969, 138–143).

Consumption of dairy produce is equally difficult to assess. At Battle Abbey cheese and milk was supplied to the monks from the manor of Marley, but the entire production of cream and butter was reserved for the abbot's household (*Batt.Accts.*, 19). At Bolton Priory the average annual consumption of the whole community during the period 1305–15 has been estimated at 115 stone of butter and 310 stone of cheese, probably about 25½ lb of dairy produce per individual, a very minor contribution to the diet (Kershaw 1973, 155).

Dairy equipment, including strainers, presses, buckets, earthenware pans and butter-crocks, figures in various monastic accounts and inventories. Concentrations of such material ought to be recognisable from excavation.

Venison

Venison very rarely receives mention in monastic account rolls, presumably because it was not often available by purchase through the market. Unusually, the fragmentary cellarer's roll from Wilton Abbey does record occasional purchases of venison in June 1299, including three carcasses for the feast for the new abbess (*Wilt.Accts.*, 148–9, 154). Normally, however, it could only be acquired from within the monastic estate, by gift, or by poaching.

Hunting was strictly forbidden by canon law, but reports of visitations of monastic houses suggest that abuses were not uncommon. Abbot Samson of Bury St Edmunds is said to have made several parks and stocked them with game, keeping a huntsman with dogs, though his biographer emphasized that these were provided for the entertainment of important visitors, and while he and his monks sometimes watched the hunt he never himself tasted venison (*Chron.Brakelond*, 28–9) (for other examples of monks and hunting, see Coulton 1960, 508–12).

A number of monastic estates included parks which could have provided a supply of game. Glastonbury Abbey had at least seven parks in three counties, while the prior of St Swithun's at Win-

chester had six in Hampshire, and many other Benedictine houses at least one. It has been estimated that monastic corporations owned some 8 or 9% of the total of all parks in the south-western counties (Bond 1994b, 139).

Where the abbey estates could not provide game, it might be aquired by other means. One of the Carthusian brothers of Witham was presented in 1270 for poaching a hart in Mendip Forest and for hunting another in Cheddar Wood (Cox and Greswell 1911, 559–60). Poachers in the Forest of Dean seem regularly to have received shelter from the monks and lay brothers of Tintern, the canons of Llanthony and the Knights Templar of Garway. Ramsey Abbey similarly received poachers according to the Rockingham Forest eyres of 1272 and 1286 (Birrell 1982, 14, 17). The Abbot of St Augustine's, Bristol, was a major receiver of stolen deer in 1270 (ibid, 20). There is no mention of venison in the Beaulieu accounts of 1269–70, but the Abbot was accused in the New Forest Pleas of *c* 1257 of harbouring deer poachers, along with the Abbot of Titchfield and the priors of St Mary's, Southampton and St Denis (*New For.Doc.*, no.83, 73). Gifts of deer to monastic houses are also recorded.

The 1492–3 menu at Winchester included an entrée of *nombles*, identified by Kitchin as a portion of venison cut from the inner side of the deer's thigh, perhaps including the liver or heart, on 17 days out of 206, plus three more occurrences as a pittance, though not in winter or Lent (*Winch. Compot.*, 307–329); the same item occurs in the Durham accounts.

Deer bones have occasionally been identified from excavations on monastic sites. The Austin Friars at Leicester produced 115 bones of fallow deer and two of red deer (Thawley 1981, 173). By contrast, only one fragment of roe antler came from the Oxford Blackfriars (Harman 1985, 191). In general venison cannot have made a major contribution to the monastic diet.

Hares and Rabbits

Hares would have been available on many estates, but again, in theory, monks and canons were not permitted to hunt them. Nonetheless we find the Augustinian William Clown, Abbot of Leicester (1345–78) earning such fame as a huntsman that Edward III and the Black Prince arranged an annual engagement of hare coursing with him; he himself declared that he would have taken no delight in such frivolity but for the need to display civility to the lords of the kingdom and to earn their goodwill and favour towards the abbey in its business affairs (Thompson 1949, 28–9, 33). Hare occasionally figures amongst purchases for the monastic kitchen (eg

Batt.Accts., 52), but was clearly never a common item of diet.

Rabbits, unlike hares, were not a native species but were introduced after the Norman Conquest. The earliest known reference to their presence in Britain occurs in 1176, when the Abbot of Tavistock successfully claimed a tithe of rabbits on the Scilly Isles (*Tavist.Ch.*, xxxii, 365). In 1280 the Abbot of Keynsham had a licence to enclose a pasture within Filwood Chase with a stone wall and to convert it to a rabbit warren (*Cal.Pat.R.*, 1272–81, 371). Sixteen rabbits were acquired at Kettering for the abbot's table at Peterborough on Jan 28th 1370–1, and they were eaten in small numbers there throughout the winter (*Pet.Accts.*, 56–83). The cellarer of Durham regularly bought 20–30 coneys a week in 1390–1 (*Durh.Accts.*, i, 49–50). In 1416–17 the kitchener at Selby accounted for 41 coneys from Crowle warren and four from Thorpe Willoughby, of which 39 were consumed in the abbey and six given away (*Selby Accts.*, 184). Quarr Abbey had six rabbit warrens on the Isle of Wight; even in the late Middle Ages when these were leased out, the monks reserved eight brace of rabbits from the Combley warren (Hockey 1970, 177). Prior More of Worcester had between 100 and 300 couples of coneys from Henwick Warren most years through the 1520s and 1530s, plus smaller numbers from his deer parks at Hallow and Battenhall (*Jnl.Pr.More*, 150, 168, 189, 289, 324, 344). He reserved the right to hunt in his warrens himself with bows, ferrets and nets.

The production of rabbits is reflected in the landscape by pillow mounds and by the remains of warreners' lodges, of which the Prior of Thetford's warrener's lodge (Fig 5.9), built soon after 1400 on Thetford Warren is the most complete surviving example. Relatively little archaeological evidence

exists for the consumption of hares or rabbits on monastic sites. Samples from Norton Priory, the Leicester Austin Friars and the Oxford Blackfriars have each produced only a few bones; at Oxford a couple of hare bones came from the mid-to-late thirteenth century claustral area and five rabbit bones from the fifteenth-century silts of the main culvert (Greene 1992, 151–2; Thawley, 1981, 173; Harman 1985, 190–2).

Conclusion

The fullest analysis of the monastic diet carried out to date has been Barbara Harvey's study of Westminster Abbey (Harvey 1993). Here in a very wealthy Benedictine house towards the end of the Middle Ages bread normally provided 35% of the energy value in the diet, ale and wine 25%, meat 17%, suet 7%, fish 6%, eggs 4.5%, dairy produce 4%, oatmeal and flour 1% and vegetables 0.5%. In Lent the contribution of bread rose to 45.5%, ale and wine to 32.5% and fish to 18%. Individual allowances were generous, though it is suggested that the average monk perhaps consumed no more than 60% of his allowance, or 75% on Fridays, leaving a surplus to be eaten by lay brothers, almsmen and servants. The quality of the diet at Westminster Abbey compared very favourably with that of other groups in medieval society, with its high protein content and high energy value; its main lack appears to have been an insufficiency of fresh fruit and green vegetables, which would have led to a deficiency in Vitamin C; the limited intake of dairy produce may also have led to some deficiency in Vitamin A.

Clearly, however, the Westminster model will not serve universally. There were considerable variations in consumption through time, between different orders and between wealthy and poor houses. Even within a single house at any one time there could be marked variations in standards of living and levels of consumption between the abbot, the monks, the sick, the corrodians, the guests, the lay brethren and the monastic servants. The ways in which dietary demands were met were even more varied, ranging from an ideal of complete self-sufficiency based upon the direct exploitation of estates to a total dependence upon the market. Further archaeological exploration alongside further study of documentary sources still has much to contribute.

Acknowledgements

My greatest debt is to the numerous authors and editors listed in the bibliography, from whose work I have quarried. My wife, Tina, has read my first draft, has translated some of it into English, and has

Fig 5.9 *The warrener's lodge at Thetford, Norfolk (photo C J Bond)*

advised on a number of points. Finally, I am grateful to Graham Keevill for inviting me to speak at the conference where the first version of this paper was delivered, and for accepting a manuscript which has developed a momentum of its own to expand considerably beyond the limits he had originally specified.

Notes

1 I owe this information to Helen Paterson.
2 I am grateful to Glyn Coppack and Steve Moorhouse for their advice on this matter.
3 I owe this reference to Frances Neale.

Bibliography

1 Published Documentary Sources

Ab.Accts.: Accounts of the Obedientiars of Abingdon Abbey, R E G Kirk (ed), 1892, Camden Society New Series 51

Ab.Chron.: Chronicon Monasterii de Abingdon, 2 vols, J Stevenson (ed), 1858, Rolls Series 2

Ann.Mon.: Annales Monastici, 5 vols, H R Luard (ed), 1864–9, Rolls Series 36

Batt.Accts.: Accounts of the Cellarers of Battle Abbey 1275–1513, E Searle and B Ross (ed), 1967, Sydney University Press

Batt.Chron.: The Chronicle of Battle Abbey, E Searle (ed), 1980, Oxford

Beaul.Accts.: The Account-Book of Beaulieu Abbey, S F Hockey (ed), 1975, Camden 4th series, 16

Brist.Compot.: Two Compotus Rolls of St Augustine's Abbey, Bristol, G Beachcroft and A Sabin (eds), 1938, Bristol Record Society 9

Cal.Pat.R.: Calendar of Patent Rolls PRO, London, commencing 1891

Chron.Brakelond: The Chronicle of Jocelyn of Brakelond, H E Butler (ed), 1949, Nelson, London

Chron.Maj.: Matthew Paris, *Chronica Majora* 7 vols, H R Luard (ed), 1872–84, Rolls Series 57

Durh.Accts.: Extracts from the Account Rolls of the Abbey of Durham, 3 vols, Canon Fowler (ed), 1898, 1898, 1900, Surtees Society 99, 100, 103,

E.H.D.ii: English Historical Documents, ii: 1042–1189, D C Douglas and G W Greenaway (eds), 1981 (2nd edn), Eyre Methuen/Oxford University Press,

Eves.Chron.: Chronicon Monasterii de Evesham, D Macray (ed) , 1863, Rolls Series 29

Eynsh.Cart.: Cartulary of the Abbey of Eynsham, 2 vols, H E Salter (ed), 1907, 1908, Oxford Historical Society 49, 51

Gesta Pont.: Willelmi Malmesbiriensis Gesta Pontificium Anglorum, N E S A Hamilton (ed), 1870, Rolls Series 52

Husb.: Husbandry in Walter of Henley and other Treatises on Estate management and Accounting, D Oschinsky (ed) , 1971, Oxford, pp 417–457,

Jnl.Pr.More: Journal of Prior William More, E S Fegan (ed), 1914, Worcs Historical Society

Mon.Ind.: Monasteriales Indicia: the Anglo-Saxon Sign Language, D Banham (ed), 1991, Anglo-Saxon Books

Much.Mem.: Muchelney Memoranda, B Schofield (ed), 1927, Somerset Record Society 42

New For.Doc.: A Calendar of New Forest Documents, AD 1244–1334, D J Stagg (ed), 1979, Hampshire Record Series 3

Pet.Accts.: Account Rolls of the Obedientiaries of Peterborough, J Greatrex (ed), 1983, Northants Record Society 33

Rule: The Rule of St Benedict, J McCann (trans), 1970, Sheed & Ward, London

Selby Accts.: Monastery and Society in the Late Middle Ages: Selected Account Rolls from Selby Abbey, Yorkshire, 1398–1537, J H Tillotson (ed) , 1988, Boydell, Woodbridge

Sibton Doc.: The Sibton Abbey Estates: Select Documents, A H Denney (ed), 1960, Suffolk Records Society 2

Tavist.Ch.: 'Some early Tavistock charters' H P R Finberg (ed), 1947, *English Hist Review* 62, pp 352–77

Wilt.Accts.: 'Fragment of an account of the cellaress of Wilton Abbey, 1299', E Crittall (ed), in *Collectanea*, N J Williams and T F T Plucknett (eds), 1956, Wiltshire Archaeological & Natural History Society Records Branch 12

Winch.Compot.: Compotus Rolls of the Obedientiaries of St Swithun's Priory, Winchester, G W Kitchin (ed), 1892, Hampshire Record Society 7

Worc.Compot.: Early Compotus Rolls of the Priory of Worcester, J M Wilson and C Gordon (eds), 1908, Worcestershire Historical Society

Worc.Reg.: Register of Worcester Priory, W Hale (ed), 1865, Camden Society 91

2 Secondary Works

Allen T G, 1994, 'A medieval grange of Abingdon Abbey at Dean Court Farm, Cumnor, Oxon', *Oxoniensia* 54, pp 219–447

Andrews D, Cook A, Quant V, Thorn J C and Veasey E A, 1981, 'The archaeology and topography of Nuneaton Priory', *Trans Birmingham & Warwickshire Archaeological Society* 91, pp 55–81

Armitage P L and West B 1985, 'Faunal evidence from a late-medieval well of the Greyfriars, London', *Trans London & Middlesex Archaeological Society* 36, pp 107–36

Astill G G, 1993, *A Medieval Industrial Complex and its Landscape: the Metalworking Watermills and Workshops of Bordesley Abbey*, Council for British Archaeology Research Report 92

Aston M (ed), 1988, *Medieval Fish, Fisheries and Fishponds in England* 2 vols, British Archaeological Reports British Series 182

Barty-King H 1977, *A Tradition of English Wine*, Oxford Illustrated Press

Biddick K 1984, 'Pig husbandry on the Peterborough Abbey estate from the twelfth to the fourteenth century AD', in C Grigson and J Clutton-Brock (eds), *Animals and Archaeology, 4: Husbandry in Europe*, pp 161–78, Oxford

Birrell J 1982, 'Who poached the kings deer? A study in thirteenth-century crime', *Midland History* 7, pp 9–25

Bishop T A M 1936, 'Monastic granges in Yorkshire', *English Historical Review* 2, pp 193–214

Black G 1976, 'Excavations in the sub-vault of the misericorde of Westminster Abbey', *Trans London & Middlesex Archaeological Society* 27, pp 135–78

Blomfield J C 1884, *History of the Deanery of Bicester, ii: The History of Bicester, its Town and Priory*, privately published, Bicester

Bond C J 1973, 'The estates of Evesham Abbey: a preliminary survey of their medieval topography', *Vale of Evesham Historical Society Research Papers* 4, pp 1–62

Bond C J 1979, 'The reconstruction of the medieval landscape: the estates of Abingdon Abbey', *Landscape History* 1, pp 59–75

Bond C J 1988, 'Monastic fisheries', in Aston M (ed), 1988, *Medieval Fish, Fisheries and Fishponds in England* 1, British Archaeological Reports British Series 182, pp 69–112

Bond C J 1989, 'Water management in the rural monastery', in Gilchrist R and Mytum H (eds), 1989, *The Archaeology of Rural Monasteries*, British Archaeological Reports, British Series 203, pp 83–111

Bond C J 1993, 'Water management in the urban monastery', in Gilchrist R and Mytum H (eds), 1993, *Advances in Monastic Archaeology*, British Archaeological Reports British Series 227, pp 43–78

Bond C J 1994a, 'Cistercian mills in England and Wales a preliminary survey', in Pressouyre L (ed), 1994, *L'Espace Cistercien*, Ministère de l'Enseignement supérieure et de la Recherche, Mémoires de la section d'archéologie et d'histoire de l'art 5, Paris, pp 364–77

Bond C J 1994b, 'Forests, chases, warrens and parks in medieval Wessex', in M Aston and C Lewis (eds), 1994, *The Medieval Landscape of Wessex*, Oxbow Monograph 46, Oxford, pp 115–58

Bond C J and Weller J B 1991, 'The Somerset barns of Glastonbury Abbey', in L Abrams and J P Carley (eds), *The Archaeology and History of Glastonbury Abbey*, Boydell, Woodbridge, pp 57–87

Brakspear H 1905, *Waverley Abbey*, Surrey Archaeological Society

Brandon P F 1972, 'The cereal yields on the Sussex estates of Battle Abbey during the later Middle Ages', *Economic History Review* 2nd series 25, pp 403–20

Cameron M L 1990, 'Bald's Leechbook and cultural interactions in Anglo-Saxon England', *Anglo-Saxon England* 19, pp 5–12

Carruthers W J 1993, 'The valley environment: the evidence of the plant remains', in Astill G G, 1993, *A Medieval Industrial Complex and its Landscape: the Metalworking Watermills and Workshops of Bordesley Abbey*, Council for British Archaeology Research Report 92, pp 204–12

Coppack G 1989, 'Thornholme Priory: the development of a monastic outer court landscape', in Gilchrist R and Mytum H (eds) 1989, *The Archaeology of Rural Monasteries* British Archaeological Reports, British Series, pp 185–222

Coppack G 1990, *Abbeys and Priories*, English Heritage/ Batsford, London

Coppack G 1994, 'The outer courts of Fountains and Rievaulx Abbeys: the interface between estate and monastery', in Pressouyre L (ed) 1994, *L'Espace Cistercien*, Ministère de l'Enseignement supérieure et de la Recherche, Mémoires de la section d'archéologie et d'histoire de l'art 5, Paris, pp 415–25

Coulton G G, 1960, *Medieval Village, Manor and Monastery*, New York, (originally published as *The Medieval Village*, Cambridge, 1925)

Courtney P 1989, 'Excavations in the outer precinct of Tintern Abbey', *Medieval Archaeology* 33, pp 99–143

Cox E H M 1935, *A History of Gardening in Scotland*

Cox J C and Greswell W H P 1911, 'Forestry', in *The Victoria History of the County of Somerset*, 2, pp 547–72

Crane E 1983, *The Archaeology of Beekeeping*, Duckworth, London

Currie C 1988, 'Medieval fishponds in Hampshire', in Aston M (ed), 1988, *Medieval Fish, Fisheries and Fishponds in England* 2, British Archaeological Reports British Series 182, pp 267–89

Currie C 1989, 'The role of fishponds in the monastic economy', in Gilchrist R and Mytum H (eds) 1989, *The Archaeology of Rural Monasteries*, British Archaeological Reports British Series 203, pp 147–72

Currie C 1991, 'Southwick Priory fishponds', *Proceedings Hants Field Club & Archaeological Society* 46, pp 53–72

Dobson R B 1973, *Durham Priory, 1400–1450*, Cambridge University Press

Donkin R A 1978, *The Cistercians: Studies in the Geography of Medieval England and Wales*, Pontifical Institute of Mediaeval Studies, Studies and Texts 38, Toronto

Dyer C 1988, 'The consumption of freshwater fish in medieval England', in M Aston (ed), *Medieval Fish, Fisheries and Fishponds*, BAR Brit Ser 182 pt I, 27–38

Dyer C 1989, *Standards of Living in the Later Middle Ages*, Cambridge University Press

Finberg H P R 1969, *Tavistock Abbey: a Study in the Social and Economic History of Devon*, David & Charles, Newton Abbot

Fox A 1958, 'A monastic homestead on Dean Moor, South Devon', *Medieval Archaeology* 2, pp 141–57

Gilchrist R, 1994, *Gender and Material Culture: the Archaeology of Religious Women*, Routledge, London & New York

Gilchrist R and Mytum H (eds) 1989, *The Archaeology of Rural Monasteries*, British Archaeological Reports British Series 203

Gilchrist R and Mytum H (eds) 1993, *Advances in Monastic Archaeology*, British Archaeological Reports British Series 227

Gray H St G 1926, 'The abbot's fish house, Meare', *Proceedings Somerset Archaeology & Natural History Society* 72.i, p xli

Gray M 1993, *The Trinitarian Order in England*, British Archaeological Reports British Series 226

Greene J P 1992, *Medieval Monasteries*, Leicester University Press

Harman M 1985, 'The animal and bird bones', in Lambrick G, 1985, 'Further excavations on the second site of the Dominican priory, Oxford', *Oxoniensia* 50, pp 190–2

Harvey B 1977, *Westminster Abbey and its Estates in the Middle Ages*, OUP, Oxford

Harvey B 1993, *Living and Dying in England, 1100–1540: the Monastic Experience*, Oxford University Press

Harvey J H 1981, *Mediaeval Gardens*, Batsford, London

Harvey J H 1984, 'Vegetables in the Middle Ages', *Garden History* 12, ii, pp 89–99

Harvey J H 1992, 'Westminster Abbey: the infirmarer's garden', *Garden History* 20, ii, pp 97–115

Hasler J and Luker B 1993, 'The site of the Bishop's Palace, Wookey', *Proceedings Somerset Archaeological & Natural History Sociey* 137, pp 111–22

Hockey S F 1970, *Quarr Abbey and its Lands, 1132–1631*, Leicester University Press

Hoffman R 1994, 'Mediaeval Cistercian fisheries natural and artificial', in Pressouyre L (ed), 1994, *L'Espace Cistercien*, Ministère de l'Enseignement supérieure et de la Recherche, Mémoires de la section d'archéologie et d'histoire de l'art 5, Paris, pp 401–14

Holdsworth C 1994, 'Barns at Cistercian granges in England and Wales', in Pressouyre L (ed), 1994, *L'Espace Cistercien*, Ministère de l'Enseignement supérieure et de la Recherche, Mémoires de la section d'archéologie et d'histoire de l'art 5, Paris, pp 353–63

Horn W and Born E 1979, *The Plan of St Gall* 3 vols, University of California Press

Hudson H and Neale F 1983, 'The Panborough Saxon charter, AD 956', *Proceedings Somerset Archaeoogical. & Natural History Society* 127, pp 55–69

Huggins P J 1972, 'Monastic grange and outer close excavations, 1970–1972', *Transactions Essex Archaeological Society*, 3rd series 4, pp 30–127

Hutchison C A 1989, *The Hermit Monks of Grandmont*, Cistercian Studies Series 118, Kalamazoo, Michigan

Jones A K G 1976, 'The fish bones', in Black G, 1976, 'Excavations in the sub-vault of the misericorde of Westminster Abbey', *Trans London & Middlesex Archaeological Society* 27, pp 170–6

Jones A K G 1989, 'The survival of fish remains at monastic sites', in Gilchrist R and Mytum H (eds) 1989, *The Archaeology of Rural Monasteries*, British Archaeological Reports British Series 203, pp 173–84

Jones A K G 1994, 'Fish remains', in Allen T G, 1994, 'A medieval grange of Abingdon Abbey at Dean Court Farm, Cumnor, Oxon', *Oxoniensia* 54, 396–8

Jones G 1994, 'Animal bones', in Allen T G, 1994, 'A medieval grange of Abingdon Abbey at Dean Court Farm, Cumnor, Oxon', *Oxoniensia* 54, pp 386–96

Keil I 1959–60, 'The garden at Glastonbury Abbey,, *Proceedings Somerset Archaeological & Natural History Society* 104, pp 96–101

Keil I 1962, 'The granger of Glastonbury Abbey, 1361–62', *Somerset & Dorset Notes & Queries* 28, part 276, pp 86–90

Kemp R 1984, 'A fish-keeper's store at Byland Abbey', *Ryedale Historian* 12, pp 44–51

Kershaw I 1973, *Bolton Priory: the Economy of a Northern Monastery, 1286–1325*, Oxford University Press

Knowles D 1963 (2nd edn), *The Monastic Order in England*, Cambridge University Press

Knowles D 1979 (new edn), *The Religious Orders in England* 3 vols, Cambridge University Press

Lambrick G 1985, 'Further excavations on the second site of the Dominican priory, Oxford', *Oxoniensia* 50, pp 131–208

Lever C 1979, *The Naturalised Animals of the British Isles*, Paladin, London

Locker A 1976, 'The animal and bird bones', in Black G, 1976, 'Excavations in the sub-vault of the misericorde of Westminster Abbey', *Trans London & Middlesex Archaeological Society* 27, pp 176–8

Lovett J 1993, 'Animal bone', in Astill G G, 1993, *A Medieval Industrial Complex and its Landscape: the Metalworking Watermills and Workshops of Bordesley Abbey*, Council for British Archaeology Research Report 92, pp 231–5

McCann J 1991, 'An historical enquiry into the design and

use of dovecotes, *Trans Ancient Monuments Society* 35, pp 89–160

McDonnell J 1981, *Inland Fisheries in Medieval Yorkshire, 1066–1300*, Borthwick Papers 60, Borthwick Institute of Historical Research, University of York

Mate M 1985, 'Medieval agrarian practices: the determining factor?', *Agricultural History Review* 33, pp 22–31

Miller E 1951, *The Abbey and Bishopric of Ely*, Cambridge University Press

Moffat B 1987, 'A curious assemblage of seeds from a pit at Waltham Abbey, Essex: a study of medieval medication', *Essex Archaeology & History* 18, pp 121–4

Moffett L 1994, 'Charred plant remains', in Allen T G, 1994, 'A medieval grange of Abingdon Abbey at Dean Court Farm, Cumnor, Oxon', *Oxoniensia* 54, pp 398–406

Moorhouse S 1989, 'Monastic estates: their composition and development', in Gilchrist R and Mytum H (eds), 1989, *The Archaeology of Rural Monasteries*, British Archaeological Reports British Series, pp 29–81

Moorhouse S and Wrathmell S 1987, *Kirkstall Abbey, 1: The 1950–64 Excavations: a Reassessment* Yorkshire Archaeology 1, West Yorkshire Archaeology Service

Morgan M 1968 (revised edn), *English Lands of the Abbey of Bec*, Oxford

Musty A E S 1978, 'Exploratory excavation within the monastic precinct, Waltham Abbey, 1972', *Essex Archaeology & History* 10, pp 121–73

Neilson N 1898, *Economic Conditions on the Manors of Ramsey Abbey*, Philadelphia

O'Connor T P 1993, 'Bone assemblages from monastic sites: many questions but few data', in Gilchrist R and Mytum H (eds), 1993, *Advances in Monastic Archaeology*, British Archaeological Reports British Series 227, pp 107–11

O'Neil T 1987, *Merchants and Mariners in Medieval Ireland*, Irish Academic Press, Dublin

Poster J and Sherlock D 1987, 'Denny Abbey: the nuns' refectory', *Proceedings Cambridge Antiquarian Society* 76, pp 67–72

Postles D 1979, 'Grain issues from some properties of Oseney Abbey, 1274–1348', *Oxoniensia* 44, pp 30–7

Pressouyre L (ed) 1994, *L'Espace Cistercien*, Ministère de l'Enseignement supérieure et de la Recherche, Mémoires de la section d'archéologie et d'histoire de l'art 5, Paris

Raftis J A, 1957, *The Estates of Ramsey Abbey*, Pontifical Institute of Mediaeval Studies, Studies & Texts 3, Toronto

Raistrick A and Holmes P F 1962, 'Archaeology of Malham Moor', *Field Studies* 1.iv, pp 1–28

Rigold S 1965, 'Two camerae of the Military Orders', *Archaeological Journal* 122, pp 86–132

Robinson M R 1985, 'Plant and invertebrate remains from the priory drains', in Lambrick G, 1985, 'Further excavations on the second site of the Dominican priory, Oxford', *Oxoniensia* 50, pp 196–201

Ryder M L 1959, 'The animal remains found at Kirkstall Abbey', *Agricultural History Review* 7, pp 1–5

Selkirk A 1968, 'South Witham', *Current Archaeology* 1.ix, pp 232–7

Seward D 1979, *Monks and Wine*, Mitchell Beazley, London

Shackley M, Hayne J and Wainwright N 1988, 'Environmental analysis of medieval fishpond deposits at

Owston Abbey, Leicestershire', in Aston M (ed), 1988, *Medieval Fish, Fisheries and Fishponds in England* 2, British Archaeological Reports British Series 182, pp 301–8

Sharpe J 1985, 'Oseney Abbey, Oxford: archaeological investigations, 1975–1983', *Oxoniensia* 50, pp 95–130

Smith R A L 1939, 'The Estates of Pershore Abbey', MA thesis, London University

Smith R A L 1943, *Canterbury Cathedral Priory: a Study in Monastic Administration*, Cambridge University Press

Smith R A L 1947, 'The Benedictine contribution to medieval English agriculture', in Smith R A L, *Collected Papers*, Longmans, Green & Co., London, pp 103–16

Thawley C R 1981, 'The mammal, fish and bird bones', in J E Mellor and T Pearce, 1981, *The Austin Friars, Leicester*, Council for British Archaeology Research Report 35, pp 173–5

Thompson A H 1949, *The Abbey of St Mary of the Meadows, Leicester*, Leicester Archaeological Society

Upton-Ward J M 1992, *The Rule of the Templars*, Boydell, Woodbridge

Vernon F G 1979, 'Bee-Keeping in 1260–70 at Beaulieu Abbey in England', *Bee World* 60 pt iv, 170–5

Watkins A 1994, 'Merevale Abbey in the late 1490s', *Warwickshire History* 9, iii, pp 87–104

Wheeler A 1984, 'Fish bones', in P Leach, 1984, *The Archaeology of Taunton*, Western Archaeological Trust Excavation Monograph 8, pp 193–4

Wilkinson M R 1985, 'The fish remains', in Lambrick G, 1985, 'Further excavations on the second site of the Dominican priory, Oxford', *Oxoniensia* 50, pp 192–3

Williams D H 1984 (2nd edn), *The Welsh Cistercians* 2 vols, Caldey

Wilson B and Allison E 1985, 'Faunal remains: Oseney Abbey', in Sharpe J, 1985, 'Oseney Abbey, Oxford: archaeological investigations, 1975–1983', *Oxoniensia* 50, pp 120–1

Wrathmell S 1987 (2nd edn), *Kirkstall Abbey: the Guesthouse*, West Yorkshire Archaeology Service

6 Monastic Water Management in Great Britain: A review

James Bond

Preface

The investigation of water management has rarely featured as a primary objective in monastic studies in Britain. In consequence information remains scanty and widely scattered through the literature. Two conferences held in York in 1988 and 1989 provided some opportunity for preliminary appraisals of the evidence in rural and urban monasteries respectively (Bond 1989, 1993), but systematic study has barely begun. The subject has fared far better on the continent. Important contributions have been made in Germany, where a series of publications under the aegis of the Frontinus Society is exploring the history and archaeology of water supply throughout Europe (see especially Grewe 1991). A conference on water supply held at Regensburg in November 1997 included several studies of monastic sites (publication forthcoming). There have also been significant advances in France, where a colloquium specifically dedicated to monastic water engineering was held at the Abbey of Royaumont in June 1992 (Pressouyre & Benoît 1996) and in Portugal, where a further symposium on monastic hydraulics took place at the Convent of Arrabida in November 1993 (publication forthcoming). The role of the Cistercians has always attracted particular attention. Some aspects of water management were touched upon at the Cistercian colloquium held at the Abbey of Fontfroide in March 1993 (Pressouyre 1994), and there have been significant further contributions since (eg Benoît 1998; Berthier & Rouillard 1998).

The following paper was not among the presentations at the Oxford conference in 1995. It emerged from a suggestion from the editors that discussions of water management on British monastic sites which have hitherto appeared only in two of the German and French language publications mentioned above (Bond 1991, 1996) might be of interest to English-speaking readers. However, rather than merely translate back into English papers which are now some years old, it was felt that a consolidated and updated review might be more in keeping with the aims of the present volume.

Introduction

The earliest monastic rules were drawn up within the political, social and economic context of the late Roman empire, when all the classical machinery of water supply and consumption was still functioning. St Augustine, writing towards the end of the fourth century, counselled his canons at Hippo to exercise restraint in their desire for clean clothing and to consult their superior before washing their clothes or taking them to a laundry; he also permitted them to visit public baths for the sake of their health, though not to go bathing simply because they enjoyed it (*Rule St A.*, 5.4, 5.5, 5.7). Even in north Africa the ready availability of such facilities was clearly taken for granted, at least in the larger towns. However, when St Benedict drew up his rule at Monte Cassino around AD 530–40, water was identified as the first of the 'necessary things' which he felt it advisable to have within the precinct (*Rule St B.*, Ch 16). Baths were to be permitted to the sick as often as was expedient, but should seldom be granted to the young and healthy (*Rule St B.*, Ch 36). Benedict placed much greater emphasis upon the seclusion of his monks, and monasteries in remote rural locations were unlikely to have access to convenient Roman aqueducts, even if such things were still functioning in the sixth century. Sources now needed to be sought close at hand. Since water was a fundamental requirement of all monastic houses, a high priority was accorded to securing satisfactory supplies.

Water was put to many different purposes within the monastic precinct, and it was exceptional for all needs to be met from a single source. Amongst the considerations were the purity of the water, the reliability of the supply, the energy of the water produced by its movement or fall, and the volume. Different uses required different combinations of these qualities (Fig 6.1):

(i)   For drinking, food preparation, and to a lesser extent for brewing and washing, the primary considerations were the purity of the water, while reliability of supply was also important.

(ii) For the purposes of flushing latrine drains and driving mills of various sorts, purity did not matter, but a significant flow of water, generating potential and kinetic energy, was a necessity.

(iii) The creation of moats around part or all of the precinct, the storage and breeding of fish, and certain industrial activities such as tanning, required a significant volume of water, but purity and flow-rate were less important.

(iv) Volume was also the main requirement when water was being used for transport, in order to provide sufficient floating depth for boats.

(v)   Irrigation of gardens was sometimes required, even in Britain, and for this purpose a reliable supply which would not fail in dry summers was the most important consideration.

The technology of monastic water management can be considered under four main headings: supply, distribution, utilisation, and removal of waste (the archaeological manifestations are summarised diagrammatically on Fig 6.2).

Water Supply

Access to water was a major consideration in the choice of sites, and few monastic houses were far from a natural watercourse. Deficiencies in local supplies were recorded as the reasons for the migrations of several communities in England, for example the Augustinian canons of Barnwell (Hertfordshire) and Wigmore (Herefordshire) (*Mon.Angl.*, v, 424; Dickinson 1950, 150; Robinson 1980, 81–2; Robinson 1981, 435–6). The short-lived settlement of the Cistercian monks of Kingswood at Hazleton on the Cotswolds is said to have been abandoned due to lack of sufficient water (Graham 1907, 100). Rivers, streams, springs and wells all contributed. Here our main concern is with man-made constructions, wells, conduits and the structures associated with them.

1 Sources of potable water

1.i: Wells

Wells within the precinct, which may date from the earliest years of the monastic settlement, were often retained as an emergency supply even after a piped water system was installed. The well-known mid-twelfth-century plan of Canterbury Cathedral Priory

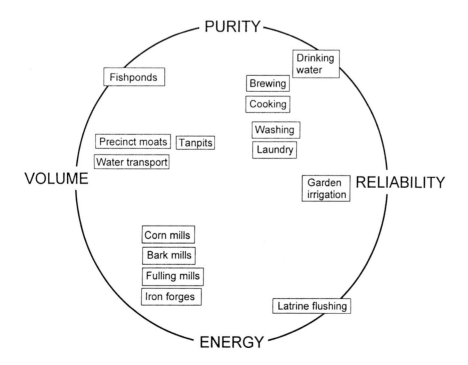

Fig 6.1 *Water quality and uses*

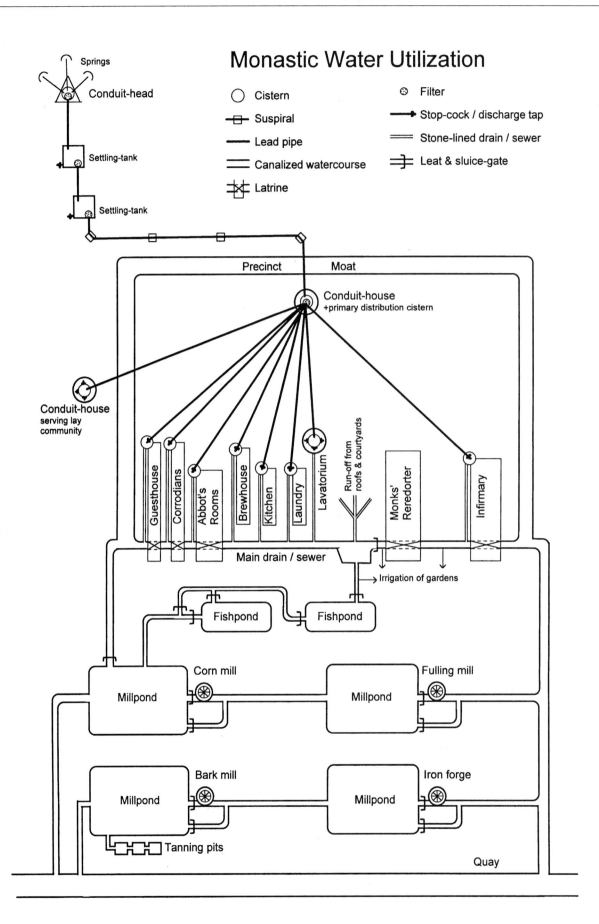

Fig 6.2 *Monastic water utilization*

shows two wells, one with a counterweight arm, located in the lay cemetery, where it was accessible to the townspeople; and one in the infirmary cloister next to a column crowned by a funnel. An annotation on the plan indicates that when the piped supply was deficient, water could be raised from the well and poured into the pipes via the funnel to supply all the priory buildings (Willis 1868). The well in the cloister at Durham was similarly used when the pipes froze up: the bursar's roll of 1338–9 records payments of 16d for drawing water from the draw-well in the cloister and for repairs to the pipe, and 2s for cleaning the well. However, the well alone was evidently unable to supply every need, since the same roll records a payment of 6s to women who carried water from the River Wear for the brewhouse, bakehouse and kitchen during the week after the Feast of the Purification (February 2nd) while the pipes remained frozen (*Durham Accts*, 100 (1898), 536). At Faversham there was a substantial stone-lined well immediately west of the claustral buildings (Philp 1968, 32). Excavation at the Benedictine nunnery of Polsloe near Exeter located a well in a room to the south of the west range, which seems to have gone out of use by the middle of the thirteenth century (*Med.Arch.*, 23 (1979), 250–1). Wells are also known within other cloisters or precincts, including St Werburgh's Abbey, Chester, St Peter's Abbey, Gloucester, the abbeys of Battle and Barlings and the priories of Woodspring and Haverholme. Some small houses may have continued to rely upon wells for their main supply. At Muchelney Abbey a well 4.3m deep cased with stone was discovered within the cloister garth towards the southern end of the east range in 1878; at the time this was believed to be the water supply for the lavatorium (Shelmerdine 1878, 72), but given the very flat nature of the site and the difficulties of bringing in water from any external source, it may have been the community's only supply of water for all purposes. However, wells had obvious limitations. They produced water in limited quantities, raising it to the levels where it was needed was laborious, they were vulnerable to pollution and they could dry up if the water table fell.

1.ii: Springs and Conduit-Heads

To secure a purer and more reliable supply and to reduce the labour required at each use, water from springs at a level higher than that of the monastic buildings was often conveyed to the monastery by conduit. Normally water from the springs was gathered into a cistern at the conduit-head before passing into the main supply conduit. The collection of spring water was sometimes augmented by driving underground tunnels into the aquifer itself.

Fig 6.3 *Raven's Well, Bristol: spring tapped by rock-cut chamber supplying the Austin Friars. The source and land for construction of the conduit was granted to the friars by Sir John de Gourney, Lord of Knowle, in 1366*

Several examples of rock-cut chambers and channels serving this purpose still survive in Bristol (Fig 6.3; see also Bond 1991, 172–3). Recent examination of the early fourteenth-century conduit-head of the Southampton Greyfriars has shown that it consists of three interconnected subterranean chambers, the northernmost of which was set in a large construction pit at least 7m wide (*Med.Arch.*, 36 (1992), 234). The conduit-head of Canterbury Cathedral Priory shown on Prior Wibert's plan still survives, containing a rectangular tank (Fig 6.4.i). The conduit-head of Canterbury's second Benedictine house, St Augustine's Abbey, a thirteenth-century polygonal stone tank fed by numerous springs, has been excavated by the Canterbury Archaeological Trust (Coppack 1990, 83–5).

The cistern at the conduit-head was normally covered and enclosed within a small stone structure. One of the earliest surviving examples, dating from the 1160s, is the conduit-head known as 'Robin Hood's Well' at the Cistercian abbey of Fountains (Coppack 1990, pl 7). Several later examples of various forms are illustrated here (Fig 6.4), and there are others at Winchcombe (Gloucestershire), Calder (Cumberland), Canons Ashby (Northamptonshire), Grantham (Lincolnshire), Waltham (Essex) and Alnwick (Northumberland), some of which have been partly or wholly reconstructed since the Dissolution. Plans and elevations of two of the three conduit-heads at Mount Grace have been published by Coppack (1990, 85). There are two contrasting examples near Gloucester. Springs on Robinswood Hill, 3.5km south of the city, were acquired by the Benedictine Abbey of St Peter in the late twelfth century and by the Franciscan friars of Gloucester soon after 1230, and a serious conflict arose between

i

iv

vii

ii

v

viii

iii

vi

Fig 6.4 *Monastic Conduit Heads*

*4.i, Canterbury, Christchurch Priory;
4.ii, Robins Wood Hill, Gloucester (St
Peter's Abbey); 4.iii, Monkton Far-
leigh Priory, Wiltshire; 4.iv, Valle
Crucis Abbey; 4.v, Lady Well, Hemp-
stead, Gloucs (Llanthony Priory); 4.vi,
Haughmond Abbey, Shropshire; 4.vii,
Edington Priory, Wiltshire; 4.viii,
Mount Grace Priory, Yorkshire*

the two houses over the use of the sources in 1355. One of the higher springs is protected by a simple conduit-head made up of stone slabs (Fig 6.4.ii), with the remains of a stone cistern or settling-tank surviving *c* 180m lower down the hill (Fulbrook-Leggatt, 1968, 116). By contrast, Lady Well at Hempstead, overlooking the River Severn 2km south-west of the city, is more elaborate architecturally, about 2.4m square at the base, with a steep gabled roof and an ogee-arched opening on the western side, suggesting an early fourteenth-century date (Fig 6.4.v). The land on which it stands belonged to the Augustinian canons of Llanthony Priory in the suburbs of Gloucester, and it is presumed to be the source of the priory's fresh water, though no specific documentation is known, and the course of the conduit has not been traced.

A few monastic houses made use of more than one conduit-head. There could be several reasons for this:

(i) In some cases a replacement or a supplement for an inadequate source was acquired at a later date. The Franciscan friars of Newgate in London acquired a spring in what is now Bloomsbury, on a site off Rugby Street, from which they laid their first conduit in 1255–6. In the early fourteenth century a second conduit-head was made by Brother Geoffrey de Camera, tapping half-a-dozen springs near the present Queen Square, and it is recorded that he also carried out repairs to the first spring-head and to the rest of the pipe. Clearly both sources remained in use, since the course of the pipes is described in considerable detail in the Grey-friars' register, and both are shown on the plan of the system made for Christ's Hospital in 1676. Both of the London Greyfriars' conduit-heads have been examined archaeologically (Norman, 1899, 1915–16; Norman & Mann 1909). Taunton Priory initially drew its water by leats from the Sherford Brook, but this source was also used by the castle and the town, and competition for the water led the canons to seek an alternative source from the Blackbrook or Stockwell Stream after 1332. The source used by the monks of St Werburgh's Abbey at Chester in 1278 was supplemented by the gift of an additional spring in 1282, while Worcester Cathedral Priory drew its water from sources at Battenhall, Swanpool and Henwick Hill in succession (references in Bond 1993, 53, 54–5, 57).

(ii) Water sources and conduits on land which was not itself in monastic ownership were always liable to disruption. Sometimes this led to a search for an alternative source over which the monks could have complete control. In 1462 the nuns of Barking Abbey had their water supply

cut off when John Rigby, husband of the heiress of Cranbrook, the manor in which the springs supplying the abbey lay, dug up and broke the pipes of a conduit leading from Cranbrook to the abbey, until the nuns agreed to pay him an annual rent of 24s. Subsequently the abbess located a new spring on the the the nuns' own land, and had a new conduit made from it to the abbey (Fowler 1907, 119).

(iii) In other cases two or more conduit-heads were clearly in contemporaneous use, serving different parts of the precinct. Fountains Abbey had separate sources for the choir monks and lay brothers: three deep reservoirs in the south-east corner of the precinct supplied water to the Robin Hood's Well conduit-head, from which water was piped to a cistern outside the infirmary from which it could be conducted to the more easterly claustral buildings, while there was a second source in the south-west of the precinct feeding another cistern or conduit-house near the lay brothers' infirmary (Coppack 1990, 85; 1993, 51, 90). The Charterhouse of Mount Grace had three separate conduit-heads supplying water to different areas for different needs. One outside the east range supplied spring water to a conduit-head in the middle of the great cloister, from which it was piped to a the surrounding cells, the kitchen and the guesthouse. Further south a second conduit-head served the outer court. The third, known as St John's Well, fed a watercourse leading towards the mill and fishponds (Coppack 1996).

2 Conduits

2.i: Open Conduits

The Roman engineer M. Vitruvius Pollio defined two basic types of conduit, both of which were employed throughout the Middle Ages in England. *Open conduits* or *free-flow channels*, in which the water flowed along an open stone trough or a mortared or clay-lined channel, were the more widely used form in the Roman world. The term 'open' does not necessarily mean that they were unprotected and exposed to the air; the watercourse could be roofed for part or all of its length. The critical point about the definition is that, even where the conduit was completely covered over, it was not entirely filled by water, but also contained some air. Open conduits could carry a considerable volume of water, and had the advantage of being more accessible for regular inspection, cleansing and maintenance, but they also had certain disadvantages. Unless they were roofed, they were vulnerable to pollution. They required a reasonably consistent gradient for their flow to be maintained. Vitruvius appears to recommend a minimum gradient of 1 in 200, while Pliny quotes 1 in 4800 (Vitruvius, Book VIII, Ch vi, 1; Pliny, Book XXXI, 57). This is a significant divergence of opinion, and although Vitruvius would normally be the more reliable authority on engineering matters, it has been argued that an early misreading of his text has been perpetuated in later copies, and that his original recommendation could have been identical with Pliny's figure (Hodge 1991, p 440, n 7). In fact, Pliny's gradient was shallower than many actual examples. Figures quoted by Hodge for the principal aqueducts supplying Rome indicate an unusually steep average gradient of around 1 in 333, falling to gradients of 1 in 666 elsewhere (Hodge 1991, 216–7). [By comparison the Dorchester aqueduct in Britain has an estimated gradient of 1 in 2400, closer to Pliny's figure]. If the gradient was too steep the energy of the water flow could erode and damage the conduit; if it was too shallow the water became stagnant and there was more sedimentation. The engineer, therefore, had to strike a balance between minimising the need for repairs and the need for regular cleansing. In fact within certain limits variable speeds of flow through steeper and shallower sections could be accommodated. Open conduits either had to follow closely the contour of the ground, which might involve an extremely long and circuitous route, or they required expensive engineering works such as tunnels, cuttings and bridge-aqueducts. Occasionally on the continent monastic aqueducts were carried over bridges in the Roman style. In 1212–21 a conduit from the stream of La Cent-Fons was constructed over a distance of 10km to the abbey of Cîteaux, passing over a bridge at Arvaux (Sonnet 1984, 285–90). However, devices of this sort do not seem to have been employed on any significant scale in Britain during the Middle Ages.

The open conduit principle was widely used for mill- and fishpond-leats, drains and sewers, but it is relatively unusual in Britain to find it employed for the main water supply. An exception is the Cistercian abbey of Stanley (Wiltshire), where the community moved to a new site alongside the River Marden in 1154. The new site provided space for the development of more extensive buildings, and it was possible to divert water from the Marden to fill the millpond and fishponds on the northern side of the precinct and to flush the reredorter drain. However, although there was a spring within the new precinct, this must have proved insufficient or unreliable, so an open conduit from the springs at the monks' previous site at Loxwell, 3.5km away, was completed by Abbot Thomas Calstone in 1214. Part of its course can clearly be followed as a ditch alongside the causeway leading into the precinct from the south (Fig 6.5, which appeared in colour in Bond 1991, 159, pl 5; see also Brakspear 1908, 544; RCHME, 1996).

Fig 6.5 *Stanley Abbey, Wiltshire, aerial view. In the foreground, to the right of the causeway approaching the abbey, is the open conduit brought from springs at Loxwell in 1214. To the left is the millpond with its overflow leat. The monastic buildings were near the river, towards the rear of this view (photo M Aston)*

2.ii: Closed Conduits

The *closed conduit* or *pressure-pipeline* principle employed airtight pipes completely filled throughout with water, which could act as an inverted syphon and were able to slope uphill or downhill at any angle, provided that their outlet was at a lower level than their intake. The overall gradient was, however, still a critical element in the calculation. From the Christleton source acquired by the monks of St Werburgh's, Chester, in 1282, there was a fall of only 3m over a distance of 3km to the conduit-house in the cloister (Burne 1962, 41). The London Greyfriars pipe had a fall of 7m in 2km, and even here the records of Christ's Hospital, which used the same supply after the Dissolution, contain many complaints that the water 'did not well come home' (Martin 1937, 204).

The main advantage of the closed conduit was its

tolerance of levels; without any need to achieve an even shallow gradient, the builder was no longer obliged to follow the natural contours, and the length of the conduit could be shortened considerably by taking a more direct route. Closed conduits were especially well-suited to use within built-up areas, as the pipes could be laid along the streets and the water was comparatively secure from external sources of pollution. The pipes could also be carried across rivers, ideally attached to bridges, where access for maintenance was easier, or, failing that, laid across the river bed. The Worcester Cathedral Priory pipes from Swanpool and Henwick Hill were carried over the Severn on the old town bridge (Habington 1897–9, ii, 403; Noake 1866, 113–4; Richardson 1955, 41), and the Canterbury plan shows the pipe crossing the town ditch by a bridge. The pipes of Reading Abbey and Lacock Abbey seem to have been laid under their respective rivers, the Thames and Bristol Avon. The drawbacks of the closed conduit system were that pipes had a smaller capacity than an open conduit; the conduit was vulnerable to bursting from water pressure if the pipe descended far below the level of either the source or the delivery point; it was more liable to become clogged with sediment; and it was less accessible for inspection, and more difficult to repair. On balance, however, the advantages of the closed conduit system generally outweighed its drawbacks, particularly for urban monasteries, and it was widely used throughout the Middle Ages.

Vitruvius and Pliny described two methods of making closed conduits, using lead pipes or ceramic pipes. Both preferred ceramic pipes because they were cheaper, because they did not require a specialist plumber to lay them, because water which had passed through them was more wholesome, and because if they were damaged it was relatively easy to replace the broken section (Vitruvius, Book VIII, Ch vi, 10; Pliny, Book XXXI, 57). However, it was more difficult to make them watertight, and special provisions had to be made for changes of direction. Vitruvius recognised that lead was harmful both to the lead workers and to those who drank water which had passed through lead pipes (Vitruvius, Book VIII, Ch vi, 10–11), and the same warning was given by Palladius (9.11.3). It is curious that knowledge of the dangers of lead seems to have been forgotten by the Middle Ages. Certainly the risks of poisoning from lead oxide were significantly reduced in hard-water areas where a scale quickly formed to insulate the water from the inner face of the pipes, and in systems where there was a constant flow; but in soft-water areas where water was stored for any length of time against a lead surface the dangers were very real.

In medieval closed conduit systems lead pipes normally had an internal diameter between 2.5cm and 10cm. The larger pipes were used to bring the water from the springs, while the use of smaller pipes regulated the quantities supplied to the various buildings within the precinct. They were often laid in a bed of clay within a stone-lined trench, for protection and to limit leakage from the soldered joints. There is a detailed contemporary account of the making of the lead conduit from Wormley to Waltham Abbey (Essex) in 1220 (Bushby 1933, 177–84). The cellarers' accounts of Battle Abbey record the regular maintenance of the lead conduit, including purchases of solder, pitch and resin for sealing the joints, and canvas and linen cloth for binding the lead pipes, perhaps for insulation against frost where they came above ground. In 1320–1 an unspecified length of fine rope was bought for the Battle Abbey conduit; it is not clear what this was intended for, unless perhaps to be pushed or pulled through lengths of pipe to remove accumulations of limescale (*Battle Cell.R.*, and see Appendix A below).

Ceramic pipes were used at least from the thirteenth century. At Kirkham Priory excavations in 1878 revealed a line of ceramic pipes bedded in clay sealed beneath part of the church dated to the 1160s, which appear to be part of the main supply conduit bringing water from springs on the hill above the priory and carrying it underneath the church to a cistern within the cloisters. However, the redistribution of water to the lavatorium and to other buildings was carried out by lead pipes, accommodated through small holes cut in the masonry (Coppack 1990, 94–5). Ceramic pipes also seem to have been used for the main supply conduit at the Cluniac priory of Thetford (Norfolk) and the Lincoln Greyfriars (Coppack 1973–6; 1990, 94).

Wooden pipes may have been more common than is generally realised, since they will only survive in exceptional conditions. Bored elm trunks were used to bring water from the conduit-head to the Cistercian abbey of Beaulieu. Examples are also known from Waverley Abbey (Surrey), Thornholme Priory (Lincolnshire) and Guisborough Priory (Yorkshire). Pipes of this sort, often charred within by dragging through a truss of burning straw, and covered with pitch externally, were still regularly used into the late eighteenth century.

Monastic conduits commonly traversed distances of 2–5km, but were rarely much longer. One exceptional case is the Dominican friary in Boston (Lincolnshire), which in 1327 acquired a licence from the king to construct a subterranean conduit bringing water from Bolingbroke, more than 20km away (*CPR* 1327–30, 182). If this was ever constructed, it would have been longer than the longest Roman aqueduct known in Britain, at Dorchester (though still much less than the 91.7km of the Aqua Marcia at Rome).

3 Settling-tanks and Filters

Water always contained some impurities, which were of three kinds:

(i) Lime was chemically dissolved, but tended to form a scaly encrustation when it came into contact with the surface of the pipes or channels. This was difficult to deal with; it could only be removed by scraping it off, or by replacing the pipes themselves whenever they became too choked to be effective.

(ii) Sand and mud was carried in suspension by water in motion, but was precipitated as sediment wherever the speed of flow was slowed down, by a reduction in gradient or change of direction. Sedimentation was easier to deal with than chemical scaling, since it could be deliberately encouraged to occur at a point where the deposit could easily be collected and removed. Settling tanks were commonly employed in medieval closed conduits. The feed-pipe brought water into the tank, where sediment was precipitated as the flow lost velocity. The exit-pipe drew off the cleaner water from the higher levels within the tank. At the base of the tank there was normally a discharge tap which would allow the tank to be drained from time to time so that the accumulated sediment could be cleaned out.

(iii) Larger floating items such as leaves and twigs could be carried into the conduit from any point where the water surface was exposed. Blockages due to floating obstructions could be prevented by placing some sort of mesh or filtering plate across the entry to any closed section of the conduit.

Both Vitruvius and Pliny describe in rather vague terms devices for purifying water either by allowing sediment to settle out in compartmented tanks or by allowing the water to percolate through a medium (Vitruvius, Book VIII, Ch vi, 15; Pliny, Book XXXI, 70). Settling-tanks and coarse filters of various kinds are known from the contemporary plans of Canterbury, Waltham and the London Charterhouse (Willis 1868, 158–206; Grewe 1991, 1996; Bushby 1933; Hope 1902; Bond 1991, 160, pl 6, 163, pl 9). The Canterbury Cathedral Priory plan shows the point of outflow from the conduit-head apparently covered by a perforated circular plate, which would have filtered out larger debris. It then shows five successive settling-tanks, each with its own discharge tap, between the source and the point where the pipe passed beneath the town wall. The thirteenth-century plan of Waltham Abbey's supply from Wormley shows two settling-tanks in which the exit-pipes appear to be flattened together at their ends with

small perforated openings to serve as a filter for larger debris in suspension, and the lower tank has a discharge tap (*purgatorium*). Sometimes there may be further filters within the internal distribution system (see below).

Occasionally an exceptionally clean source might be tapped which would allow the system to function without settling-tanks or filters. The Lichfield Cathedral pipe, constructed in the later twelfth century, appears to have fallen into this category (Gould, 1976)

4 Suspirals

The 15th-century plan of the London Charterhouse water-supply and the 1676 plan of the former London Greyfriars pipe, then used by Christ's Hospital, both show a number of suspirals. These were plugged vents which could be opened to admit air and allow the draining of the water for repairs and maintenance. They provided the possibility of clearing the pipes of blockages by using some sort of pull-through device. They were used to release any air which became trapped within the siphon, being closed as the pipe refilled with water. They could also serve as safety-valves where the level of the pipe dipped, since their plugs could be designed to blow off when the pressure rose to dangerous levels. Examples were noted on the Lichfield Cathedral pipe where it ran near a stream (Gould 1976, 76).

Distribution

Water brought to the precinct needed then to be distributed to the various offices where it was needed. Potable water might require storage, and further filtering devices might be installed. In some circumstances the monastic water supply might be extended beyond the precinct for the convenience of lay consumers.

1 Reservoirs and Cisterns

Where no great volume of water was required, and where disposal of the overflow presented no difficulty, it would be quite possible to operate a system of supply whereby the water ran continuously from the source through various outlets in the monastery 24 hours a day. The quantities passing through to particular buildings could be regulated simply by the diameter of the different pipes.

Where the internal distribution system was a complex one, however, the water was often piped into one or more storage reservoirs at sufficient height to provide a good head of water. The water

Fig 6.6 *Canterbury, Christ Church Cathedral Priory: Prior Wibert's Water Tower in the Infirmary court*

tower built by Prior Wibert in the middle of the twelfth century to house the main storage cistern in the infirmary court at the Benedictine cathedral priory of Christ Church, Canterbury, is a rare survival of this type of building (Fig 6.6; see also Willis 1868; Grewe 1991, 1996). There are also indications of cisterns in several other monastic infirmaries, for example at Fountains, Waverley and Beaulieu, and this may have been the preferred location for the main distribution reservoir (Hope 1900a, 330; Brakspear 1905, 89–90; Hope & Brakspear 1906, 178–9; Bond 1989, 86; Coppack 1990, 85).

Carthusian houses tended to have their main reservoir in a tower in the middle of the cloister, from which water could be piped to each individual cell. The 15th-century plan of the London Charterhouse shows a polygonal tower in this position, and excavations at Mount Grace in 1900 and 1987 revealed the timber pile foundations of the building with sufficient fragments of the superstructure to permit a reconstruction drawing to be attempted. In this instance the reservoir is at a higher level than the source, and it is difficult to see how it can have

worked without a pump or some other device to raise the water by non-gravitational means (Coppack 1996, 160–2).

Elsewhere cisterns occur which were at too low a level to provide a head of water to serve the main buildings, and they can only have been used as dipping-tanks. Excavations at Polsloe nunnery have revealed a sunken rectangular cistern to the south of the refectory, built towards the end of the fifteenth century. This was walled and floored in ashlar, and was fed by earthenware pipes. Access to the cistern was provided by steps descending from the east (*Med Arch.*, 23 (1979), 250–1).

2 Internal distribution

The conveyance of water from the storage cisterns to the various parts of the precinct where it was needed was normally carried out by closed conduits. Lead pipes were most frequently used; the lead was usually robbed at the Dissolution, but short lengths have been recovered from many sites. Despite the difficulties of bringing a supply into Muchelney Abbey posed by its very flat site, several short lengths of lead pipe of 19mm bore, running for some 4.1m, were discovered beneath the south transept of the church in 1874; it was interpreted at the time as a drain from the cloister lavatorium (Shelmerdine 1878, 70–71), but a function as a supply or distribution pipe seems more likely. Ceramic pipes have been recovered from the kitchen area of the Chelmsford Blackfriars. At the Cistercian abbey of Glenluce (Wigtownshire) much of the system of both lead and ceramic pipes was found *in situ* during clearance in the 1930s (Fig 6.7.i). One feature of particular interest at Glenluce, so far without known parallel in Britain, were the hemispherical ceramic junction boxes sited where the course of the pipeline turned through a sharp angle. Since the break in flow was likely to cause a precipitation of sediment, these were equipped with lids to give access for periodic cleaning-out (Fig 6.7.ii). The ends of the pipes and the sockets at the junction boxes have matching tally marks, indicating that they were made and laid to a preconceived plan (Cruden 1950–51, 177–8, 185, 193–4).

In 1214 the canons of Waltham Abbey managed to obtain a second-hand washbasin from King John, which had originally been installed in Westminster Palace by Henry II, but had later been removed (*Rot.Litt.Claus.*, i, 140; *Chart.Waltham*, 27, no 38). Its transfer to Waltham may have prompted the construction of a new conduit in the early 1220s (see Appendix A below).

The internal distribution system might be altered several times during the life of the monastery, as new sources were acquired or new buildings

i

ii

Fig 6.7 *i, Ceramic pipes from Glenluce Abbey, Wigtown-shire; ii, Glenluce Abbey, junction box sited where pipeline changes direction.*

erected. At Glastonbury the rebuilding of the abbey after the great fire of 1184 may have provided an opportunity for the reorganisation of the water system (see Appendix A). At St Peter's Abbey, Gloucester, the first water brought into the precinct was the Fulbrook, an artificial canal constructed in the time of Abbot Serlo (1072–1104) (*Hist.Glouc.*, i, 154–5, ii, 186). This was diverted from the River Twyver just over 400m upstream from the north-east corner of the city wall, forming a ditch immediately outside the north wall and entering the precinct from the east. As the name implies, this was unfit for drinking and served only to cleanse the drains and drive the abbey mill below the inner court. Within the precinct water from the Fulbrook was led through at least three successive culverts. The southernmost course appears to have been the earliest, since it led beneath the dormitory and cloister garth. The middle culvert passed beneath the Little Cloister and ran along the north side of the

refectory serving the kitchen, then forked, one arm continuing westwards directly to the abbey mill, the other arm turning sharply south to link up with the southern culvert near the Norman abbot's lodging, subsequently the prior's house, north-west of the church, before turning west again, uniting with the tail-race of the mill and leaving the precinct just north of St Mary's Gate. This may date from around 1218, when the precinct was extended northwards for the building of the new kitchen larder and bakehouse. The northernmost course diverged from the second culvert just south of the infirmary and served the new abbot's house north-west of the infirmary, the replacement for the Norman lodging, before rejoining at the mill. The new abbot's lodging was first occupied by Abbot John Wigmore (1329–37), and this may date the northern culvert as the latest of the sequence. Further adjustments must have been made following the acquisition of the first piped supply of pure water from Robins Wood Hill, granted to Abbot Reginald (1163–84) by Philip, son of Philip of Matson. A further source on Robins Wood Hill was acquired from William Geraud of Matson in around 1230. The record in the abbey's chronicle of the death of the sacrist, Helias of Hereford, on November 9th 1237, mentions in passing that he was responsible for making the conduit of 'living water', ie fresh spring water, to the abbey, presumably as a result of the second grant (*Hist.Glouc.*, i, 28). An ashlar-lined cistern with stone roof supports discovered within the cloister garth in 1888 and visible until the redesign of the cloister garden a few years ago (Fig 6.8) has been attributed to Helias the sacrist. Although it clearly antedates the existing cloisters, however, it is on the line of the first culvert, and seems more likely to be part of the

Fig 6.8 *St Peter's Abbey, Gloucester: cistern formerly visible within the cloister garth, on the line of the first conduit from the Fulbrook; often attributed to Helias the sacrist, c. 1230, subsequently used as the drain from the lavatorium.*

drainage system than any sort of reservoir for the fresh water supply. A sluice at the west end of the cistern was clearly designed to release a flush into the culvert beyond, but it is not clear what function this can have served; it lies below the monks' reredorter, and although it would be in the right position to serve a latrine in the Norman abbot's lodging, subsequently used by the prior, there is no direct evidence for such a structure having existed at that particular point. By the beginning of the fourteenth century it had been relegated to serve as a drain for the waste from Abbot Frocester's new lavatorium (Fulbrook-Leggatt 1968, 113–4; Heighway 1988; Welander 1991, 104–5; Bond 1993, 54, 67)

3 Settling tanks and filtering systems

Archaeological evidence for settling-tanks and filters within the internal distribution system has been recognised on several sites. Within the south-eastern quarter of the cloister at Kirkstall Abbey a stone cistern, which must originally have been lead-lined, was entered by a pipe from the east, with the outlet to the south some 30cm higher, drawing off clean water probably to supply the original lavatorium. The pipe system was extended after about 1175, and a further stone cistern was set just outside the south wall of the warming-house in the angle of its junction with the dormitory range. This, too, must originally have been lead-lined, and served as a settling-tank for a further range of buildings to the south (Moorhouse & Wrathmell 1987, 8–11, 45–9).

The filters shown on the handful of medieval plans were all fairly crude devices, and no documentary evidence is known for the use of more sophisticated filtering systems in the Middle Ages. However, evidence recovered from a recess on the mezzanine landing of the service stairway adjoining the refectory at Westminster Abbey enabled Micklethwaite (1892) to produce an ingenious and plausible reconstruction of a more refined and effective filtering apparatus. The presence here of a slab pierced by four holes clearly intended for pipes, together with other debris left lying on the floor nearby, suggested an arrangement whereby the feed-pipe brought water into a cistern containing a sand-trap which filtered out impurities before the service pipe drew off the clean water, there also being provision for a waste outlet.

4 Distribution of Potable Water beyond the Precinct

Sometimes lay people living outside the monastic precinct made direct use of the monastic supply. This was clearly not a satisfactory option. At the time of

Bishop Alnwick's visitation to Daventry Priory in 1442 the prior, Robert Man, complained of the women who regularly came through the cloister to draw water from the conduit, and requested that such access should be restrained (*Visit.Dioc.Linc.*, II.i, 60).

As an alternative, a number of urban monasteries and secular cathedrals permitted extensions from their own supply to serve other monasteries, hospitals, inns, shops, private houses and town communities nearby. Waltham Abbey provided a separate supply from its conduit to the townspeople in the early 1220s (*Chart.Waltham*, 279–85, no 413). Bishop Beckington of Wells in 1451 granted the surplus from the cathedral supply for the use of the burgesses, and a public conduit-house was erected in the market-place of the town; he also provided a piped supply to the New Works, the terrace of twelve shops which he had built on the north side of the market-place. Similarly, the conduit to St Augustine's Abbey, Bristol, was extended to serve houses in Trinity Street belonging to the canons. The fifteenth-century London Charterhouse plan shows pipes passing beyond the great cloister to four buildings outside the precinct, which appear to be inns or taverns (Bond 1993). Since 1236 the city of London had been piping water from springs at Tyburn, but in 1439 it acquired a second source from Westminster Abbey. In this year Abbot Richard granted to the mayor and commonalty of the city a piece of ground 26 perches long by one perch in width containing springs in a close called Oxlease on the abbey's manor of Paddington (probably on what is now the north-west side of Craven Road near its junction with Westbourne Terrace) with the right to erect all necessary cisterns and to carry pipes above or below ground to the city through any intervening land belonging to the abbey outside its manor of Hyde, saving the rights of the abbey's tenants in Paddington and subject to an annual payment of 1lb of pepper. A proviso was added that if the abbey's own ancient supply from the manor of Hyde was in any way disturbed, the abbey would be entitled to reclaim the head and springs it had granted to the city (Davies 1913). The friars, who, of all the orders, perhaps took the most practically philanthropic stance, were especially prominent in providing public water supplies. Two or three of the friaries in Bristol extended their conduits into the town, and others in Boston, Gloucester, Scarborough and Southampton also entered into agreements with the town authorities (Bond, 1993).

The extent to which monastic granges had independent piped water supplies of their own is another question which requires further investigation. So far documentary evidence has been discovered only for the Fountains Abbey grange at Malham (see Appendix A, below).

Utilization of Water

1 Ritual and Ceremonial Uses

Water played an important part in the regular rituals of the church, most obviously in the sacrament of baptism, but also in the cleansing of vessels used in the Mass, and in ritual washing by monks and clergy. So much of the monastic routine was surrounded by ceremonial that it is often difficult to separate the symbolic from the utilitarian. However, the Anglo-Saxon observances codified in the *Regularis Concordia* contain some obvious symbolic acts involving water, including the *asperges*, the solemn processional blessing of the cloister with holy water after Sunday Matins, and the sprinkling of the dormitory with holy water (Symons 1926, 167, 171). Lanfranc's Constitutions required the sacrist to wash the chalices twice a week, or more often if need be, and also to wash the corporals (the linen cloths on which the consecrated elements were placed during the Mass) before Easter and as often as was necessary at other times of year, in bronze vessels used for no other purpose. The water used for washing the chalices and corporals was to be disposed of in a special place (Lanfranc, 83).

1.i: Holy Wells

Springs were venerated long before the arrival of Christianity, and many of the 'holy wells' of the Middle Ages and, indeed, some of the sources tapped by monastic houses, were almost certainly originally sites of pagan worship. A Roman altar significantly inscribed *Nymphis et Fontibus* was discovered close to the Abbot's Well at Christleton, which supplied St Werbergh's Abbey in Chester. Early missionaries made every effort to sanctify them.

Outside the monastic precincts holy wells associated with local saints and hermits were especially characteristic of the western parts of Britain where traditions derived from Celtic Christianity were stronger; but they occur throughout most of the country, often covered over like a normal conduit-head, but issuing into a bath or dipping-tank. Such wells are, of course, not confined to monastic properties. However, examples on monastic estates were sometimes energetically promoted as places of pilgrimage and centres of healing, and more substantial structures were developed to enclose them. Holy wells under monastic management often had chapels or other structures built directly over the spring, so that their use could be regulated. Land on the Clent Hills containing the spring which reputedly arose at the site of St Kenelm's martyrdom formed part of the foundation endowments of Halesowen Abbey in 1215. There was already a chapel by the well, and in the fourteenth century the east end of the

building was reconstructed in two storeys, with a crypt below the chancel enclosing the spring. In 1473 the abbey had licence to acquire lands or rents to the value of £10 for the repair of the chapel and the maintenance of a chaplain there (*CPR* 1467–77, 396). Oblations at the chapel were valued at £10 in 1535. St Margaret's Well and the adjoining chapel at Binsey (Oxon), legendary refuge of St Frideswide, was under the care of the canons of St Frideswide's priory in Oxford, and miracles associated with the site brought many pilgrims. A stone building over the well was pulled down in 1639 (Wood 1773, 320–2). Dupath Well near Callington (Cornwall) was acquired by the canons of St Germans in 1432, who built a small chapel over the basin and maintained it until the Dissolution. Water from St Aldhelm's Well at Doulting (Somerset), which belonged to Glastonbury Abbey, appears to have been channelled into some sort of small pool or bath with a building over it.

The most renowned well-shrine in Britain was St Winifred's Well at Holywell in Flintshire, which came into the hands of St Werburgh's Abbey at Chester in 1093, was lost to the Welsh, and was then granted by Dafydd ap Llywelyn in 1240 to the Cistercians of Basingwerk, who maintained it until the Dissolution. Offerings at the well were worth £10 in 1535. The present ornate building over the spring succeeded an earlier structure, and was built towards the end of the fifteenth century in the time of Abbot Thomas Pennant, with a substantial benefaction from Margaret Beaufort, Countess of Richmond. It is of two storeys, with a chapel above entered from ground level on the southern side, and a vaulted well-chamber below which is open on the northern, downhill side. The spring rises in a central star-shaped basin, with a bath on the northern side. The central roof-boss over the well depicts scenes from the life of St Winifred. There was originally a stone screen between the well itself and the tank where pilgrims could bathe. The larger pool below is of more recent origin (Hole 1954, 53–7; Jones 1954, 49–50; Hall 1965, 18–44; Charles-Edwards n.d.; David 1971).

1.ii: Baptistries

Baptistries became widespread in the Mediterranean regions between the third and seventh centuries (their origins are discussed further below). At a period when adult baptisms were common and total immersion was employed, significant quantities of water were required, and facilities for supply and disposal required careful consideration. Although the evidence from Britain is relatively meagre, a few early examples are known or suspected. Recent excavations at Hoddom in southern Scotland, a site associated with the late sixth-early-seventh-century mission of St Kentigern and later occupied by an important Northumbrian monastery, revealed a rectangular structure built of re-used Roman masonry. A radio-carbon date points to its construction around AD 600, and a well-built stone-lined drain and soakaway suggests its possible use as a baptistry (Selkirk 1993). Eadmer records the construction of a baptistry immediately east of the cathedral at Canterbury dedicated to St John Baptist by Archbishop Cuthbert (740–60), which would also serve as a mausoleum for the archbishops; and there may already have been a similar arrangement in the church of SS Peter & Paul in St Augustine's Abbey nearby (Taylor 1969, 102). The eighth-century crypt at Repton may also have served a similar dual function. Baptistries do not appear to have been limited to the greater churches. The suggestion made by Micklethwaite in 1896 that the late tenth-century western annexe to the tower at Barton-on-Humber was built to serve as a baptistry was confirmed by excavations in 1978–81, which located the base and soakaway of the font (Micklethwaite 1896; Rodwell & Rodwell 1982, 298–9, Pl XLIa). The plan of a pre-Conquest timber chapel including a baptistry with a setting for a font has also been excavated near the parish church of Potterne in Wiltshire, and the massive tub font within the present church almost certainly came from it (Davey 1964).

From about the tenth century baptisms normally took place in relatively small fonts which could be filled by hand. Fonts were a feature of English monastic churches only where they also fulfilled parochial functions, and will not be considered further here.

2 Water for Drinking, Cooking and Brewing

Fresh water was used for drinking, cooking, brewing and washing. Control of water at the points of usage was achieved by bronze or brass taps: examples from six different monastic sites dating from the late twelfth to the late fourteenth century have been illustrated by Coppack (1990, 92–3). Ale-brewing is well-documented on many sites, but few monastic brewhouses have yet been examined by excavation, apart from those at Fountains and at Nuneaton Priory (Hope 1900a, 393–7; Andrews *et al*, 1981, 61, 64–5).

3 Washing

The Rule of St Benedict makes no direct reference to washing, but the *Regularis Concordia* required the brethren to wash their hands and faces before entering the church for Terce, and to wash their feet on Saturdays before the evening meal. On Saturdays there was also a ceremonial washing of the feet of

the incoming and outgoing ministers. Moreover, every day the feet of three poor men selected from amongst those dependent upon the abbey were washed, the task being undertaken by the boys of the choir and their masters on Saturdays and Sundays and by the monks for the remainder of the week; no-one was to be excused, and even the abbot was exhorted to assist whenever he was able (Symons 1926, 164, 170–1). Lanfranc's Constitutions prescribed daily washing at the lavatorium prior to Terce and in summer also before None. There were special arrangements for certain days. On Christmas night the chamberlain's servants were required to provide a good fire, with basins, towels and warm water for the brethren vesting for Mass; and the washing of feet took place in the cloister following the Rogation Day procession between Sext and None (Lanfranc, xxxv–xxxvii, 4, 13, 20, 26, 49, 52).

Washing facilities for the monks were required from the first communal monastic foundations up to the Dissolution, and the lavatorium or washing-place, normally located near the refectory entrance, is the most distinctive structure connected with fresh water utilisation. The form of the lavatorium will be discussed below, where differences between the monastic orders are explored.

4 Bathing

The attitude of the Benedictine rule towards bathing is clearly stated (Ch 36): 'Let the use of baths be afforded to the sick, as often as may be expedient; but to the healthy, and especially to the young, let them be granted seldom'. The Augustinian rule (Ch 5.5) recognised that bathing was beneficial to health, but discouraged bathing for enjoyment. However, the presence of baths is well attested at early continental monasteries, such as Vivarium in Calabria and St Gall in Switzerland (Lillich 1982, 127). In England Lanfranc's Constitutions made provision for optional baths to take place on the vigil of St Thomas the Apostle just before Christmas, when the arrangements are described in some detail, and during Holy Week (Lanfranc, 9–10, 26, 62). Occasional documentary references imply that bathing facilities were present in some English monasteries, as at Abingdon, where the chronicle records Abbot Vincent (1121–30) building baths for the monks. A feature excavated near the warming-house at Kirkstall was initially interpreted as a bath, though it is now seen merely as a water cistern (Moorhouse & Wrathmell 1987, 13–17). Malcolm Lyne's recent publication of excavations at Lewes Priory has discussed the possibility that in some Cluniac houses part or all of the ground floor of the reredorter block may have served as a bath-house (Lyne 1997, 38–9).

5 Laundry

The Benedictine rule offers no advice on the washing of clothing, but the Rule of St Augustine (Ch 5.4) requires any canon wishing to have his clothes washed to consult with his superior, 'lest an exagerrated desire for clean clothes sully your character'. The *Regularis Concordia* set aside time on Saturdays for the brethren to wash their shoes, stockings and clothes (Symons 1926, 170). Monastic laundries remain elusive archaeologically, although this function has been suggested for the ground-floor room of the later reredorter at Lewes Priory (Lyne 1997, 59). The washing of clothes may often have been undertaken by external servants: it was recorded at Canterbury in 1267 that the washerwoman was given a meal every time the laundry was returned (Urry 1967, 157).

6 Utilization of water as a power source

Water power was used to drive mills of various kinds, both within the precinct and on the estates. Such uses, demanding volume and fall of water rather than purity, were normally supplied by open conduits or contour leats diverted off natural watercourses. The most substantial monastic precinct mill building to survive is at Fountains (Hope 1900a, 399–400; Coppack 1990, 115–7; Coppack 1998), but there are fragmentary architectural remains of several others, for example at Abbotsbury (Dorset) and Furness (Lancashire) (Graham 1986; Hope 1900b, 290). Many more are known from earthworks or documentary evidence (Bond 1989, 102–4; 1993, 72–3; 1994). The vast majority of medieval watermills were engaged in grinding grain for flour, but on several Cistercian sites mills used for other industrial purposes have been identified. These will be discussed further in a later section. Considerable diversions of natural watercourses could be involved in the construction of mills at all periods. The making of the Clack Beck at Mount Grace around 1420 was the culmination of a complex history of water management on the site, primarily to drive the mill, but also serving the fishponds (Coppack 1996).

7 Moats and Fishponds

Moats enclosing part or all of the monastic precinct have been identified on a number of sites (Bond 1993, 73–4). At Abingdon excavations in 1990 located the convent ditch, some 10m wide, to the north-east of St Nicholas Church. This is first documented in 1369–70, and is shown surrounding the precinct on a sixteenth-century map in Abingdon Guildhall. If its observed alignment from north-

east to south-south-west continued, it would have crossed the low gravel interfluve between the River Thames and its northern tributary, the Stert, protecting the abbey within the confluence of the two rivers. It is tempting to suggest that a work on this scale might date from the reformation of the community by Abbot Aethelwold in the tenth century, particularly given Aethelwold's apparent interest in water management implied by the abbey chronicle's ascription of the reredorter drain and the long mill-leat to him. An alternative possible historical context for its construction might be the aftermath of the riots of 1327, when the abbey was attacked and fired by the townspeople. Unfortunately, repeated cleansing of the ditch meant that most material from it was late medieval or later, and there was no archaeological evidence for the date of its first construction. Two trestles of a timber bridge were found spanning the moat, and this structure has yielded a date of c1510 through dendrochronology (Allen, 1990).

Fishponds, sometimes occurring in groups of eight or more covering up to 4–5 hectares, are a prominent feature of many monastic precincts, while on the granges of Byland Abbey (Yorks.) ponds up to 20 hectares in extent have been recorded (Bond 1988; McDonnell & Everest 1965; McDonnell 1981, 24–7, 30–33). However, despite the considerable labour and engineering skills required for the construction of such ponds, they do not seem to have been especially productive, because supplementary feeding was rarely practised. Most monasteries, therefore, even deep in the English midlands, continued to rely upon marine fish for their staple diet. Freshwater fish were regarded as a luxury for feast-days and for the entertainment of important guests (Currie 1989). Fishponds have been discussed at some length in the references quoted, and cannot be pursued further here.

Further examples of both moats and fishponds on monastic sites and granges have been recorded by survey by the Royal Commission in Lincolnshire (Everson *et al* 1991); however, a cautionary note is sounded there about the not uncommon reuse of monastic sites as grand post-dissolution residences. Moats and ponds were often constructed as garden features, and where sites were reoccupied we need to be aware that not all of the earthworks we now see were necessarily of monastic origin.

8 Canalisation of watercourses for transport

The construction of artificial canals for the transport of building materials and other bulky commodities may also be important considerations on some monastic sites. Evidence for this can be seen as early as the tenth century. Charles and Nancy Hollinrake

(1991, 1992) have discussed the possibility that an early canal 1.5km long connected Glastonbury with the River Brue in Dunstan's time. Cnut's Dyke in the Fenland may also date from the tenth century, built to assist the construction of Ramsey Abbey (Hall 1992, 42). The course of the River Thames at Abingdon appears to have undergone a number of alterations during the eleventh and twelfth centuries (Bond 1979, 61). There is clear evidence for more than one diversion of the River Rye at Rievaulx, and Henry Rye was the first to suggest that a series of land grants made to the abbey between 1142 and 1203 may have been designed to permit the making of canals in order to bring in building stone from its quarries both upstream and downstream (Rye 1900). The evidence has since been reassessed by Weatherill (1954) and Coppack (1990, 95–6), but the changes in the valley are still not fully understood. The Monks' Lode on the edge of the Fens was cut by the monks of Sawtry in order to bring building stone from Barnack up from the River Nene, over 7km away, and was confirmed to them in 1176. The Eschedike, which runs in a straight line for over 2km from the River Hull to Meaux Abbey was cut between 1160 and 1182, partly as a drain, but was also used for transport of stone to the abbey (Sheppard 1958). In Lincolnshire there is evidence for short canalised watercourses connecting with the River Witham at the Premonstratensian abbeys of Barlings and Tupholme, the latter documented to the time of Henry II. Glastonbury Abbey was continuing its programme of water management in the Somerset moors, with several major projects undertaken during the thirteenth century, including the diversion of the River Brue away from the Bleadney gap into Meare Pool, the construction of the Pilrow Cut linking the Brue and Axe valleys west of the Wedmore island, and possibly also the new outlet of the Brue to the sea near Highbridge (Williams 1970). It is hoped to examine some of these works in more detail in a future study.

Disposal of Waste

A distinction should be drawn between drains designed to remove waste or surplus water, which might occur anywhere within the precinct, and sewers which were directed specifically to carry away waste from latrines. In addition to the main reredorter there may be further latrines attached to the lay brothers' quarters, abbot's or prior's lodging, guesthouse, corrodians' quarters and infirmary (Fig 6.2).

1 Drains

Rainwater run-off from roofs and courtyards was normally channelled into open surface drains. Sometimes the position of such drains indicates that they were intended to receive eaves-drip directly or channelled through gargoyles, in other cases there are indications that lead or wooden guttering and down-pipes had been employed. The cellarers' accounts of Battle Abbey record payments to plumbers for mending gutters above the stable and other buildings (*Battle Cell.R.*, 72, 82, 157) and for clearing the drains in the court (ibid, 70). Excavations east of the Battle Abbey chapter house, parlour and dormitory undercroft and north and east of the reredorter have discovered a considerable complex of drains conducting storm-water southwards off the plateau. Initially open gulleys were utilised, two of which were then blocked by the east end of the reredorter. Some time after the major reconstruction and extension of the buildings in the thirteenth century, a new system of stone-lined and stone-roofed drains was developed. This included a new drain around the north side of the reredorter which had stone rainwater hoppers adjoining three of the buttresses, presumably marking the positions of gargoyles or down-pipes (Hare 1985, 24, 35–7).

The cloister garth, surrounded on all four sides by extensive areas of roof, represented a particular problem, since it could turn into a sump in wet conditions. Prior Wibert's Canterbury plan shows a drain around all four sides of the main cloister, and it is known that Prior Chillenden (1390–1411) and Prior Goldston (1495–1517) both extended the system of gutters and drains carrying off rainwater (Willis 1868, 170). Excavations at Haverfordwest Priory (Pembrokeshire) have exposed a stone-lined drain in precisely this position, carrying the run-off from the surrounding pent roofs down to the river; the main drain of the latest cloister had intersected two earlier drains running into the cloister interior (*Med.Arch.*, 35 (1991), 230). A similarly enclosed area north of the original church at Denny Abbey, serving in the later Middle Ages as a garden, contained a clunch-built cistern with a smaller inner tank and a brick roof set into the natural gravel. Four stone-lined culverts with rounded heads fed into the cistern from all four sides of the enclosure (Christie & Coad 1980, 189–91). The lack of any continuation of surface drains around the perimeter of the garden may suggest that here water was collected from the surrounding roofs by lead or wooden drainpipes or gargoyles which fed directly into the culverts. Surface drainage from the small cobbled garth of the 15th-century infirmary cloister was fed into a circular stone-lined cistern in the centre (*Med.Arch.*, 1, (1957), 153). At Faversham three drains cut diagonally across the cloister garth. The source and outlet of one remains unclear. The second, its floor and walls constructed of unmortared ragstone blocks with a roof of rubble and tile set in mortar, appears to have served the lavatorium. The third, made with a bed of roofing-slates and tiles, walls of unmortared ragstone blocks and flints and a capping of stone, led from the mid-point of the south cloister walk, either taking rainwater from the roof or serving the workshop area located between the cloister and nave. The second and third drains united in the north-east corner of the thirteenth-century cloister, and passed on beneath the refectory range and past the probable site of the kitchen to join the main sewer (Philp 1968, 22–3). Ceramic pipes were also used for drains: two types of earthenware pipe dated to the mid-fifteenth century have been recorded at Thetford Priory (Norfolk) (Coppack 1973–6).

Apart from the removal of surface run-off, provision had to be made for disposing of waste water from the lavatorium, the kitchen, and other buildings to which it was supplied. Drains from the kitchen at Tintern into the main sewer are clearly visible. Evidence for the stone-lined drains carrying waste water away from the kitchen, scullery and west range at Kirkstall has been recovered by excavation (Moorhouse & Wrathmell 1987). A narrow drain 46cm across, running parallel with the main sewer at Little Marlow Nunnery, was blocked when the infirmary was built. Although it was suggested that this might have served as an overflow to the reredorter sewer, it seems more likely that its original purpose was to remove waste water and runoff from the kitchen area and the open space south of the refectory (Peers 1902, 321).

2 Sewers

The main sewers serving the monastic latrines are still a spectacular feature on many sites, such as Furness and Tintern (Figs 6.9, 10, 11). At Melrose (Roxburghshire) water was diverted into a leat from the River Tweed over 500m east of the abbey, driving the abbey mill. From this leat a second loop was constructed to serve the latrines of both the lay-brothers and monks, reinforced by the outfall of subsidiary drains, roughly-lined through most of its length with pebbles and covered with flags, but constructed of ashlar where it passed beneath the reredorter itself, to aid cleansing (Richardson & Wood 1981, 29; Fawcett 1994, 114–5). Normally a single sewer channel passed along the inner face of one wall of the reredorter building, with the main range of privy seats above at first floor level. Not infrequently there were one or two additional privies in the ground floor of the building. In large

Fig 6.9 Furness Abbey, Lancashire: branches in the main sewer

Fig 6.10 Furness Abbey, Lancashire: the reredorter

Fig 6.11 Tintern Abbey, Monmouthshire: branches in the main sewer

monasteries the reredorter could be of considerable length: the later twelfth-century reredorter at Lewes was nearly 48m long internally, accommodating a row of 59 cubicles, while that at Christ Church, Canterbury, was nearly 43m long, with 55 cubicles. Occasionally the sewer passes along the central axis

Fig 6.12 *Cleeve Abbey, Somerset: drains approaching the reredorter with sluicegate positions at the junction*

Fig 6.13 *Tintern Abbey, Monmouthshire: positions of sluicegates in the main sewer*

of the building, with the seats arranged back-to-back down the middle of the room; this appears to have been the original arrangement at both Shap and Fountains, though in both cases the sewer was subsequently re-routed; it was also employed in the lay brothers' reredorter at Jervaulx and Fountains. Alternatively the sewer may divide to pass along the inner face of both walls, accommodating two rows of seats backed against the walls facing each other across the centre of the building; this arrangement was used at Westminster (Micklethwaite 1876, 31), Durham and Glastonbury. Other buildings within the precinct, particularly the infirmary and guesthouse, often had sizeable latrines of their own (Bond 1989, 91–7; 1993, 69–71, q.v. for further references). Special arrangements were required at Carthusian houses, where each cell had its own garderobe, and at Mount Grace a spring rising to the north-east of the great cloister, which did not contribute to the piped supply, was conducted in a stone-lined channel to flush the latrines of six cells along the north range (Coppack 1996).

The positions of sluicegates which could either divert the flow or could hold back a volume of water to be released in a flush are visible at the Cistercian abbeys of Cleeve (Somerset) (Fig 6.12) and Tintern (Fig 6.13). The frame of a wooden sluicegate controlling the flow through the canons' latrine was discovered during the excavations of the Augustinian priory of Norton (Cheshire) (Greene, 1989, 35–6). Penstocks or sluices have also been recorded at Shap, Monk Bretton and Boxley.

3 Land drainage and flood control

The drainage of marshland for agricultural purposes lies beyond the scope of the current enquiry, but the diversion of streams to secure dry sites for monastic settlement is of more immediate relevance. The most impressive example of this is at the final site of the Cistercian abbey of Byland (Yorks), settled in 1177, where considerable alterations to the natural drainage seem to have been carried out. This involved the interception of a series of streams which originally flowed eastwards off the Hambleton Hills towards the River Rye and their diversion into a new watercourse, the Long Beck, draining south-westwards towards the River Swale (McDonnell & Everest 1965).

The choice of valley-bottom sites, dictated by the needs of water supply, nevertheless often necessitated considerable engineering works to control the flow of water and to reduce the risk of flooding. The diversion of the River Arrow into a canalised course at Bordesley Abbey, enabling the old valley bottom to be used for fishponds and millponds, has long been recognised (Aston 1972; Aston & Munton 1976, 28–32). Grenville Astill has recently shown that, contrary to earlier hypotheses, this operation had been completed within a few decades of the first Cistercian settlement. Moreover, increasing difficulties in maintaining the complex water management system in the valley by the early fifteenth century led to the mill becoming choked with flood silt and the entire eastern part of the precinct being abandoned (Astill 1993, 85–95, 103–7). Watercourse diversions made in order to gain more space for buildings are also evident at Dieulacres, Cleeve and Strata Marcella (Fisher 1969, 13; Gilyard-Beer 1960, 16; Williams 1990, 21, 89).

Future Questions

So far our main concern has been simply to collect and collate information about a wide range of monastic water-engineering activities. The accumulation and evaluation of such data is a necessary preliminary, from which many questions now arise:

questions about the origins, chronology and historical context of developments in water management, the extent to which the monasteries can be seen as innovators compared with secular society, and whether particular orders can be seen to have any special or distinctive role.

Origins, Chronology and Historical Context

1 The Classical Tradition of Water Technology

The basic need for water to serve at least some of the uses listed above must have been faced by the earliest monastic communities in Britain, but archaeological and documentary evidence remain limited before the middle of the tenth century. Where did the technological inspiration come from?

Around the Mediterranean a long tradition of constructing artificial watercourses for a variety of purposes had been developed by the Greeks, Etruscans and Romans. The Cloaca Maxima in Rome, which served the threefold function of draining the marsh around the Forum, collecting rainwater runoff and removing sewage, is traditionally attributed to Tarquinius Priscus (616–578 BC) (Bauer 1989). Between 312 BC and AD 226 eleven major aqueducts were built across the Campagna to the city of Rome from distant sources, including the Aqua Marcia, built in 144–140 BC, 91.7km long, of which 81km ran below ground, and the Aqua Anio Nova in AD 35–49, 86.8km long with 71.8km underground. The baths of the city were the major consumers, but the aqueducts also supplied private houses and public fountains. Although no major new works were undertaken after the completion of the Aqua Alexandriana by Alexander Severus (AD 222–35), the existing aqueducts were the subject of regular maintenance, with repairs undertaken under Diocletian, Constantine, Honorius and Arcadius (Hodge 1991). Major Roman aqueducts can still be seen in Gaul, Spain, North Africa, and in other provinces of the Empire. Irrigation, agricultural drainage and the reclamation of swamps had also long been matters of concern around the Mediterranean, and various aspects are described in some detail by Roman agricultural writers such as Cato, Varro, Pliny and Columella (White 1970, 146–72). The water-mill seems to have made its first appearance around 100 BC, early references occurring in the works of Antipater of Thessalonica and Strabo, while Vitruvius gives a clear description of the use of a vertically-mounted water-wheel geared to turn a millstone (Vitruvius, Book X, ch v; Syson, 1965, 18–27; Holt 1988, 1). The Gaulish poet Ausonius, writing around AD 360, mentions mills on the Mosel near Trier (Guillerme 1988, 80). Vitruvius also describes the

Archimedean screw, a type of pump and other devices for raising water (Book X, chs iv, vi, vii). Artificial fishponds were another form of water utilisation which had a long tradition of use in the Roman world (Higginbotham 1997).

Roman systems of water supply and water utilisation were developed in the remotest corners of the empire. Most Roman towns in Britain were served by aqueducts. These rarely achieved the impressive size or technical sophistication of their continental counterparts, partly because the need was less in a wetter country with abundant springs and wells, partly because the smaller urban communities in Britain did not have the financial resources to construct and maintain anything over-elaborate. Nevertheless, the British aqueducts are not insignificant works. The longest known was at Dorchester (18.2km), though it has been argued that the Lincoln aqueduct may have been even longer (32km) if it was not employing some lifting device to raise water into the town from springs closer to hand. These two, along with the Wroxeter aqueduct, employed open leats which may have delivered sufficient water for domestic supplies as well as public bathhouses. Other conduits consisted simply of single pipelines. Many military forts were similarly equipped, and some military aqueducts were more advanced technically, for example at Housesteads and South Shields, where deep inverted syphons were used. Some villas had a piped supply. The gold-mines of Dolaucothi were served by an aqueduct 13km long bringing water for ore-washing. The main consumers of water were the numerous military and public bathhouses, but stone basins from public drinking fountains are known from Leicester, Lincoln, York and Catterick. Roman forts such as Housesteads had elaborate sewerage systems. Lincoln had a comprehensive network of stone drains, and other towns, particularly Cirencester, Verulamium and Colchester, may have done. At least 27 Roman water-mills are now known or claimed in Britain. There were navigable canals in eastern England, the Car Dyke and Foss Dyke (see Stephens 1985 and Bond 1991, 180–1 for full references). Evidence for Roman fishponds in Britain has been summarised by Zeepvat (1988). Thus, even in Britain, Roman systems of water management and utilization anticipate many of the monastic techniques and usages.

2 Survival and Resurrection of Roman Water Technology in Continental Europe

How much of this Roman technology survived, either in working order or in recognisable form, to a time when it might have inspired or influenced monastic builders? Roman aqueducts around the

Mediterranean often involved much more substantial constructions than anything built in Britain, and some of them remained in use long after the withdrawal of imperial government from Britain (Greenhalgh 1989, 109–11). Procopius records the cutting of all the aqueducts of Rome by the Ostrogoths during the siege of AD 537, when the defenders blocked with masonry all those which might have given access to the city. However, neither action was irreversible, and it is believed that the supply was restored once the immediate threat was past. There is good archaeological evidence for Byzantine repairs, and a letter of Pope Gregory I to the praetorian prefect in Ravenna shows that the aqueducts were still functioning in AD 602. While the great public baths fell out of use, the ancient conduits continued to supply mills, fountains, baptistries, private houses and latrines. New papal undertakings included the construction by Pope Honorius I (625–38) of a branch off the Aqua Traiana to work a mill on the Janiculum ridge west of the Tiber and the restoration of the water supply to the baths of the church of San Lorenzo fuori le Mura by Gregory II (715–31). The aqueducts were further damaged during the siege by the Lombards in AD 756, and early on in his reign Pope Hadrian I (772–95) requisitioned labour to restore four of the aqueducts, the Aqua Claudia, Virgo, Traiana and Jovia, which had been put out of action or had been working only fitfully for the last twenty years. Eighth-century repairs have been identified archaeologically both on the Aqua Claudia, which supplied the Lateran Baptistry amongst other works, and on the Aqua Alexandrina, which is identifiable with the Aqua Jovia of the written sources. The official record of papal undertakings, the *Liber Pontificalis*, records continuing repairs on the Aqua Jovia and Aqua Traiana by Popes Sergius I (687–701) and Nicholas I (858–67). A fountain continued to function outside St Peter's, which so impressed Charlemagne that he had a copy made for his own seat at Aachen (Ward-Perkins 1988). There is evidence from other sources that the Aqua Claudia, Aqua Anio Novus and Aqua Traiana from Tivoli and Subiaco were still working into the eleventh century. It is not until the twelfth century that the Roman aqueducts finally ceased to function, and the city's population became increasingly concentrated in the low-lying quarters by the Tiber (Coates-Stephens 1998). The exile of the popes in Avignon between 1305 and 1378 removed any prospect of further repair, and it was not until the sixteenth century that renewed papal initiatives finally resulted in the successful restoration of the Aqua Virgo (1570), part of the Aqua Alexandrina (1585) and the Aqua Traiana (1611).

Elsewhere in the former western Empire the city of Pavia retained its Roman drainage system in full working order. Piped water supplies continued to supply small baths in Milan and Brescia (Ward-Perkins 1988). The Roman aqueduct of Segovia was brought back into use and was still working until recently. Continental bishops sometimes played a significant part in the reconstruction of water supplies in the early Middle Ages. Vienne had a water supply in the time of Bishop Avitus (d.c.520), while at Cahors Bishop Desiderius had restored the Roman aqueduct by about 630 (Grewe 1991, 26).

3 Post-Roman Water Technology in Continental Western Europe

In the early eighth century the Moors imported an advanced knowledge of water technology into Spain, using dams and irrigation systems and waterwheels for grinding grain and raising water. Much may have been learned from their works during the Reconquista when new monastic houses were established in Castile, Navarre and Aragon. Of more immediate significance for Britain were developments taking place within the Carolingian empire. The Norman background also needs to be considered.

3.i: Aqueducts

Bishop Aldric of Le Mans is reported to have made an aqueduct over 7km long to serve the city in the ninth century (Gies & Gies 1994, 69). Few other civic examples are known before the late thirteenth century. The city of Siena built an underground aqueduct in the 1330s, some 25km long. A few medieval aqueducts were carried in part on bridges in the Roman style, notably at Morella in Aragon (built between 1273 and 1318), at Perugia in Umbria (completed in 1277–81) and at Coutances in Normandy (1322). Later medieval examples survive at Spoleto in Umbria and at Elvas and Evora in Portugal. The ruined Roman aqueduct of Segovia was repaired after four centuries of neglect in 1483–9. Most aqueducts continued to operate by gravity, and devices for raising water are rare; however, in the late thirteenth century a chain of buckets powered by a treadmill was installed at the Waterhuis in Bruges, from which water was then distributed to public conduit-houses within the city through underground pipes.

3.ii Immersion Baptistries

The earliest Christian adult baptisms took place in a fairly ad-hoc way utilising whatever natural pools or watercourses were available. The requirement of total immersion, which appears to have been general within the early church, derives from the Jewish ceremony of ritual purification, and many early synagogues adjoin artificial pools where this could be performed. As Christianity gained strength during the third century, more emphasis was placed upon preparation for the ceremony, and to this end secular bath-houses were being adapted or purpose-built baptistries constructed. Over 400 baptistries dating from between the third and seventh centuries have been recognised, the earliest known example being in a house-church at Dura-Europos (Es-Salihiyeh in modern Iraq), dating from *c*240. A number of early baptistries survive in western Europe, particularly in Italy and France. The lower courses of the baptistry of St John built at Poitiers in AD 356–68 survive, the building having been heightened and extended by the addition of three apses in the seventh century. The octagonal baptistry of St John in the former Basilica of St Tecla in Milan, where Bishop Ambrose baptised Augustine of Hippo in 387, was revealed by excavations beneath the Duomo during the 1960s. The south aisle of the Cathedral of St-Sauveur at Aix-en-Provence, itself the nave of an eleventh-century church, incorporates another late fourth- or early fifth-century baptistry, while excavations immediately north of the Cathedral of St Jean at Lyon have uncovered the foundations of the baptistry of St Etienne, of similar date but rebuilt in the eleventh century. In Ravenna Bishop Neon converted a late fourth-century bath-house to a baptistry in the third quarter of the fifth century; this is a spectacularly-decorated octagonal building 11m across containing an octagonal font 3.5m wide and 0.8m deep. A late fifth-century baptistry survives at Fréjus, octagonal in plan with four apses and eight granite columns with marble capitals, while at Venasque the late sixth-century baptistry of St Siffrein is square with an apse on each side. A mid-fifth-century baptistry at Terrassa in Catalonia, partly rebuilt in the ninth century, is cruciform in plan, with re-used Roman marble columns surrounding a polygonal basin. Around the end of the seventh century Venantius Fortunatus describes water being brought to the baptisty of St Julien at Viviers by a lead conduit (Ferguson 1990, 131–7; Grewe 1991, 20–26). Many later examples are well-known, for example at Florence and Pisa.

The evidence discussed earlier for the appearance of a limited number of baptistries in Britain from the seventh century onwards may reflect continental influences.

3.iii Water-Mills

Whether any water-mills of Roman construction survived the disintegration of the empire, and if not, when they first reappeared, remains uncertain. Written records begin from the late sixth century, when Gregory of Tours described the River Suzon at Dijon 'turning mill-wheels with a wondrous speed outside the gate' (*History of the Franks*, III, 19, quoted in Rahtz & Bullough 1977, 20). Numerous water-mills were erected throughout the Frankish world between the seventh and ninth centuries (Bloch 1935; Champion 1996). Archaeologically the earliest evidence comes from Ireland, where at least a dozen horizontal-wheeled water-mills have been dated by dendrochronology to various dates between the 630s and 920s (Baillie, 1980). After the middle of the tenth century there appears to have been a further rapid spread of water-mills through France, which continued into the thirteenth century. Guillerme (1988, 82), who was concerned primarily with urban mills, identified 82 examples built between 950 and 1083, 2 between 1083 and 1106, 8 between 1107 and 1119, and 125 between 1120 and 1275. In Picardy the number of known mills increased from 40 in 1080 to 245 by 1175, and there may have been a thousand or so examples in the Paris basin around the middle of the eleventh century (Duby 1974, 187; Gimpel 1988, 10). The Domesday total of around 6,000 mills in England in 1086 is impressive by comparison. In general the water-mill was slow to replace the hand quern entirely; the capital outlay and cost of repairs would only be worthwhile if there was a sufficiently large quantity of grain to be ground, and at first it was only the great landowners who could afford the expense.

3.iv Navigation and Drainage Canals

In 793 Charlemagne embarked upon an ambitious scheme to make a navigable connection between the Rhine and the Danube, by linking two of their headstreams, the Rivers Rezat and Altmühl, with an artificial canal 1.6km long, over 27m wide and up to 6m deep near Weissenburg. In the event the project was defeated by heavy rainfall during the autumn of that year which undermined the sides of the canal, but some traces of the works can still be seen (Gies & Gies 1994, 69).

In Normandy drainage works were undertaken at Rouen under Duke Rollo in the beginning of the tenth century, when the city was extended over land reclaimed from the Seine (Guillerme 1988, ix). Following the selection of Caen by William the Conqueror as his principal residence and the foundation of the two abbeys of St Etienne and la Trinité there in 1062–3, Lanfranc, then abbot of St Etienne, began the improvement of the River Orne and its tributary, the Odon, in order to develop a port suitable for sea-going ships. The Odon was diverted into a canalised course, the Nouvel Odon, cutting off a large meander loop along the southern side of the town between the abbey and the bridge of St Pierre, an operation probably completed between 1066 and 1083. Further works were undertaken under Robert Curthose, including the diversion of the Orne into two separate channels and the construction of the Robert Canal along the eastern side of the marshy Ile St Jean on the southern side of the town, completed in 1104. The Robert Canal (later enlarged into what is now the Bassin St Pierre) provided further dock space in the twelfth century, and also helped to drain the marshes of the island, although no significant settlement developed in that area before the fourteenth century (Guillerme 1988, 38–9, 54–6).

3.v City moats and ditches

Guillerme (1988) points to a significant development of urban water networks in France between the ninth and eleventh centuries. The threat of Norman invasion appears to have prompted Charles the Bald (843–877) to undertake a series of river diversions to create defensive moats at Senlis, Noyon and Chartres. Further activity took place in the later tenth and early eleventh centuries when new watercourses were dug at Châlons-sur-Marne, Beauvais, Étampes and Caen.

3.vi Garden irrigation

In Moorish Spain the Caliphs of Cordoba developed an immense complex of pleasure-gardens at Mdina Azahara between 936 and 976, with baths, pools, marble basins and a lavatory. This was supplied by a conduit from the north which ran mostly underground, but emerged in places as a bridge-aqueduct on horseshoe arches, and fed into a water-tower, from which the water was distributed in lead pipes (Barrucand & Bednorz 1992, 61–9). At Cordoba itself water was raised from the River Guadalquivir to the gardens of the Alcazar by a great wheel, which worked up to 1492. Palace gardens at Toledo and Seville were irrigated with pools and fountains in the eleventh century. Spanish water gardens achieved their most elaborate form in the Alhambra and Generalife in Granada in the fourteenth century, but there is some evidence for a spread of skills and knowledge into northern Europe from Spain long before this (Harvey 1981, 8, 37–54; Grewe 1991, 11).

Early medieval evidence from northern Europe is more limited. However, in 1015 Constance, wife of King Robert II of France, deliberately chose a site for her new palace at Étampes-les-Nouvelles so that it could be surrounded by gardens and served by water. Two diversion channels were led off the River Chalouette for over 1km to serve the new palace and to enclose the new town. By 1046 the church of Notre Dame, founded by Robert around 1020, had two mills on the Chalouette (Guillerme 1988, 37, 53).

4 Early Monastic Water Management in Continental Europe

The general spread of post-Roman mills in Europe has been mentioned above, and the monasteries as big landowners played some part in this. One of the earliest references to a monastic mill occurs in the late sixth-century *Liber Vitae Patrum* of Gregory of Tours, where a mill built by Abbot Ursus of Loches on the River Indre is described 'with wooden stakes packed with large stones and sluice-gates controlling the flow of water into a channel where the mill-wheel turned' (quoted in Rahtz & Bullough 1977, 20). Frankish monastic houses seem to have embarked upon a programme of investment in water-mills in the seventh century, examples appearing on the lands of the abbots of St Lucien at Auxerre in c665, St Benoît-sur-Loire in 651 and St Pierre-le-Vif at Sens. The polyptych of the abbey of St Germain-des-Prés, made around AD 801–820, lists 59 mills on the abbey estate, including eight new and two recently repaired (quoted in Duby, 1968, 17). Around 845 the abbey of Montier-en-Der in Champagne had 11 mills along the River Voire. Others are recorded in the ninth century on the lands of the Abbeys of St Pierre-de-Lobbes, St Bertin, St Rémy at Reims, Wissembourg and Prüm (Champion 1996). Of the dozen or so urban watermills in France known before AD 950, all were owned by large Benedictine monasteries (Guillerme 1988, 80, 87).

More elaborate monastic water systems are implied by the sixth-century description of the monastery of Cassiodorus at Vivarium, where it is stated that the waters of the River Pellena flowing into the precinct were 'skilfully directed wherever it is considered necessary', irrigating the gardens and working the mills, and it is also recorded that pleasant fishponds and baths for the sick had been made (quoted in Lillich 1982, 127). The idealised plan made in the early ninth century for the rebuilding of the Abbey of St Gall in Switzerland marks the positions of washing fountains, a laundry, bathhouses for the monks, for the abbot, for the sick and for the novices, brewhouses for the monks and for the two guesthouses, a mill and a tannery. It also shows seven separate latrine blocks, the largest attached to the nobles' guesthouse for the servants (18 stalls), others attached to the external school (14 stalls), the abbot's house (6 stalls), the bleeding-house (7 stalls), the infirmary (6 stalls), the novitiate (6 stalls) and the monks' own reredorter (9 stalls), in addition to a number of single garderobes. Although the plan does not show watercourses as such, it must have been envisaged that some, if not all, of these facilities would have been served by water (Horn 1975; Horn & Born 1979). The contemporary biography of the Bavarian Abbot Sturm of Fulda (744–

779), a disciple of St Boniface who had been sent to Monte Cassino to learn the Benedictine observance, describes how he surveyed the river in order to divert part of its course some distance above the monastery, which he then canalised beneath the various workshops of the abbey (Talbot 1954, 189–90). Sturm's biography was composed by one of his own disciples, Eigil, in about 790, and although it contains many of the conventions common to such documents, it cannot be doubted that the new monastery of Fulda already had significant water diversions before the end of the eighth century. An anonymous cleric who accompanied Peter Damian, the reforming Cardinal-Bishop of Ostia, on his visit to Cluny in 1063, describes how 'in all the workshops and wheresoever necessary water is sought, it marvellously flows out at once and of its own accord from hidden channels' (quoted in Braunfels, 1972, 55, 240); the original date of these works is not known. At Chartres the River Eure had been artificially divided into two courses before 1060, when Abbot Lanfry of St Pierre at the southern end of the town had a ditch cut from the river to enclose and irrigate his garden (Guillerme 1988, 28).

Even on the continent, however, significant new efforts towards improved water supplies and sewerage remained relatively rare before 1100. From then on, just as in England, the quantity of evidence increases dramatically, reaching its apogee during the twelfth and thirteenth centuries (Benoît 1996). The Chronicle of St Lambert describes Abbot Hillinus (*c*1118) making a watercourse below the reredorter at Lüttich (Kosch 1991, 91). Abbot Peringer II (1177–1201) made a lead aqueduct at St Emmeric, Regensburg (ibid). In Paris the abbey of St Laurent first piped water from its reservoir at Pré-St-Gervais into the city in lead pipes around 1190, while the Cluniac abbey of St Martin-des-Champs in the same city is said to have repaired and employed 1100m of the masonry of the old aqueduct of Belleville (Singer *et al*, 1956, ii, 691). Kosch (1991) quotes a number of similar records from the same period, including the making of an aqueduct by Abbot Berthold at the abbey of Gosek in Thuringia in the late twelfth century.

5 Water Management in Britain before the Norman Conquest

Even in Britain there is evidence that some Roman town water-supplies continued to function into the fifth century or even later. In a few places the first generation of Christian monks may have witnessed the wonders of Roman hydraulic technology at first hand. Excavations at St Albans have revealed an unusually late water-main of Roman type, consisting of wooden tubes jointed with iron collars,

laid over a sequence of late fourth- and early fifth-century buildings. Here the Roman town aqueduct was clearly still functioning after AD 450, perhaps considerably later. When Bishop Cuthbert of Lindisfarne visited Carlisle in AD 685 he was shown a well or fountain (*fons*) 'wonderfully built by the Romans', still working (Colgrave, 1940, 122–3, 242–5). Generally, however, there seems to have been a complete breakdown in the organisation of public water supplies in Britain during the fifth century. No instance of continuity of use of Roman conduits into the Middle Ages, or of medieval repair of Roman systems, has yet been discovered in Britain.

Hagiologies of the holy men of the Celtic church occasionally attribute to their intervention the miraculous appearance of springs, and there are a significant number of mentions of water-mills in the biographies of sixth- and seventh-century bishops, monks and priests in Brittany and Ireland. However, authentic evidence for the manipulation of water resources in Britain remains very limited between the end of the Roman administration and the tenth century. Excavations at Whithorn have yielded fragments of a couple of large millstones of Roman type which may point to the use of a water-mill by the monastic community as early as the sixth century AD, perhaps even a survival of Roman technology, though this does not seem to have survived for very long; from the tenth to the fourteenth centuries querns were used instead (Hill *et al* 1997, 29, 459–61). There is no clear evidence for the renewed use of water-mills in England before the seventh century. The first authentic documentary record of a mill in monastic hands occurs in AD 762, when a charter of King Aethelbert II of Kent records a receipt of half the rent of an already-existing mill at Chart, near Dover, from the minster community of St Peter & St Paul in Canterbury, in exchange for rights to graze swine in the Weald (Sawyer, *Chart.*, no 25). In 883 the monastic community at Berkeley surrendered part of their lands at Stoke Bishop in Gloucestershire in exchange for exemption from supplying food-rents to the king, and the bounds of the property included a mill-pool (Sawyer, *Chart.*, no 218; bounds, Grundy, *Gloucs.*, ii, 223–31). The site of this mill can still be recognised amidst the modern suburbs of Bristol above Millpill Bridge, where the Shirehampton road crosses the River Trym.

Although Anglo-Saxon monasticism was portrayed as insular and backward by the Norman reformers, it never developed in isolation, and there is ample evidence of many contacts with the continent from its very beginnings. Augustine of Canterbury had himself come from Rome, where his own monastery of St Andrew on the Caelian Hill (on the site of the existing church of S. Gregorio Magno) lay little more than 200m from the monumental nymphaeum and aqueduct built by Nero after the fire of AD 64. Abbot Hadrian, who accompanied Theodore of Tarsus to Britain in 668–9 and took over the abbacy of St Peter's at Canterbury, was a native of Africa and was previously abbot of Niridano near Naples. In 680 John, abbot of the monastery of St Martin, was sent from Rome to the Northumbrian abbey of Wearmouth to teach the chant for the liturgical year as practised at St Peter's in Rome. The pages of Bede and the Anglo-Saxon Chronicle record the names of many nobles and churchmen who made the arduous pilgrimage down through France, Burgundy and Lombardy to Rome. King Caedwalla of Wessex (d.688) and his successor Ine (d.726), King Coenred of Mercia and Prince Offa of Essex, all died in Rome. Others returned, including the young Prince Alfred, who was sent with an embassy to Rome at the age of four or five in 853–4, and accompanied his father, King Aethelwulf, on a second journey in 855–6.

Two of the great Northumbrian churchmen of the seventh century, Wilfrid and Benedict Biscop, embarked upon the first of their several journeys to Rome together in AD 653, when Biscop was about 25 years old and Wilfrid about 18. Biscop visited Rome six times during his lifetime, and after his second visit spent some time as a monk at the monastery of St Honoratus at Lérins off the coast near Cannes, where he took the name Benedict. He came back to Britain with the mission of Theodore of Tarsus after his third visit in 667–8. Wilfrid, on his first visit, had been been much impressed by the ceremony of the Roman church and the grandeur of the imperial city even in its reduced state, which must have provided a striking contrast with the material poverty of Lindisfarne and the asceticism of the Christian tradition there. Wilfrid took instruction at Augustine's old monastery, St Andrew's, and then studied at Lyon for two years, where he took the tonsure. On his return to Northumbria he was instrumental in securing the victory of the Roman party at the synod of Whitby in 664, and introduced the Roman rite at Ripon. He journeyed to France for his consecration as Archbishop of York. Following his exile by King Ecgfrid he fled first to Friesland in 678–9 and then to France before going to Rome again to seek the help of the Pope, returning in 680. He made a third journey to Rome after 691. Bede also mentions the journeys to Rome of Bishop Mellitus of London in 610, of the archbishop-elect Wighard in 664, of Oftfor of Whitby, later bishop of the Hwicce, of Acca, bishop of Hexham, and of Nothelm, later Archbishop of Canterbury (735–9).

English churchmen travelling abroad through this period must have gained some impression not just of the relics of the imperial past, but also of contemporary new works involving various aspects of water technology. Whether any of their journeys bore fruit in terms of the application of such technology is another matter. Benedict Biscop is known to have sent for various craftsmen to help with the building of his new churches at Wearmouth and Jarrow, and he also brought back many books for the libraries of those monasteries, which may have included technical as well as religious texts. One of the early buildings excavated at Jarrow, interpreted as the refectory, was surrounded on three sides by shallow eaves-drip drains, while another contained a shallow well in one room and a sink or washing-place in another. One of the early buildings at Whitby also seems to have contained a sink, and stone-covered drains and small wells were also present. However, archaeological work has not, so far, revealed any more sophisticated system of water supply and distribution (Cramp 1976, 223–9, 234–41). Wilfrid, too, is said to have brought back artists, masons and artisans from Italy and France, and all of his early biographers describe his building of the new church at Hexham. Among them, Prior Richard's history of the church of Hexham also mentions the existence of an aqueduct to the monastic buildings, consisting of a stone-lined trough running through the middle of the town, with the implication that this was Wilfrid's work (*Hist.Hexham*, 13). However, Prior Richard was writing around the middle of the twelfth century, and none of the earlier biographers, Eadmer of Canterbury, Frithegode, or, most importantly, Wilfrid's own contemporary, Eddius Stephanus, credit him with this work (*Hist.Ch.York*). On present evidence there is little indication that the journeys of the early Anglo-Saxon churchmen resulted in any practical application of the water technology they must have witnessed.

Renewed contacts were made during the reforms of the tenth century. When Dunstan was exiled by King Eadwig in 956 he took refuge at the abbey of *Blandinium*, St Peter's in Ghent, where he remained for more than a year; and he travelled to Rome in 960 to receive the pallium from Pope John XII. Aethelwold of Abingdon, denied the opportunity to study the continental monastic reforms at first hand by King Eadred, sent one of his monks to study at Fleury instead. Oswald of Worcester was sent to Fleury in about 950 by Archbishop Oda of Canterbury to absorb the lessons of continental monasticism, returning to England in 958, but travelling to Rome in his turn in 972; and it was Oswald's request which resulted in the visit of Abbo of Fleury to Ramsey in 985–7.

The Benedictine reform of the tenth century may mark a new beginning, with the initiation of larger-scale works. The number of mills seems to have increased very considerably during the tenth century. For example, Abingdon Abbey appears to have acquired mills in Tadmarton (Oxfordshire) in 956 and in Sutton Courtenay (Berkshire, now in Oxfordshire) shortly after 1002. The first known chronicle reference for a major alteration to a watercourse on a monastic site also occurs at Abingdon, where the diversion of part of the River Thames into a leat for the new mill is attributed to Abbot Aethelwold (*c*954–963). Although the written record dates from two centuries after the event, there is no particular reason to doubt its veracity, and it seems likely that the present leat to the abbey mill, over 1km in length, still follows the course of its tenth-century predecessor. The same abbot is also said to have dug a sewer from the abbey reredorter down to the River Ock, although this would have involved a quite lengthy and devious cut, and it is difficult to see why it was not aligned to drain directly into the Thames (*Chron.Ab.*, i, 480–1, ii, 270, 278–80, 282, 285; Bond, 1979, 69–71). At Winchester, to which Aethelwold moved as bishop in 963, there was already a complex system of open channels and mill leats fed from the River Itchen, passing from north to south through the streets of the town by the late ninth century, and Aethelwold seems to have undertaken further works there, including the diversion of a stream through the Old Minster precinct (Biddle & Keene 1976, 282–4). Evidence for monastic canals at Dunstan's own abbey at Glastonbury and at Ramsey, both possibly dating from the tenth century, was noted earlier (Hollinrake & Hollinrake 1991, 1992; Hall 1992, 42), as were the eleventh-century diversions of the Thames around Abingdon.

6 Classical Literature on Water Management and its Survival in Britain

If there is no evidence for the continuing use or reuse of Roman water systems in Britain, could knowledge of Roman technology have been preserved through books? Four principal Roman works are known. M. Vitruvius Pollio, writing in the early part of the 1st century AD, devoted Book VIII of his *De Architectura* to water-supply, aqueducts, wells and cisterns and part of Book X (Ch v–ii) to engines for raising water, water-wheels, water-mills, water screws and pumps. S. Julius Frontinus, former Governor of Britain, was appointed by Nerva to be curator of the water supply for the city of Rome in AD 97, and his treatise *De Aquaeductu*, which is a description of the administration of the system with recommendations for its improvement rather than an engineering document, was a product of his tenure of this post (Evans 1997). Some information on civil engineering and hydraulics was also to be found in Pliny the Elder's *Historia Naturalis*. Pliny describes some of the Roman aqueducts, discusses methods of prospecting for water, the construction of wells, the laying of earthenware

or lead pipes to carry water, and the construction and use of conduits for washing gold and silver ore. He also discusses the channel cut through a mountain by Claudius to drain the Fucine Lake into the River Liris, a major operation undertaken between AD 41–52 (Pliny, Book III, 53–5; Book XXXI, 43–6, 48–9, 57–8; Book XXXIII, 74–6; Book XXXVI, 121–4). There are also brief sections on prospecting for water and the construction of wells and aqueducts in the *Opus Agriculturae* of the late fourth-century agronomist Rutilius Taurus Aemilianus Palladius (Palladius, IX, viii–i).

Many aspects of classical learning were preserved and transmitted through copies of ancient works held in monastic libraries. Books were valued from the earliest days of monasticism, and scientific and technical texts found their place alongside scriptural and devotional works. Benedict Biscop is known to have collected a considerable library for his foundations at Monkwearmouth and Jarrow, including books from the monastery at Vivarium, where Cassiodorus is known to have valued the agricultural recommendations of Palladius (White 1970, 30). There was a further influx of books from central France in the wake of the tenth century reform, and after the Norman Conquest the libraries of some English abbeys included hundreds of volumes.

Of the four classical authorities mentioned above, Pliny's interests ranged widest, and it was his encyclopaedia which became the most widely copied and consulted during the Middle Ages. By the ninth century copies of Pliny were present in many European monastic libraries, including Monte Cassino, Reichenau, Lorches, Corbie and St Denis. In England Bede is known to have had access to about half the books of Pliny's encyclopaedia, and the work was also used by Alcuin of York. In 1141 Robert Cricklade edited an abridged version of Pliny's encyclopaedia at Oxford, and it was also known to William of Malmesbury and cited in Bartholomew de Glanville's encyclopaedia *De Proprietatibus Rerum* compiled around 1240. A copy was transcribed for Abbot Henry of Blois around 1170 and given to the library of Glastonbury Abbey, where it appears in the 1247–8 catalogue (Williams 1897, 49, 66). A union catalogue of books in British cathedral and monastic libraries made by the Franciscans of Oxford in the early fourteenth century lists further copies of Pliny at St Albans, Bury St Edmunds, Canterbury Cathedral Priory and Exeter Cathedral (*Reg.Anglie*, 226). Vitruvius was less well-known in medieval England, but the same fourteenth-century catalogue identifies copies of *De Architectura* at the libraries of both Christ Church and St Augustine's in Canterbury, Bury St Edmunds, Ely and the Austin Friars in York (ibid, 225; Humphreys, 1990, 115). Leland recorded one or two copies of another work of Frontinus, the

Strategematicon, but no copies of *De Aquaeductu* appear to be listed in any English monastic library catalogues. Copies of Palladius are known from the libraries of both Christ Church and St Augustine's in Canterbury, from Waltham Abbey, Worcester Cathedral Priory, Byland, Durham, the Austin Friars in York and the Oxford Blackfriars (*Reg.Anglie.*, 249; Ker 1964, 22, 42, 193, 208; Humphreys 1990, 115, 205), and the text was translated into English around 1420 (Palladius, ed. Lodge 1873, 1879).

It would not be possible on present evidence to claim that the classical texts provided any direct inspiration for the initiation of new water systems in English monasteries; but they were available as works of reference, and remained without rivals until the late Middle Ages, when the first new books on water supply were published by Konrad Kyeser (1405) and Giovanni da Fontana (1420) (Singer *et al* 1956, 691–2).

7 Monastic Water Supply in Britain after the Norman Conquest

Given the Anglo-Saxon background described above, the Norman Conquest was clearly not responsible for the introduction of a knowledge of water engineering, and there seems little evidence at present that it gave any immediate boost to the employment of such skills. The diversion by Abbot Serlo (1072–1104) of part of the River Twyver into the Fulbrook to drive the mill and flush the latrines of St Peter's Abbey at Gloucester (*Hist.Glouc.*, i, 154–5, ii, 186) appears to be the only major undertaking recorded between the Conquest and the second quarter of the twelfth century. At present we know of no more than four or five records of water supply conduits being made for English monasteries before about 1150 (Fig 6.20).

There must be some question whether the general lack of early evidence for monastic conduits is simply a result of the shortcomings of the available documentation. Detailed contemporary written records of a type likely to yield such evidence do not become available in quantity before the mid-twelfth century. Moreover, the well-known plan of Canterbury illustrating the system installed by Prior Wibert (1152–67) already shows a completely evolved water supply, distribution and drainage system of considerable complexity (Willis 1868, 158–206; Grewe, 1991)

However, on present evidence both archaeology and written sources do support the view of a considerable upsurge of activity in the twelfth century. There are probably four main reasons for this:

(i)   For monastic houses in towns, the lowering of the water table through increased consumption by the surrounding urban population and increasing pollution of local ground water through proximity to cesspits was becoming a serious problem by this period. The tapping of purer supplies from more distant springs was becoming a matter of urgency.

(ii) The preferred material for making conduits was becoming more readily available as the output of lead from surface mines increased. Lead had been used occasionally for roofs as early as the seventh century, but early lead mining in the north of England was mainly a subsidiary process in the search for silver. Productive new surface workings opened up in Derbyshire in the 1170s and in the Mendip Hills in the 1190s (Salzman 1913, 38–61; Blanchard, 1981; Homer, 1991). English lead was being exported to continental houses before the end of the twelfth century: shortly after 1180 a monk from the Benedictine abbey of Mortemer-en-Lyons in south-eastern Normandy was sent to England to buy lead for its conduits (Lillich 1982, 146).

(iii) The twelfth century witnessed many major new building and rebuilding projects taking place in cathedrals and monastic precincts throughout England, and this may have provided a particular opportunity for improving the water supply.

(iv) The strongly centralised organisation developed by the new reformed orders during the twelfth century may have facilitated the more rapid diffusion of technological knowledge. David Williams (1998, 180–1, 246–7, 253–4, 322–3, 332–5) has provided a valuable summary of Cistercian water supply and utilization, drainage and irrigation practices and milling throughout Europe.

Several further documentary records of conduit construction have come to light since the last catalogue was published in 1993 (Appendix A), and a summary list of all references identified to date in England and Wales is given in Appendix B. The impression from the documentary record is that the introduction of conduits gained momentum during the later twelfth century, became most frequent in the thirteenth and early fourteenth centuries when the town-based orders of friars were especially active, but then tailed off into the later Middle Ages. The chronology of construction as currently known is illustrated by Fig 6.20, which has been updated from the version published in the Fontfroide colloquium proceedings to take account of subsequent discoveries. However, it must be emphasized that our present knowledge of the chronology of conduit construction remains woefuly inadequate. The subject index of one of the major printed sources, the *Calendar of Patent Rolls*, inadequate at its best, omits all references to aqueducts, conduits and water-courses after the volume for 1317–21, and many more mentions must still await discovery in the later volumes. The same can be said for many published chronicles and other accounts. Investigation of unpublished manuscript sources has not begun. The sample of sites for which we have some knowledge of the date of the water supply remains very low, in the region of ten per cent of all monastic sites in England and Wales.

The Monasteries as Technological Innovators

Monastic water management has attracted more attention than water management in the secular world because it is usually better documented and more closely focussed. However, on present evidence it would be difficult to claim for the monastic orders any particularly innovative role in terms of technological development. The form of lead pipes employed on monastic water conduits is in all significant respects identical with that of the pipes produced by Roman plumbers over a thousand years before, while stone-lined channels, ceramic pipes and bored wooden pipes were also abundantly used in the Roman world. The monastic orders do seem to have played a significant part in the reintroduction of the water conduit to medieval Britain: as indicated above, at least four examples are documented on Benedictine and Augustinian houses before 1160, whereas the first known instance of a conduit to a royal palace (Westminster) is not recorded until 1169–70 (Bond 1991, 168). However, the scale of medieval secular and monastic conduits pales into insignificance compared with some of their Roman predecessors.

It is almost universally agreed that medieval monastic conduits worked entirely on gravity flow. Although various kinds of pumps were known in the classical world, it is generally assumed that the technology was lost after the collapse of the Roman empire, and that pumps did not make any further appearance before the fifteenth century, when they were being employed in mines. However, Glyn Coppack has drawn attention to the problem at Mount Grace, where the water-tower in the great cloister rose to a higher level than the nearby source, and suggests that a pump may have been installed there (Coppack 1996, 162). The published *History of the King's Works* contains a tantalising passing mention of one Edmund of St Andrew, a canon of Newstead Abbey, who had constructed some sort of primitive machine for raising water at Worksop

Priory which attracted much attention in the middle of the fourteenth century (Brown *et al* 1963, i, 520).

The earliest post-Roman revival of water engineering skills in Britain can be seen with the reintroduction of the water-mill, but it is unclear to what extent monastic houses were in the forefront of this development. The first English record of a water-mill in monastic hands is the charter of 762 already quoted, referring to a mill at Chart (Kent). This charter contains no implication that the minster community at Canterbury had actually been responsible for building the mill. The earliest archaeological evidence for the introduction of the water-mill occurs on the royal estates, for example at Old Windsor (Berkshire), where a triple vertical-wheeled mill powered by a leat taken off the River Thames has been dated by dendrochronology to the late seventh century, and at Tamworth (Staffordshire), where a horizontal-wheeled mill has been dated to *c*850 (Holt 1988, 3–5). These precede Aethelwold's mill at Abingdon Abbey by a considerable margin. Charter evidence suggests that water-mills were becoming widespread on monastic and secular estates alike by the tenth century, but many of the early examples may well have been small horizontal-wheeled structures requiring minimal water diversion.

The application of water power to processes other than corn-milling is more fully attested on monastic than on secular estates. The earliest firmly-dated fulling-mills in England are those at Newsam (Yorks) and Barton by Guiting (Gloucs), both recorded in the survey of the properties of the Knights Templar made in 1185, and within five years fulling-mills had appeared on both Benedictine and Cistercian estates (Carus-Wilson 1941, 44–5). Structures interpreted as fulling-mills have been excavated within the Cistercian precincts at Fountains (Coppack 1986, 59–60) and Beaulieu. The Cistercian monks of Kirkstall are claimed to have been pioneers in the introduction of the water-powered hammer forge (*Mon.Angl.*, v, 536; Donkin 1978, 172), and at Bordesley (Worcestershire) a succession of mills between the late twelfth and late fourteenth centuries operated trip-hammers or bellows for metal-working (Astill 1993). Another water-powered forge of early fourteenth-century date has been excavated at Chingley, which belonged to the Cistercian abbey of Boxley (Kent) (Crossley 1975, 2, 6–17). One of Kirkstall Abbey's mills was employed in crushing oak bark for leather tanning in 1288, while Battle Abbey had a bark-mill near Sedlescombe (Sussex) in 1384–5 (Carus-Wilson 1941, 46; Searle 1974, 301). Other bark mills are documented at Beaulieu and Fountains, but this type of mill has not yet been recognised archaeologically. Once again, however, it would be unwise to overstress either the general importance of industrial mills in the Middle Ages, or the role of the monasteries in their introduction. Their overall numbers remained small. Even the wealthiest monasteries, which could afford to take a long-term view, displayed caution in investing their resources in ventures whose economic returns were unproven.

Although fishponds are documented on a few monastic sites by the late eleventh century, they do not become widespread before the thirteenth century, and here once again it has been argued persuasively by Currie (1989) that the introduction of artificial fishponds in England owes far more to royal and aristocratic initiative than to monastic innovation.

Only in the field of sewage disposal, where water-flushed drains appear much earlier on monasteries than on any kind of secular site, do the religious orders have a clear lead.

Differences Between the Monastic Orders

Were there significant differences between the orders in their management of water resources? Obviously the distinctive way of life of the Carthusians imposed special requirements, with water supply and sewage disposal facilities needed for every cell (Coppack 1996). Leaving them aside, the basic needs were common to all monastic communities. However, there are differences of emphasis. These seem to be more a product of the topographical potential of the sites of individual houses, rather than of any fundamental differences of approach engendered by the orders themselves. The main concern of houses

within larger towns, which included both the ancient Benedictine monasteries founded before the eleventh century and the new mendicant friaries of the thirteenth century, was the securing of reliable supplies of fresh, unpolluted water from outside the urban areas. By contrast, houses in the open countryside, including those of the twelfth-century reformed orders such as the Cistercians and Premonstratensians, for whom isolation from human habitation was a requirement, usually had little difficulty in obtaining potable water, but had more space and opportunity to undertake extensive works for drainage and the construction of overshot mills and extensive ranges of fishponds (Bond 1989, 1993).

1. Lavatoria

In terms of architectural innovation, the most distinctive building form connected with water utilisation is the lavatorium. On the continent this often takes the form of a tiered circular basin in the form of a fountain, housed in a square, circular or polygonal building projecting into the cloister-garth (Grüger 1984). A polygonal building serving this function is relatively well-preserved at the Cistercian abbey of Mellifont (Co.Louth, Ireland) (Fig 6.14). This type does occur in Britain in the twelfth century, but it is less common, and is primarily associated with the older Benedictine houses such as Durham and Battle and Cluniac houses such as Lewes, Exeter and Much Wenlock (Godfrey 1949; Bond 1993, 68–9; Anderson,1996). At Durham the original late twelfth-century lavatorium was a square building containing

Fig 6.14 *Polygonal lavatorium building at Mellifont Abbey, Co Louth, Ireland*

a circular basin set within the south-west angle of the cloister garth. When the cloisters were rebuilt on a larger scale in the early thirteenth century this was replaced by a larger free-standing building, circular within and octagonal with angle buttresses externally (Hope 1903). Further examples can now be added. At Faversham the original arrangement is unclear, but when the claustral ranges north of the church were rebuilt in around 1220, a new lavatorium was built in the north-west corner of the cloister. Emergency excavations in 1964–5 located the robber-trenches of a circular or polygonal lavatorium with an internal diameter of 5.5m, together with an associated soakaway and drain (Philp 1968, 22). At Glastonbury evidence for a free-standing octagonal lavatorium with a covered paved walk surrounding a circular central basin was recorded in 1959 in the south-east corner of the twelfth-century cloister (Radford 1960, 254) Portions of a marble basin between 20–30ft in circumference were discovered at Peterborough in 1896. A further instance has recently been excavated by Graham Keevil at the Benedictine abbey of Eynsham (Oxfordshire) (*Med.Arch.*, 35, 1991, 183). The projecting form was still being used occasionally into the later Middle Ages: an excavated example at Elstow Abbey (Beds) dates from the mid-fourteenth century and a re-erected example at Sherborne (Dorset) was originally built in the time of Abbot John Mere (1504–35) (Fig 6.15) (Baker 1971; Godfrey 1949, 97).

Another alternative, employed by Abbot Walter Frocester (1381–1412) in his rebuilding of the north alley of the cloister garth at St Peter's Abbey, Glou-cester, was to incorporate a straight washing-trough within a narrow building, four bays long, aligned parallel with the refectory wall and projecting one bay forward from the western half of the garth wall of the cloister alley. This is an especially attractive structure, lit by eight two-light windows facing the garth and by windows at either end, with a fan-vaulted roof. A stone ledge along the whole length of the building originally carried a lead tank fitted with spigots from which water flowed into the trough below, which then drained into the culvert and cistern previously described (Welander 1991, 231) (Figs 6.16, 6.17).

Fig 6.16 The lavatorium built under Abbot Walter Frocester (1381–1412) at St Peter's Abbey, Gloucester: the south side, facing the cloister, showing the drain outlets

Fig 6.15 Polygonal lavatorium from Sherborne Abbey, Dorset, built in the time of Abbot John Mere (1504–35), dismantled and re-erected in the Parade after the Dissolution. The absence of tracery from one arch indicates the face which originally abutted against the cloister alley

Fig 6.17 The lavatorium of St Peter's Abbey, Gloucester, interior view

More commonly in Britain from the thirteenth century the lavatorium was incorporated into a recess on the outer face of the refectory wall. It has been suggested by Lillich (1982) that the recessed trough type of lavatorium may have been invented by the Cistercians in the thirteenth century to cope with the cold winters which they encountered in northern Britain, where the water would freeze in a more exposed projecting basin. Superficially this is an attractive idea; certainly the early Cistercian abbeys in Yorkshire, such as Rievaulx and Fountains, could expect seven or eight more days of air frost per annum than the first Cistercian settlement in the south of England at Waverley, and seventeen or eighteen more days of air frost than the order's first settlement in south Wales, at Tintern. Many Cistercian houses throughout Britain had a pair of arcades or a pair of broad single alcoves containing troughs on one or both sides of the refectory entrance (Fig 6.18). However, free-standing lavatoria of fountain-house type were still occasionally used by the Cistercians even further north, such as at Melrose (Roxburghshire), where the circular basin was placed in a square

iii

i

iv

ii

v

Fig 6.18 *Cistercian alcove lavatoria recessed against the refectory wall: i, Rievaulx Abbey, Yorkshire; ii, Whalley Abbey, Lancashire; iii, Tintern Abbey, Monmouthshire; iv, Cleeve Abbey, Somerset; v, Hailes Abbey, Gloucestershire*

building projecting into the cloister garth (RCAMS 1956, 2, 282; Richardson & Wood 1981); and by the Tironensians at Arbroath (Angus), where a similar example was built within the south-west angle of the garth (Fawcett 1994, 105).

Whatever the reason for its origin, the recess form of lavatorium was soon widely employed by all orders in Britain. In several cases their structure shows evidence of substantial alteration during their period of use. At the house of Augustinian canonesses at Lacock (Wiltshire) the original lavatorium of *c*1235 was contained within a tall arched recess immediately east of the refectory entrance; when the cloister garth was rebuilt in the fifteenth century the arch was too

high to be contained within the new roof. It was, therefore, filled in and partly blocked by one of the springers of the new vault (Fig 6.19.i), and a new projecting trough with a richly-panelled pedestal was built, only to be destroyed after the Dissolution (Brakspear 1900, 139). At the Cistercian abbey of Hailes (Gloucestershire) the original tall lavatorium recess was similarly replaced by a lower recess when the cloister walk was remodelled in the mid-fifteenth century (Fig 6.18.v). At the Cistercian abbey of Forde (Dorset) the thirteenth-century arcading of the original lavatorium was blocked by the traceried panelling of the new cloister walk inserted by the last abbot, Thomas Chard (1527–39) (Fig 6.19.ii).

i

ii

Fig 6.19 *Alcove lavatoria disrupted by later alterations. i, Lacock Abbey, Wiltshire: The arch of the original lavatorium, built around 1235, was blocked in order to accommodate a vault springer when the cloister alley was re-roofed in the fifteenth century, preserving mural paintings behind. ii, Forde Abbey, Dorset: The original thirteenth-century lavatorium was concealed behind the traceried panels inserted by Abbot Thomas Chard (1527–39).*

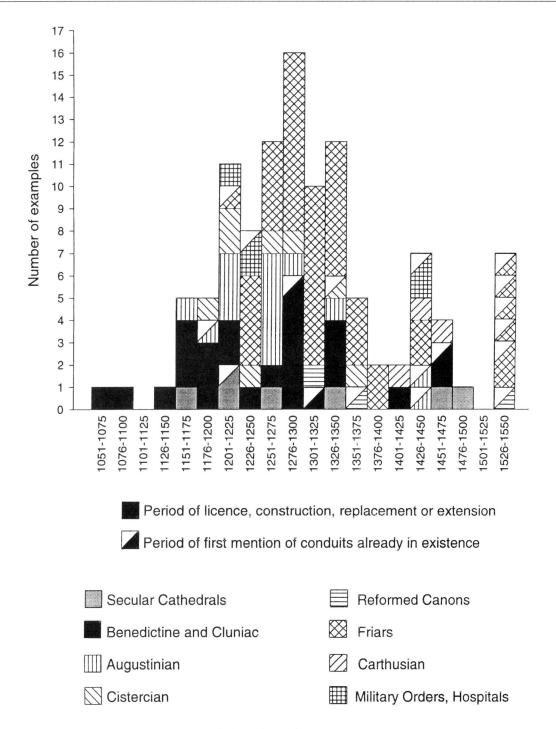

Fig 6.20 *Provisional chronology of water conduit construction*

2 Reredorters

It has sometimes been suggested that the Cluniacs paid particular attention to sanitation. Certainly the large size of some Cluniac houses produced some impressive facilities. The early eleventh-century reredorter at Cluny itself crossed the southern end of the dormitory range; according to the Farfa Customary it was 70ft long x 23 ft wide (21m x 6.9m), containing 45 wooden seats with a small window above each cubicle and a range of 17 larger windows at first-floor level (Hunt 1967). The plan of Cluny shows the seats arranged in two rows, discharging into both sides of a central sewer. A bath-house with 12 rooms each containing a wooden bath-tub was attached to the west end of the block (Conant 1973). This was subsequently rebuilt, and a description in 1623 describes the Cluny latrine as 105 ft long by 48 ft wide (32m x 14.6m) (Evans 1938, 146; Lillich 1982, 129–31).

The arrangements at Lewes Priory have recently been clarified by Malcolm Lyne's publication of the excavations carried out by Richard Lewis between 1969 and 1982 (Lyne *et al* 1997, 33–40, 55–68). The first reredorter at Lewes, built between 1077 and 1140, is probably the oldest major monastic reredorter to survive in England. Located across the southern end of the original dormitory, it was 28.8m long by 7.5m wide, orientated from east to west, with a sewer just over 1m wide along the southern side, separated from the main part of the building by an internal longitudinal wall. Brakspear's plan shows that the western end of the building was closed off (Hope 1906), and the discovery of a fragment of a Devon slate slab with a perforation for a faucet nearby has prompted the suggestion that this room may have served, as at Cluny, as a bath-house. In the main room there were seats at ground-floor level, set in embayments in the long transverse wall with chutes debouching into the sewers at basement level. Enough survived of one embayment to indicate that the cubicles were around 0.77m wide and 1.38m high. Traces of four chutes remain, and if the entire length of the building accommodated latrines, there would be room for an absolute maximum of 18 seats; if the western room was used as a bath-house, there would be space for ten cubicles in the remainder. There was some evidence for the passage over the sewer containing a stairway from first-floor level and being used as a corridor to both the latrines and the suggested bath-house. This would clearly negate any possibility of further latrines at first-floor level. The sewer was cleansed by a watercourse diverted off the Upper Cockshut stream to the west, which was originally an earth-banked channel through marshy ground. Problems with flooding necessitated raising the ground level by dumping, and the sewer was then walled with greensand blocks and vaulted over, some time between about 1100 and 1170. Finds of two fragments of window glass in the sewer raise the possibility that the windows were glazed.

In about 1180, following the extension of the dormitory southwards over the original reredorter, a new branch was taken off the main sewer and realigned 27m to the south, and the building of the second and much larger reredorter was begun. This building was 51.3m long by 10.4m wide externally, and at least 7m high up to the eaves. Like its predecessor it was aligned with its long axis east-west, crossing the southern end of the eastern claustral range at right-angles, the main difference being that the new reredorter was physically detached from the east range at ground level, with access from the dormitory over a bridge. The internal arrangements were also similar, with the sewer channel 1.2m wide, running along the inner

face of the south wall, separated from the ground floor room by a longitudinal internal wall, 4.8m thick. The absence of any evidence for latrine chutes within the sewer suggests that, in contrast to its predecessor, the seats of the second reredorter were all at first-floor level. The lower part of the south wall of the building contained four small rectangular openings midway between each pair of external buttresses. Since these can have lit only the sewer itself, their function would have been as vents rather than windows. Beyond the north wall of the sewer, the ground floor room was undivided and had a beaten earth floor and a wooden ceiling. The original excavator suggested that it may have served as a laundry and / or bath-house, though there appears to be little clear evidence for either function. The upper part of the south wall shows the remains of 60 small windows arranged alternately with the springers of 60 arches spanning the sewer channel at a slighly lower level, and it was this which led St John Hope to suggest that each window lit a single cubicle about 0.7m wide perched directly over the sewer, with another cubicle lit from the east gable wall, making 61 seats in all (Hope 1886, 27; Lillich 1982, 129–31). However, Lyne's reinterpretation places the cubicles within bays in the 1.5m thickness of the north wall of the sewer, with the windows lighting an access corridor over the sewer itself, as in the earlier reredorter; with this arrangement the spacing of the arches over the sewer implies a maximum of 59 cubicles. The sewer broadened just as it approached the west end of the reredorter, and at the point where it passed beneath it, the stumps of a pair of wooden posts were found set in the bed of the sewer on either side, with the remains of an oaken sluice gate. The low-lying position of the new reredorter, on reclaimed ground, with little natural gradient, may have made it impossible to secure an adequate continuous flow of water, and the sluice-gate would have held back water at high tide, to be released on the falling tide. Immediately below the sluicegate there was a sill or raised weir 0.45m high, with a rectangular stone tank inserted within the bed of the sewer immediately below the weir. A water conduit and a box drain discharged into the tank from the northern side wall. The function of this tank is unclear; one suggestion is that it served as a trap for the salvage of items lost in the laundry. From the east end of the building the sewer emptied into a catchment pond, which then drained into the estuary.

At Thetford the reredorter was built around 1120–40 in an east-west alignment, projecting westwards from the southern end of the dormitory, originally 20.7m by 4m internally, with the drain on the southern side. There was access from the ground floor, where the remains of five chutes are visible, and almost certainly access directly from the dormitory to seats at first-floor level. In the fourteenth century the west end was sealed off and abandoned, the length of the reredorter being reduced to about 14.6m. Was the west end here also used as a bathhouse? At Castle Acre the reredorter is 31m long, the northern part spanning a natural watercourse, with a sewer diversion channel running along the southern side. Here twelve ground-floor latrine cubicles were set across the thickness of the internal longitudinal wall, with their backs sealed with wooden partitions. At Monk Bretton the reredorter was free-standing, detached from the south wall of the dormitory and accessible from it by a short bridge. The splayed end of one chute is visible at the western end. Excavations at Bermondsey Priory carried out by Dave Beard in 1984–8 revealed an initial phase of reredorter construction in the late 11th century producing a building 66ft long by 40ft wide with a central line of round piers and an undercroft floored with plain ceramic tiles. In the late 12th century a wall was built to function as a cutwater round the piers, and the area within the wall around the foot of the piers was infilled with clay. In the early 13th century the main drain was redirected to run to the south, a wall built to separate the north half of the building from the drain, and the building was used as a cesspit. Dumps of kitchen refuse indicate that the cesspit went out of use in the late fifteenth century (*London Archaeologist*, 6.iii (1989), 76).

From the evidence of extant and excavated Cluniac reredorters in England it is clear that they were often substantial buildings. The possible use of part of the building as a bath-house, and the arrangement of ground-floor seats set within the thickness of the internal wall from which splayed chutes debouch into the sewer, may be something of a speciality of the order.

When material was being gathered for previous syntheses the rather primitive latrine arrangements of some sites were noted. At the Benedictine nunnery of Higham (Kent), for example, there was only a single privy linked with the dormitory, with a stone- and tile-paved drain leading from it, but no evidence of any mechanism for regular flushing (Tester 1967, 148–9). It was assumed that such limited arrangements might be characteristic of small, poor houses on flat sites where natural watercourses could not easily be diverted, and it was not anticipated that there would be any sigificant differences between the quality of provision in monasteries and nunneries. However, Roberta Gilchrist has pointed to other cases where the standards of sanitation in female religious houses appear to have been distinctly inferior to those of male houses. Even Elstow Abbey (Bedfordshire), a relatively wealthy nunnery, had a small reredorter only slightly wider than the dormitory itself, flushed by a single drain (Baker 1971). She suggests that this may be more a matter of deliberate intent than a mere consequence of their relative poverty: just as the long-term accumulation of kitchen refuse within the nunnery precinct may reflect the much stricter attention given to closure, poor sanitary facilities may reflect a deliberate mortification, a more ascetic and eremitic way of life (Gilchrist 1994, 113–5, 125–6).

This is an interesting idea, and is certainly worthy of further exploration. However, we should be cautious about drawing too many conclusions from rather scanty evidence. Many nunnery precincts had private quarters with their own separate garderobes, and a clear distinction needs to be made between these and the communal latrines used by the nuns themselves; we should not assume that the one is similar to the other. At Denny Abbey a garderobe tower was added to the west face of the south transept of the original Benedictine and Templar church, which was converted to residential use when the premises were taken over by the Franciscan nuns moved there from Waterbeach in 1351. The high quality of the conversion suggests that this accommodation may have been designed for the regular use of the nuns' patron, Mary de Valence, Countess of Pembroke, perhaps later becoming used as a guesthouse or as the abbess's own dwelling, so the garderobe here is essentially that of a private dwelling. The countess built a new church for the nuns to the east of the Benedictine and Templar church, with a new cloister and refectory beyond an open court to the north, and the nature and position of the nuns' latrine remains unknown (Christie & Coad 1980).

Even where we are certain that we are dealing with the nuns' own latrines, few examples have received more than partial excavation, and we should not be too dismissive of them without knowing more of their extent. At Polesworth rescue excavation in 1959 revealed a fragment of paved drain, narrowing as it passed beneath a wall between two angle buttresses. Interpretation was difficult because of the very limited area exposed, but this may represent the east end of a reredorter flushed by water taken from the River Anker to the west and returned to the river further east (Mytum 1979, 81) At Nuneaton part of the reredorter was exposed by excavation of the east claustral range in 1949–50. The reredorter projected at right-angles eastwards from the east wall of the dormitory range, with an ashlar-faced drain running along the interior of its south wall (Brown 1951, 40–3). The relieving arch over the lintel of the drain in the east wall of the warming-house below the dormitory and part of the drain itself was exposed in a further trench cut in 1981 (Andrews *et al* 1981, 65–6). Little or nothing is known of the arrangements at other major nunneries such as Shaftesbury, Amesbury, Wilton, Romsey or St Helen's in London.

Some nunneries do appear to have had sanitary facilities which were just as elaborate and efficient as those in any house of monks. Of the larger Benedictine nunneries only the reredorter at Barking Abbey has been investigated archaeologically. Here, already in the twelfth century, the nuns had a separate latrine block, 6m x 18m internally, west of the dormitory, linked with it by a passage, and flushed by a great culvert divided into two channels through the length of the building (Clapham 1913). Little Marlow had a detached reredorter apparently connected by bridge to the dormitory range, and although this was relatively short and the site is more or less surrounded by marshland, a well-built sewer 0.7m wide, floored with hard gravel, was conducted through the building beneath tiled arches in either end wall; an annexe to the infirmary block contained a second latrine flushed by a sewer (Peers 1902, 320–22). At Burnham Abbey a vestibule leading from the north end of the dormitory gave access to a reredorter 7.8m long by 2.3m wide, with the sewer along the internal face of the north wall, and the same sewer served a garderobe adjoining the infirmary hall (Brakspear 1903, 532–3, 540). The Augustinian sisters at Lacock also had a large reredorter block which had a row of cubicles at first-floor lever in addition to a single ground-level garderobe perched over the drain. Admittedly this was reduced to half its original size in the fourteenth century, when the dormitory was extended northwards (Brakspear 1900, 149). A substantial culvert can be traced at Godstow (see Appendix A, below), though the precise site of the reredorter itself cannot be identified. As is evident at Little Marlow and Burnham, attention to efficient sewage removal was not limited to the main latrines. The eulogy listing the achievements of Abbess Euphemia (1226–57) in the cartulary of the Benedictine nunnery of Wherwell (Hampshire) describes how she built a new infirmary, beneath which 'she constructed a watercourse, through which a stream flowed with sufficient force to carry off all refuse that might corrupt the air' (VCH Hants ii, 1903, 132–3).

Equally, there are examples of houses of monks where the sanitary facilities left much to be desired. For all the grandeur of the 55–seater reredorter at Canterbury Cathedral Priory, the sewer beneath it seems to have been flushed solely by runoff from the roofs and waste water from drains, and this was not sufficient on its own. A list of about a hundred monastic servants in the priory, made in 1267 but referring back to the twelfth century, includes among the part-time staff a man responsible for cleaning out the main drain, who worked on Mondays only (Urry 1967, 157). The surviving reredorter of Muchelney Abbey (Somerset) has five arched openings alongside the sewer on its western side, with a slight sill above the sewer floor. There is no visible gradient, and even if run-off from roofs could somehow have been stored and released periodically, this can never have been very efficient at cleansing the sewer. The function of the arches has been described as ventilation, but it seems equally likely that their purpose was simply to provide access at regular intervals for a servant with a shovel. The position of Battle Abbey on its ridge top also posed special difficulties, and the cellarers' accounts record regular payments between 1369 and 1513 for scouring and cleaning out the 'longhouse', i.e. the main reredorter, as well as the abbot's own latrine and the latrines in other offices and chambers (Battle Cell.R., 63, 106, 111, 116, 158). Here a new reredorter was built in the thirteenth century, 30.6m long by 8.3m wide, extending eastwards from the south-east corner of the east range. The principal range of latrines was accessible from the dormitory level, but at the west end there was a small tower containing two single garderobe chambers, one at intermediate level reached by staircase from the novices' quarters, the other at ground level reached by external pentice from the common room. Excavations in 1978–80 showed that the sewer ran along the southern side of the building, with a row of six arches on its outer side, larger than those at Muchelney, slotted to accommodate wooden shutters. Although the sewer floor was inclined slightly downhill eastwards, it is difficult to see how it can have been water-flushed on any regular basis, and it has been speculated that the wooden shuttering may have been a means of containing solid waste within the arches until it could be cleaned out manually (Hare 1985, 30–33). At Worcester the impossibility of directing a watercourse to flush a reredorter in the normal position in the east range led to the relocation of the late eleventh-century dormitory to an east-west alignment on the west side of the cloister. The reredorter, largely rebuilt in the later twelfth century, occupied the top floor of a narrower three-storey building running on towards the Severn, its north wall continuing the alignment of the dormitory wall. It contained space for a single row of 23 privies each 0.9m wide, with seats 0.46m high. Each privy was lit and ventilated by a single small unglazed window, of which six remain. Sockets in the walls mark the position of the wooden partitions. The sewer takes the form of a stone-lined channel 0.66m wide, with a semicircular-section floor, running down a steep incline at an angle of 21 degrees, from above the level of the dormitory sub-vault down towards the river. This too can only have been flushed by rainwater runoff from the dormitory roof, aided by its exceptionally steep angle (Brakspear 1916, 198, 202).

Conclusions

This discussion has attempted to synthesise and update the present state of knowledge, and to pose a few questions which arise from it, but it does not pretend to be a product of much original research. Living at a considerable distance from an adequate library, and with very limited time in which to pursue a personal interest which yields no income and pays no bills, I am well aware that my investigation even of secondary sources remains extremely patchy. Much remains to be done, even at the most basic level of data collection from published works.

The study of monastic water management in Britain as a whole is still in its infancy. Much uncertainty remains about the origins and development of water technology in general, and about its diffusion and application within the monastic world. There have been many excavations on monastic sites, some of them quite extensive, and numerous portions of pipes and drains have been uncovered; but we could hardly point to a single site where we could claim that the water system was known in its entirety. The robbing of leadwork after the Dissolution has meant that many features connected with water supply and utilisation are poorly preserved, and the fragmentary remains that do survive are often inadequately understood.

A multi-disciplinary approach will be essential if our understanding of this topic is to make any real progress in the future. The study of monastic water management requires the combined skills of archaeologists, architects, historians, hydraulic engineers, geologists and ecologists.

Acknowledgements

As usual, my greatest debt is to the numerous archaeologists and historians who have gone before, and whose works are listed in the bibliographies which follow. I am grateful to Grenville Astill, Mick Aston, Graham Brown, Glyn Coppack, Chris Currie, Hazel Dodge, Martin Foreman, Malcolm Lyne, Don and Dorothy Miller, Steve Moorhouse, Martin Watts and Charmian Woodfield for various references and for discussing with me sites on which they have worked. All errors of commission and omission are mine alone.

I am grateful to Mick Aston for the use of his photographs in Figs 6.4.iii, 6.4.iv and 6.5, and to my wife, Tina, for reading the text and for persuading a computer to disgorge much neater versions of Figs 6.1, 6.2 and 6.20 than I could possibly have drawn myself.

Appendix A
Additional Documented Examples of Monastic Conduit Construction

The following list contains further references to the construction or modification of monastic water supply conduits which have come to my notice since the previous discussions of water supply to rural and urban monasteries were published (Bond 1989, 85–8; 1993, 50–64). My intention was to list only references to the bringing of fresh water for the lavatorium and kitchen, and not to include stream or river diversions for mills, fishponds or the flushing of reredorters; but the records are sometimes ambiguous, and the precise purpose of the conduit is not always stated. Indeed, the surplus from the fresh water supply often contributed towards these other uses. In a few cases where separate sources were used for different purposes, stream diversions used as sewers are noted below to avoid confusion. All examples currently known to me are listed chronologically with sources in Appendix B. Many further references undoubtedly still await discovery, even within published sources.

Benedictine Houses

BARKING ABBEY, Essex
The nuns of Barking had a conduit leading from Cranbrook to the abbey, which was broken in 1462 by John Rigby, who had married the heiress of Cranbrook manor, forcing the abbess and nuns to pay him a yearly rent of 24s before the supply was restored. Subsequently the abbess discovered a new spring on the abbey's own land, and caused a new watercourse to be made from it to the abbey (Fowler 1907, 119).

BATH PRIORY, Somerset
In 1263 Prior Walter de Anno purchased a plot of ground measuring 12ft by 8ft (3.6m x 2.4m) just within the South Gate of the city on which to build a cistern, replacing an earlier one. The water supplying it appears to have been piped over the Avon from Beechen Cliff on the south bank,

the pipe probably being attached to the old St Lawrence's Bridge, which was removed in 1754. Following the building of St James's Church just east of the South Gate in around 1280, it became known as St James's pipe or cistern. In 1616, when the former porter's lodge, steward's chamber and rooms over the abbey gate were leased, they were said to be supplied with water from the ancient priory conduit. The gate referred to stood near the east end of the present Abbeygate Street. There were several walled gardens immediately to the north, and in the same year one of these was leased for building with permission to demolish the 'little conduit-house'. This is probably to be identified with a small structure shown in the north-east corner of one of the gardens on Henry Savile's map of Bath (*c*1600). St James's cistern was evidently a public conduit-house drawing from the priory's pipe. The 'little conduit-house' must have been a different structure, located within the priory precinct, and probably serving both the bishop's palace and the laundry, the latter probably built by Prior Walter around 1279. The kitchen, refectory and claustral buildings lay some 30–50 m. further to the north-east.

A second supply from the north appears to have been tapped soon after 1280, when Prior Walter permitted the citizens to bring a water conduit from Broadwell on Beacon Hill across Barton Fields in Walcot to the cemetery stile on the north side of the priory church, probably in the present High Street. This, too, probably served both the town and the monastic community (Manco 1993, 94).

Although Leland does not specifically mention the priory's role, approaching Bath from the south he noted the 'rocky hill full of fair springs of water' (Beechen Cliff), and went on to describe the supply of pure water from various springs rising on the hills around the city, conveyed 'by divers ways' into the city, where many individual houses were supplied by lead pipes (Leland i, 139–40).

BATTLE ABBEY, Sussex

No references to the date of construction of the conduit of Battle Abbey, or to the location of its source, have yet been found. However, the cellarer was charged with the duty of maintaining the conduit, and the account rolls of this office contain numerous references to the wages of the plumbers and the costs of materials for repairs between 1320 and 1513. The making of an unspecified length of new pipe cost 108s 10d in 1385–6 (*Battle Cell.R.*, 82). Expenditure on lead pipes for mending the broken conduit on many occasions in the year 1440–1 came to 13s 4d, while further repairs to the pipes cost 4s in 1478–9 and 5s in 1512–13 (ibid, 130, 150, 159). A boy was paid 2d for shovelling the earth back into the trench to cover the pipe in 1465–6 (ibid, 144). Canvas was purchased for the binding of the pipe in 1399–1400, 1409–10, 1412–13, 1420–21, 1464–5, 1465–6, and 1478–9 (ibid, 93, 102, 111, 136, 140, 144, 150). On one occasion, in 1465–6, the quantity of canvas bought for 9d is recorded as 9lb: this was almost the smallest sum spent on this material during the years over which such purchases are recorded; in the previous year canvas had cost 5s (ibid, 140, 136). Linen cloth for the same purpose was a separate purchase costing 2s 6d in 1464–5 (ibid, 136). Solder cost 6s in 1399–1400 (ibid, 93). Pitch and resin for the conduit cost 2s 5d in 1464–5, and subsequent purchases of resin alone

cost 22d in 1465–6 and 12d in 1478–9 (ibid, 136, 144, 150). Fine rope costing 10d was bought for the conduit in 1320–1 (ibid, 50). The likely use of these materials has been discussed in the main text.

BURTON ABBEY, Staffs

Burton Abbey is said to have laid down pipes for a water supply early in the reign of Henry VI (Hibbert 1909, 38). Although the River Trent flows within 35m of the east end of the abbey church, it is difficult to believe that this would have supplied all the abbey's needs prior to that date. However, the Staffordshire antiquarian Stebbing Shaw in 1798 reproduced a copy of a plan of the abbey buildings, apparently originally made around the middle of the sixteenth century, which contains a caption in the middle of the cloister garth, "In all the Place there is no water" (Shaw, i, 1798, f.p.9)

BURY ST EDMUNDS ABBEY, Suffolk

Walter de Banham was appointed sacrist of Bury St Edmunds in about 1200, and he is recorded to have 'enclosed in lead the water-supply (*aqueductum*) from its head and spring from a distance of 2 miles [3.2km], and brought it to the cloister through ways hidden in the ground' (*Mem.St Edm.* ii, 292).

DURHAM CATHEDRAL PRIORY

Leland's note of the conduit in 1433 and the 1593 description of the lavatorium were mentioned in a previous summary (Bond 1993, 53, 68). Originally the square lavatorium in the south-west corner of the twelfth-century cloister was supplied by lead pipes from a stone-lined well within the cloister, and this was retained as an emergency supply after the enlargement of the cloister and the building of a new octagonal lavatorium in the early thirteenth century. However, a new water supply seems to have been secured at that time from springs around Elvet Hill outside the city. These springs fed into a cistern on higher ground a mile to the south, on the further side of the River Wear. From this point the water was conveyed by pipes to a conduit-house standing on the highest part of the precinct a short distance south of the kitchen, thence by a pipe laid in a stone-lined trench passing below the refectory into the new lavatorium (*Rites of Durham*, 261; Hope 1903, 453; Coppack 1990, 86–8).

EARL'S COLNE PRIORY, Essex

Earl's Colne was a dependency of Abingdon Abbey, and the chronicle of that abbey records how Prior William (1204 x 1221) made a conduit and lavatorium, and repaired it subsequently when it was broken (*Chron.Ab.*, ii, 294).

GLASTONBURY ABBEY, Somerset

In the twelfth century the abbey was drawing a water supply from a source or sources somewhere to the north of the church. A channel bringing water into the original reredorter drain was found running obliquely beneath, and blocked by, the foundations of the new east range. The new reredorter was flushed by a supply drawn from the south, or from the south-east, the direction of the Chalice Well. The rebuilding after the great fire of 1184, which continued into the early thirteenth century, may have been seen as an opportunity for reorganising and improving the water supply.

The Chalice Well consists of a square well-shaft, 1.04m square internally, 1.7m externally, and 2.7m deep, built of large squared blocks of blue lias. The lias blocks resemble the stonework used in the abbey before the 1184 fire, but it is equally likely that they were salvaged and reused from the damaged buildings at a later date. Two holes, possibly for lead pipes, were drilled through the stones on the southern face of the shaft, the downhill side. From this position pipes could have been led around the flank of Chalice Hill, turning north-westwards into the abbey precinct, 30m below. An irregular pentagonal inner chamber, possibly used as a sedimentation tank, is of post-medieval construction, being related to the exploitation of the site as a spa in the eighteenth and nineteenth centuries. The outer face of the well was also of dressed stone, and trial excavations around the well in 1961 suggested that what now appears as a well-shaft may originally have been built as a free-standing conduit-head standing up to 2.4m high. Its construction put a stop to the scouring effect of the spring, and as a result it fairly rapidly became engulfed in hill-wash from higher up the slope (Rahtz 1963-4).

GODSTOW ABBEY, Oxon

Two undated charters summarised in the mid-fifteenth-century cartulary record grants for the construction of a conduit for the nuns of Godstow. Robert FitzVincent, lord of Wytham, gave the nuns a place to make a conduit-head on his land, which lay between Wytham church and the land of John of Appleford in the second furlong of the long moor towards Wytham, along with the right to bring the conduit to the nunnery across his arable land and meadows and the lands of his tenants, on condition that any damage caused in the construction or repair of the conduit was made good (*Reg.Godstow*, i, 44, no 28). The second charter is a confirmation that Robert Calamunt (was this the same man, or a neighbour?) had granted to the nuns free licence to make a conduit over his arable land and meadow to their court of Godstow, subject to the same conditions (ibid, i, 45, no 29). The original date of both charters appears to be around 1135. A third undated charter of about 1200 records a grant by Robert Newman of Wytham of a parcel of land 12 feet by 10 feet, giving the nuns rights of free entry and re-entry for enlarging and augmenting the conduit-head and for building a conduit-house thereupon, and for carrying out all subsequent necessary repairs (ibid, i, 45, no 30). Maintenance was not always adequately carried out. At the time of Bishop Alnwick's visitation in 1445 one of the sisters, Dame Juliana Weston, requested that the conduit should be repaired with all speed, 'inasmuch as by reason of default in repair they suffer great scarcity of water within the cloister' (*Visit.Dioc.Linc.* II.i, 114). The nuns' conduit tapped the same aquifer in the Corallian hills within the great bend of the Thames which, in the thirteenth century, also supplied Oseney Abbey and the Oxford Blackfriars from springs in Hinksey. The Godstow conduit must have been a little over 1km in length, crossing the Seacourt Stream of the Thames.

Andrew Clark, the editor of the register of the abbey,

traced the course of a straight artificial canal known as the 'Sanctuary Stream' southwards from the 'Wytham Brook' (apparently the branch of the Thames followed for the lower part of its course by the old county boundary between Oxfordshire and Berkshire, which ultimately joins the Seacourt Stream not far from Binsey Church). This then ran parallel with the west boundary of the convent, turning sharply eastwards near the south-western corner, passing beneath the west wall by a fourteenth-century arch, filling two ponds on either side within the inner court, passing beneath the east wall to fill further fish-ponds, and then debouching into the Thames. Some parts of this course can still be traced, but a further complex of fishponds immediately south of the precinct, which is said to have had one arm 65 yards by 9 yards (59m x 8m) and another 23 yards by 8 yards (21m x 7m), both 4 feet (1.2m) deep, were all filled in in 1887, while the lower part of the Sanctuary Stream was itself filled in a couple of years earlier. These features can all clearly be recognised on a map made by Herbert Hurst (Bodl. MS Top.Oxon, a 18/2), and Hurst's own description had previously noted beyond the former guesten hall 'a rather straight artificial brook' spanned by a small thirteenth-century arch at the limit of Sanctuary Field and walled at the side, which could be traced first southwards and then westwards (*sic*), passing into the walled precinct of the nunnery near a small cowshed. 'A few years ago its exit might still have been seen close to the one doorway which opens towards the river' (Hurst 1899, 119).

At the point where the Sanctuary Stream left the Wytham Brook, some 130 m west of Godstow Bridge, the foundations of a rectangular building were brought to light by the trampling of cattle after an elm tree blew down in 1899. Hurst suggested that this may have been the early twelfth-century conduit-head, but it seems too far from Wytham church on the wrong side of the Seacourt Stream, and there is no evidence that any part of the intervening meadows were ever under arable cultivation. This confusion appears to result from the conflation of two separate artificial watercourses. The conduit from Wytham must have been piped to get it across the Seacourt Stream, and there would be no reason for it to reappear as an open conduit. On the other hand, the canalised Sanctuary Stream was clearly bringing river water from the Wytham Brook into the precinct, partly to fill the ponds, and very probably also to flush the reredorter.

HIGHAM PRIORY al. LILLECHURCH PRIORY, Kent

In 1346 the prioress and nuns of Higham by Rochester received licence to make an underground conduit from a well in 'Lorkynescroft at la Gore' as far as the highway leading from Cliffe to Chalk, and beyond that to a way below the priory leading from Oakleigh to Higham, and thence to the priory (*CPR* 1345-8, 46). The source must be somewhere near Gore Green, about 1.3km to the south of the priory.

Cistercian Houses

KINGSWOOD ABBEY, Gloucs

In 1301 the monks of Kingswood acquired rights to use a

spring in Haw Park, which belonged to the Berkeley family, with leave to convey water from it to the abbey, 'provided always that, when the abbot and convent mend their pipes, they should bring with them neither bows, arrows, crossbows, nets or other engines or doggs to kill the Deere in that parke'. Despite this provision, access to the source may have created some friction, since around 1365 Maurice, son and heir of Sir Thomas Berkeley, gave the abbey leave to remove their water-conduit from his park to a new position outside it, agreeing to uncover it for its removal, with the right to repair the conduit and conduit-house given due notice and on condition that the land through which the conduit passed remained unharmed. (Lindley 1954, 165; 1955, 39).

LOUTH PARK ABBEY, Lincs
Water was brought to the abbey by a canal from St Helen's Spring in the town of Louth (*Chron.Parc.Lud.*, lxi)

MEAUX ABBEY, Yorks.
Abbot Richard of Ottringham (1220–35) is said to have begun construction of wells and conduits in the monastery, as well as causing to be made several ditches or canals for the carriage of goods to the abbey (*Chron.Melsa*, i, 433). Earlier ditches had been made by the monks in the Hull valley, including the Eschedike, dug in 1160–82 to link the abbey directly with the river, and the 20–ft (6m) wide Monkdike, dug in 1210–20 to divert part of the Lambwath stream through the abbey precinct into the Eschedike. The main undertaking in Abbot Richard's time seems to have been the cutting of the Forthdike, 5m (16ft) wide, diverting more of the flow of the Lambwath stream well to the south of the abbey between Wawne and Sutton. 15km higher up the valley the monks of Meaux cut another artificial watercourse to the river from near Skerne Grange in 1210–20 (Sheppard 1958).

Houses of Regular Canons

CIRENCESTER ABBEY, Gloucs (Augustinian canons)
Several undated charters refer to the making of a conduit some time between 1200 and 1225. Geoffrey the Clerk of Stratton gave the canons the spring called Letherwell and the right to build a conduit from it to their lavatorium. Richard of Bagendon gave them his land adjoining the Letherwell spring and the watercourse as far as the River Churn, with free access to the water through his land. Arnold of Bagendon gave his land adjoining the Letherwell spring from the high road down to the river; and his son John confirmed this gift (*Cart.Ciren.*,1, 225–8, nos 235/284, 236/285, 237/286, 238/287). Possibly there was some adjustment to the course in the late thirteenth century, when Richard of Hampton, lord of Stratton, granted a new charter to the abbot and canons of Cirencester permitting them to place their aqueduct for their lavatorium through the middle of his and his mens' meadow at Stratton, with free access to lay, improve or mend the pipes and channels as necessary; at the same time a grant in similar terms was made by five free tenants of Stratton (ibid, 3, 808–9, nos 288–9).

CONISHEAD PRIORY, Lancs (Augustinian canons)
By an undated charter the monks of Furness granted formal permission to the canons of Conishead to conduct the water of the spring called 'Trankeld' along a dyke 12 feet [3.7m] wide to their house, together with a grant of fishing privileges (*Furness Coucher Bk*, I.ii, 423). The source, now called Trinkeld, is to the south-west of Ulverston, 3km west of the priory, and part of the open conduit can still be seen.

HEXHAM PRIORY, Northumberland (Augustinian canons)
Some time around the middle of the nineteenth century 'a connected chain of earthenware pipes lying *in situ* ' was found near the Manor Office in Hexham, and a couple of the pipes were preserved in the cathedral library at Durham. At the time J Collingwood Bruce believed them to be Roman, but later writers (Raine 1863, 13n; Hinds, iii, 1896, 106n) were tempted to link them with the works supposedly undertaken by Wilfrid in AD 674–8, despite the fact that the aqueduct ascribed to him was said to be a stone trough. However, as described in the main text above, the first contemporary mention of a conduit occurs only in the history of the church of Hexham compiled by Prior Richard, who became prior in 1142. There does not seem any over-riding reason for assuming the ceramic pipe conduit to be earlier than the conversion of Hexham to a house of regular canons in the second decade of the twelfth century; indeed, it is more likely to have been laid in place as part of the major reconstruction work begun towards the end of the twelfth century. Yet the church used by the canons in Prior Richard's time was still essentially Wilfrid's church, and the problem is to determine whether the stone conduit that he mentions could really also have been Wilfrid's work, or whether it dates from any time in the intervening period while Hexham served as a cathedral and then a house of secular canons.

KNARESBOROUGH PRIORY, Yorks W.R. (Trinitarians)
Leland (*Itin.*, i, 86) relates that there was once a stone conduit conveying water from the Dropping Well over the River Nidd to the priory at Knaresborough, but it had fallen into decay before the dissolution of the house.

THURGARTON PRIORY, Notts (Augustinian canons)
Some time between 1258 and 1280 Richard Criol of Horspool granted to the canons of Thurgarton the right to dig a ditch on his land across a furlong called *Kyrielwong* in Thurgarton field abutting the park to the south of the priory, and to lay lead pipes there to conduct water, with rights of access to carry out repairs without hindrance (*Cart.Thurgarton*, 42–3, no 69).

WALTHAM ABBEY, Essex (Augustinian canons)
The making of a conduit from Wormley over a distance of nearly 5km to Waltham Abbey in 1220–2 was noted previously (Bond 1993, 46, 57). Its course and construction are documented in considerable detail in the Waltham Abbey charters. In 1220 Henry, son of William of Wormley, granted the canons a plot of ground to the south of his court, 9 perches long by 2–3 perches broad (45m x 10–15m) with the sources of water rising there, along with the right

to enclose the plot and to construct and repair a conduit across his land, with two reservations: that the canons should leave Henry and his heirs a portion of the water sufficient for their own use, and that they should pay compensation for any damage caused to crops (*Chart. Waltham*, 268–9, no 400). The precise location of this source has been the subject of much debate; a field on the northern boundary of Wormley called Smallwells, another field called Conduit Croft or Conduit Close beyond the southern boundary of the parish, and Springs House at Turnford in Cheshunt have all been suggested. Subsequently Henry granted the canons a messuage and croft alongside the spring in exchange for land and meadow elsewhere, quitclaimed any share in the water, and undertook that he would never dig or work his land there in any way which might cause damage to the spring, the conduit or its enclosure (ibid, 269–71, nos 401–2). There follow transcripts of further charters from neighbouring landholders granting the canons consent to build, maintain and repair the conduit across specified lengths of their land, subject to compensation for any damage caused to their crops, grass or hay. Several of these charters limit the width of land over which access was permitted to a maximum of 10ft (3m) (ibid, 271–9, nos 403, 405–11). A further strip of land running north-south, containing another spring, and bounded on the east by the land given by Henry of Wormley, was granted by John of Stewkley, son of William of Broxbourne, with the consent of his lord (ibid, 272–3, no.404). This grant was probably made after 1222, and may reflect some concern about whether the original sources would provide a sufficient supply. The new spring may be the one shown alongside the first settling-tank on the contemporary plan, although this is shown as lying east rather than west of the other springs (Harvey 1968, 1986; reproduced also in Bond 1993, fig 5.2). Towards the lower end of the conduit there seems to have been some sort of balancing reservoir: in 1221 Henry, son of William Portingale, granted the canons the right to dig in his meadow in Frithey beside Hooks Marsh, to place there, and to alter whenever they wished, an overflow cistern of their conduit, and to raise a mound there to a height of 10ft (3m) and at least 1 perch 2ft (5.9m) square (ibid, 279, no 412). A detailed narrative of the work undertaken at the springs, the manufacture and design of the lead pipes and the progress of laying the pipes underground then follows. Work began on 25th March 1200 under the direction of Master Laurence of Stratford, who located three springs at the source and led the water through stone conduits into the first settling-basin. From this tank an overflow pipe of lead, 10ft (3m) long and as thick as a man's thigh, with a perforated end to serve as a rough and ready filter, led beneath a thick clay bank (designed to deflect flood-water) into a second tank, 4ft deep, 5ft from north to south and 3ft 6ins across (1.2m x 1.5m x 1m), built of polished white mortared freestone with a marble slab on top. The main outflow pipe led eastwards from halfway up the side of this tank. The intention had been to make the main pipe to Waltham 7ins (178mm) in circumference, but as the springs turned out to produce more water than had been expected, the circumference of the pipes was increased to 8ins (203mm). Two other pipes exited from this second tank, an overflow pipe near the top providing surplus water to the

donor, Henry of Wormley, and another at the bottom which could be opened to purge the tank of sediment. The pipes were then led across the fields, meadows and marshes of the various donors, including crossings of three millponds and the main stream of the River Lea. The narrative records the length of each section of pipe laid down up to the autumn of 1220. Master Laurence then seems to have taken a break for the winter, and when work resumed in the spring of 1221 the narrative no longer records lengths, but describes how many days it took to lay each section. There were 16 cisterns or settling-tanks along its course, each with overflow pipes. The conduit brought the first water to the lavatorium and kitchen on 10th February 1222. Master Laurence suffered a stroke and died very shortly after the completion of the conduit, and the deaths of his sons Ralph and William, and of John Curiol, all of whom assisted him in the work, are also commemorated in the document. There then follows a further description of the site of the three springs with the basins and pipes constructed there, to which the well-known contemporary plan is attached; the plot is here described as 3 perches wide at the west end, 8 perches long (slightly at variance with the 9 perches of Henry of Wormley's charter) and 2 perches wide at the east end (ibid, pp 279–86, no 413; see also Bushby 1928–33; Bascombe 1973).

Friaries

BRISTOL, Austin Friars

The grant of Ravenswell in Totterdown to the Austin Friars by Sir John de Gourney, lord of Knowle, was previously noted (Bond 1993, 57). A date of 1366 for this grant is provided by Barrett (1789, 553), who also quotes a deed of 1404 in the vestry of Temple church by which Thomas Lyons permitted the friars to bring their conduit through his land called Brandiron Close or Long Close. Barrett dates the extension of the conduit to the Neptune fountain beyond the Temple church to 1561, and describes the course in some detail.

COLCHESTER, Franciscans

In 1279 Edward I granted licence to the Greyfriars of Colchester to make an underground conduit from the spring granted to them by Nicholas de la Warde through his demesne lands and meadows and beneath the town wall to the friary, provided that they fill up the excavated trench and repair the wall at their own cost (*CPR* 1272–81, 299).

NOTTINGHAM, Franciscans

A licence for the Nottingham Greyfriars to make an underground conduit from their spring of 'Athewell' to the priory was noted previously (*CPR* 1301–7, 131, quoted in Bond 1993, 61). In 1311 the friars received a renewal of their licence, this time to carry their conduit through the king's lands and parks there (*CPR* 1307–13, 383). The borough records in 1395 mention the spring or conduit under the name 'Frere watergang'.

STAFFORD, Austin Friars

The licence granted for Ralph, Lord Stafford, to found a

house of Austin Friars in the suburb of Forebridge beyond the River Sow to the south of the town also included a licence for Humphrey de Hastang, Archdeacon of Coventry, to grant to the friars a well or spring in Forebridge which he held of Lord Stafford, and for the friars to make an underground conduit from the well to their church and houses (*CPR* 1343–5, 321).

Hospitals

OXFORD, St John's Hospital

The final publication of the excavations undertaken by the Oxford Archaeological Unit at Magdalen College in 1987 has clarified a number of problems related to this site. It was known that in June 1246 Henry III had permitted the brethren of St John's Hospital to take water from the spring called Crowell in the north-east corner of the city ditch and to convey it to the hospital (over a distance of 400m) by an aqueduct (*CCR* 1242–7, 438). This conduit from Crowell may have been used to flush the five projecting buttress-like garderobes recorded by Buckler on the north side of Magdalen College's cloisters, a range believed to incorporate a surviving part of the hospital buildings (Gunter 1916, 399–402).

The excavation revealed a further culvert conveying water through the eastern annexe to the infirmary hall, which is interpreted as a probable chapel. This may have been fed by another branch of the conduit carrying water from the Crowell spring, although it is also possible that a leat was fed into the building directly from the nearby River Cherwell. The culvert was of high-quality ashlar, originally spanned by five arches within the infirmary annexe. Both the position of the culvert within the putative chapel and the presence of a flight of steps leading down into it from the interior of the building seem to negate the obvious interpretation as a latrine; it has been suggested, therefore, that it may have played some part in the process of ritual cleansing or healing. There were signs that the infirmary culvert had been quite deliberately abandoned after the middle of the thirteenth century.

The reason for its abandonment may be indicated by the documentary record. In 1267 the king, with the consent of the warden and brethren of St John's Hospital, gave Merton College permission to take water from the River Cherwell above the Chapel of St Cross at Holywell, passing above or below ground through the area of the chapel and courtyard of the hospital, across the 'great road' (the modern High Street) outside the city's East Gate, then south of the barton of St Frideswide's Priory, skirting the city wall, and entering the college by a gutter, leaving by another gutter. The brethren of the hospital were also to have reasonable use of the water as it passed through their property. This new water supply system must have intersected and disrupted the line of the 1246 conduit from Crowell. The stated aim of the new watercourse system was to provide water for cleansing the college's courtyard, and for this purpose river-water would have sufficed; but the presence of a lavatorium in the middle of the cloister, which the College repaired in 1483, suggests that purer water from the Holywell spring above St Cross church may also have been tapped. Loggan's map of 1675 shows a complex of ditches which may be part of this system, and during excavation work a large ditch which may be the outfall from the later 13th-century water system was discovered along the southern side of the infirmary, choked with fine silt which accumulated in the 14th–15th century (Durham *et al*, 1991, 22, 29–34, 66–70, 72–3).

Cistercian Granges

MALHAM GRANGE, Yorks W.R.

Fountains Abbey's grange at Malham had its own piped water supply by the middle of the thirteenth century. In 1257 Richard de Otterburn quitclaimed to the monks all lands and possessions in Malham given or sold to them by Thomas, son of William de Malham, also granting them 'the conduit of their water of Malham' where it crossed his land, with consent for them to dig the land to repair the conduit whenever necessary without hindrance by him or his heirs (*Chart.Fountains*, ii, 475, no 63). The Fountains Cartulary contains a further confirmation and quitclaim to the monks by Thomas, son of Matilda, daughter of William de Malham, of all lands and tenements with their appurtenances, liberties and easements granted by his ancestors, including 'free transit through his land for examining and repairing their lead water conduit for the water flowing to their grange of Malham, they making good any damage they do in digging (ibid, ii, 476, no 69). Finally, in 1298 William, son of Thomas de Malham, inspected and confirmed the charter granted by his father 'which the Abbot and Convent have respecting their lead conduit to be laid and repaired through the middle of his land in the vill and territory of Malham' (ibid, ii, 477, no 70).

Appendix B
Summary of References to Cathedral and Monastic Water Conduits

This list includes both records of conduit construction and, where these are not available, first records of conduits being in existence. Later references are tabulated only if they seem to imply the tapping of supplementary sources, or extensions or alterations to the course of existing conduits. Fuller details for all sites listed can be found in Bond, 1989, 85–8; 1993, 50–64; or in Appendix A of the present article.

Date	Site	Order	Nature of Record	Source
11th Century				
?1042 x 66	Westminster Abbey	Ben.	?Grant of source	see Bond 1993, 54
1072 x 1104	Gloucester, St Peter's Abbey	Ben.	River diversion	*Hist.Glouc.* i, 154–5, ii, 186
12th Century				
*c*1135	Godstow Abbey, Oxon.	Ben.N.	Licence to make conduit	*Reg.Godstow*, i, 44–5
1140 x 1166	Lichfield Cathedral, Staffs	Sec.	Making of conduit	Gould 1976
1148 x 62	Canterbury, Christ Church Priory	Ben.	Grant of source	Willis 1868
1158	Taunton Priory, Somerset	Aug.	Grant of watercourse	see Bond 1993, 57
1161 x 89	Evesham Abbey, Worcs.	Ben.	Making of conduit	*Chron.Evesham*, 100
1163 x 84	Gloucester, St Peter's Abbey	Ben.	Grant of source	Fulbrook-Leggatt 1968
1179	Waverley Abbey, Surrey	Cist.	Completion of conduit	Brakspear 1905, 89–90
*c*1184 x 94	Winchcombe Abbey, Gloucs.	Ben.	Grant of source	*Winchc.Landboc*, i, 239
post-1184	Glastonbury Abbey, Somerset	Ben.	Making of new conduit	See Appendix A
1186 x 1216	Bristol, St John's Hospital, Redcliffe	Hosp.	Concession from parish	Latimer 1901, 173
Late C12	Hexham Priory, Northumberland	Aug.	Mention of conduit	See Appendix A
13th Century				
Early C13	Wells Cathedral	Sec.	Construction of conduit	see Bond 1993, 52–3
Early C13	Durham Cathedral Priory	Ben.	New conduit	see Appendix A
*c*1200	Bury St Edmunds Abbey, Suffolk	Ben.	Improvement of conduit	*Mem.St.Edm.* ii, 292
1200 x 25	Cirencester Abbey, Gloucs.	Aug.	Grant of source	*Cart.Ciren.*, i, 225–8
1204 x 21	Earls Colne Priory, Essex	Ben.	Making of conduit	*Chron.Ab.*, ii, 294
1205 x 21	Oseney Abbey, Oxon.	Aug.	Grant of source	*Cart.Oseney*, iv, 472–3
1214	Stanley Abbey, Wilts.	Cist.	Making of conduit	Brakspear 1908, 544
1215	Waverley Abbey, Surrey	Cist.	Replacement of conduit	Brakspear 1905, 89–90
1220–2	Waltham Abbey, Essex	Aug.	Making of conduit	*Chart .Waltham*, 268–86
1220 x 35	Meaux Abbey, Yorks.	Cist.	Making of conduit	*Chron.Melsa*, i, 433
1221	Oxford, Greyfriars	Fran.	Conduit in existence	Little 1891, 28n
pre-1226	Exeter Cathedral	Sec.	Conduit in existence	see Bond 1993, 50–1
*c*1230	Gloucester, St Peter's Abbey	Ben.	Grant of source	Fulbrook-Leggatt 1968
*c*1230	Gloucester, Greyfriars	Fran.	Grant of source	Fulbrook-Leggatt 1968
1232	Bristol, Blackfriars	Dom.	Licence to make conduit	*GRB Bristol*, ii, 191ff.
*c*1240	Bristol, St Mark's Hospital, Billeswick	Hosp.	Existence of conduit	Lobel 1975, 9
1244	Exeter, Blackfriars	Dom.	Grant of source	Little & Easterling 1927
1244	Stamford, Blackfriars, Lincs.	Dom.	Grant towards cost of making conduit	CLR ii, 250
1246	Oxford, St John's Hospital	Hosp.	Licence to make conduit	CCR 1242–7, 438
1251	Kenilworth Priory, Warwicks.	Aug.	Licence to make conduit	CPR 1247–58, 93
1255–6	London, Newgate, Greyfriars	Fran.	Grant of source	CLR iv, 274
1256 x 1310	Pershore Abbey, Worcs.	Ben.	Grant of source	*VCH Worcs*, iv, 171
1257	Malham Grange, Yorks.	Cist.	Grant of conduit	*Chart.Fountains*, ii, 475–7
1257 x 87	Lacock Abbey, Wilts.	Aug.S	Making of conduit	*Chart. Lacock*,25, 49–51
1258 x 80	Thurgarton Priory, Notts.	Aug.	Consent to make conduit	*Cart.Thurgarton*, 42–3
*c*1259	Lichfield Cathedral	Sec.	Grant of new source	Gould 1976
1259	London, Holborn, Blackfriars	Dom.	Licence to make conduit	CLR iv, 484
1260	Lincoln, Blackfriars	Dom.	Licence to make conduit	CCR 1259–61, 37; CPR 1258–66, 67
1260 x 96 (1284)	Malmesbury Abbey, Wilts.	Ben.	Making of conduit	*Reg.Malm.*, ii, 361, 376
1263	Bath Priory, Somerset	Ben.	Building of cistern	Manco 1993, 94
1263 x 84	Gloucester, St Oswald's Priory	Aug.	Extension from St Peter's	Fulbrook-Leggatt 1968
1267	Oxford, Blackfriars	Dom.	Grant of source	CPR 1281–92, 165
1271	Warter Priory, Yorks.	Aug.	Licence to make conduit	CPR 1266–72, 579

Date	Site	Order	Nature of Record	Source
1276	Chester Blackfriars	Dom.	Licence to make conduit	CPR 1272–81, 16
pre-1277	Bristol, Greyfriars	Fran.	Grant of source	CPR 1370–74, 471
1278	Chester, St Werburgh's Abbey	Ben.	Licence to make conduit	CPR 1272–81, 279
1279	Northampton, Blackfriars	Dom.	Grant of source	CPR 1272–81, 322
1279	Colchester, Greyfriars	Fran.	Licence to make conduit	CPR 1272–81, 299
post-1280	Bath Priory, Somerset	Ben.	Making of additional conduit	Manco 1993, 94
1282–3	Chester, St Werburgh's Abbey	Ben	Grant of additional source Licence to make conduit	*Chart.Chester*, 224, no.340 CPR 1281–92, 75
1283	Scarborough Greyfriars, Yorks.	Fran.	Grant of source	VCH Yorks iii, 275
1283	Scarborough Blackfriars, Yorks.	Dom.	Request for use of source	Yorks.Inq.ii, 9
1290 x 1310	Southampton Greyfriars, Hants.	Fran.	Licence to enclose source	see Bond 1993, 62
1291	Northampton Greyfriars	Dom.	Licence to make conduit	CPR 1281–92, 442
1293	Kings Lynn Blackfriars, Norfolk	Dom.	Grant of source	CPR 1292–1301, 15
1294	Daventry Priory, Northants	Clun.	Breaking of conduit	CPR 1292–1301, 115–6
Late C13	Cirencester Abbey, Gloucs.	Aug.	? Alteration to conduit	*Cart.Ciren.*, iii, 808–9

14th Century

Date	Site	Order	Nature of Record	Source
C14	Bristol, St James's Priory	Ben.	Concession from Greyfriars	Lobel 1975
Early C14	London, Newgate, Greyfriars	Fran.	Making of 2nd conduit head	Norman 1899
1301	Kingswood Abbey, Gloucs.	Cist.	Grant of source	see Appendix A
1301	Lichfield Greyfriars, Staffs.	Fran.	Grant of source	see Bond 1993, 60
1303	Nottingham Greyfriars	Fran.	Licence to make conduit	CPR 1301–7, 131
1306	Lincoln, St Catherine's Priory	Gilb.	Licence to make conduit	CPR 1301–7, 482
1313	Grimsby Greyfriars, Lincs.	Fran.	Licence to make conduit	CPR 1307–13, 597
1314	Kings Lynn Greyfriars, Norfolk	Fran.	Licence to make conduit	CPR 1313–17, 128
1314	Grantham Greyfriars, Lincs.	Fran.	Grant of source	*Reg.Pal.Dunelm.* ii, 1255–6, iv, 385–6
1315	Exeter Greyfriars, Devon	Fran.	Grant of new source	CPR 1313–17, 398
1319	Scarborough Greyfriars, Yorks.	Fran.	Licence to make conduit	CPR 1317–21, 376–7
1320	Oseney Abbey, Oxon.	Aug.	Confirmation of rights	CChR 1300–26, 424–6
1320–1513	Battle Abbey, Sussex	Ben.	Repairs to conduit	*Battle Cell.R.*
1327	Boston Blackfriars, Lincs.	Dom.	Licence to make conduit	CPR 1327–30, 182
1327	Cambridge, Greyfriars	Fran.	Construction of conduit	RCHM Camb.ii, 233
1329	Beaulieu Abbey, Hants.	Cist.	Confirmation	
1332	Taunton Priory, Somerset	Aug.	Licence to make conduit	CChR iv, 312–18
1341	Chelmsford Blackfriars, Essex	Dom.	Licence to make conduit	CPR 1340–3, 227–8
1341	Gloucester, Whitefriars	Carm.	Grant of source	CPR 1340–3, 255
1344	Stafford, Austin Friars	Aus.F.	Licence to make conduit	CPR 1343–5, 321
1346–9	Exeter Cathedral	Sec.	Replacement of conduit	see Bond 1993, 50
1346	Exeter, St Nicholas's Priory	Ben	Extension from cathedral supply	see Bond 1993, 53
1346	Higham al. Lillechurch Priory, Kent	Ben.N.	Licence to make conduit	CPR 1345–8, 46
1347	Exeter Greyfriars, Devon	Fran.	Making of new conduit	CPR 1345–8, 424
1358	Kings Langley Blackfriars, Herts.	Dom.	Licence to make conduit	CPR 1358–61, 34
1363	Huntingdon, Austin Friars	Aus.F.	Licence to make conduit	CPR 1361–4, 306
1365	Kingswood Abbey, Gloucs.	Cist.	Alterations to source	See Appendix A
1366	Bristol, Austin Friars	Aus.F.	Making of new conduit	See Appendix A
1373	Bristol, St Augustine's Abbey	Vict.	Mention in charter	*Bristol Chart.*, i, 155
1376	Bristol, Whitefriars	Carm.	Concession to parish	*GRB Bristol*, i, 114–7
1380	Sudbury Blackfriars, Suffolk	Dom.	Licence to make conduit	CPR 1377–81, 534
1391	Bristol, Blackfriars	Dom.	Exchange of supply	*GRB Bristol*, ii, 191ff

15th Century

Date	Site	Order	Nature of Record	Source
pre-1407	Worcester Priory	Ben.	Confirmation of rights	see Bond 1993, 54–5
1414–5	Sheen Charterhouse, Surrey	Carth.	Grant of source	Cloake 1977, 151
post-1422	Burton Abbey, Staffs.	Ben.	Making of new conduit	Hibbert 1909, 38
1430	London Charterhouse	Carth.	Grant of source	Hope 1902, 296
pre-1433	London, St Bartholomew's Priory, Smithfield	Aug.	Concession to hospital	Norman 1899, 256
1433	London, St Bartholomew's Hospital, Smithfield	Hosp.	Concession from priory	Norman 1899, 256
c1438	Gloucester Greyfriars	Fran.	Extension to serve town	Fulbrook-Leggatt 1968

Date	Site	Order	Nature of Record	Source
1440–1	Exeter Blackfriars	Dom.	Extension to serve town	Little & Easterling 1927
Mid-C15	London, St Mary's Priory, Clerkenwell	Aug.S.	Shown on map	Hope 1902, 303, 305
Mid-C15	London, St John's Priory, Clerkenwell	Kts.H.	Shown on map	Hope 1902
1451–3	Wells Cathedral	Sec.	Extension to serve town	see Bond 1993, 52
1462	Barking Abbey, Essex	Ben.N	Breaking of conduit	Fowler 1907, 119
1466	Sheen Charterhouse, Surrey	Carth.	Licence to make new conduit	CPR 1461–7, 513
Later C15	Barking Abbey, Essex	Ben.N.	Making of new conduit	Fowler 1907, 119

16th Century

1535	Lincoln, Greyfriars	Fran.	Licence to make new conduit	*Cal.Linc.MSS*, 33
1538	Bridgnorth Greyfriars, Salop.	Fran.	Conduit out of order	*Inv.Salop*, 378–9
1538	Chichester Greyfriars, Sussex	Fran.	Listed in inventory	*Inv.Sussex*, 71
Dissoln.	Coventry Greyfriars, Warwicks.	Fran.	Description at Dissolution	L & P Hen.VIII, 13(2), 257
Dissoln.	Richmond Greyfriars, Yorks.	Fran.	Existence of conduit	Leland, *Itin.*, iv, 25
Dissoln.	Knaresborough Priory, Yorks.	Trin.	Conduit in decay	Leland, *Itin.*, i, 86
Dissoln.	Stamford Greyfriars, Lincs.	Fran.	Survival of conduit	*VCH Lincs*, ii, 228–9

Undated

	Conishead Priory, Lancs.	Aug.	Licence to make conduit	*Furness C.B.*, I.ii, 423
	Louth Park Abbey, Lincs.	Cist.	Existence of conduit	*Chron.Parc.Lud.*, lxi
	Pontefract, Blackfriars	Dom.	Existence of conduit	VCH Yorks iii, 272
	Reading Abbey	Ben.	Existence of conduit	Hurry 1901, 23

Key to Orders:

Aug.	= Augustinian canons	Aug.S.	= Augustinian sisters	Aus.F.	= Austin friars
Ben.	= Benedictine monks.	Ben.N.	= Benedictine nuns	Carm.	= Carmelite friars
Carth.	= Carthusians	Cist.	= Cistercian monks	Clun.	= Cluniac monks
Dom.	= Dominican friars	Fran.	= Franciscan friars	Gilb.	= Gilbertine canons
Hosp.	= Hospitals	Kts.H.	= Knights Hospitallers	Sec.	= Secular cathedrals
Trin.	= Trinitarian canons	Vict.	= Victorine canons		

References

1 Published Documentary Sources

Battle Cell.R.: The Cellarers' Rolls of Battle Abbey, 1275–1513, ed Searle, E & Ross, B (Sussex Record Soc, 65, 1967)

Bristol Chart.: Bristol Charters, 1155–1373, ed. Harding, N D (Bristol Record Soc, 1, i–iii, 1930)

CCR: Calendar of Close Rolls (HMSO, London)

CChR: Calendar of Charter Rolls (HMSO, London)

CLR: Calendar of Liberate Rolls (HMSO, London)

CPR: Calendar of Patent Rolls (HMSO, London)

Cal.Linc.MSS: The Manuscripts of the Corporation of Lincoln (Historical MSS Commission, 37, 14th Report, Appendix, part viii (1895)

Cart.Ciren.: The Cartulary of Cirencester Abbey, 3 vols; 1–2, ed Ross, C D (Oxford University Press, 1964); 3, ed Devine, M (Oxford University Press, 1977)

Cart.Oseney: The Cartulary of Oseney Abbey, ed Salter, H E (6 vols, Oxford Hist Soc, 89, 1929, 90, 1929, 91, 1931, 97, 1934, 98, 1935, 101, 1936)

Cart.Thurgarton: The Thurgarton Cartulary, ed. Foulds, T. (Paul Watkins, Stamford, 1994)

Chart.Chester: Chartulary of the Abbey of St Werburgh, Chester, ed Tait, J (2 vols, Chetham Soc, new ser, 79 (1920), 82 (1923)

Chart.Fountains: Abstracts of the Charters and other Documents contained in the Chartulary of the Cistercian Abbey of Fountains in the West Riding of the County of York, 2 vols, ed Lancaster, W T (Leeds, 1915)

Chart.Lacock: Lacock Abbey Charters, ed Rogers, K H (Wilts Record Soc, 34, 1978)

Chart.Waltham: The Early Charters of the Augustinian Canons of Waltham Abbey, Essex, 1062–1230, ed Ransford, R (Boydell, Woodbridge, 1989)

Chron. Ab.: Chronicon Monasterii de Abingdon, 2 vols, ed Stevenson, J (Rolls Series, 2, 1858)

Chron.Evesham: Chronicon Abbatiae de Evesham, ed Macray, W D (Rolls Ser 29, 1863)

Chron.Melsa: Chronicon Monasterii de Melsa, ed Bond, E A (3 vols, Rolls Ser 43.i, 1866; 43.ii, 1867; 43.iii, 1868)

Chron.Parc.Lud.: Chronicon Abbatiae de Parco Lude, ed Venables, E (Lincs Record Soc. publications, 1 (1891)

Durham Accts: Extracts from the Account Rolls of the Abbey of Durham, ed Fowler, J T (3 vols, Surtees Soc, 99, 1898, 100, 1898, 103, 1900)

Frontinus: *The Stratagems and the Aqueducts of Rome*, ed

Bennett, C E (Loeb Classical Library Harvard University Press, Cambridge, Mass, no.174, 1925). (A more recent translation with a wider consideration of some of the aqueducts of Rome is provided by Evans (1997), see below)

Furness Coucher Bk: The Coucher Book of Furness Abbey, ed Atkinson, J C (Part ii, Chetham Soc, new ser, 11, 1887)

GRB Bristol: The Great Red Book of Bristol, edVeale, E W W (Bristol Record Soc, 4 (1933), 8 (1938))

Gregory of Tours, *The History of the Franks*, trans Lewis Thorpe (Penguin, Harmondsworth)

Grundy, *Gloucs: Saxon Charters and Field-Names of Gloucestershire* (2 vols, Bristol & Gloucestershire Archaeological Soc, 1935, 1936)

Habington: T Habington, *A Survey of Worcestershire*, ed Amphlett, J (2 vols, Worcs Historical Soc, 1893–5, 1897–9)

Hist.Ch.York: Historians of the Church of York and its Archbishops, ed Raine, J (Rolls Series, 71.i, 1879) (contains biographies by Eddius Stephanus, 1–103, Frithegode, 105–59, and Eadmer of Canterbury, 161–226)

Hist.Glouc.: Historia et Cartularium Monasterii Sancti Petri Gloucestriae, ed Hart, W H (2 parts, Rolls Series, 33, 1863, 1865)

Hist.Hexham: Prior Richard of Hexham, History of the Church of Hexham, in Raine, J (ed), *The Priory of Hexham: its Chroniclers, Endowments and Annals*, Vol 1 (Surtees Soc, 44, 1863), 1–6

Inv.Salop.: Inventories of the Religious Houses of Shropshire at their Dissolution (Trans.Salop Archaeol.& Nat Hist Soc, 3rd ser, 5 (1905), 377–92)

Inv.Sussex: Inventories of Goods of the Smaller Monasteries and Friaries of Sussex at the Time of their Dissolution (Sussex Archaeol Collns, 44 (1901), 55–72)

L & P Henry VIII: *Letters & Papers of Henry VIII* (HMSO)

Lanfranc: *The Monastic Constitutions of Lanfranc*, ed Knowles, D (Thomas Nelson, London, 1951)

Leland, *Itin.: The Itinerary of John Leland, c.1535–1543*, 5 vols, ed Toulmin Smith, L (Centaur Press, London)

Mem.St Edm.: Memorials of St Edmunds Abbey, ed Arnold, T (Rolls Series, 96.i (1890), ii (1892), iii (1896))

Mon.Angl.: Dugdale, W, *Monasticon Anglicanum*, ed Caley, J, Ellis, H & Bandinell, B, 6 vols (Record Commissioners, London, 1817–30)

Palladius: *Opus Agriculturae de Veterinaria Medicina de Insitione*, ed Rodgers, R H (BSB B.G. Teubner Verlagsgesellschaft, Leipzig, 1975); *On Husbondrie*, ed Lodge, B (Early English Text Society, 52, 1873; 72, 1879)

Pliny: *Natural History*, ed Rackham, H, Jones, W H S & Eichholz, D E (Loeb Classical Library, Harvard University Press, Cambridge, Mass, 37 books in 10 vols, nos 330, 352–3, 370–1, 392–4, 418–9, 1940–80). A convenient abridged translation is Pliny the Elder, *Natural History: a Selection*, ed Healey, J F (Penguin Books, London, 1991)

Reg.Anglie: Registrum Anglie de Libris Doctorum et Auctorum Veterum, ed Mynors, R A B, Rouse, R H & Rouse, MA Corpus of British Medieval Library Catalogues (British Library / British Academy, London, 1991)

Reg.Godstow: The English Register of Godstow Nunnery near Oxford, 3 vols, ed.Clark, A. (Early English Text Soc, 129, 1905; 130, 1906; 142, 1911)

Reg.Malm.: Registrum Malmesburiense, ed Brewer, J S (2 vols, Rolls Ser, 72.i (1879), 72.ii (1880))

Reg.Pal.Dunelm: Registrum Palatinum Dunelmense, ed Hardy, T D (4 vols, Rolls Ser, 62.i (1873), 62.ii (1874), 63.iii (1875), 63.iv (1878))

Rites of Durham: Rites of Durham, being a description or Brief Declaration of all the Ancient Monuments, Rites and Customs belonging or being within the Monastic Church of Durham before the Suppression, written in 1593, ed Fowler, J T (Surtees Soc, 106,1902)

Rot.Litt.Claus.: Rotuli Litterarum Clausarum in Turri Londinensi asservati (2 vols, Record Commissioners)

Rule St.A.: The Rule of St Augustine, ed Van Bavel, T J, trans Canning, R (Darton, Longman & Todd, London, 1984)

Rule St.B.: The Rule of St Benedict, trans McCann, J (Sheed & Ward, London, 1976)

Sawyer, *Chart.: Anglo-Saxon Charters: an Annotated List and Bibliography* (Royal Historical Soc, Guides & Handbooks no 8, 1968)

Visit.Dioc.Linc.: Visitations of Religious Houses in the Diocese of Lincoln, II: Records of Visitations held by William Alnwick, Bishop of Lincoln, AD 1436 to AD 1449, i, ed Thompson, A Hamilton (Lincolnshire Record Soc, 14, 1916)

Vitruvius: Marcus Vitruvius Pollio, *The Ten Books of Architecture*, ed Morgan, M H (Harvard University Press, 1914); for a more recent edition, ed Granger, F (Loeb Classical Library, Harvard University Press, Cambridge, Mass.; Books I–V, no.251, 1931, reprinted 1998, Books VI–X, no.280, 1934, reprinted 1999).

Winchc.Landboc: Landboc sive Registrum Monasterii de Winchelcumba, ed Royce, D (Exeter)

Yorks.Inq.: Yorkshire Inquisitions, ed. Brown, W. (4 vols, Yorks Archaeol Soc Record Ser 12 (1891), 23 (1897), 31 (1902), 37 (1906))

2 Secondary Works

Allen T 1990, 'Abingdon', *Current Archaeology*,121, pp 24–7

Anderson F 1996, 'Le système hydraulique et le lavabo du prieuré de Lewes (East Sussex, Grande-Bretagne)', in Pressouyre & Benoît (1996), 55–64

Andrews D, Cook A, Quant V, Thorn J C & Veasey E A 1981, 'The archaeology and topography of Nuneaton Priory', *Trans Birmingham & Warwicks Archaeol Soc*, 91, 55–81

Astill G G 1993, *A Medieval Industrial Complex and its Landscape: the Metalworking Watermills and Workshops of Bordesley Abbey* (Council for British Archaeology, Research Report, 92)

Aston M 1972, 'The earthworks of Bordesley Abbey, Redditch, Worcs', *Medieval Archaeology*, 16 (1972), 133–6

Aston M (ed) 1988, *Medieval Fish, Fisheries and Fishponds in England* (2 vols, British Archaeological Reports, Oxford: British Series, 182)

Aston M & Munton A P 1976, 'A survey of Bordesley Abbey and its water control system', in Rahtz, P A & Hirst S, *Bordesley Abbey* (British Archaeological Reports, Oxford: British Series, 23), 24–37

Baillie M 1980, 'Dendrochronology: the Irish view', *Current Archaeology*, 73, 61–3

Baker D 1971, 'Excavations at Elstow Abbey, Bedfordshire, 1968–70', *Beds Archaeol Jnl*, 6, 55–64

Barrett W 1789, *The History and Antiquities of the City of Bristol* (Bristol)

Barrucand M & Bednorz A 1992, *Moorish Architecture in Andalusia* (Rolf Taschen, Cologne)

Bascombe K N 1973, 'A water-conduit head at Wormley', *Herts.Archaeology*, 3, 124–5

Bauer H 1989, 'Die Cloaca Maxima', *Leichtweiss-Institut für Wasserbau der Technishcen Universitat Braunschweig*: Mitteilungen, 103, 43–68

Benoît P 1996, 'Vers une chronologie de l'hydraulique monastique', in Pressouyre & Benoît (1996), 475–86

Benoît P 1998, 'Les aménagements hydrauliques de l'abbaye de Cîteaux du XIIe au XIXe siècle', in Plouvier M & Saint-Denis A (eds), *Pour une Histoire Monumentale de l'Abbaye de Cîteaux* (1098–1998) (Vitreux-Dijon).

Berthier K & Rouillard J 1998, 'Nouvelles recherches sur l'hydraulique cistercienne en Bourgogne, Champagne et Franche-Comté', *Archéologie Médiévale*, 28, 121–47

Biddle M & Keene D J 1976, 'Winchester in the eleventh and twelfth centuries', in Biddle M (ed), *Winchester in the Early Middle Ages: an Edition and Discussion of the Winton Domesday* (Winchester Studies, 1, Oxford), 241–448

Blair J & Ramsay N (eds) 1991, *English Medieval Industries: Craftsmen, Techniques, Products* (Hambledon Press, London)

Blanchard I S W 1981, 'Lead mining and smelting in medieval England and Wales', in Crossley (1981), 72–84

Bloch M 1935, 'Avènement et conquêtes du moulin à l'eau', *Annales d'Histoire Economique et Sociale*, 36, 538–563

Bond C J 1979, 'The reconstruction of the medieval landscape: the estates of Abingdon Abbey', *Landscape History*, 1, 59–75

Bond C J 1988, 'Monastic fisheries', in Aston (1988), i, 69–112

Bond C J 1989, 'Water management in the rural monastery', in Gilchrist & Mytum (1989), 83–111

Bond C J 1991, 'Mittelalterliche Wasserversorgung in England und Wales', in Grewe (1991), 147–83

Bond C J 1993, 'Water management in the urban monastery', in Gilchrist & Mytum (1993), 43–78

Bond C J 1996, 'Le système hydraulique monastique au moyen age en Grande-Bretagne', in Pressouyre & Benoît (1996), 457–73

Brakspear H 1900, 'Lacock Abbey', *Archaeologia*, 57.ii, 125–58

Brakspear H 1903, 'Burnham Abbey', *Records of Bucks*, 8.vi, 517–40

Brakspear H 1905, *Waverley Abbey* (Surrey Archaeological Society, Guildford)

Brakspear H 1908, 'Stanley Abbey', *Wiltshire Archaeology & Natural History Magazine*, 35, 541–81

Brakspear H 1916, 'On the dorter range at Worcester Priory', *Archaeologia*, 67, 189–204

Braunfels W 1972, (trans, Laing A) *Monasteries of Western Europe* (Thames & Hudson, London)

Brown H E 1951, 'Nuneaton Priory: a record of excavation of the eastern range of conventual buildings, 1949 and 1950', *Transactions of Birmingham Archaeological Soc*, 69, 40–3

Brown R A, Colvin H M & Taylor A J 1963, *The History of the King's Works*, 1: *the Middle Ages* (HMSO, London)

Burne R V H 1962, *The Monks of Chester* (SPCK, London)

Bushby G H 1928–33, 'The holy springs of Waltham Abbey at Wormley', *Trans East Hertfordshire Archaeol Soc*, 8, 177–83

Carus-Wilson E M 1941, 'An industrial revolution of the thirteenth century', *Economic Hist Review*, 11, 39–60

Champion E 1996, 'Les moulins à eau dans les polyptiques carolingiens d'entre Loire et Rhin', in Pressoure & Benoît (1996), 321–35

Charles-Edwards T (nd), *Saint Winefride and her Well* (Holywell)

Christie P M & Coad J G 1980, 'Excavations at Denny Abbey', *Archaeol Jnl*, 137, 138–279

Clapham A W 1913, 'The Benedictine Abbey of Barking', *Essex Archaeol Trans*, 12, 69–89

Cloake J 1977, 'The Charterhouse of Sheen', *Surrey Archaeol Collns*, 71, 145–98

Coates-Stephens R 1998, 'The walls and aqueducts of Rome in the early Middle Ages, AD 500–1000', *Jnl of Roman Studies*, 88, 166–78

Colgrave B 1940, *Two Lives of St Cuthbert* (Cambridge University Press)

Conant K J 1973, *Carolingian and Romanesque Architecture, 800–1200* (Pelican History of Art)

Coppack G 1973–6, 'Two late medieval pipe drains from Thetford Priory', *Proc Suffolk Institute of Archaeology*, 33, 88–90

Coppack G 1986, 'The excavation of an outer court building, perhaps the wool-house, at Fountains Abbey, North Yorkshire', *Medieval Archaeol*, 30, 46–87

Coppack G 1990, *Abbeys and Priories* (English Heritage/ B T Batsford, London)

Coppack G 1993, *Fountains Abbey*, B T Batsford/English Heritage, London

Coppack G 1996, 'La chartreuse de Mount Grace (North Yorkshire, Grande-Bretagne): le système hydraulique du XVe siècle: adduction, distribution et évacuation des eaux', in Pressouyre & Benoît (1996), 157–68

Coppack G 1998, 'The water-driven corn mill at Fountains Abbey: a major Cistercian mill of the twelfth and thirteenth centuries', in Lillich M P (ed), *Studies in Cistercian Art and Architecture*, 5, 270–96

Cramp R J 1976, 'Monastic Sites', in Wilson, D M (ed), *The Archaeology of Anglo-Saxon England* (Cambridge), pp 201–252

Crossley D W 1975, *The Bewl Valley Ironworks, Kent, c.1300– 1730 AD* (Royal Archaeological Institute Monograph, London)

Crossley D W (ed) 1981, *Medieval Industry* (Council for British Archaeology, Research Report, 40)

Cruden S 1950–1, 'Glenluce Abbey: recent finds discovered during excavations, part 1', *Trans Dumfries & Galloway Nat Hist & Archaeol Soc*, 3rd ser, 29, 177–94

Currie C K 1989, 'The role of fishponds in the monastic economy', in Gilchrist & Mytum (1989), 147–72

Davies A Morley 1913, 'London's first conduit system – a topographical study', *Trans London & Middlesex Archaeological Soc*, new ser, 2, 9–59

Davey N 1964, 'A pre-Conquest church and baptistry at

Potterne', *Wilts Archaeological & Natural History Mag*, 59 (1964), 116–23

David C 1971, *St Winifride's Well: a History and Guide*

Dickinson J C 1950, *The Origin of the Austin Canons and their Introduction into England* (SPCK, London)

Donkin R A 1978, *The Cistercians: Studies in the Geography of Medieval England and Wales* (Pontifical Institute of Mediaeval Studies, Studies & Texts 38, Toronto)

Duby G 1968, trans Postan C, *Rural Economy and Country Life in the Medieval West* (Columbia, SC)

Duby G 1974, trans. Clarke H B, *The Early Growth of the European Economy* (Ithaca, New York)

Durham B, *et al* 1991, 'The infirmary and hall of the medieval hospital of St John the Baptist at Oxford', *Oxoniensia*, 56, 17–75

Evans H B 1997, *Water Distribution in Ancient Rome: the Evidence of Frontinus* (Univ of Michigan Press, Ann Arbor, 2nd edn, 1997)

Evans J 1938, *The Romanesque Architecture of the Order of Cluny* (Cambridge)

Everson P L, Taylor C C & Dunn C J 1991, *Change and Continuity: Rural Settlement in North-West Lincolnshire* (Royal Commission on Historical Monuments, England)

Fawcett R 1994, *Scottish Abbeys and Priories* (Scottish Heritage / BT Batsford, London)

Ferguson E 1990, 'Baptism' and 'Baptistery', in Ferguson E (ed), *Encyclopaedia of Early Christianity* (St James Press, Chicago & London), pp 131–4, 135–7

Fisher M J C 1969, *Dieulacres Abbey, Staffordshire* (Stafford)

Fowler R C 1907, 'Religious houses', in Page W & Round J H (eds), *The Victoria History of the County of Essex* (London)

Fulbrook-Leggatt L E W O 1968, 'The water supplies of the abbey of St Peter and the priory of the Grey Friars, Gloucester, from Robinswood Hill', *Trans Bristol & Gloucs Archaeol Soc*, 87, 111–18

Gies F & Gies J 1994, *Cathedral, Forge and Waterwheel: Technology and Invention in the Middle Ages* (Harper Collins, New York)

Gilchrist R 1994, *Gender and Material Culture: the Archaeology of Religious Women* (Routledge, London & New York)

Gilchrist R & Mytum H (eds) 1989, *The Archaeology of Rural Monasteries* (British Archaeological Reports, Oxford: British Series, 203)

Gilchrist R & Mytum H (eds) 1993, *Advances in Monastic Archaeology* (British Archaeological Reports, Oxford: British Series, 227)

Gilyard-Beer R 1960, *Cleeve Abbey, Somerset* (HMSO)

Gimpel J 1988, *The Medieval Machine: the Industrial Revolution of the Middle Ages* (2nd edn, Wildwood House, Aldershot)

Godfrey W H 1949, 'English cloister lavatories as independent structures', *Archaeol Jnl*, 106, Supplement

Gould J 1976, 'The twelfth-century water supply to Lichfield Close', *Antiq Jnl*, 56.i, 73–79

Graham A H 1986, 'The Old Malthouse, Abbotsbury: the medieval watermill of the Benedictine Abbey', *Proc Dorset Nat Hist & Archaeol Soc*, 108, 103–25

Graham R 1907, 'Abbey of Kingswood', in *The Victoria History of the County of Gloucestershire*, 2, 99–101

Greene P 1989, *Norton Priory: the Archaeology of a Medieval Religious House* (Cambridge University Press)

Greenhalgh M 1989, *The Survival of Roman Antiquities in the Middle Ages* (Duckworth, London)

Grewe K (ed) 1991, *Die Wasserversorgung im Mittelalter* (Frontinus-Gesellschaft, Geschichte der Wasserversorgung, 4: Verlag Philipp von Zabern, Mainz)

Grewe K 1991, 'Die Wasserversorgungsplan des Klosters Christchurch in Canterbury (12 Jahrhundert)', in Grewe (1991), 229–36

Grewe K 1996, 'Le monastère de Christchurch à Cantorbery (Kent, Grande-Bretagne): interpretation et signification du plan du réseau hydraulique (XIIe siècle)', in Pressouyre & Benoît (1996), 123–34

Grüger H 1984, 'Cistercian fountain houses in central Europe', in Lillich, M M (ed), *Studies in Cistercian Art and Architecture*, 2 (Cistercian Studies 69, Kalamazoo, USA), 201–222

Guillerme A E 1988, *Les Temps de l'Eau: la Cité, l'Eau et les Techniques* (Editions du Champ Vallon, Seyssel, 1983; transl as *The Age of Water; the Urban Envionment in the North of France, AD 300–1800* (Texas A & M University Press, College Station, 1988)

Gunter R T 1916, 'On the architecture of the Hospital of St John', in Salter, H E (ed), *A Cartulary of the Hospital of St John the Baptist*, 3 (Oxford Historical Soc Vol 69), 393–434

Hall D 1992, 'The Fenland Project no 6: The South-Western Cambridgeshire Fenlands', *East Anglian Archaeology*, 56 (1992), 42)

Hall D J 1965, *English Mediaeval Pilgrimage* (Routledge & Kegan Paul, London)

Hare J N 1985, *Battle Abbey: the Eastern Range and the Excavations of 1978–80* (Historic Buildings & Monuments Commission for England, Archaeological Report no 2)

Harvey J 1981, *Mediaeval Gardens* (BT Batsford, London)

Harvey P D A 1968, 'A thirteenth-century plan from Waltham Abbey, Essex', *Imago Mundi*, 22, 10–12

Harvey P D A 1986, 'Wormley, Hertfordshire, 1220x1230', in Skelton, R A & Harvey P D A (eds), *Local Maps and Plans from Medieval England* (Clarendon Press, Oxford), 59–70)

Heighway C 1988 'Archaeology in the precinct of Gloucester Cathedral, 1983–5', *Glevensis*, 22, 29–37

Hibbert F A 1909, *Monasticism in Staffordshire* (Stafford).

Higginbotham J 1997, *Piscinae: Artificial Fishponds in Roman Italy* (University of North Carolina Press, Chapel Hill)

Hill P *et al.* 1997, *Whithorn and St Ninian: the Excavation of a Monastic Town, 1984–91* (Whithorn Trust & Sutton Publishing, Stroud)

Hinds A B 1896, *A History of Northumberland*, 3, *Hexhamshire*, part i (Newcastle-upon-Tyne)

Hodge A T 1991, *Roman Aqueducts & Water Supply* (Duckworth, London)

Hole C 1954, *English Shrines and Sanctuaries* (Batsford, London)

Hollinrake C & Hollinrake N 1991, 'A late Saxon monastic enclosure ditch and canal, Glastonbury, Somerset', *Antiquity*, 65, 117–8

Hollinrake C & Hollinrake N 1992, 'The abbey enclosure ditch and a late-Saxon canal: rescue excavations at

Glastonbury, 1984–1988', *Proc Somerset Archaeol & Nat Hist Soc*, 136, 73–94

Holt R 1988, *The Mills of Medieval England* (Basil Blackwell, Oxford)

Homer R F 1991, 'Tin, lead and pewter', in Blair & Ramsay (1991), 57–80

Hope W H St J 1886, 'The archaeological history of the Cluniac priory of St Pancras at Lewes', *Sussex Archaeological Collns*, 34, 71–106

Hope W H St J 1900a, 'Fountains Abbey', *Yorks Archaeol Jnl*, 15, 269–402

Hope W H St J 1900b, 'The abbey of St Mary in Furness, Lancashire', *Trans Cumberland & Westmorland Antiq & Archaeol Soc*, old ser, 16, 221–302

Hope W H St J 1902, 'The London Charterhouse and its old water supply', *Archaeologia*, 58, i, 293–312

Hope W H St J 1903, 'Recent discoveries in the Cloister of Durham Abbey', *Archaeologia*, 58, ii, 437–60

Hope W H St J 1906, 'The Cluniac priory of St Pancras at Lewes', *Sussex Archaeological Collns*, 49, 66–88

Hope W H St J & Brakspear H 1906, 'The Cistercian abbey of Beaulieu in the County of Southampton', *Archaeol Jnl*, 58, 129–86

Horn W 1975, 'Water Power and the Plan of St Gall', *Jnl of Medieval History*, 1, 219–57

Horn W & Born E 1979, *The Plan of St Gall: A Study of the Architecture and Economy* (California Studies in the History of Art, 19, 3 vols, Berkeley, California)

Humphreys K W 1990, *The Friars' Libraries* (Corpus of British Medieval Library Catalogues; British Library / British Academy)

Hunt N 1967, *Cluny under St Hugh, 1049–1109* (London)

Hurry J B 1901 *Reading Abbey* (Eliot Stock, London)

Hurst H 1899, *Oxford Topography* (Oxford Historical Soc, 39)

Jones F 1954, *The Holy Wells of Wales* (University of Wales Press, Cardiff)

Ker N R (ed) 1964, *Medieval Libraries of Great Britain: a List of Surviving Books* (Royal Historical Soc Guides & Handbooks, 3, 2nd edn)

Kosch C 1991, 'Wasserbaueinrichtungen in Hoch-Mittelalterlichen Konventanlagen Mitteleuropas', in Grewe (1991), 89–146

Latimer J 1901, 'The Hospital of St John, Bristol', *Trans Bristol & Gloucs Archaeol Soc*, 24, 172–8

Lillich M P 1982, 'Cleanliness and Godliness: a discussion of medieval monastic plumbing', in Chauvin B (ed), *Mélanges a la Mémoire du pere Anselme Dimier*, 3, v, (Arbois), 123–49

Lindley E S 1954, 1955, 'Kingswood Abbey, its lands and mills', *Trans Bristol & Gloucs Archaeological Soc*, 73, 115–91, 74, 36–59

Little A G 1891, *The Grey Friars in Oxford* (Oxford Historical Soc, 20)

Little A G & Easterling R C 1927, *The Franciscans and Dominicans of Exeter* (History of Exeter Research Group, Monograph 3)

Lobel M D 1975, 'Bristol', in Lobel, M D & Johns W H (eds), *The Atlas of Historic Towns*, 2 (Johns Hopkins University Press, Baltimore)

Lyne M 1997, *Lewes Priory: Excavations by Richard Lewis, 1969–82* (Lewes Priory Trust, 1997)

McDonnell J 1981, *Inland Fisheries in Medieval Yorkshire, 1066–1300* (Borthwick Papers, 60, York)

McDonnell J & Everest M R 1965, 'The "waterworks" of Byland Abbey', *Ryedale Historian*, 1, 32–9

Manco J 1993, 'The buildings of Bath Priory', *Proc Somerset Archaeol & Nat Hist Soc*, 137, 75–109

Martin A R 1937, *Franciscan Architecture in England* (Manchester University Press)

Med Arch, Annual summaries of work in *Medieval Archaeology*

Micklethwaite J T 1876, 'Notes on the abbey buildings of Westminster', *Archaeological Jnl*, 33, 15–48

Micklethwaite J T 1892, 'On a filtering system of the fourteenth century at Westminster Abbey', *Archaeologia*, 53, 161–70

Micklethwaite J T 1896, 'Something about Saxon church building', *Archaeological Jnl*, 53, 333–5.

Moorhouse S & Wrathmell S 1987, *Kirkstall Abbey, 1: The 1950–64 Excavations: a Reassessment* (West Yorkshire Archaeological Service, Wakefield)

Mytum H C 1979, 'Excavations at Polesworth', *Trans Birmingham & Warwickshire Archaeol Soc*, 89, 79–90

Noake J 1866, *The Monastery and Cathedral of Worcester* (Longman & co, London)

Norman P 1899, 'On an ancient conduit-head in Queen Square, Bloomsbury', *Archaeologia*, 56, 251–66

Norman P 1915–16, 'Recent discoveries of medieval remains in London', *Archaeologia*, 67, 1–26

Norman P & Mann E A 1909, 'On the White Conduit, Chapel Street, Bloomsbury, and its connexion with the Grey Friars' water system', *Archaeologia*, 61, 347–56

Peers C 1902, 'The Benedictine nunnery of Little Marlow', *Archaeol Jnl*, 59, 307–25

Philp B 1968, *Excavations at Faversham, 1965* (Kent Archaeological Research Group Council, 1st Research Report)

Pressouyre L (ed) 1994, *L'Espace Cistercien*, Proceedings of Fontfroide Colloqium, 24–27 March 1993 (Comité des Travaux Historiques et Scientifiques, Mémoires de la Section d'Archéologie et d'Histoire de l'Art, 5, Paris)

Pressouyre L & Benoît P (eds) 1996, *L'Hydraulique Monastique: Milieux, Réseaux, Usages*, Proceedings of Royaumont Colloqium, 18–20 June 1992 (Collection "Rencontres à Royaumont", Editions Créaphis, Grane)

Radford C A R 1960, 'The excavations at Glastonbury Abbey, 1959', *Somerset & Dorset Notes & Queries*, 27, 251–5

Rahtz P A 1963–4, 'Excavations at Chalice Well, Glastonbury', *Proc Somerset Archaeol & Nat Hist Soc*, 108, 145–63

Rahtz P A & Bullough D 1977, 'The parts of an Anglo-Saxon mill', *Anglo-Saxon England*, 6, 15–37

Raine J (ed) 1863, *The Priory of Hexham: its Chroniclers, Endowments and Annals*, i (Surtees Soc, 44)

Richardson L 1955, 'The geology of Worcester', *Trans Worcester Naturalists' Field Club*, 11.i, 29–67

Richardson J S & Wood M 1981, *Melrose Abbey* (HMSO)

RCHM Camb 1959, *An Inventory of Historical Monuments in the City of Cambridge* (3 parts, Royal Commission on Historical Monuments, England)

RCHME 1996, *An Earthwork Survey at Stanley Abbey*

RCAMS Roxburgh 1956, *An Inventory of the Ancient and Historical Monuments of Roxburghshire*, 2 (Royal Commission on Ancient Monuments of Scotland, Edinburgh

Robinson D M 1980, *The Geography of Augustinian Settlement in Medieval England and Wales* (British Archaeological Reports, Oxford: British Series, 80)

Robinson D M 1981, 'The site changes of Augustinian communities in medieval England and Wales', *Mediaeval Studies*, 43, 425–55

Rodwell W & Rodwell K 1982, 'St Peter's Church, Barton-upon-Humber: Excavation and Structural Study, 1978–81', *Antiquaries Jnl*, 67.i, 283–315

Rye H 1900, 'Rievaulx Abbey, its canals and building stones', *Archaeol Jnl*, 57 (2nd ser., 7), 69–88

Salzman L F 1913, *English Industries of the Middle Ages* (Constable & Co., London)

Searle E 1974, *Lordship and Community: Battle Abbey and its Banlieu, 1066–1538* (Pontifical Institute of Mediaeval Studies, Toronto, Studies & Texts, 26)

Selkirk A 1993, 'Hoddom', *Current Archaeology*, 135, 88–92

Shaw S 1798, 1801, *History and Antiquities of Staffordshire* (2 vols, reprinted 1976, ed Greenslade, M W & Baugh G C)

Shelmerdine T 1878, 'Notes on the excavations at Muchelney', *Proceedings of Somerset Archaeology & Natural History Soc*, 24, ii, 67–74

Sheppard J 1958, *The Draining of the Hull Valley* (E Yorks Local Hist Soc)

Singer C, Holmyard E J, Hall A R. & Williams T I (eds, 1956) *A History of Technology*, 2: *The Mediterranean Civilizations and the Middle Ages* (Oxford University Press)

Sonnet B 1984, 'Le pont des Arvaux', *Mem de la Comm des Antiquités de la Cote d'Or*, 34 (1984–6)

Stephens G R 1985 'Civic aqueducts in Britain', *Britannia*, 16, 197–208

Symons Dom T 1926, 'The monastic observance of the Regularis Concordia', *Downside Review*, 44, 157–71

Syson L 1965, *British Water-Mills* (B T Batsford, London)

Talbot C H 1954, *The Anglo-Saxon Missionaries in Germany* (Sheen & Ward, London & New York)

Taylor H M 1969, 'The Anglo-Saxon cathedral church at Canterbury', *Archaeological Jnl*, 126, 101–30

Tester P J 1967, 'Excavations on the site of Higham Priory', *Archaeologia Cantiana*, 82, 143–61

Urry W 1967, *Canterbury under the Angevin Kings* (Athlone Press, London)

VCH various dates, *The Victoria History of the Counties of England*

Ward-Perkins B 1988, 'The towns of northern Italy: rebirth or renewal ?', in Hodges R & Hobley B (eds), *The Rebirth of Towns in the West, AD 700–1050* (Council for British Archaeology, Research Report 68), 16–27

Weatherill J 1954, 'Rievaulx Abbey: the stone used in its building, with notes on the means of transport, and a new study of the diversion of the River Rye in the twelfth century', *Yorks Archaeol Jnl*, 38, 333–54

Welander D 1991, *The History, Art and Architecture of Gloucester Cathedral* (Alan Sutton, Stroud)

White K D 1970, *Roman Farming* (Thames & Hudson, London)

Williams D H 1990, *Atlas of Cistercian Lands in Wales* (University of Wales Press, Cardiff)

Williams D H 1998, *The Cistercians in the Early Middle Ages* (Gracewing, Leominster)

Williams M 1970, *The Draining of the Somerset Levels* (Cambridge University Press)

Williams T W 1897, *Somerset Medieval Libraries* (Somerset Archaeological & Natural History Soc., Bristol)

Willis R 1868, 'The architectural history of the conventual buildings of the monastery of Christ Church in Canterbury', *Archaeol Cantiana*, 7, 1–206

Wood A. ed Peshall J 1773, *The Antient and Present State of the City of Oxford* (J & F Rivington, London)

Zeepvat R J 1988, 'Fishponds in Roman Britain', in Aston (1988), i, 17–26

7 Pieces of Patterns – Archaeological Approaches to Monastic Sites in Oxfordshire

G D Keevill

Abstract

This paper examines the extent to which pre-determined concepts of what a medieval monastic site looked like influence contemporary attitudes to their archaeological study. In particular it addresses attempts to assess such sites, whether through excavations up to the 1980s or through projects of various sizes including evaluations during the 1990s. The emphasis on sampling is questioned through an appraisal of archaeological fieldwork results on Oxfordshire's abbeys.

Introduction

Archaeology and monastic sites

Archaeological approaches to the study of monastic sites have varied substantially over the last hundred years. The initial concentration during the late 19th and early 20th century on delineating the central monastic buildings (the church and, to a slightly lesser extent, the cloister) was often driven by contemporary requirements for (and concepts of) display (Coppack 1990, 18–30). Regrettably post-medieval deposits were often cleared without any significant attempt to make an archaeological record, an omission which cannot now be rectified on the relevant sites. The discovery of three lead ingots under post-Dissolution rubble at the west end of Rievaulx Abbey's nave in 1920 provided a hint of the information which could be gleaned from such deposits (Dunning 1952).

The second half of the 20th century has seen an increasing realisation that the wider monastic landscape is equally worthy of study, in many ways pre-figured by St John Hope's remarkable study of Hulne Abbey, Northumberland (St John Hope 1890). Our sights have been raised above the altar and our gaze has extended beyond the cloister, and more projects have examined the service buildings of the inner and outer wards/courts of the precinct. Projects have included structural, earthwork and documentary surveys as well as excavations, and have looked at associated sites such as granges as well as the abbeys themselves.

The trend towards site evaluations in the last decade or so, especially following the publication of PPG16 (DoE 1990), has seen a number of monastic sites subjected to trial trenching, although this is scarcely a new approach to such sites (see below). This strong emphasis on site evaluation has led to further increases in the amount of monastic archaeology being undertaken, but the generally small scale of these projects has made them more difficult to interpret, and analysis has been at a premium. At the same time, financial pressures in a sluggish economy, and the pervasive atmosphere of 'preservation by record', have made it more difficult to establish large-scale excavation and survey projects.

The phrase 'Pieces of Patterns' in the title of this paper is therefore deliberately double-edged. The raw material will not only be monastic sites themselves, and patterns within them, but also patterns within archaeological studies of the sites, and their advisability or otherwise in some cases. The city and (modern) county of Oxford has been chosen as a starting point largely for pragmatic reasons, but some of the issues raised may be more generally applicable.

Oxfordshire monasteries and their archaeology

The city and county of Oxford contain numerous monastic sites, and these have received varying degrees of archaeological attention: some little or none, others extensive surveys and excavations. The various abbeys, priories and other sites received relatively little attention from 19th- and early 20th-century antiquarians, and even in Oxford itself more effort was expended on documentary and architectural research despite the early steps then being taken towards a recognisably modern archaeology (Hassall 1987, 3–4). The efforts of Rev Chambers and others at the turn of the century in publishing the Cartularies and other documentary archives of the major abbeys in the county provided an invaluable resource for anyone studying these sites, but a comparable campaign of archaeological research was not forthcoming. Pioneering work was undertaken at Abingdon in the 1920s, however, and most of the county's monasteries have received some archaeological attention since then.

The limits of the county set during local government reorganisation in 1974 have been used in preparing this study. This creates some anomalies compared to the historic structure of Berkshire and Oxfordshire, the most serious of which is the inclusion of Abingdon Abbey in Oxfordshire. This approach reflects other recent studies of the county (most notably Briggs *et al* 1986) as well as the reality of the archaeological database for the modern shire, centred on the County Sites and Monuments Record. The latter represents the most important source consulted for the study, although other resources used include the Victoria County History volumes for Berkshire and Oxfordshire, published excavation reports, and archives held by the Oxford Archaeological Unit. Much of the initial work on this survey was carried out by Nicoletta Vollu, whose assistance is gratefully acknowledged.

This case study is intended to provide a brief introduction to the sites, the ways they have been studied, and the results of the studies. Space does not permit detailed descriptions of the sites, but the paper will seek to assess the relationship between study methods and the results and interpretations thereby generated. The following sections therefore provide an outline of studies on the major sites (mostly undertaken by the Oxford Archaeological Unit), with an assessment of the validity of interpretations where relevant. The final section discusses the wider implications of this study and attempts to set the Oxfordshire evidence in a wider context.

Oxford

The history of Oxford is inextricably linked with monasticism. This paper concentrates mostly on monasteries *per se*, although the monastic aspect of collegiate Oxford can scarcely be overstated. There were several major abbeys and friaries in and around the city (such as Oseney and Rewley Abbeys, and the houses of the Blackfriars, Greyfriars

and several more besides), as well as monastic colleges and hospitals. The vast majority of these establishments post-date the Norman conquest, although there is strong evidence for a 9th-century priory associated with the legend of St Frideswide (Blair 1987; Scull 1990), and there was a broadly contemporary minster church at Binsey to the west of the (later) urban area (Blair 1987 and 1990a). At least 24 monastic establishments existed in and around Oxford by the 14th century. There were colleges and hospitals within the walls, but more importantly there was a ring of major abbeys, friaries and colleges around the defences (OAU 1994). These sites formed a buffer zone of largely open ground outside the walls, preventing extensive suburban development around much of the south and west sides of the circuit until the post-medieval period (Hassall *et al* 1984).

It is also true that many of these sites survived so well as archaeological sites precisely because they lay immediately outside the core of the city and thus only fell under serious threat from development in recent decades. Most of the city's monastic sites have received some archaeological attention, often on a small but valuable scale (cf Hiller 1994 on Godstow Abbey to the north of the city). Unfortunately in several cases (including those which have seen the most extensive work) redevelopment occurred during the 1960s and 1970s, before archaeology had attained the strong position within the planning and development control process that it now enjoys. Consequently much of the archaeological work was poorly-funded and supported, and relied upon developers' and authorities' goodwill. It is a very real tribute to the perseverance and dedication of those who were involved in archaeology at this time, in Oxford and elsewhere, that so much information was retrieved. Nevertheless one cannot help but lament the lost opportunities for more extensive work on these sites.

St Frideswide's Priory

The Saxon and medieval priory dedicated to St Frideswide (a figure known from local hagiography: Blair 1987) underlies and is partly encapsulated in Christchurch Cathedral, which lies within the city defences immediately to the east of the South Gate. The cathedral and priory have been the subject of extensive archaeological and architectural surveys (see papers in Blair 1990b). There have also been several significant excavations (Scull 1990; Sturdy 1990), although these have not been on a large scale and they have provided few data on the monastic configuration. The most important work was undoubtedly the cloister excavation of 1985. This revealed fourteen pre-Conquest inhumations, four of which were radiocarbon-dated to the 9th-10th centuries (Scull 1990, 60–2). Burials pre-dating the refoundation of the priory as a house of Augustinian Canons in 1122 were found in and outside the north-east chapels of the Cathedral in 1963 (Sturdy 1990), while graves excavated in Tom Quad during 1972 (Hassall 1973) may belong to the same cemetery. Other discoveries have not been as significant, although the substantial stone-built foundations of a 16th-century possible belfry/campanile are of more than local interest (Scull 1990, 66–72) and the information on successive arrangements within the Cathedral's Latin Chapel is useful (Sturdy 1990).

Rewley Abbey

Few people who enter modern Oxford by train realise that the station is adjacent to one of the city's most important religious houses, but Rewley Abbey spreads eastward from the railway towards the Castle Mill Stream. Rewley was a Cistercian foundation of 1282, and it enjoyed something of a double life as abbey and *studium*. Although many of the monastic buildings survived the Dissolution and were used into the 19th century, only a stretch of the medieval curtain wall survives today, including a fine gate. Much of the precinct was used as a coal depot in modern times, accounting for a thick layer of rubble over most of the site. Rewley is protected as a Scheduled Ancient Monument, but it has been the subject of a major redevelopment at the end of the second millennium.

There have been several trial excavations at Rewley Abbey, usually because of proposed developments, and the trenches have revealed parts of the church, claustral ranges, and an encircling moat. The results have undoubtedly been valuable, and the most recent work by David Wilkinson in 1993–4 produced important evidence for the domestic buildings, including a reredorter spanning the moat. The evaluation was largely intended to establish how the current redevelopment could be designed within the Scheduled area so as to minimise impact on the monastic archaeology, and it has been demonstrably successful in this respect. The work does, however, highlight the frustrations of evaluation by trial trenching and the necessarily limited extent of excavation (and therefore interpretation) on such projects (Wilkinson 1994): the presumption that remains should be preserved for the future is laudable, but it does mean that we still only have a very broad outline plan of this very important abbey even after several seasons of quite extensive work. Equally seriously, trial trenches can only provide a glimpse into the wider context of the remains, and the interpretative potential of the data recovered is severely limited.

Oseney Abbey (Fig 7.1)

Oseney, separated from the city by the St Thomas suburb, was an Augustinian abbey founded in 1129. It became one of the wealthiest houses of the Order in England, but once again very little has survived to the present day, although a medieval building does represent an important survival (Bond 1986, 144). There is much useful documentary, cartographic and pictorial evidence for the site, although most of the drawn evidence post-dates the Dissolution (Sharpe 1985, 109–17). Small-scale excavations and observations added further data during the 1970s and 1980s (Sharpe 1985), while a number of evaluation trenches were excavated in 1994 (Booth 1994). This work has shown that the archaeology survives in a variable, but often extremely good condition, with evidence for buildings, floors, surfaces and other features. Unfortunately the work has been so piecemeal that the archaeological data are extremely difficult to interpret meaningfully in their own right. The interpretative building plan published by Sharpe (1985, fig. 8) relies strongly on documentary, cartographic and pictorial sources, and the archaeological information it contains does not always accord well with the other evidence.

The Blackfriars and Greyfriars sites (Figs 7.2 and 7.3)

The two friaries on the south side of the city defences between the South Gate and the Castle have been the subject of the most intensive archaeological work on Oxford's monasteries. This was largely dictated by the pace of development from the early 1960s through to the 1980s, especially on the Westgate precinct and its associated car parks, and the published reports demonstrate the considerable restrictions of time, funding and access which inevitably affected what could be achieved on the projects. The two sites were founded within a few years of each other: the Blackfriars in 1221 (strictly speaking a refoundation, as the Dominicans had previously occupied a cramped site in the city's Jewish quarter), and the Greyfriars in 1224. There is little to be seen of either site now, although the Blackfriars' gateway does survive (Lambrick, in Lambrick and Woods 1976, 200–2).

The excavations from the 1960s to 1980s were usually small-scale in any one year (Lambrick and Woods 1976; Lambrick 1985; Hassall *et al* 1989, 140–94), although they often conjoined to make larger composite areas (most notably on the Greyfriars' church; Hassall *et al* 1989, especially fig. 25). It is remarkable that so much information was retrieved from these excavations given the constraints already referred to, and the general plans of the Blackfriars' site as a whole (Fig 7.2) and the Greyfriars' church

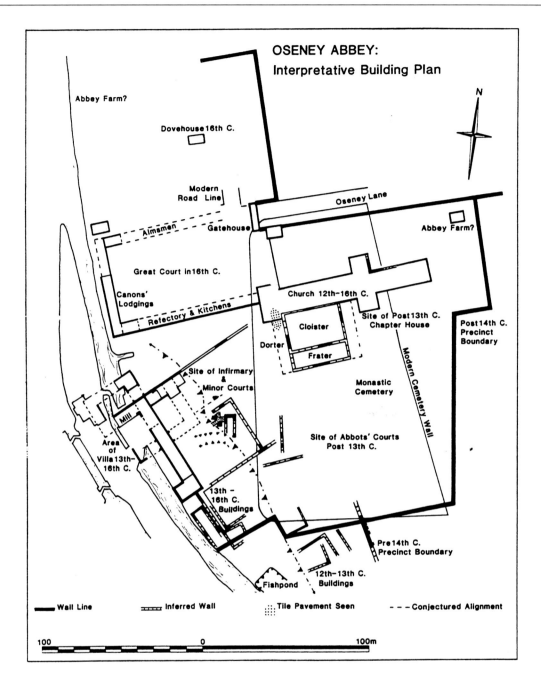

Fig 7.1 *Summary plan of Oseney Abbey excavations (after Sharpe 1985; copyright Oxfordshire Architectural and Historical Society)*

(Fig 7.3) are fairly well understood (although some details of interpretation may be questionable) because of the work. Nevertheless the excavations suffer from many of the difficulties which bedevil Rewley and Oseney, and interpretation of the Blackfriars' groundplan is at least partly predicated upon preconceived notions of medieval monastic layouts which go back to the work of Brakspear, St John Hope and others, along with presumptions about the Order itself. The further one gets from the claustral heart the more hazy the interpretation becomes. Moreover, interpretation of the internal monastic context is extremely difficult (eg the detailed arrangements within most buildings), whether within the sites or between them. The layout of the Greyfriars' site south of the church itself is virtually incomprehensible; as Hassall states (1989, 193):

> The area trenched to the south-west [referring here to the cloister] also contained substantial wall remains, but only open-area excavation could satisfactorily explain the layout of the building. In fig. 42 the walls of

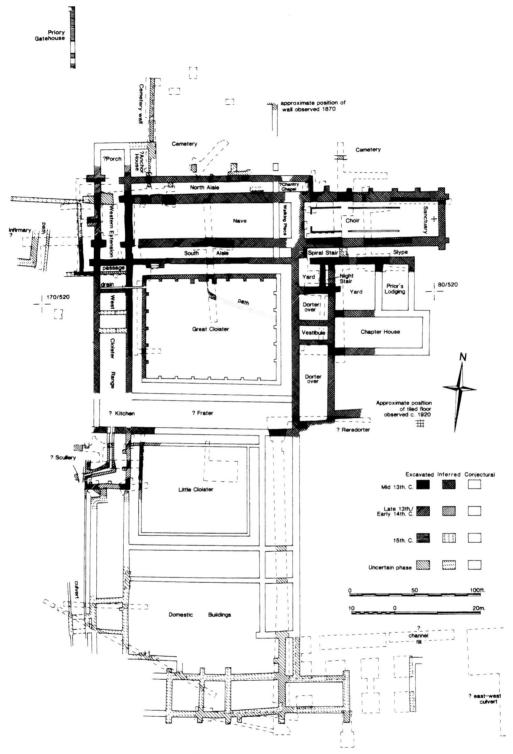

Fig 7.2 *Summary plan of the Oxford Blackfriars excavation results (after Lambrick 1985; copyright Oxfordshire Architectural and Historical Society)*

the conventual building have been projected and joined up when they aligned. While this has produced a schematic plan, detailed interpretation of function is not possible.

Much the same was said about Blackfriars (Lambrick 1985, 133):

These [rapid trenching and salvage] methods are less than ideal, but have again proved reasonably cost-effective in recovering basic information, though this is certainly at the expense of much valuable detail which might have been recovered had resources been available for larger-scale work.

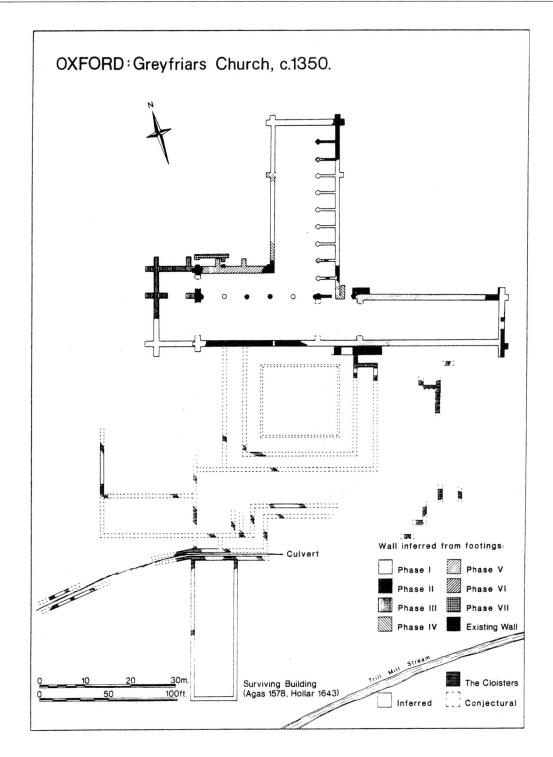

Fig 7.3 *Summary plan of the Oxford Greyfriars excavation results (after Hassall et al 1989; copyright Oxfordshire Architectural and Historical Society)*

The report goes on to emphasize that "the skeleton of the plan – the church and great cloister – was built to a regular, predictable pattern", though "numerous irregularities and some puzzles" were admitted (Lambrick 1985, 207). Interestingly, and certainly more contentiously, on the same page Lambrick suggests that larger-scale excavation could have been less cost-effective in terms of data retrieval. Unfortunately this contention cannot now be challenged in the substantial area of the nave and north-west cloister which was destroyed during the development. The resourcing difficulties of the Blackfriars and Greyfriars excavations were common to many projects of that era, however, and there is an inevitable limit to what the archaeologist can achieve in such circumstances.

Abingdon

The Benedictine abbey at Abingdon was one of the most important of all English religious houses, with a tradition stretching (however unreliably) into the early years of Anglo-Saxon Christianity. The house enjoyed considerable wealth and importance in the post-Conquest period, becoming "by far the wealthiest monastic house in the Upper Thames region" (Bond 1979, 143). Its importance is reflected in the attention it has received from historians and archaeologists alike. Stenton (1913) produced an important study of the main documentary evidence for the Saxon foundation (but see Lambrick, 26–34, in Biddle 1968), and Jope (1948) wrote an important study of building supplies to the abbey making strong use of the 14th- and 15th-century Obedientiaries' Accounts. More recently James Bond, a pioneer of landscape archaeology, has produced a seminal analysis of the abbey's estates, incorporating much new and detailed survey work (Bond 1979). The extensive excavation of the abbey's grange property at Dean Court, Cumnor, on the west edge of Oxford adds a further dimension to our understanding of the house (Allen 1994).

There have been several studies, then, which have sought to place the abbey within its wider historical and landscape context, but what of the precinct itself? Here too Abingdon has been the subject of intensive investigation. Gabrielle Lambrick (in Biddle 1968, 42–59) produced a detailed documentary survey of the disposition of buildings etc within the precinct through the Saxon and medieval periods. The first significant excavations took place in 1922, when the Berkshire Archaeological Society formed a small committee to organise trial excavations under the general supervision of Charles Peers and Alfred Clapham (Biddle 1968, 60). Numerous long, narrow trenches were excavated across the church buildings and cloister, with the main aims of establishing the plan (at least in outline) and assessing the survival of any evidence for the Anglo-Saxon abbey (see Biddle 1968, 62–5, for a full summary of the limited but important discoveries). This much was achieved with reasonable success (at least in the church; very little significant information was retrieved in the cloister), but still we know little beyond the outline of the plan.

The reconstructed trench plan (Biddle 1968, fig 12) is remarkable for being so reminiscent of many modern evaluation trench plans and the work on the Oxford Blackfriars and Greyfriars (above). The method of laying out the trenches was scarcely subtle:

"the excavators ... cut [trenches] at right-angles across the probable site of the walls. Once rubble-filled [robber] trenches had been found, parallel cuts were taken and if rubble filling appeared at corresponding points, lines connecting these rubble fillings ... were thought to give the lines of the required walls." (Biddle 1968, 65)

and the recording was "inadequate even by comparison with other amateur excavations of its day" (Biddle 1968, 61). Nevertheless important data were recovered at relatively little expense in terms of damage to the site, and no further work has been undertaken which would improve the published plan. The abbey church and surrounding area is now a Scheduled Ancient Monument with the legal protection that affords, and it is hard to see any significant excavation taking place here in the foreseeable future.

Having said that, very extensive excavations have taken place within the non-Scheduled part of the precinct known as the Vineyard during the late 1980s and the 1990s. Tim Allen has revealed important structural evidence such as: part of a chapel (probably that of the Holy Cross: Lambrick, 50, in Biddle 1968); a free-standing belfry/campanile similar to that at Christchurch, Oxford (above): the Convent ditch with the timber footings of a bridge preserved in its base by waterlogging; and the lay cemetery on the far side of the Convent ditch from the abbey buildings. Evidence for about 1000 medieval graves was revealed by these excavations (Allen 1990). This work provides important information about the arrangement of the outlying church buildings within the inner part of the precinct, forming an invaluable adjunct to and test of Gabrielle Lambrick's documentary work mentioned above. Furthermore the skeletal remains from the lay cemetery are an extremely important resource, especially as the excavations also revealed a separate Civil War cemetery from which about 250 skeletons were excavated (Allen 1990, 27). More recently a geophysical survey in 1998 by Alister Bartlett for Tim Allen and the Oxford Archaeological Unit has provided a very detailed plan of the monastic church.

Other Oxfordshire Monasteries

With the exception of the recent project at Eynsham Abbey (below), the remaining monastic sites in the county have received relatively low-level attention. The Augustinian abbey at Dorchester-on-Thames, for instance, has received negligible investigation, comprising antiquarian work in the 17th and 19th centuries and three small trenches of limited value dug in 1961–2 (Cunningham and Banks 1972; Doggett 1986). At Bicester Priory (Augustinian) work was restricted to a watching brief by a local schoolboy, who recorded structural evidence for the church and claustral ranges. Detailed interpretation of the observations is inevitably difficult because operational constraints meant that recording was largely restricted to the location of walls and foundations, though fragments of floors and other features were also seen. Without this individual dedication (and no little skill in recording) "all record of the site would have been completely lost" (Hinton 1968, 22), but establishment of the general plan layout and identification of individual buildings must rely once again on assumptions regarding the "typical" abbey plan.

The alien Benedictine priory at Cogges, Witney, has been investigated more extensively, although the site is atypical and resembled a grange as much as a priory (Blair and Steane 1982). The remains of a nunnery at Minchery Farm to the south of Oxford are well-known and were surveyed by Pantin (1970). The Benedictine priory at Wallingford has not been investigated archaeologically, and a Cistercian grange at Swalcliffe has fared little better, although the owners apparently revealed foundations over an extensive area (Oxfordshire Sites and Monuments Record PRN 10449). Finally unpublished excavations at the Augustinian priory at Wroxton are said to have revealed conduits and foundations of outbuildings (in 1956) as well as part of the church in 1964 and 1966 (Oxfordshire Sites and Monuments Record PRN 4819).

The Eynsham Abbey Project

Such small excavations as have just been described are inevitably frustrating (even where they have been published) because they provide a glimpse of what is often far greater potential (cf the conduits etc at Wroxton Priory). This problem has been tackled in recent years at Eynsham Abbey, where a major project from 1989–93 studied the evidence for a middle Saxon minster, a late Saxon Benedictine abbey and its post-Conquest successor, and the post-medieval use of at least part of the site as a manorial centre. The work has involved evaluations, small-scale and large open-area excavations, geophysical and earthwork surveys, and a brief survey of the (Church of England) parish churchyard (Fig 7.4). Detailed post-excavation analysis took place during 1995–8. The basis of the project and some of its results are relevant to the current discussion.

Background to the project

Eynsham was one of the last foundations of the late Saxon monastic reformation. As elsewhere it would be more correct to speak of a refoundation, because the Benedictine house established by ealdorman Æthelmaer in 1005 replaced a minster which had existed since the 9th century at least. Its origins may be much earlier than this (Blair 1987, 87–93). The new abbey underwent a period of great uncertainty after the Conquest, and the community seems to have been dispersed; the abbey's lands were transferred to Stow, Lincolnshire (Crossley 1990, 104). The community was refounded in the early 12th century, again under the Benedictine Rule, and flourished to become one of the richest houses in the county. An extensive series of legal documents (the Eynsham Cartulary) is preserved in the library of Christchurch College, Oxford, and these were transcribed (with additional documents) at the beginning of the 20th century (Salter 1907, 1908). After the Dissolution part of the abbey was occupied by the Stanley family (Crossley 1990, 119). The monastic precinct was extensive, and included a cemetery, farm, fishponds and open fields (Bond 1992; Keevill 1995, 2–28). Sporadic investigations took place during the 1960s (Keevill 1995, 2–3), and trial trenches excavated in 1971 revealed significant archaeology including the late Saxon abbey cemetery (Gray and Clayton 1978). This led to an area known as the Nursery Field being designated as a Scheduled Ancient Monument. Despite this very little was known of the location and disposition of the monastic buildings of either the Inner or Outer Courts.

Study methods

The Eynsham Abbey project was established by the Oxford Archaeological Unit in 1989. Proposed extensions to the Church of England and Roman Catholic cemeteries would destroy an area of open ground to the west of the Scheduled part of the site. The open ground was thought to contain some part of the abbey buildings, and OAU therefore funded an evaluation in 1989. A single long trench was opened and, although excavation was kept to the minimum possible, it established that archaeology was well-preserved, deeply-stratified, and that monastic buildings of some sort were present. English Heritage therefore agreed to fund the excavation of an area of approximately 3200 m^2 during 1990–92 (Fig 7.4). The excavations provided extremely detailed information about the medieval abbey's Great Cloister (including a free-standing, two-phase lavatorium), the fratry and kitchen to its south, and the dorter and reredorter to the east (Fig 7.5). Parts of the Anglo-Saxon abbey were also found, centring on what seems to have been a cloister (Keevill 1992, 1993). Further excavation in

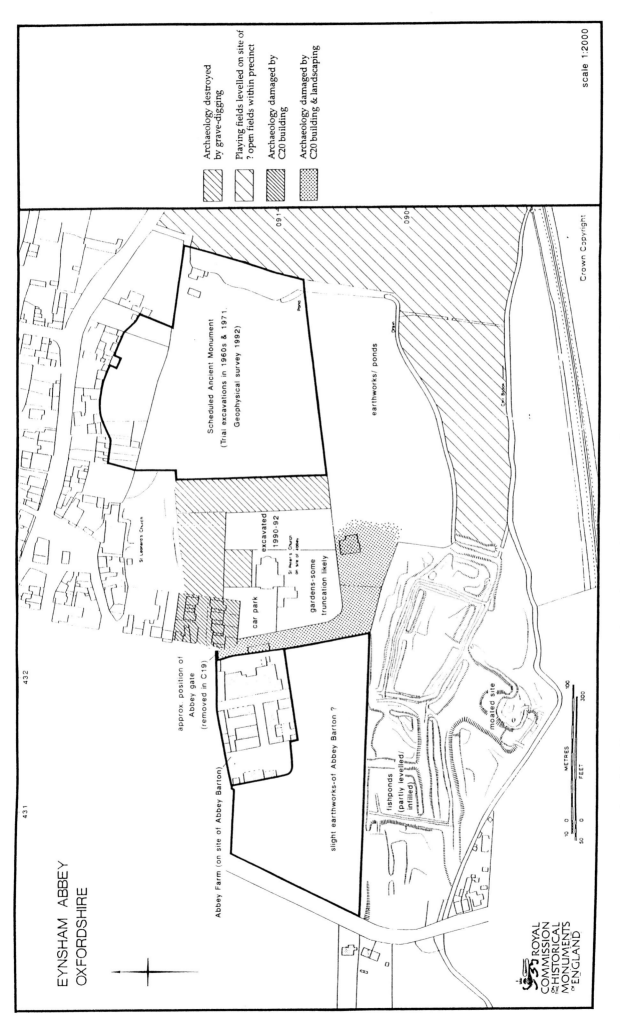

EYNSHAM ABBEY
OXFORDSHIRE

ROYAL
COMMISSION
ON THE HISTORICAL
MONUMENTS
OF ENGLAND

Archaeology destroyed
by grave-digging

Playing fields levelled on site of
? open fields within precinct

Archaeology damaged by
C20 building

Archaeology damaged by
C20 building & landscaping

scale 1:2000

Scheduled Ancient Monument
(Trial excavations in 1960s & 1971.
Geophysical survey 1992)

earthworks / ponds

excavated
1990-92

St Peter's Church
on site of abbey

gardens-some
truncation likely

car park

approx. position of
Abbey gate
(removed in C19)

Abbey Farm (on site of Abbey Barton)

slight earthworks of Abbey Barton ?

fishponds
(partly levelled/
infilled)

moated site

St Leonard's Church

Pond

Drain

Crown Copyright

Fig 7.4 Plan of the abbey precinct at Eynsham, showing the main surviving features and areas of fieldwork (OAU/RCHME)

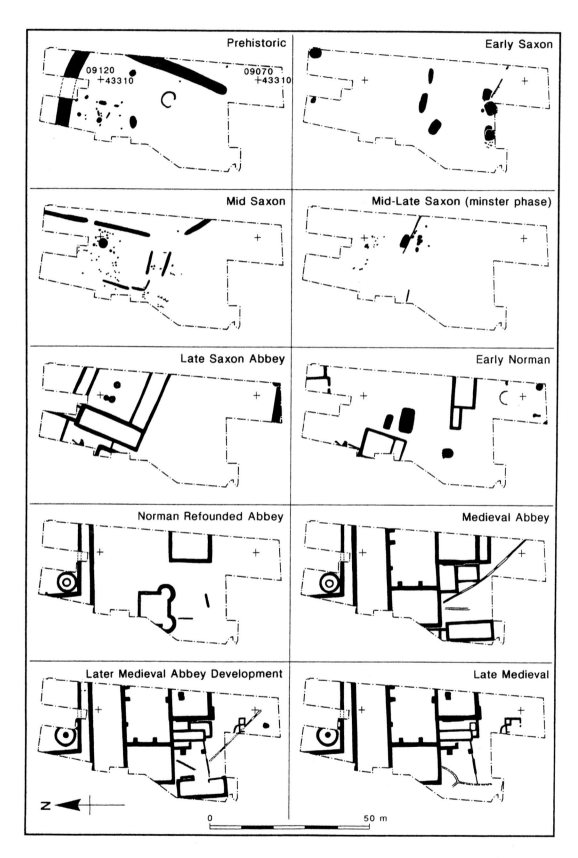

Fig 7.5 *Summary plan of the Eynsham Abbey excavations (OAU)*

1993 produced more information regarding arrangements on the west side of the medieval cloister (Keevill 1995, 30–45). Nationally significant assemblages of pottery, animal bone and small finds have been recovered.

A wider context for the excavations was provided by a series of related projects elsewhere in the precinct. These included a detailed survey by the Royal Commission on the Historical Monuments of England of fishponds in the south-west corner of the precinct (see Keevill 1995, fig. 2) along with various other earthworks (including the probable boundary between the abbey and the medieval parish church to its north). The fishponds were also examined ecologically by the Berkshire, Buckinghamshire and Oxfordshire Naturalists' Trust, while their environs were studied extensively during an evaluation, excavation and watching brief on a Thames Water pipeline which also traversed parts of the open fields on the eastern edge of the precinct (Keevill 1995, 2–28). Finally a geophysical survey was carried out in the Nursery Field by the Archaeometry Branch of English Heritage's Ancient Monuments Laboratory (Cole 1993). This survey provided evidence for extensive ranges of buildings, probably arranged around courtyards or cloisters, and perhaps representing the infirmary ranges of the abbey. Taken together the fieldwork represents a substantial (but not exhaustive) study of the abbey precinct (evidence for the abbey church and the north-east quadrant of the cloister ranges has been destroyed by grave-digging in St Leonards churchyard).

Discussion

Evaluation: pieces of patterns?

Defining the shape, disposition and extent of a monastic site may seem to be a relatively straight-forward matter, and evaluations would appear to be ideally suited to such an exercise. Such projects are, after all, designed to characterise the date, extent, state of preservation and (to a degree) significance of archaeological remains on any given site and use well-established and reasonably rigorous methods to do so. There are some limitations, of course, not least that evaluations usually occur within the context of development control and are confined to a site or area where a development might impact on archaeological remains. The concordance of such an area with all or even a reasonable proportion of a monastic precinct is likely to be a matter of chance in most cases (the case of Rewley Abbey, noted above, must be exceptional in that the relevant development proposal included virtually the whole of the abbey's core precincts within its compass), and the wider extent of monastic estates are most unlikely to fall

within the boundaries of an evaluation. This is not necessarily to belittle the value of evaluations, but more to highlight what is probably an inevitable limitation.

The point can be made by reference to the remains of Oxfordshire's monasteries. Many of these are now well-known archaeologically, having benefitted from some (and often extensive) archaeological fieldwork. This has sometimes taken the form of substantial area excavations (as at the Oxford Greyfriars and Blackfriars, albeit in piecemeal fashion, and at Eynsham Abbey), but just as frequently work has been on a smaller scale. Even where such projects have not been formal evaluations they often combine with other observations to become the equivalent of such an exercise, as at Oseney Abbey. In other cases – most notably Rewley Abbey – one site has been the subject of several episodes of evaluation or trial trenching. Yet an adequate understanding of the dynamics of the abbey and its precincts through time is only available at a few of these sites (arguably only Eynsham and Abingdon, where large-scale work has been undertaken in the 1990s) and numerous questions remain to be answered about all of the monasteries in Oxford itself. It is therefore worth briefly reconsidering the methods employed during the various programmes of fieldwork.

Studying Oxfordshire sites: potential and limitations

The common theme which is apparent across all of the sites is all too obvious: larger-scale fieldwork brings about exponential leaps in understanding and interpretability. Conversely the piecemeal approach necessarily adopted at many Oxford abbeys because of the exigencies of development programmes has led to fragmented pictures of the places where some parts of the abbey (including the core buildings) can only be sketched in with the absolute minimum of interpretation. This is true of all the city's great monastic sites – St Frideswide's, Oseney and Rewley Abbeys, the Blackfriars and the Greyfriars. In some cases such as the latter's cloisters the problem is extreme, and even the excavator was unable to mount any realistic attempt at defining the buildings and spaces which had been revealed. It is difficult to overstate the difficulties under which the excavations were executed, and it has to be accepted that even less would have been found without the remarkable dedication of those who undertook the work. Nevertheless it is equally difficult to avoid a deep sense of regret at how much could *not* recorded for posterity.

It is hard to believe that such unrecorded or scantily-recorded losses could occur now. The whole concept of development control and site preservation has changed to a remarkable degree since the late 1980s, and archaeology is now routinely considered as a major factor in development proposals. Once again one can point to the recent work at Rewley Abbey as a good case in point. This is not to say that monastic sites are not under threat, of course – far from it. The two largest projects of all, at Eynsham and Abingdon Abbeys, resulted directly from the threat (now being carried out) of extensive destruction within the precincts. Admittedly the circumstances at Eynsham are unusual (graveyard extensions are not normally quite so destructive), while at Abingdon the large-scale redevelopment of the Vineyard area was sponsored by the local council as a major urban regeneration initiative. The point, though, is that in both cases the threats led directly to large-scale excavations and associated surveys, with evaluation being but one stage in the process of archaeological mitigation.

Sample excavations, no matter when undertaken or under what circumstances, by definition provide only a partial picture of any given site. This is usually an accepted and acceptable fact of archaeological life, and site interpretations are coloured accordingly. This need not be a huge problem where essentially domestic or industrial archaeology is concerned, because a certain amount of gap-filling may be possible and plausible. The question must be whether such an approach is feasible for religious sites; this may be relevant for any period of human endeavour, but our concern is with medieval monastic sites. In that context there are widespread assumptions, both implicit and explicit, about what a monastic site should contain and even look like. Some of these, of course, are entirely reasonable: an abbey without a church or cloister would be highly unusual. The greater problem arises when one wishes to attempt more detailed interpretations based around the daily pattern of liturgy and life within the monastic community, and this of course is by no means confined to the core of the abbey itself. The interpretative benefits derived from large-scale fieldwork at sites such as Bordesley Abbey have more than justified the extent of the work involved, and the level of interpretation achieved there would not be possible without large-scale excavation and survey (Hirst et al 1993). The point can be made well enough by comparison with any of Oxford's monasteries, where interpretation must necessarily remain at a much more crude level because of the limitations of the available evidence. Even the apparently obvious patterns of the monastic plan can be difficult to establish from sampling alone. This is certainly apparent on the great Oxford monasteries already mentioned, where not only the detail but in some cases even the outlines of the plan remain obscure. The difficulties involved can be

appreciated readily through an exercise first carried out by the author with an evening class in Oxford. This involved taking a reasonably well-understood ground plan of an Irish Cistercian monastery and overlaying it with an array of trenches such as one might expect to see in an archaeological evaluation. The walls in between the trenches were 'rubbed out', leaving only those fragments of masonry which lay within the trenches behind. The students then had to flesh out these outlines into an interpretative plan, and were then able to compare this against the actual plan. With a little prompting most students were able to identify the position and general layout of the church and cloister, but no details could be filled in and even the cloister ranges were difficult to pick out. Admittedly the exercise was somewhat unfair on the students because they had not been prepared for it and had less than an hour in which to look at the plan, but it was interesting nevertheless and one which anyone interested in site interpretation should repeat for themselves.

Lessons for the future

It seems clear enough that there is little substitute for large-scale fieldwork if one is to attempt detailed interpretation of a monastic site from archaeological evidence. The fieldwork need not always be intrusive, and work at Eynsham and Abingdon has shown the value of non-destructive survey techniques where ground conditions permit their use. Nevertheless there is no substitute as of yet for excavation where high-level archaeological interpretation is desired, and to that end trial trenching can only be a means to an end. Some interpretation may still be possible, and will certainly be better than nothing where larger excavation is unlikely to be feasible or acceptable (eg at the Scheduled Ancient Monument of Rewley Abbey). It should be possible, however, to target some sites in any given region where extensive fieldwork would be both acceptable and possible, and to target these for extensive research excavation. The best examples will be those where large areas of the precincts are available so that the core buildings of the abbey can be examined in the wider context of the monastic landscape. A multi-disciplinary approach is also recommended, drawing in archaeologists, historians, landscape specialists and others as appropriate to study the totality of a place. Only then will we be able to test assumptions about patterns (and pieces of them) on the basis of thorough and rigorous data sets.

Acknowledgements

I am grateful to many colleagues, especially at the Oxford Archaeological Unit, for discussing their work with me at various times and providing information about the sites. Alan Hardy (Eynsham), Tim Allen (Abingdon), Brian Durham, Dave Wilkinson and George Lambrick (Oxford) have been especially helpful, while Julian Munby has been a consistent fount of information and wisdom on the subject. John Blair's advice was also most valuable, especially with regard to Eynsham in the later Saxon and Norman periods but also concerning several other sites. It goes without saying that any errors made here are my own, not theirs. Finally I would like to thank (and apologise to) the students who had to endure my monastic plan exercise, and who actually seemed to enjoy it!

Bibliography

Allen T G 1990, Abingdon, *Current Archaeology* 121, 24–7

Allen T G 1994, A medieval grange of Abingdon Abbey at Dean Court Farm, Cumnor, Oxon, *Oxoniensia* 59, 219–447

Biddle M 1968, The excavations at Abingdon Abbey, 1922, *Med Archaeol* 26/27, 70–201

Blair J 1987, Saint Frideswide Reconsidered, *Oxoniensia* 52, 71–128.

Blair J 1990a, Thornbury, Binsey: a probable defensive enclosure associated with St Frideswide, in J Blair (ed) 1990, 3–20

Blair J (ed) 1990b, *Saint Frideswide's Monastery at Oxford: Archaeological and Architectural Studies*, Alan Sutton, Gloucester (reprinted from *Oxoniensia* 53)

Blair J and Steane J M 1982, Investigations at Cogges, Oxfordshire, 1978–81: the priory and the parish church, *Oxoniensia* 47, 37–125

Bond C J 1979, The reconstruction of the medieval landscape: the estates of Abingdon Abbey, *Landscape History* 1, 59–75

Bond C J 1986, The Oxford region in the Middle Ages, in G Briggs *et al* 1986, 135–59

Bond C J 1992, The fishponds of Eynsham Abbey, *The Eynsham Record* 9, 3–17

Booth P 1994, Oseney Abbey field evaluation, in OAU 1994

Briggs G, Cook J, and Rowley T 1986, *The Archaeology of the Oxford Region*, OUDES, Oxford

Cole M 1993, *Report on geophysical survey at Eynsham Abbey, Oxfordshire*, Ancient Monuments Laboratory Report 5/93

Coppack G 1990, *Abbeys and Priories*, English Heritage/Batsford, London

Crossley A 1990, *A history of the County of Oxford: volume 12, Wootton Hundred (south) including Woodstock*, Victoria County History

Cunningham C J K and Banks J W 1972, Excavations at Dorchester Abbey, *Oxoniensia* 37, 158–64

DoE 1990, *Planning and Policy Guidance 16: Archaeology and Planning*, HMSO, London

Doggett N 1986, The Anglo-Saxon See and cathedral of Dorchester-on-Thames: the evidence reconsidered, *Oxoniensia* 51, 49–61

Dunning 1952, A lead ingot at Rievaulx Abbey, *Antiq J* 32, 199–202

Gray M and Clayton N 1978, Excavations on the site of Eynsham Abbey, 1971, *Oxoniensia* 43, 100–122

Hassall T G 1973, Excavations in Oxford 1972: fifth interim report, *Oxoniensia* 38, 270–2

Hassall T G, Halpin C E and Mellor M 1984, Excavations in St Ebbe's, Oxford, 1967–1976: Part I: post-medieval domestic tenements and the post-Dissolution site of the Greyfriars, *Oxoniensia* 49, 153–275

Hassall T G 1987, *Oxford: the Buried City*, Oxford Archaeological Unit, Oxford

Hassall T G, Halpin C E and Mellor M 1989, Excavations in St Ebbe's, Oxford, 1967–1976: Part I: late Saxon and medieval domestic occupation and tenements, and the medieval Greyfriars, *Oxoniensia* 54, 71–277

Hiller J 1994, A watching brief at Godstow, in OAU 1994

Hinton D 1968, Bicester Priory, *Oxoniensia* 33, 22–52

Hirst S M, Walsh D A and Wright S M 1983, *Bordesley Abbey II*, BAR 111

Jope E M 1948, Abingdon Abbey craftsmen and building stone supplies, *Berks Archaeol J* 51, 53–64

Keevill G D 1992, The rediscovery of Eynsham Abbey, Oxfordshire: archaeological investigations 1989–92, *Medieval Europe 1992 Pre-Printed Papers: Religion and Belief*, 195–200

Keevill G D 1993, Abbeys and archaeology in Eynsham, 1989–92, *The Eynsham Record* 10, 5–17

Keevill G D 1995, *In Harvey's house and in God's house: excavations at Eynsham Abbey 1991-3*, Thames Valley Landscapes Monograph No 6, Oxford

Lambrick G 1985, Further excavations on the second site of the Dominican Priory, Oxford, *Oxoniensia* 50, 131–208

Lambrick G and Woods H 1976, Excavations on the second site of the Dominican Priory, Oxford, *Oxoniensia* 41, 168–231

OAU 1994, *Oxford and the Religious Orders*, OAU News (Autumn issue), Oxford

Pantin W A 1970, Minchery Farm, Littlemore, *Oxoniensia* 35, 19–26

St John Hope W H 1890, On the Whitefriars or Carmelites of Hulne, Northumberland, *Arch J* 47, 105–29

Salter H E 1907 and 1908, *The Cartulary of the Abbey of Eynsham Vols I and II*, Oxford Historical Society 49 and 51

Scull C 1990, Excavations in the Cloister of St Frideswide's Priory, 1985, in J Blair (ed) 1990, 21–73

Sharpe J 1985, Oseney Abbey, Oxford: archaeological investigations 1975–83, *Oxoniensia* 50, 95–130

Stenton F M 1913, *The Early History of the Abbey of Abingdon*, University College Reading, reprinted 1989 by Paul Watkins, Stamford

Sturdy D 1990, Excavations in the Latin Chapel and outside the East End of Oxford Cathedral, Winter 1962/3, in Blair (ed) 1990b, 75–102

Wilkinson D 1994, Rewley Abbey, *Oxford Archaeological Unit Annual Report 1993-4*, 19–21

8 Romsey Abbey: Benedictine nunnery and parish church

Ian R Scott

Introduction

The intention of this short paper is to consider the evidence for the relationship between the developing town of Romsey and the Benedictine nunnery at Romsey, in particular as it relates to the precinct of the nunnery.[1] It is important to give due weight to the dynamics of the relationship between the town and abbey which has always been close, and the abbey church survives today because it was purchased by the town in 1545 to serve as its parish church. Today the church is dedicated to Saints Mary and Aethelflaeda.

The parish church, which was dedicated to St Lawrence, had been situated within the north aisle of the abbey prior to the Dissolution. It is uncertain when the parish first began to use the north aisle. The first vicar was appointed by Bishop Asser in 1321, but a deed of the Abbess Cecilia (1238–47) refers to Adam, a canon of Romsey, who was also rector of St Lawrence, and there is a later thirteenth century reference to 'The Prebend of the Church of St Lawrence the greater in the House or Church of the Monastery of Romsey' (Luce 1948, 30). Indeed there had been presbyters and *clericuli* recorded at Romsey Abbey as early as 1130 (Liveing 1906, 125). The foundation of the Benedictine nunnery at Romsey is attributed to Edward the Elder and traditionally dated to 907 (Liveing 1906, 11). The foundation by Edward is recorded in a twelfth-century source, Florence of Worcester. He recorded that in 967 Edgar 'placed nuns in the monastery at Romsey founded by his grandfather, Edward the Elder' (Coldicott 1989, 6–7). Dumville (1992) has recently presented a case for seeing the reforms of the reign of Edgar as a culmination of a process begun as early as the reign of Alfred and continuing through the tenth century. The foundation of Romsey in 907 would fit into this context. The context of Edgar's refoundation of 967 is clear: the late tenth century was a period characterised by monastic reform and new foundations.

It has recently been suggested that Romsey may have been the site of a minster pre-dating Edward's 907 foundation (Hase 1988, 46). Hase argues that Romsey is better placed spatially than Nursling in relation to the known minsters at Eling and Southampton. Secondly he suggests that the possibility of a collegiate minster church at Romsey is given support by the fact that in the later medieval period there were prebends attached to the abbey for the cure of the souls of the parish rather than of the nuns (Coldicott 1989, 55–58). Thirdly, Hase infers the existence of a royal manor, or hundred, centred on Romsey, from the 14 hides held by the nuns prior to the Norman invasion in 1066 (Berrow 1978, 6), and from the privileges enjoyed by the abbess within Romsey Infra. The abbess held the Manor of Romsey, which consisted of both Romsey Infra and Extra. There were distinct differences of jurisdiction between the two parts of the Manor. Within *Romsey infra pontem* the abbess enjoyed hundredal privileges, independent of the King's Hundred of Somborne (Berrow 1978, 11–14). Romsey Extra, on the other hand, was subject to the manor court of Romsey but within the King's Hundred of Somborne. These privileges seem to go back at least to the reign of William I, as is indicated in the confirmation of privileges granted by Henry I (Liveing 1906, 35–6). The abbess also had the right to hold a market every Sunday; this privilege goes back at least to the reign of Henry II.

There are two possible explanations for these privileges. On the one hand it can be argued that these franchises indicate the origins of Romsey's foundation in a royal estate. This argument is strengthened, not only by the royal foundation in the tenth century, but also by the continuing involvement with Romsey of princesses of the royal house of Wessex. The alternative argument is that these privileges are comparable to the privileges, or banleucas, granted to other abbeys and churches at their foundation. Hase's arguments are tempting because they would give support to the idea that the middle Saxon settlement was the centre of a royal estate, but the evidence is slight.

Topography of Romsey (Figs 8.1 & 8.2)

The present town of Romsey is situated on the edge of a gravel terrace overlooking the flood plain of the Test. The town spreads out to the north, south, and east of the abbey. The abbey itself lies near the edge of the terrace which is marked by the 17 m (or 50 ft) contour. To the west the terrace drops steeply down to the flood plain of the Test. To the south of the abbey the ground slopes gently until it reaches the low-lying peat deposits at the south end of Bell Street. The historic core of the town centres on the abbey and Market Place. Immediately east of the Market Place is the course of the Fishlake/ Holbrook, which in the nineteenth century marked the borough boundary. It also marks the historic division between Romsey Infra, centred on the abbey, and Romsey Extra to the east. The name Romsey Infra derives from the medieval description of *Romesie infra pontem* (*Calendar of Charter Rolls 1257–1300*, 102). The bridge in this instance being

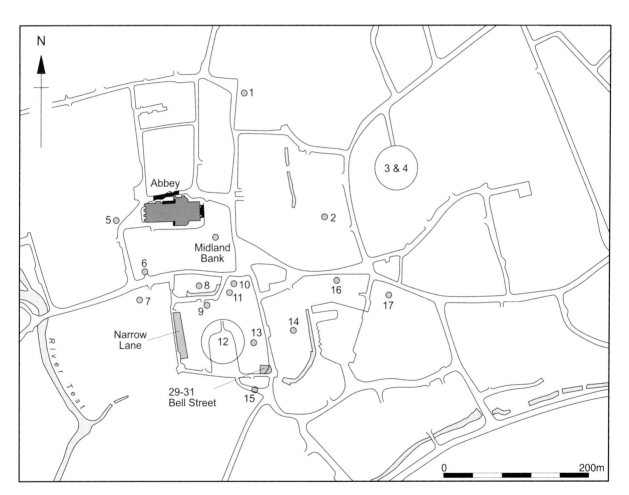

Fig 8.1 *Site location and central Romsey: Location of sites mentioned in text. (c) Crown copyright.*

1	Whitbread Brewery (A 1986.8)	9	10, Abbey Water (A 1986.7)
2	Latimer Street Car Park	10	4, Market Place ("Creatures") (A 1986.12)
3	Orchard House (A 1985.25)	11	Town Hall Car Park
4	Orchard House Car Park (A 1990.3)	12	Newton Lane Car Park
5	Abbey West, 1988 (A 1988.6) (including Abbey Green Soakaway)	13	Angel Hotel, Bell Street (A 1984.4)
6	21–23, The Abbey (A 1990.4)	14	Baptist Chapel, Bell Street (A 1992.27)
7	La Sagesse Convent (A 1988.31)	15	Newton Lane Link (A 1989.16)
8	Abbey United Reformed Church (A 1989.14)	16	11, The Hundred (A 1988.4)
		17	35, The Hundred ("Waitrose" extension) (A 1988.15)

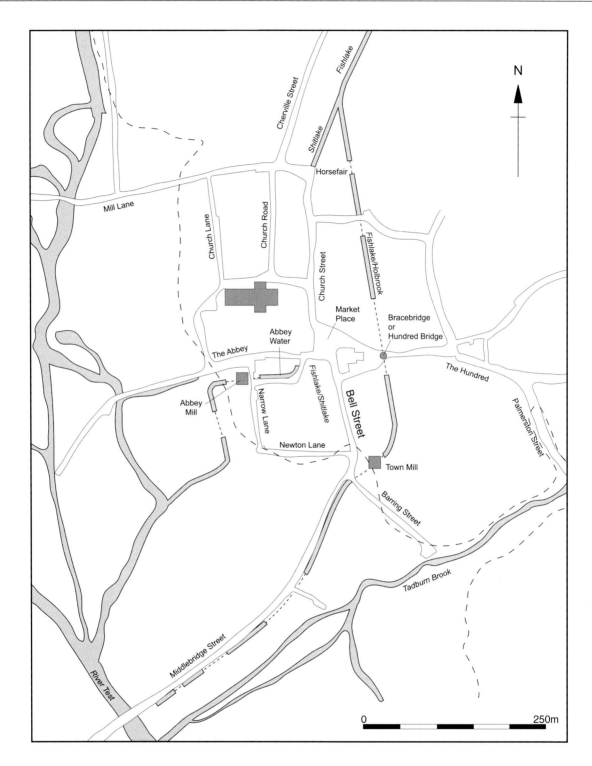

Fig 8.2 *Topography of Romano-British and Saxon Romsey (Based upon the 1967 Ordnance Survey 1:2500 map with permission of the Controller of Her Majesty's Stationery Office (c) Crown copyright).*

Bradebrigge (or Broad Bridge), which is identified with the later Hundred Bridge which crosses the Fishlake, at the eastern edge of the Market Place.[2]

The Fishlake separates from the main course of the Test 1.75 km north of the abbey, just above Greatbridge, where the road north to Stockbridge

crosses the river. After meandering in its upper reaches, the stream runs parallel to Cherville Street, before splitting into two about 250 m north of the abbey. The eastern branch of the Fishlake, also known as the Holbrook, runs behind the properties on the east side of Church Street, forms the boundary of Romsey Infra, and is crossed by the Hundred Bridge. It continues down the back of properties on the east side of Bell Street, before turning sharply west south-west towards the Town Mill, which was sited near the bottom of Bell Street. Bell Street was formerly known as Mill Street. From the town mill the stream flows south west alongside Middlebridge Street, until it turns south to join the Tadburn Brook, and then flows back into the Test.

The western arm of the Fishlake, which now runs in a culvert under Church Street, may have flowed down the east side of the street in the Saxon period. Excavations in 1989 revealed the edge of a stream fronting the early medieval tenements (A 1989.15).[3] If the stream did flow down the east side of Church Street, it must have crossed under the street where it entered the Market Place, because the stream flows along the western edge of the Market Place. It divides at the south-west corner of the Market, just beyond the abbey gateway, and one part – now known as Abbey Water – flows west to serve the Abbey Mill. This stream was probably a later creation. The second arm forming the main course flowed parallel to Bell Street and is also known as the "Shitlake". It has been canalised on different courses over the centuries and its precise route in the Saxon period is unclear. No trace of a stream was observed during the Town Hall Car Park salvage work, but a possible late Saxon stream was identified in excavations behind 4 The Market Place ('Creatures' pet shop) (A 1986.12). The Fishlake/ Shitlake stream flowed down the backs of properties on the west side of Bell Street. It may have continued parallel to Middlebridge Street until it rejoined the Test. The branch which served the Abbey Mill flowed west to the mill before turning sharply south and then west again to rejoin the Test downstream of Middlebridge.

It is likely that both branches of the Fishlake were artificial creations. The evidence from 29–31 Bell Street (A 1981.126) (Rees 1994, 24–6 and fig 5) clearly indicates that there was a stream adjacent to Bell Street in the later Bronze Age and earlier and that there was an early, and presumably natural, precursor to the Shitlake in the area of Bell Street. On topographical grounds, it is unlikely that the Fishlake/Holbrook was a natural stream, but the fact that it formed the boundary between Romsey Infra and Extra indicates that this stream was a comparatively early feature of the settlement's topography. It served as the leat to the original town mill.

Saxon Settlement

Archaeological fieldwork has been undertaken over much of the historic core of Romsey. Mainly this has taken the form of watching briefs and small scale salvage excavations. Much of the evidence recorded is limited in extent but taken together the various pieces of information present a coherent pattern albeit with some gaps. The major lacuna concerns the area to the north of the abbey between Church Lane on the west and Church Street on the east and including Church Road. On the north it is delimited by Mill Lane and the Horsefair. The only excavation within this area (Church Street 1977–78) explored the late medieval and post-medieval deposits only. A more recent small scale evaluation, immediately north of the 1977–78 excavation and east of and adjacent to Church Road, revealed a substantial stream bed with water-lain deposits. There was no evidence for medieval or earlier activity. Later activity was represented by a deep topsoil confirming the presence of gardens. However, excavations immediately east of the Horsefair (A 1986.8) did reveal successive ditches probably of late Saxon date. These were aligned east-west and may have marked the northern boundary of the Saxon settlement.

Evidence for the extent of the middle Saxon settlement

The earliest post-Roman occupation attested in Romsey is of middle Saxon date, and consists of four elements. The limited extent of the excavations from which the evidence is derived makes interpretation difficult. The four elements are:

(i) Structures and burials pre-dating the Norman abbey

In excavations on the present abbey a number of earlier phases of activity were recognised. Few of them were directly dated, but there are radiocarbon determinations for some features and phases (Table 8.1). In the report of the excavations on the abbey, Phases 6, 7 and 8 have been identified as late Saxon, while Phases 3, 4 and 5 can be dated as middle Saxon (Scott 1996).

Evidence for timber-built structures and associated floors (Phase 5) was found in a soakaway excavated near the west end of the abbey on its north side (A 1988.7). These structures were orientated east-north-east to west-south-west. A grave on a similar alignment to the structures may also have belonged to this phase. The phase 5 structures were cut into a soil horizon (Phase 4) which contained substantial quantities of animal bone representing food waste (Bourdillon nd) and which gave radiocarbon determinations of middle to late Saxon date (Table 8.1). Traces of structures and metalled sur-

Table 8.1 *Romsey Abbey radiocarbon dates (1σ = 68 % confidence; 2σ = 95 % confidence. Calibration of Phase 3 and 4 dates is after van der Plict and Mook 1989: other calibrations are after Stuiver and Pearson 1986)*

Phase	Site	Cxt	Cxt type	Sample ref	Sample type	¹⁴C age BP	CAL AD 1σ	CAL AD 2σ
3	A 1988.9	128	Layer	OxA 2313	Pig bone	1215 ± 80	690 – 890	665 – 970
3	A 1988.9	122	Layer	OxA 2314	Cattle ribs	1355 ± 80	610 – 770	545 – 875
4	A 1988.7	6030	Layer	OxA 2319	Cattle bone	1125 ± 80	810 – 990	690 – 1030
7	RA 1979	5119	Grave fill	HAR 3675	Charcoal	1170 ± 70	775 – 960	680 – 1010
8	RA 1975	6030	Grave fill	HAR 2527	Charcoal	1050 ± 70	895 – 1025	830 – 1155
8	RA 1979	5127	Grave fill	HAR 3670	Charcoal	1100 ± 70	885 – 1010	780 – 1030

faces pre-dating the phase 4 soil horizon were found in small scale excavations within the west end of the nave. These have been assigned to Phase 3. There is no dating evidence for these features, and no plan of the buildings can be re-constructed from the tantalisingly fragmentary pieces exposed.

(ii) Animal bone

In addition to the animal bone from the 1988 excavations on the north side of the abbey, another small excavation to the south-east of the abbey behind the Midland Bank (A 1988.9) produced more material (Bourdillon 1988). This small trench revealed two superimposed horizons containing quantities of food waste in the form of animal bone. The animal bone in the upper layer was associated with debris from iron-smelting. Whereas the animal bone from the north of the abbey consisted of basic domestic material, the range of species represented in the Midland Bank trench was altogether more varied. It included bones of Roe deer, and of various birds. It gives a tantalising glimpse of a high status site. Radiocarbon determinations for this animal bone gave dates firmly in the middle Saxon period (Table 8.1).

(iii) Iron smelting

Excavations have revealed evidence for iron smelting activity in an area to the south of the abbey. The major evidence has come from excavations in Narrow Lane (A 1981.125), and includes possible hearths and at least one furnace, in addition to substantial quantities of slag.

The area in which smelting was carried out can be defined with some confidence. No substantial *in situ* slag deposits have been found to the north, around the abbey itself. Slag was found in the Midland Bank excavation to the south-east of the abbey. This is the most northerly occurrence and the

only substantial occurrence north of Abbey Water. It is significant that the iron smelting activity does not appear to have respected this stream because it suggests that the stream was later in date. No slag was found during excavation of the later Saxon cemetery in the United Reformed Church excavation (A 1989.14: see below), but substantial deposits were recognised to the south of the Market Place in excavations behind 4 The Market Place ('Creatures' pet shop, A 1988.12) and in salvage work in the nearby town hall car park (A 1988.2). Observations during the construction of the Newton Lane Car Park also revealed extensive deposits of charcoal-rich soil and slag blocks. No evidence for iron smelting activity was recovered from the 29 Bell Street site (A 1981.126) at the corner of Bell Street and Newton Lane.

The area covered by the iron smelting does not extend northwards as far as the abbey, but there is some evidence that smelting activity extended north of Abbey Water. It extends westward to the edge of the gravel terrace, and eastward no further than Bell Street. It is possible that the 'Shitlake' marked the eastern boundary of the activity. Its south end falls short of Newton Lane.

The iron was smelted using the *Schlackenklotz* (slag block) technique (McDonnell, 1988), which would fit best in a middle Saxon context (McDonnell, 1989). The dating evidence for the iron industry in Romsey is contradictory. The pottery found with the slag deposits ranges in date from Romano-British to nineteenth-century. The RB pottery is certainly residual and derived from the underlying settlement. The iron smelting deposits have clearly been re-worked through horticultural activity in the medieval and post-medieval periods with the result that the pottery has been largely mixed. A possible middle Saxon date for the iron smelting activity is suggested by the distribution and its relationship to topographical features and to the distribution of middle Saxon pottery (see below).

A further piece of evidence also suggests an early date: there is no reference to iron smelting in the Romsey Domesday entry suggesting that smelting had ceased well before the Conquest.

The very limited quantity of smithing slag, and the absence of any other evidence for the production of iron tools, weapons or other equipment should be noted, and suggests that the iron was produced for finishing elsewhere. The trading network which sustained the middle Saxon *emporium* of Hamwic would be an obvious context for iron production at Romsey.

(iv) Pottery

The final piece of evidence for the existence and location of a middle Saxon settlement at Romsey is the presence of pottery comparable to that from Hamwic (Rees in Scott *et al*, forthcoming). Little, or no, middle Saxon pottery is found to the east of the Fishlake/Holbrook stream, and most comes from west of the Shitlake. Its distribution is limited to the excavations at the abbey and the areas to the south. Insufficient data exist for the areas to the north of the abbey. The distribution strongly suggests that any middle Saxon settlement was within the later Romsey Infra and centred to the south of the abbey.

The nature of the middle Saxon settlement

The conclusion has to be that there was middle Saxon occupation in the area under the present abbey and to the south, and that to the south of the abbey smelting of iron was carried out on a substantial scale. The limited evidence, particularly for structures, makes interpretation difficult, but the likelihood is that the middle Saxon settlement was an estate centre, and given that the nunnery was a royal foundation, it is reasonable to further suggest that it was a royal estate centre. The arguments put forward by Hase (1988) would support this idea.

Late Saxon Romsey
(i) The abbey

The survival of the footings of the late Saxon predecessor to the present abbey has been known since the turn of the twentieth century. This abbey (Phase 8) lay directly beneath the present abbey (Fig 8.3) and a number of graves were associated with it, including charcoal burials, on an east-west alignment. Radiocarbon dates from the charcoal burials confirmed their late Saxon date. The evidence for Phase 7, which preceded the late Saxon abbey, consisted of two substantial chalk footings found

sealed beneath the nave south aisle wall of the present abbey and a number of burials on an east-west alignment cut by the foundation trench of the north transept of the late Saxon abbey. The chalk footings were orientated east-west on the same alignment and were of similar length. Their north-south extent was obscured by the present abbey. Unfortunately nothing is known of the structures built on the chalk footings, and it is not clear whether they formed parts of a single building, or of separate buildings. The Phase 7 graves found on the north side of the abbey cut Phase 6 burials on a northwest-southeast alignment. No evidence was found for associated structures on this northwest-southeast alignment. In addition to the features recovered in and around the abbey church, in 1989 part of an early cemetery was investigated some 60 m south of the abbey (United Reformed Church excavation A 1989.14). All the investigated graves in this cemetery were orientated east-west, and one grave contained a charcoal burial. The activity in this cemetery has been assigned to Phases 7 and 8.

(ii) Houses, boundaries, roads and the market

The three main roads – Bell Street, Church Street and The Hundred – meet by the abbey, at the point now occupied by the Market Place. This lies outside the abbey gateway, and immediately beyond the Fishlake/Shitlake. It is almost certain that the Market Place is sited where the late Saxon market controlled by the abbess was held.

Apart from the structures associated with the abbey, the evidence for late Saxon buildings is limited to one site – 29–31 Bell Street – where three buildings have been identified. Pottery from the postholes and foundation trenches of these buildings is of eleventh- to twelfth-century date. This site lies on the west side of Bell Street and between the two arms of the Fishlake. A ditch, possibly a property boundary, excavated adjacent to the Baptist Church (A 1992.27) also lies within this area, but on the other side of the street. Bell Street, formerly Mill Street, was the road to the New Forest and the south-west, via the bridge at Middlebridge, and it is probable that the route came into use during the late Saxon period, if not earlier. It was certainly a road in the time of Edward I (WCM 16083). It is possible that Banning Street, which ran south from Bell Street, was the main route to Southampton until the Tudor period when it was replaced by Palmerston Street, formerly Southampton Road (Berrow 1977, 13–14). Banning Street is known from at least 1247 (WCM 16348).

A large east-west ditch possibly of late Saxon date was uncovered to the north of the abbey in the Brewery excavation. It had been cut by a smaller

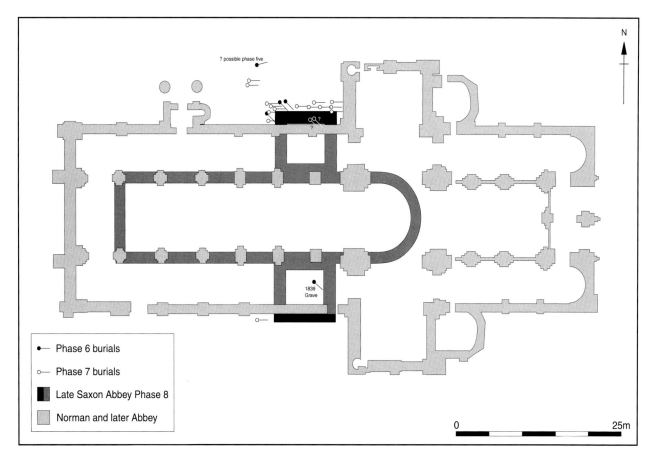

Fig 8.3 *Plan of Romsey Abbey with Phase 8 late Saxon Abbey and Phase 6 and 7 Saxon graves*

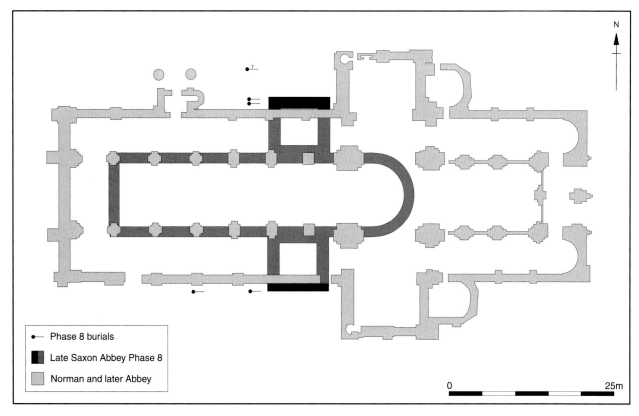

Fig 8.4 *Plan of Romsey Abbey with Phase 8 late Saxon Abbey and Phase 8 graves*

ditch on the same alignment. Both ditches contained late Saxon pottery in their fills. They were on the south side of the Horsefair, and very near to the Fishlake. They were also close to the road north to Stockbridge and Andover. The relationships of the ditches to the road were not established. It is possible that the road from the north originally continued straight down towards the abbey, along the line of the present Church Road, and that the Horsefair was a creation of a later date. The large ditch may have marked the northern extent of the Saxon settlement before the creation of the Horse-fair, and the smaller ditch was probably a property boundary associated with the later street arrangement. It is possible that the large ditch was a middle Saxon feature, infilled in the later Saxon period.

Late Saxon pottery and a north-south boundary ditch have been found to the east of the Market Place (ie beyond the Fishlake/Holbrook) in Romsey Extra, at 11 The Hundred (A 1988.4). Other possible property boundaries were located near Orchard House (A 1990.3) and in the Latimer Street car park. Both the latter ditches were aligned approximately east-west and were a similar size to the ditch at 11, The Hundred. Dating evidence was lacking from these two ditches. Late Saxon pottery found to the east at 35 The Hundred (A 1988.15) was probably spread as the result of manuring, and this site may well have been a field or garden in the late Saxon period.

Interpretation of the Late Saxon evidence

The evidence for houses and boundaries leads to a tentative suggestion that domestic occupation grew up alongside the three main roads out of Romsey. The most substantial evidence comes from Bell Street. The evidence from 29–31 Bell Street suggests that the occupation of plots was not urban in character, in the sense of deep narrow tenements running up to the street frontage. Rather the evidence accords with that from late Saxon Thetford and Northampton (Williams 1984, 31), with wide plots alongside roads. The buildings within the plots are well spaced out and not aligned on the street frontage. Traces of possible boundary ditches beside The Hundred and the Stockbridge road may hint at similar plots on the roads to the east and the north. Although the late Saxon abbey church (Phase 8) has been identified and much of its plan recovered, little or nothing is known of its domestic buildings. A small number of graves have been identified both south and north of the abbey, and further burials have been found in what is assumed to be a separate cemetery adjacent to the present United Reformed Church Manse (A 1989.14). The extent of the Saxon precinct is not known but some indication of its extent and nature can be derived from a consideration of the later precinct and the relationship between abbey and town.

The Later Medieval Nunnery and its Precinct

The later medieval town developed out of the later Saxon settlement and grew up alongside the roads established in the late Saxon period. Prior to the thirteenth century, there is little evidence for dense occupation or for the development of urban tenements and the excavated evidence suggests a continuation of the pattern of occupation observed in the late Saxon period. The deep narrow tenements, which form the basis of property boundaries down to the present day, only appear in the thirteenth century. The fact that the first vicar of Romsey was appointed in 1321 by Bishop Asser may have been a reflection of the needs of a growing population in the town. The town appears to have continued to grow despite the Black Death, for in 1403 a faculty was granted by Bishop William of Wykeham for the enlargement of the parish aisle. It is within this context that the later medieval precinct must be considered.

Part of the bounds of the medieval precinct can be identified, or at least suggested. A stone-built wall with a chamfered quoin was identified in the cellar of the old vicarage and this has been interpreted as the north-west corner of the precinct. The north-south run marking the western boundary appears to follow the line of the 17 m (50 ft) contour. It lay only 40 m west of the abbey church. The east-west return of the wall was aligned on the north-west corner of the abbey and formed part of the northern boundary of the precinct. Its seems likely that the abbey itself lay on the northern edge of the precinct. The presence of the parish aisle in the northern part of the abbey church, with access through the north porch lends support to this idea. Furthermore it is known that the free-standing campanile for the parish church stood to the north of the abbey adjacent to Church Road. It is likely that this stood outside the precinct. The location of the north-east corner of the precinct is not known, but probably lay close to the line of the Fishlake/ Shitlake. The east side of the precinct will have been marked by the line of this stream or of Church Street. The position of the abbey gateway at the south-west corner of the Market Place is known and the Fishlake/Shitlake flows in front of it. The present gateway is a nineteenth-century rebuilding. The south side of the precinct is less clearly defined. It is possible that the line of Abbey Water, the leat

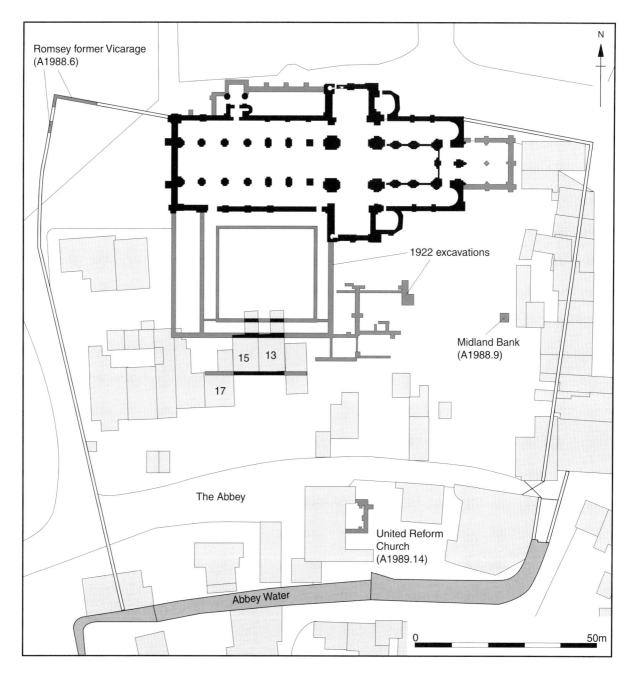

Fig 8.4 Romsey Abbey with plan of buildings uncovered in 1922.

serving the Abbey Mill, defined the precinct. More probably this leat marked the south edge of the inner court, and the land to the south of Abbey Water, between Narrow Lane and the Shitlake, formed an outer court. The evidence from the Narrow Lane excavations indicated that there were no structures built on this site before the seventeenth century and that it was given over to horticulture. The presence of fishponds just to the west on the flood plain of the Test perhaps confirms that the western wall may have marked the limit of the inner court.

The medieval precinct as defined above was quite small even if it included the land to the south of Abbey Water. This is to be expected given the antiquity of the foundation and the parallel development of the abbey and town in such close proximity. The documentation produced at the Suppression does not dispel this idea. Many of the parcels which are described and which formerly belonged to the abbey are small and apparently interlocked with secular tenements.

Those parcels that were clearly within the precinct such as the abbess' lodging are comparatively small. The accounts of Henry Warner, the King's Bailiff, quoted by Liveing (1906, 264) contain the following description of the abbess's lodging:

> ...a dwelling house called Chabbey's lodginge, containing 51 feet in length (between a hall called the Household Hall) from the west end of the same to the chapel of S. Peter at the East end of the said house, together with the said chapel, a kitchen, granary, stable and a new barn in a court called the 'utter courte of the monastery'.

The location of the 'utter court' is not known certainly, but it is suggested above that it may have been to the south of Abbey Water. Adjacent to the abbess's garden and the outer court was the tenement known as the Clerk's chamber. It is described, again in Henry Warner's accounts (here quoted from Liveing 1906, 265):

> A tenement commonly called the 'Clerkes Chamber', with all chambers, houses, and buildings between the said tenement and the stone wall of the outer gate of the monastery, and a parcel of the said outer court, containing 60 ft in length from the end of the said stone wall to the end of the garden called 'Chabbes Garden', and 26 feet in breadth, and a parcel of land at the end of the said tenement called 'Paradise', containing ... in length from the said tenement to the water course in the parcel in the parcel called Paradise, including part of the same water.

The water course next to the Paradise may have been the stretch of the Fishlake which lay between the abbey precinct and the Market Place, or perhaps more probably the Shitlake. Another small parcel was the '*Receyvours lodginge*' consisting of the chambers over the abbey gateway and the tenement next to the gate.

The Clerk's chamber, the Paradise and the Receiver's lodging were the only parts of the abbey site *not* rented after the Suppression by Francis Fleming, who had been the nunnery's lawyer. The portion rented by Fleming included gardens, orchards, a cemetery, ponds and waters (Coldicott 1989, 150). The ponds probably lay to the west of the precinct, on the flood plain of the Test. It would be tempting to identify the cemetery rented by Fleming with that found during excavations by the United Reformed Church Manse in 1989 and to suggest that the gardens and orchards lay nearby. Among the lay officers of the nunnery at the Dissolution, there is mention of John Calkyn 'keeper of the swans', whose presence suggests that the ponds and waters of the abbey were more than merely utilitarian. In 1541 the 'farm of the swans on the rivulet' was let to John Foster (Liveing 1907–1910, 144).

One final site is mentioned in the documentary sources of the Suppression. In 1544 'a messuage called le Systers house at the gate of Romsey abbey

... in the tenure of Peter Westbroke' was amongst properties granted to John Foster and Richard Marden (*Letters and Papers* Vol XIX part 2 (1544), Item 800 [24]). This messuage need not have been within the precinct, since its description as being 'at the gate' leaves open the possibility that it might have been *outside* the gate.

Conclusion

The history of the relationship between the nunnery and town came to an end at the Suppression. The nunnery had begun as a royal foundation and flourished with royal patronage. Royal princesses were educated at Romsey, and some even served as its abbesses. Aethelflaeda, daughter of Edward the Elder was at Romsey, possibly as abbess. Her sisters were married to the Emperor Otto the Great and Charles the Simple, king of the West Franks (Collier 1990, 46–7). Later, in the late eleventh century Matilda (Eadgyth) and Mary the daughters of Margaret and Malcolm, king of Scotland were educated at Romsey. Margaret's sister Christina was a nun at the abbey. Margaret and Christina were the daughters of Edmund Ironside, and the sisters of Edward Atheling. Matilda herself was to marry Henry I. Henry granted seven charters to the abbey. These included granting the privileges of holding fairs and markets (Liveing 1906, 44–5)

In 1105, and again in 1110 or 1114, Henry I visited Romsey. His queen, Matilda, died in 1118. It has been argued that Romsey might have been rebuilt in memory of Henry's wife who had been educated in the nunnery (Luce 1948, 18–19). However, since the king was just starting to build the monastery of Reading in 1120, it might seem unlikely that he embarked on another major building project at this time. In the Victoria County History (VCH Hampshire, Vol 2, 126) it was suggested that the building work was started a little later in the time of Abbess Mary (*c*1160) and that Henry de Blois, Bishop of Winchester (1129–71), was responsible. Mary was the daughter of King Stephen and the niece of Bishop Henry de Blois. An early twelfth-century date for the start of the work on the Norman abbey is more probable on stylistic grounds.

There was still active royal interest in Romsey as late as the thirteenth century. In 1231 Henry III gave the abbess five good oaks from the wood of 'Milchet' (Melchet) '*ad planchias faciendas ad dormitorium reparandum*'. He gave six oaks from Clarendon Forest to the abbey in November 1271 (*Cal Close Rolls, 1268–1272*, 448). In January 1275 Edward I visited Romsey for two days (Liveing 1906, 70) possibly on the occasion of the consecration of the rebuilt Lady Chapels.

The nunnery appears to have flourished until the

early fourteenth century. In 1333, ninety-one nuns are recorded at the election of a new abbess. Following the Black Death, which struck in the middle of the fourteenth century, the nunnery appears to have gone into decline. In 1478 there were only eighteen nuns, and the number never rose above twenty-five thereafter.

The town had developed around the abbey and the market which had been granted to the abbess, but long before the Suppression the town had developed to the point where it was the more powerful partner. Following the Dissolution it was able to purchase the abbey church to serve as its parish church.

Acknowledgements

Particular thanks are due to Francis Green, Director of TVAT, and Barbara Burbridge for sharing their local knowledge, and discussing specific points about Saxon Romsey. They are not responsible for any errors. Helen Rees provided spot dates for most of the sites mentioned and discussed the pottery and stratigraphic record from the Narrow Lane excavations. Jennifer Bourdillon provided information of the animal bone from the various excavations and discussed their significance. Thanks are due to Steve Cheshire who prepared the illustrations.

Abbreviations

WCM   *Winchester College Muniments*, 3 volumes (editor Sheila Himsworth) (Chichester, 1976–84)
LTVASG   Lower Test Vally Archaeological Study Group

Notes

1 The detailed archaeological evidence on which this paper is based will be presented in two monographs respectively on the excavations on Romsey Abbey (Scott 1996) and the town (Scott *et al*, forthcoming). These are to be published as Hampshire Field Club monographs.

2 Living 1906, 175, identified Bradebrigge, or Broad Bridge, with the crossing of the Fishlake at the bottom of Bell Street where Banning Street joined it and Middlebridge Street. The identification with the important crossing adjacent to the market seemed inherently more likely, and this is now confirmed by a recently discovered deed of October 1622 confirming the identification ("Deed of the Town Hall No 28": Hampshire County Records Office: Tylee, Mortimer and Attlee Collection, Acc. No. 4M92, uncatalogued). The deed is concerns the acquisition of a property adjacent to the Hundred Bridge by the Borough as the first town hall, and refers to the tenement *"neere a bridge there called broade bridge al[ia]s the hundred bridge & adioyninge to the watercourse there leadinge to the Towne Milles..."*. I am grateful to Barbara Burbridge of LTVASG and Test Valley Archaeological Trust for

drawing my attention to this reference, and to Ann Thick of the Hampshire Archives Trust for details of the Hampshire Record Office accession code.

3 The code A 1989.15 and similar numbers throughout the text are Hampshire County Museum Service accession numbers (and Test Valley Archaeological Trust site codes) for both paper and material archives from excavations.

Bibliography

Berrow P 1977, *Drawing the Map of Romsey* (LTVASG Occasional Papers, No 1, Romsey)

Berrow P 1978, *When the Nuns ruled Romsey* (LTVASG Occasional Papers, No 2, Romsey)

Bourdillon J nd, *Animal bones from three sites at Romsey Abbey* (Archive report to the Ancient Monuments Laboratory)

Bourdillon J 1988, *The animal bones from the Midland Bank site at Romsey* (Test Valley Archaeological Trust Archive Report 1/88)

Coldicott D K 1989, *Hampshire Nunneries* (Chichester)

Collier C R 1990, Romsey Minster in Saxon times *Proc Hampshire Fld Club Archaeol Soc* 46, 41–52

Dumville D 1992, King Alfred and the tenth-century reform of the English Church, in D Dumville, *Wessex and England from Alfred to Edgar* (Woodbridge)

Hase P 1988, The mother churches of Hampshire, in J Blair (ed), *Minsters and Parish Churches – the Local Church in Transition, 950–1200* (Oxford Univ Committee for Archaeology Monograph 17, Oxford)

Liveing Rev H G D 1906, *Records of Romsey Abbey* (Winchester)

Liveing Rev H G D 1907–10, Romsey Abbey and Town, a transition document, 1539–1541, *Proc Hampshire Fld Club Archaeol Soc* 6, 140–51

Luce Sir R 1948, *Pages from the History of Romsey and its Abbey* (Winchester)

McDonnell J G 1988, *The Ironworking Residues from Romsey, Hampshire* (Ancient Monuments Laboratory Report No 72/88)

McDonnell J G 1989, Iron and its alloys in the fifth to eleventh centuries AD in England, *World Archaeology* 20, No 3, 373–81

Plict J van der and Mook W J 1989, Calibration of radiocarbon ages by computer, *Radiocarbon* 31, 805–60

Rees H 1994, Later Bronze Age and early Iron Age settlement in the Lower Test Valley, *Proc Hampshire Fld Club Archaeol Soc* 49, 19–46

Scott I R 1996, *Excavations on Romsey Abbey, 1973–1991*, (Hampshire Fld Club Archaeol Soc Monograph 8)

Scott I R, Bourdillon J and Rees H forthcoming, *Excavations in Romsey, 1973–1993* (Hampshire Fld Club Archaeol Soc Monograph)

Stuiver M and Pearson G W 1986, High Precision Calibration of the radiocarbon time scale, *Radiocarbon* 28, 805–38

VCH *Hampshire* Vol 2 1903, *Victoria County History, Hampshire and the Isle of Wight*, Vol 2 (London)

Williams J H 1984, A review of some aspects of late Saxon urban origins and development, in M L Faull (ed.), *Studies in Late Anglo-Saxon Settlement* (Oxford University, Department of External Studies, Oxford), 25–34

9   The Planning and Development of a Carthusian Church – the example of St Anne's Charterhouse, Coventry

Iain Soden

The centre of Carthusian life was, and still is, the individual cell of each monk. All were arranged around the great cloister and conformed to a general layout which was designed to facilitate the pursuit of an extremely austere lifestyle. Although subsidiary to the cell in its importance, a church was nevertheless a necessity, if only for attendance to perform the offices of the day. Recent excavations at St Anne's Charterhouse in Coventry (NGR: SP 345 783) indicate that the structure of the church building may have been as much subject to the strict planning principles and architectural traits that are peculiar to the order, as were the monks' cells. On occasion this appears to have been to the detriment of structural integrity.

In its final form at about 1500 the church at Coventry Charterhouse was a long thin rectangle, oriented east-west, with a central bell-tower and a large chapel on the north side. Its south side was contiguous with the great cloister. It comprised six bays, with various internal divisions reflecting both the strict segregation of quire monks from lay brethren and the series of former chantry chapels which were established at regular intervals within the nave. However, five individual phases of construction had altogether created the church in a process of accretion from a small simple 'two-cell-type' plan, where the eastern half was originally for the quire monks and the west for the lay brothers (Fig 9.1). In every way this is closely comparable to the Carthusian church at Mount Grace Priory in North Yorkshire (Coppack 1990, 52–4).

At Coventry's Charterhouse, which was the earlier foundation (1381–5 as opposed to 1398 at Mount Grace), there is evidence that some of the structural phases were anticipated long before they were in fact built. Both the east and west end walls of the earliest rectangular church appear to have been of timber and were set on relatively flimsy foundations in contrast to the buttressed stone side walls which were wider and more sturdily founded. It is not possible to say whether enlargement was always envisaged, assuming that appropriate benefaction would be forthcoming, or if the shortcomings in the building-methods were due to financial constraints such as are known to have been a major bar to development throughout the early 15th century (Soden 1994, 159).

The close similarity between the individual phases of construction at Coventry and Mount Grace implies a common long-term development plan that was regulated and overseen by the order. There are some differences, however, chiefly in the dates of each building phase. At Mount Grace the quire was extended eastwards in the 1420s (Coppack 1990, 52–3) but at Coventry a similar extension was only made in about 1475, and then accompanied by a corresponding westward extension of the nave. There are at least two possible reasons for this additional extension. Firstly, there may have been the need to create space for new intra-mural burials of benefactors: this part of the nave contained 18 of the 27 inhumations which can be dated post-1475 (the church contained an overall total of 41 burials). The historical context for such need exists in the plagues which are attested to have swept through Coventry and Warwickshire in 1478–9, killing almost 4500 people (CRO 201/1). Secondly, the unparalleled foundation of a school 'for twelve poor clerks' within the precinct of St Anne's in the early 15th century may eventually have required a discrete place for worship, separated from the quire monks and possibly from the lay brothers, particularly as they were not to be educated as Carthusians. Their very presence contravened the Carthusian rule (Soden 1995, 24–5).

The erection of a central bell-tower at Mount Grace in the 1420s is also parallelled at Coventry,

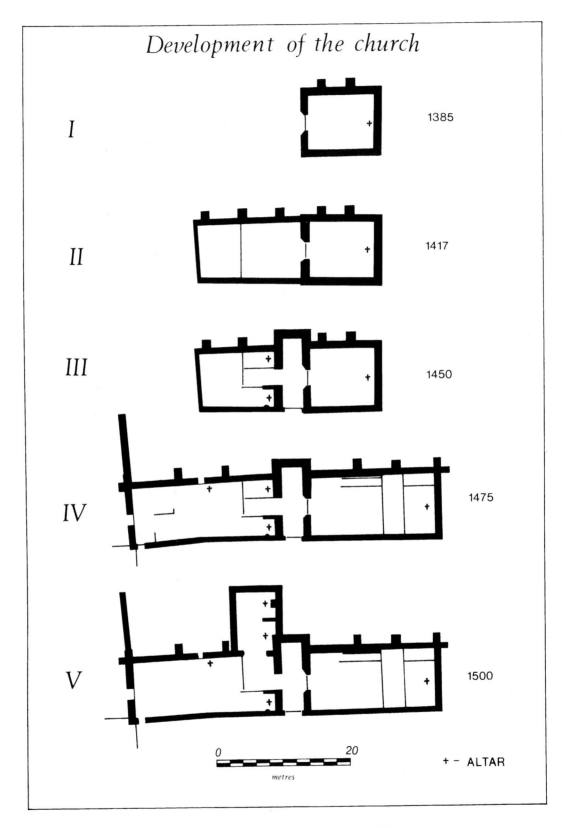

Fig 9.1 *Coventry Charterhouse: development of the church.*

Fig 9.2 *Mount Grace Charterhouse: the bell-tower.*

although the foundations, which are all that survive, cannot be more closely dated than to the period *c*1417–1475 (Fig 9.2). Its purpose, as at Mount Grace, is linked with the enlargement of the community. At Coventry this happened twice as the result of specific benefaction, in 1386 and again in 1398, by which time the priory may have reached its full complement. It is not known why the building of the tower should have taken so long but the financial hardship which the house experienced until at least 1439 cannot be overlooked (Soden 1994, 159). A date of perhaps 1450 or soon after might therefore be suggested for the tower's construction.

When built the new tower and its rood loft may have caused chaos since they breached the ridge line of the existing church. The problems were exacer-

bated when the quire and nave were later extended.

The tower had been standing for between ten and thirty years when the major programme of extension took place. Besides the removal of the old east and west walls, the new works required the entire structure to be re-planned. What had been a 30m x 10m rectangle of five unequal bays, subsequently punctuated by the insertion of a central tower at the centre bay position, was now turned into a 50m x 10m rectangle of six more-regular bays, with three at each side of the tower. Old buttresses were torn down and new ones built, some only slightly offset. The effects of this work on the integrity of the overall structure can only be surmised but all geometry would have been lost and it is likely that a total reworking of the fenestration scheme took place.

Such drastic actions might betoken the severity of the effects caused by inserting a bell-tower into a structure which was never designed to accommodate such an ungainly mass.

Evidence has survived at Coventry for at least five chantry chapels. With the nave already full of chantries by perhaps 1500, there came a need to extend beyond the body of the church. This was achieved by building a large chapel on the north side of the nave, springing partly from the end of the bell-tower and covering an entire bay of the church. A large opening was created, probably with no dividing doors, and the space was given over to two new chantry chapels in which the altar bases partly survive, together with the screen wall dividing them.

This was the last addition to the church, and it may be significant that no burials took place in the chapel before the house was dissolved. Perhaps the patron and his family were still alive at the Dissolution, and thereby unable to claim burial rights subsequently.

The inviolable segregation of quire monk from lay brother meant the enforcement of the quire/nave division and thus when there was no longer room for chantries in the nave, side chapels were the only option. At Mount Grace there were three side chapels, the last being almost identical to that at Coventry (two altars, side by side but with a tomb between) and of similar date (Coppack 1990, 52–3; cf HBMCE 1986, 9).

Throughout their histories the Charterhouses of Coventry and Mount Grace display great similarities. Both grew at similar rates, with similar structures. The builders at Coventry seem not to have foreseen the effects of their methods however, and the monks there may have made poor decisions owing to their penury. Similarities of design enacted at similar times may suggest a movement towards a common church development plan in the English Carthusian Chapter. But the rigidity of layout long-accepted in relation to the individual monk's cell and the great cloister may almost have come to grief when rigidly, and on occasion retrospectively, applied to a complicated church building which was already evolving along lines dictated by the structure. For a monastic order which had so much of its house-layouts pre-planned, leaving the church to evolve initially in an almost organic manner and then to impose restrictions was a recipe for total structural failure. If the church at Mount Grace remains a well-preserved testament to the rigour and order of Carthusian life, then the remains excavated at Coventry lie in total contrast, where the planning almost came to grief.

Acknowledgements

My thanks to Brian Dix, formerly Chief Archaeologist of Northamptonshire Archaeology, for his comments on the text of this paper.

Bibliography

1 Historical sources
CRO 201/1: Coventry Record Office, Diary of John Whittingham, 1746–95.

2 Secondary Works
Coppack G 1990, *Abbeys and Priories*, Batsford, London
HBMCE 1986, *Mount Grace Priory*, HMSO London
Soden I 1994, 'The propaganda of monastic benefaction: Statement and implication in the art of St Anne's Charterhouse, Coventry', in Locock M P (ed), 1994, *Meaningful architecture: social interpretations of buildings*, Worldwide Archaeology Series 9, Aldershot, Hants and Vermont, USA.
Soden I 1995, *Excavations at St Anne's Charterhouse, Coventry, 1968–87*, Coventry museums monograph

10   The Demolition and Conversion of former monastic buildings in post-dissolution Hertfordshire

Nick Doggett

"Mergate was a nunnery of late tyme. It standith on a hil in a faire woode hard by Watheling streate on the est side of it; Humfray Boucher, base sunne to the late lorde Berners, did much coste in translating of the priorie into a maner-place".[1]

Despite the vast amount written on the dissolution of the monasteries, relatively little has been published on the demolition and conversion of former monastic buildings.[2] It is therefore not yet possible to say with certainty which parts of a monastic establishment were most likely to survive the dissolution and whether any significance should be attached to the re-use of different buildings at sites of varying size and complexity. Nevertheless, there is considerable potential for study and it is a field in which documentary, archaeological and architectural evidence can all be used. Moreover, by examining in detail the religious houses of a single county, in this case Hertfordshire, some light may be shed on the social and economic implications of this undoubtedly important but as yet improperly understood process.

With the exception of the Benedictine Abbey of St Albans, which was the fourth wealthiest monastery in the country in 1535,[3] Hertfordshire never had any monastic houses of the first rank; there is no spectacular ruin like Fountains, Glastonbury or Rievaulx. This was partly due to the ownership of large tracts of land by St Albans in the south and west of the county and to the existence of the considerable estates of Westminster Abbey and St Paul's Cathedral in the north and east. Similarly, the relatively high population level in the county meant that the more austere orders like the Cistercians and Carthusians were not attracted here. On the contrary, Hertfordshire was a county of friaries and hospitals, usually situated in towns and many of them late foundations, only the friary at King's Langley being of more than local significance.

Considering the comparative unimportance of Hertfordshire's religious houses and their relatively high density within a small county, it is not surprising that many of them ceased to exist well before the dissolution. The casualties included the collegiate house of Thele, which closed in 1431 and the preceptories of Temple Dinsley and Standon, which were the properties of the Knights Templar and the Knights Hospitaller respectively.[4] The alien priory of Ware was suppressed as early as 1414,[5] while the Trinitarian friary at Hertford, the Benedictine priories of Redbourn and Salburn in Standon and the Benedictine nunneries at Rowney and St Mary de Pré had all disbanded before the First Act of Suppression.[6]

This act, passed in 1536, proclaimed that as a result of 'manifest sin, vicious, carnal and abominable living' all 'the little and small abbeys, priories and other religious houses ... where the congregation ... is under the number of twelve persons should be utterly suppressed.'[7] This was to lead to the fall of all remaining Hertfordshire houses with the exception of Ashridge, St Albans and its dependent cell of Hertford.

Many of the foundations dissolved in 1536–7 were already in a poor state, both morally and physically. For instance, at the Augustinian priory of Wymondley although the prior had repaired the refectory and spent 100 marks on rebuilding the belfry in 1530, many other parts of the buildings were in need of refurbishment.[8] Similarly, the low values assigned to the great majority of the county's houses in the *Valor Ecclesiasticus* suggest that many of them would have disappeared even without the passing of the 1536 Act.

Naturally, when there were already derelict buildings and a house had almost ceased to function, the task of the royal commissioners appointed to superintend the suppression and demolition of the monasteries was very much easier. Only two Hertfordshire foundations, the Benedictine nunneries of Cheshunt and St Margaret's, Nettleden were in fact dissolved in 1536. This was probably due to their extreme poverty: the commissioners valued Cheshunt's lead at only £2, which suggests that the church was already in ruins.[9]

In 1537 the Benedictine nunneries of St Giles in the Wood, Flamstead, Markyate and Sopwell and the Augustinian priories of Royston and Wymondley capitulated to be joined in the following year by the Dominican friary of King's Langley and the Franciscan friary at Ware. Also in 1538 the Carmelite friary of Hitchin, to which Henry VIII himself had made a gift of 40s as late as 1530,[10] was suppressed. By the end of 1539 Hertfordshire's three remaining monasteries, the college of Bonhommes at Ashridge, St Albans and its dependent cell of Hertford had all surrendered.

Before demolition could begin all goods of value had, of course, to be removed from the church and domestic buildings. Their values having been recorded by the king's commissioners, the plate and jewellery were sent to the royal treasury in London. Even the smallest house could provide the crown with considerable revenue as the following extract from the inventory made at the suppression of St Giles in the Wood, Flamstead shows:

'Itm the glasse in the Wyndowes in the church...20s
Itm a sensor of Latten and a Shippe...4d
Itm the pavement stone in the churche...10s
Itm the Tymber in the quyre...26s 8d
Itm a Table of Alabaster for o'r Ladye aulter...3s 4d
Itm the Stuffe in the Backhowsse sold for 26s 8d
Itm a salte of sylver wt a cover p'cell gilte...44s
Itm 6 sylver spones white 20s
Itm a chalice wt a patent gilte...48s 6d
Itm the garnysshynge of a masor band gilte...12s 1d
Sma Totalle of alle the goods Cattalle and plate belongynge to the said late priory of Seynt Gyles in the Woode...£44 8s 3d'[11]

The goods valued and removed and the monks dispersed, demolition could begin in earnest. Despite the king's instructions to his commissioners that they should 'pull down to the ground all the walls of the churches, stepulls, cloysters fraterys, dorters, chapter howsys and the like',[12] it seems that the demolition of a monastic house was rarely total and this certainly seems to have been the case in Hertfordshire. For the most part, the commissioners appear to have been content to 'deface' the church and to render the domestic buildings uninhabitable by removing their roofs and stairs. For example, at Hitchin Priory the steeple of the church was knocked down, stripped of its bells, lead, glass and stone and the building soon fell into disrepair.[13] However, for fear that 'the birds (ie the religious) should build therein again',[14] the east range of the cloister was commonly razed to the ground as it contained the chapter house, dormitory and library essential for the maintenance of monastic life.

At two Hertfordshire sites physical evidence of the demolition process has been recovered through excavation. At Sopwell traces of hearths for the melting of lead have been found.[15] Lead was obviously one of the most valuable commodities to be obtained from former monastic buildings (its exact value always being recorded by the commissioners in their inventories) and was quickly removed to prevent its falling into the hands of unscrupulous local people. Such lead was often later to be re-used elsewhere. For instance, lead from Sopwell was re-used at the king's manor house of The More near Rickmansworth during the 1540s, while lead valued at £150 from King's Langley was re-used in the 1550s for royal building works at Windsor.[16]

Also at King's Langley, excavation has revealed evidence for the deliberate acts of vandalism, which were all too frequent at this time. On the site of the friary church, fragments of late 14th-century glass have been found on the south side of the lady chapel and the south chancel chapel.[17] This suggests that the windows were smashed from within, presumably soon after the friary was dissolved and perhaps with the aim of preventing the friars from returning to hold services. It is therefore somewhat ironic that a new religious community was established here during Mary's reign, although it was a group of seven Dominican nuns from Dartford (Kent) rather than friars, which formed the new foundation. This community was, however, short lived, moving back to Dartford within a year of its creation in 1557, only to be suppressed on the accession of Elizabeth in November 1558.[18]

Elsewhere, too, it seems that there may have been hopes (or should it be fears?) of a revival of monastic life. At St Albans, after plans in 1539 to make it the seat of a bishopric had come to nothing,[19] the last abbot, Richard Boreman, who in the event of a change in the political and religious climate apparently held hopes of being re-appointed to the abbacy, continued, with several other ex-religious, to live in the town. Indeed, Dugdale suggests that shortly before her death Mary intended to refound the abbey. In November 1551 Boreman, probably with Mary's help, had bought the site from Sir Richard Lee – ostensibly for the grammar school he had been authorised to establish – and in December 1556 made it over to her, no doubt with this very purpose in mind.[20] Nothing more, however, seems to have come of the scheme. Elsewhere, apart from some fighting talk at Ashridge, Hertfordshire's religious seem to have accepted their capacities and pensions with little complaint and among the lay population there seems to have been little sorrow at their departure.

To return to the buildings; these were most

vulnerable to plunder by local people for their materials after the commissioners' work was complete and while the sites awaited transfer to lay ownership. There are no recorded cases in Hertfordshire of individuals suffering from moral scruples in profiting from the fall of the monasteries in this way; rather they seem to have shared the often-quoted contemporary attitude adopted by Michael Sherbrook's father towards the despoliation of Roche Abbey in Yorkshire: 'What should I do ... might I not as well as others have some Profit of the spoil of the Abbey? For I did see all would away; and therefore I did as others did.'[21]

Following the 1536 and 1539 Acts of Suppression, the former monastic properties were taken into royal hands. Some, such as Royston, Wymondley and Ware were leased or sold to new tenants or owners almost immediately, while others were to remain with the crown for a number of years. In either case, the wholesale disposal of church property represented the biggest change in land ownership since the Norman Conquest.

Although relatively little is known of some of the beneficiaries of the royal grants and leases in Hertfordshire, it is clear that a significantly and perhaps atypically high proportion were favourites of the crown. This can be contrasted with the situation in counties such as Devon and Norfolk, remote from London's influence, where the former monastic lands were just as, if not more, likely to be acquired eventually by lesser members of the gentry or of the aspiring yeoman farmer class.[22] Several men who took an active role in the dissolution of the monasteries profited directly from their fall. One such was Richard Yngworth, the last prior of King's Langley, who as a royal commissioner supervised the suppression of many friaries in England and Wales. He was also made suffragan bishop of Dover and in 1540, after much supplication to Cromwell, was further rewarded with the grant of his old house, the richest Dominican friary in the country.[23]

Other royal officials who benefited in a similar way include Thomas Birch, an accountant and agent of Cromwell, who was granted the site and lands of Ware Priory in 1544, his father, Robert, having been lessee there since 1538.[24] Sir Anthony Denny, a privy councillor and great royal favourite, succeeded in building up a considerable estate in Hertfordshire and Essex on the spoils of the monasteries.[25] In 1538 he was granted the buildings and lands of Hertford Priory, although its formal suppression was postponed until the following year when St Albans itself fell. As well as acquiring further St Albans lands, he had already obtained possession of Cheshunt Nunnery in 1536 and in 1540 he was granted a messuage in Hertford called 'le Trynitie', the site of the former Trinitarian friary.[26]

Sir John Tregonwell, another privy councillor and legal adviser to Henry VIII, who had superintended the surrender of many monasteries throughout the country, was, however, rather less fortunate – at least in Hertfordshire. The former nunnery of St Giles in the Wood, Flamstead and its manor of Beechwood were conveyed to him in 1537 but two years later Henry, wishing to obtain Sir Richard Page's manor of Molesey (Surrey), turned him out and gave Beechwood to Page.[27] It is said that Tregonwell often complained bitterly of his lot,[28] but the rich prize of Milton Abbas in Dorset, which he bought for £1000 on its dissolution, must have proved some compensation.

There is only one other instance of a royal lease in Hertfordshire being revoked. This was at Ashridge, leased in 1541 to John Norrys for 21 years, but which was granted in 1550 to Princess Elizabeth by her brother, Edward, probably because they had spent considerable parts of their childhoods there.[29]

Other royal favourites, although they had not been actively engaged in the suppression of the monasteries also benefited from their closure. Sir James Nedeham, surveyor of the king's works, builder of the Jewel house at the Tower of London (1535–6) and who also converted the former monasteries of Dartford and Rochester (Kent) into royal residences,[30] was leased and then granted Wymondley in 1538.[31] Sir Richard Lee, the military engineer, successor to Nedeham as surveyor of the king's works (1544–7) and later architect of the artillery defences at Berwick-upon-Tweed, was in 1538 granted Sopwell, of which he had been bailiff since 1534, and also bought much of the land of St Albans Abbey.[32]

In 1537 Robert Chester, gentleman usher of Henry VIII's chamber and subsequently sheriff of Essex and Hertfordshire, was leased the site and lands of Royston Priory, which were then sold to him in 1540,[33] while Humphrey Bourchier, the illegitimate son of the second Lord Berners, who had translated Froissart's Chronicles and was deputy of Calais until his death in 1533,[34] acquired the lease of Markyate in 1539.[35]

There seems to be little evidence for property speculation among the new owners, although the activities of Sir Anthony Denny could perhaps be construed as such. For the most part, rather, they seem to have been anxious to hold onto their new possessions, with the intention of building up country estates. Indeed, from the mid-16th century onwards, Hertfordshire was to experience a considerable influx of new families, be they those of courtiers or merchants, drawn from London by the combined attractions of pleasant countryside and good, wholesome air. This trend was so widespread that by the mid-17th century Fuller could comment wittily that 'such who buy a house in Hertfordshire pay two years' purchase for the air'.[36] It has also been noted that 'of 295 manors or similar estates, whose successive owners can be traced through the county histories, 168 (42.5%) were in the hands of the crown in 1540. By 1550 only twelve (7%) of these 168 properties remained in the hands of the crown',[37] although it should be pointed out that the number of manors owned by the crown in 1540 had been artificially inflated by the temporary appropriation of monastic manors between 1536 and 1540. However, it is probably significant that by 1700 only 42 of the 395 properties were owned by the same family or institution as in 1540.

This remarkable transfer of ownership was partly due to the widespread sale of privately owned manors, beginning in the 1540s, but the dispersal of former monastic lands through the king was largely responsible. Indeed, it is significant that with the exception of Ashridge – held until 1575 – the crown did not retain for any significant time its ownership of any of the former monastic houses in Hertford-shire. This was no doubt partly caused by the need to reward favourites in order to ensure their continuing support, but the far greater need to gain revenue, especially after the first rash of sales and leases was over, was perhaps even more important. To the lessees or purchasers, be they courtiers, merchants or members of the gentry, the proximity of Hertfordshire to the capital, where the court was becoming increasingly permanently based would have been essential.[38]

Once a former religious house had been granted to its new owner it was, of course, his to do with as he thought fit. In some cases the new owner was no more than an absentee landlord, interested in the property only as a source of income. In this event the surviving buildings were likely to be further plundered by local people for those re-usable materials which had not already been removed by the new owner or tenant, and it is worth emphasising that vandalism and theft did not cease with the transfer from royal to private ownership.

In many places the despoliation was so complete that virtually all traces of the monastic buildings probably disappeared within a generation or so of the dissolution. For instance, at Cheshunt the buildings were almost certainly partly derelict at the time of the dissolution and, although the refectory seems to have survived until the early 19th century, little else was left by the early 18th century.[39] There appears to have been a similar sequence of events at St Margaret's, Nettleden, where only a building likely to have been the monastic refectory remained in the early 19th century.[40] The site at Cheshunt was totally destroyed by gravel quarrying in the 1950s, but relatively substantial earthwork remains can still be seen at St Margaret's.

The conventual church of St Mary de Pré appears to have been in use as a farmhouse by the early 18th century,[41] while the site of Rowney Priory, Great Munden is occupied by a Victorian building, albeit one almost certainly containing fragments of its monastic predecessor.[42] At The Biggin, Hitchin, the church and claustral buildings were converted into a house in the mid- to late 16th century, sub-sequently being adapted as a school in the 17th century and as a poorhouse in the 18th century. There are still substantial remains of the medieval crown-post roof structure in the present timber-framed building and its four ranges around a small central courtyard probably reflect the layout of the monastic cloister.[43]

Although a comparatively substantial free-standing 14th-century two-storey rectangular building and a well-preserved gatehouse embedded in a post-medieval building survive at King's Langley, the site never seems to have been used as anything more than a farm and its history after the Dissolution is illustrative of the fate that befell many monastic houses. In 1553 a survey was carried out there by John Pygot, steward general of the county, which shows the buildings to be in a very poor state of repair,[44] suggesting that there had been systematic slighting of the friary. However, the following buildings remained, even if defective 'bothe in timber and tylinge':-

The Church
Our Ladyes Chappell
The Cloister (including the sore decayed frater and dorter)
Vestry
Great Kitchen and Housse of effyce
A Fayre gate housse and fayre stables (probably the existing buildings)
Brewe Housse and Back Housse
Garner
Barn
Great Housse
Olde Housse for Stables
A Little Mancion House standing in the orchards
A sore decayed dove house

Surprisingly, some lead remained on the church roof, 'although the glass and the iron work bothe of the chaunsell and the belfry (were) taken away',[45] but this too was soon to be removed for the royal building works at Windsor referred to earlier.

There is no evidence to suggest that either Yngworth or his successor to the property, John Lord Russell of Bedford, who was the owner between 1546 and 1556, ever lived here and they must have been aware of, and perhaps actively encouraged, the despoliation of the buildings. Possibly the reason why the nuns of Dartford returned thither only a year after the reintroduction of monastic life at King's Langley was that many of the buildings were barely inhabitable. In any case, Edward Grimston, who bought the site in 1573, effectively prevented the majority of them continuing in use and by 1607, when the site passed to Edward Newport, the church was totally in ruins.[46] William Houlker carried out further demolition in the late 17th century, but the surviving buildings continued to be used as a farmhouse in the 19th and early 20th centuries, as a number of illustrations show.[47] In 1831 Farmer Betts had removed the last traces of the church, its foundations being observed in the process by the young George Gilbert Scott.[48]

But such a sorry tale is not typical of the post-Reformation history of all of Hertfordshire's monasteries. Although there is perhaps nothing to match the daring conversions to domestic use of Sir Thomas Wriothesley's Titchfield (Hants) or Sir Richard Grenville's Buckland (Devon),[49] a significant proportion were transformed into imposing town or country residences and it is to these that we now turn.

Indeed, even if converted monastic houses were eventually to become 'curses upon the Families and Estates of their owners' as Clement Spelman, writing over a century later, would have it,[50] there was no reluctance at the time to adapt them to domestic purposes, as the new owners rushed to take advantage of the suppression of the monasteries in this way.

At Redbourn, Richard Reade is reputed to have built Place House on the site of the priory,[51] and at Beechwood, Markyate and Royston, completely new structures were built nearby using materials from the former monastic buildings.[52] Elsewhere, the church or the conventual buildings were used to form an integral part of new residences. The claustral ranges were particularly attractive to the new owners for, not only had they been especially built for domestic purposes – often including the superior's own lavish lodgings – but in many cases they had only comparatively recently been reconstructed to high standards. These buildings could then, in theory at least, be converted with the minimum of effort into the fashionable courtyard houses so characteristic of Tudor and early Elizabethan architecture. In practice, the frequently different dates and varying floor and roof levels of the individual claustral ranges made conversions into a unified whole more difficult to achieve than might at first sight appear. However, where circumstances did allow, such conversions could be very fine indeed, as is shown at Ashridge, Lacock (Wilts) and Newstead (Notts).[53] Certainly, a conversion of this kind, particularly one made in the period from the 1540s to 1560s, would have provided a highly desirable and fashionable dwelling, and it cannot be coincidental that several other major newly-built or extensively remodelled houses in Hertfordshire at this time were also of courtyard plan, including Broxbourne Bury (1544 ff), Gorhambury

(1563–8), Knebworth (c 1563) and, on a slightly smaller scale, Standon Lordship (1546–61).[54]

Occasionally, moral scruples may have prevented an owner from converting the church itself to residential use but several well-known examples, like Netley and Mottisfont in Hampshire, show that this was by no means always the case. Indeed, the supposed rarity of church conversions has almost certainly been greatly exaggerated. Earlier studies such as Copeland's work on Buckland,[55] tended to over-emphasise the alleged unsuitability of the church for domestic purposes, but more recent examinations of a number of individual buildings, such as Denny and Hinchingbroke in Cambridgeshire, have suggested that the re-use of the church was relatively widespread.[56] Moreover, the tendency to insert first floors into the open halls of secular buildings from the early 16th century onwards would have established a precedent for similar work to churches and the technical problems posed by such an operation would have been easily overcome by the Tudor builder.

Hertfordshire has at least two major conversions of this sort in Sopwell and Wymondley. There is also less conclusive evidence for the residential adaptation of the churches at The Biggin and Hitchin Priory into two-storey halls, while at Ashridge it appears that the west end of the church may have been re-used as domestic apartments.[57] The physical transformation of a monastic church into a house is, however, most clearly seen at Wymondley where, through the insertion of first and second floors and fireplaces, the west end of the aisleless nave formed the nucleus of the house created by Sir James Nedeham in the 1540s. The thick 13th-century walling of the church has now been much disturbed, but extensive if ill-conceived 'restoration' in 1973–4 revealed two lancets in the south wall of the present building. A processional north doorway suggests that the cloister probably lay to the north. Much of the work now visible in the house was probably carried out by Nedeham's grandson, George, around 1600, when there is also some suggestion that the house was much reduced in size. The three prominent gables on the north front, much of the square and rectangular oak panelling in the ground-floor rooms and a wall painting of Roman soldiers, discovered in 1973–4, are all likely to be of this date.[58]

Of the other former monastic buildings here, a fine timber-framed and weather-boarded late 15th-century barn of nine aisled bays survives within the moated platform on which the house stands. There is also a dovecote, which may in fact just post-date the dissolution, to the north-west. This was converted into a cottage in the late 19th century. Very little now remains of the 16th-century conduit house, from which water was once piped to the house and which the late 17th-century historian, Sir Henry Chauncy, tells us provided 'sufficient water to turn the spit in the kitchen (of the house) upon all occasions'.[59]

At Ashridge all physical evidence for the conversion carried out after the dissolution has been destroyed by Wyatt's Gothic fantasy of 1808–13. One of the most important sources for establishing the lay-out of the 16th-century house, and that of its medieval predecessor, is a survey of 1575 which shows that the cruciform church was on the south side of the cloister, the refectory on the north (the late 13th-century undercroft of which survives in the cellars of the present mansion), the chapter house and dormitory on the east and a hall on the west.[60]

Although there is some uncertainty as to precisely which of the ex-monastic buildings were then still in use, the survey gives the impression that the buildings were generally in a good state of repair. In fact much rebuilding had taken place in the 15th century as a result of gifts from Cardinal Beaufort, bishop of Winchester and his clerk, Richard Petworth.[61] This and the post-dissolution royal interest in the former monastery probably explains the survival of its buildings after the suppression. Although there is no evidence that the surveyor of the king's works was ever concerned with Ashridge during Henry VIII's reign, there are clear indications that efforts were made to improve the buildings for royal use after they were granted to Princess Elizabeth in 1550.[62] A survey of 1560 remarks that, although £55 3s 8d had been spent on repairs since the first year of Elizabeth's reign, 300 marks would still not make it fit for the queen.[63] In 1564 further repairs costing £67 10s 7d were carried out by the surveyor of the queen's works in connection with a royal progress in the county.[64]

In 1598 Norden notes that 'this place is lately beautified by the Lord Cheyney', although perhaps simply in deference to his monarch he acknowledges that the house was more 'stately' when 'Elizabeth lodged (there) as in her owne'.[65] More extensive work, however, took place in 1604–7 following the acquisition of the property by the lord chancellor, Sir Thomas Egerton, in 1603.[66] A new gatehouse was built and wings added to the former monastic refectory, which had become the great hall of the post-dissolution house. The church had by then been largely, if not completely demolished and a maze was laid out in the grounds for the enjoyment of Sir Thomas and his guests. Work seems to have been finished in 1607 for in that year there are copious references in the family papers to furniture being 'bought and exchanged' for Ashridge. The items included tapestries, hangings, cushions, screens and curtains. Two tapestries depicting the stories of Alexander and Elias for 'the purple bed-chamber' alone cost £132 15s.[67]

A number of 18th- and early 19th-century drawings show the north front of the house with the great hall sandwiched between the two projecting wings, showing the way in which the house presented a fashionable H-plan front to the outside world.[68] In front was a large courtyard, in the centre of which stood the three-storey gatehouse referred to above. Behind the great hall the former monastic cloister formed the inner courtyard of the new house, its walks raised in height to form corridor galleries between the connecting ranges. On the ground floor, however, the cloister largely, and somewhat remarkably, retained its medieval appearance until all was swept away by Wyatt in the early 19th century. Thomas Baskerville, a visitor in 1681, considered it notable for 'having in paint upon the walls some scriptures and monkish stories'.[69] Todd in his *History of Ashridge*, written during the period in which the post-dissolution house was being demolished, says that the scenes depicted were from the life of Christ, including the raising of Lazarus and the betrayal, although by then the paintings were much damaged by water as the claustral walks surround a reservoir.[70]

Apart from Ashridge, the most ambitious conversion in Hertfordshire was Sir Richard Lee's Sopwell, shown by excavation (as yet not properly published) to have taken place in two distinct phases.[71] The first occurred during the late 1540s and 1550s when Lee, spending almost a decade of retirement in the county, built a house on the ground-plan of the church and claustral buildings of the former nunnery. Although he appears to have used additional materials from the domestic buildings of St Albans Abbey, which he bought in 1550,[72] the monastic plan was retained, perhaps with a timber-framed superstructure, the church being used as the great hall and the cloister as a courtyard. In the late 1560s or early 1570s all this was swept away and the work on a house of fashionable double-courtyard plan began. This consisted of a long hall range linking east and west wings, the latter of which was of double width at its northern end and forms the principal surviving ruin on the site today. To the east lay a formal garden and to the west a forecourt with low buildings, in front of which was an outer courtyard entered through the main gateway on the road.[73]

The house was surrounded by a large park, for the creation of which Lee diverted the London road. Parts of the wall enclosing this still survive and incorporate moulded stonework which may come from the former nunnery church.[74] Work on the house was never completed, however, probably as a result of Lee's death in 1575. Lee's pride in his new house is, nevertheless, reflected by his will, drawn up in 1570, which states that 'if any of the persons mentioned in this entail do alter, change, transforme digge cutt dowen or deface the said howses, edifices, buyldynges or walles of the mansion house of the said Syr Rycharde called Lee Hall or Sopwelle Hall.. the sd persons so doing shall forfeit their interest in the premises'.[75]

A series of plaster and stone medallions now at Salisbury Hall in the neighbouring parish of Shenley are said to have been purchased by Sir Jeremiah Snow from Sir Harbottle Grimston, who bought Sopwell in 1669 and who is believed to have demolished at least some of its buildings.[76] The medallions are of very fine quality and depict the busts of Roman emperors and other figures from classical antiquity. They are almost certainly of English workmanship and would seem to have been expressly commissioned for Lee's Sopwell, but even their general context within the house is unknown. Their exact date is also uncertain. Although their fine quality would seem in some ways to be more in keeping with the lavish second phase of Sopwell, they are precisely the kind of work associated with the mid-Tudor Renaissance of Protector Somerset and his circle and were perhaps ultimately inspired by the very similar terracotta roundels of the 1520s at Hampton Court.[77] As such, they are useful confirmation that even in its first, comparatively modest phase, Sopwell is likely to have been a house of more than local significance.

At Markyate no direct use was made of the former monastic buildings, but their materials were almost certainly re-used in the new house built higher up the hillside there. Some of Humphrey Bourchier's 'costly translating of the priorie into a maner place' may still survive in the present building, but most of it was extensively remodelled in a neo-Elizabethan style by Robert Lugar in 1825–6.[78] Moreover, what 16th century work does survive in the house, notably in the short wing to the north-east, may date to after c1580. Parts of the east and north walls of this wing are faced with alternating squares of flint and Totternhoe clunch, a fashionable technique which was also employed on the now-demolished Berkhamsted Place (c1580) a few miles away.[79] This suggests that this part of the house may have been the work of the Ferrers family, who had acquired the property in 1548 and who held it for about 100 years.[80] Indeed, Leland comments that Bourchier, who died in 1540, having unsuccessfully tried to buy the estate, left the house 'nothing endid'.[81]

The 16th-century house, whether mainly the work of Bourchier or the Ferrers family, must have been considerably more impressive than the present building, and plans and illustrations made before Lugar's remodelling show it to have been much larger.[82] Its reconstructed appearance is conjectural but it seems to have had a large forecourt to the south and a long hall range, probably of two storeys above an undercroft, aligned roughly east-west with cross-wings projecting to the north. A plan of 1805 shows the reputed position of the east end of the monastic church, some 12m to the west of the terrace to the north of the present house.[83]

The survival rate of former monastic buildings in towns is mixed in Hertfordshire. At St Albans the domestic buildings of the abbey were retained by the crown as it appears to have been Henry VIII's intention to use the abbot's lodgings as an occasional residence, as at St Augustine's Canterbury.[84] With this purpose in mind the stables and other offices in the great court were put into the care of John Palmer, who as 'surveyor of the king's barnes and other out-houses within the late monastery of St Albans' in 1541 submitted an account for repairs amounting to £49. Further repairs were carried out in 1543 to the 'king's mansion' and in the following year St Albans was one of the royal houses visited by Robert Sylvester, the master mason to the Court of Augmentations.[85]

Royal interest in St Albans seems to have waned with Henry's death in 1547 and, as we have seen, in 1550 the majority of the former conventual buildings were sold to Sir Richard Lee. The church, discussed below, and the great court, however, remained with the crown and during Elizabeth's reign the stables were repaired several times, either by the surveyor of the royal estates in the county, or, in the event of a visit from the queen, by the surveyor of the works. As late as 1607 a joint survey by the officers of the works and the officers of the horse called for repairs costing nearly £100,[86] suggesting that the stables were still in frequent use.

Meanwhile the great gatehouse had become the sessions house, which it remained until 1631 when the decision was taken to turn it into a prison. It continued in this use until 1871, when it was comprehensively restored and taken over by the grammar school.[87] Another gatehouse by the river was demolished in 1772.[88]

At St Albans' dependent cell of Hertford it would seem that the majority of the buildings were demolished soon after the dissolution, although there is some tentative evidence to suggest that Priory House, which was not demolished until the late 19th century, was a post-suppression remodelling of the former prior's house.[89] At Royston parts of the priory's domestic buildings survived to be recorded by William Cole and William Stukeley in the mid-18th century,[90] but the present Priory House, which appears to have originated as a timber-framed structure in the late 16th century, perhaps as part of the courtyard house considered as a stopping-place for Elizabeth on a royal progress in 1578,[91] does not seem directly to overlie the site of any of the claustral ranges.

At Hitchin the conventual buildings appear to have remained largely intact after the dissolution, a survey of 1546 listing a 'mansion house' with frater and dorter over the cloister, the church, the old hall, the prior's lodging, two chambers for the brothers, a kitchen and a barn. All except the 'mansion house', which had been repaired since the suppression, were severely dilapidated, 'ruinous both in timber and tile',[92] while, as referred to earlier, the commissioners had already 'defaced' the church.[93]

How long the site remained in this condition is not known. The Palladian-style south range of the existing house, which is said to have been built to a design by Robert Adam in the 1770s,[94] conceals a courtyard incorporating substantial elements of the medieval cloister, its 15th-century arcades surviving in the north and west wings. That there was an immediate post-dissolution conversion of the former monastic buildings is indicated by some surviving 16th- and early 17th-century work. By the late 17th century, if not before, the claustral arches on the south side of the north wing had been blocked and an arcade inserted in the north, entrance front. One of the arches remained open, however, and formed the main access through to the courtyard.[95] Both phases of post-medieval work were carried out by the Radcliffe family, who originally obtained the site in 1553.[96] The 17th-century Oxford antiquary, Anthony Wood, records the tradition that Ralph, the first member of the family to own the site, opened a school here and converted one of the rooms into a stage, where he taught pupils to act Latin and Greek comedies, some of which he wrote himself.[97]

The cloister was also used to form the basis of the 16th-century house created at the Franciscan friary of Ware by the Birch family. The present house, which was formerly considerably larger, consists of nearly all of the south claustral range probably originally the monastic refectory, half the west range and the great hall or guest range, which runs westwards at right-angles to the west range. Again it is significant that, as at Hitchin, the buildings had been reconstructed only in the late 15th century. Both the south range and hall range retain scissor-braced roofs, the latter with crown posts.[98]

Three former monastic churches in Hertfordshire became parish churches at the dissolution, the most well-known example being that of St Albans Abbey, which in 1553 was sold by Edward VI to the borough, the old parish church of St Andrew, which had adjoined the north-west corner of the abbey, being pulled down as a result.[99] For a brief period the lady chapel of the abbey church appears to have been in the possession of Richard Boreman, the last abbot who, shortly before buying the majority of the former conventual buildings from Sir Richard Lee in November 1551, acquired it from the crown with permission to found a school in it.[100] That Boreman was merely acting on behalf of the town, however, is suggested by the fact that in 1553 the corporation was given licence to hold a school in the abbey church.[101] Ironically, the borough's ownership of the church was probably the main stumbling block to plans for the re-foundation of the abbey when Boreman gave his portion of the site to Mary in December 1556.[102]

At Hertford, excavations in 1893 and again in 1988–9 have revealed the lay-out of the monastic church, which appears also to have served as a parish church in the medieval period, to have consisted of a long aisleless nave with transepts and a possible tower to the crossing.[103] This church seems to have been in poor condition by the time of the dissolution and, after a period of apparent abandonment, it was totally rebuilt on a much smaller scale in the 1620s, the rebuilt structure in its turn being demolished before the end of the 17th century.[104]

Before the dissolution, the town of Royston, a deliberate 'plantation' of the 12th century,[105] lay in five separate parishes, but an act of parliament in 1540 made it into a parish in its own right.[106] Consequently, the former priory church, the advowson of which along with the priory buildings and lands had been granted to Robert Chester,[107] was converted exclusively to parochial use. The part transformed in this way was, somewhat unusually, the eastern end of the church, the nave being demolished. The present nave therefore consists of the aisled chancel and choir of the 13th-century monastic church, the current chancel having been added only in 1891. The 16th-century and later western tower presumably stands on the site of the medieval central tower.[108] Indeed, to the west of the church and on line with its south wall can still be seen the ruined wall of the south aisle of the monastic church.

This catalogue of conversions to domestic or parish use leads to a consideration of other purposes to which monastic buildings could be put. It is said that Henry VIII used the chapel of the London Charterhouse as a store for his tents and garden gear, while at Blackfriars, Gloucester Thomas Bell, 'clothmaker and draper', turned many of the buildings into workshops.[109] Nothing of this sort appears to have occurred in Hertfordshire, however, and it remains only to look briefly at the fate which befell the former monasteries' agricultural buildings, many of which must have remained in farming use after the dissolution. We have already examined the situation at Wymondley and a very similar barn remains at the preceptory of Standon.[110] There is also a late 15th century close-studded timber-framed barn at Ashridge, although this was gothicized by Wyatville in 1821 and converted to residential accommodation in the 1970s.

Of fittings and furnishings from former monastic buildings even less survives. The 16th-century fireplace at the essentially early 18th-century house of Beechwood may be pre-dissolution in date and may have come from the former nunnery,[112] while a screen and some apparently 15th-century panelling at Little Gaddesden Manor are reputed, on no particularly reliable grounds, to have come from Ashridge.[113] It is known, however, that the monument to Sir Ralph Verney (d.1546) and the fine chest-tomb in Aldbury church to Sir Robert Whittingham (d.1452) and his wife with its surrounding stone parclose screen came from Ashridge after it finally left royal ownership in 1575.[114] Similarly, the late 14th-century tomb of Edmund of Langley (†1402), a notable bene-factor of the friary at King's Langley, was transferred to the local parish church after the dissolution.[115]

The wider question of what happened to the buildings on former monastic manors and whether the dispersal of former monastic lands among new lay landlords and tenants was in any way respon-sible for Hoskins's 'great rebuilding' in the late 16th and first half of the 17th century remains open, and can only be answered by further research, both on a regional and national scale.

Abbreviations

Arch J	*Archaeological Journal*
BL	British Library
Bodl	Bodleian Library
Cal Pat R	*Calendar of Patent Rolls*
DNB	*Dictionary of National Biography*, 22 vols (revised edition 1921/2)
Dugdale	William Dugdale, *Monasticon Angli-canum* (eds J Caley & H Ellis), 6 vols (1817–30)
Herts Arch	*Hertfordshire Archaeology*
HRO	Hertfordshire Record Office
J Brit Arch Assoc	*Journal of the British Archaeological Association*
LP	*Letters and Papers of Henry VIII* (eds J S Brewer & J Gairdner), 21 vols (1862–1920)
Med Arch	*Medieval Archaeology*
PRO	Public Record Office
RCHM	Royal Commission on Historical Monu-ments, Hertfordshire (1911)
VCH	*Victoria County History* for Hertford-shire, 4 vols (1902–14)

Notes

1 Lucy Toulmin Smith (ed), *The Itinerary of John Leland in or About the Years 1535–43* (revised edn, 1964), 104.

2 But see, for example, G W O Woodward, *The Dissolu-tion of the Monasteries* (1966) and J C Dickinson, 'The buildings of the English Austin canons after the dissolution of the monasteries', *J Brit Arch Ass*, 31 (1968), 60–75. More recent studies include Maurice Howard, *The Early Tudor Country House* (1987), ch 7; J H Bettey, *Suppression of the Monasteries in the West Country* (1989), ch 7; Glyn Coppack, *Abbeys and Priories*

(1990), ch 6 and Patrick Greene *Medieval Monasteries* (1992), chs 2, 8 and 9.

3 David Knowles, *The Religious Orders in England*, 3 (1959), app iv.

4 *VCH*, iv, 454 (Thele); ibid, 444–5 (Temple Dinsley) and 444 (Standon).

5 For a general account of the suppression of the alien priories, see Colin Platt, *The Abbeys and Priories of Medieval England* (1984), 173–8.

6 *VCH*, iv, 453 (Hertford); ibid, 418 (Redbourn), 422 (Salburn in Standon) and 435 (Rowney); Eileen Power, *Medieval English Nunneries* (1922), 604 (St Mary de Pre).

7 C H Williams (ed), *English Historical Documents, 1485–1588* (1967), 171.

8 *VCH*, iv, 442.

9 PRO, E 117/12/30.

10 *LP*, v, 751.

11 PRO, E 117/12/30.

12 *LP*, xi, 242.

13 PRO, SC 12/8/29.

14 Thomas Fuller, *The Church History of England*, vi (1655), 258.

15 *Med Arch*, 10 (1966), 177–8.

16 Bodl, MS Rawl D 809; Martin Biddle, 'The excavations of the manor of The More, Rickmansworth, Hert-fordshire', *Arch J*, 116 (1959), 196–9 (Sopwell); W H St John Hope, *Windsor Castle* (1913), 257 (King's Langley).

17 St John O. Gamlen, 'Medieval window glass from the priory, King's Langley', *Herts Arch*, 3 (1973), 73.

18 Dugdale, vi, 1486.

19 *LP*, xiv (2), 151–2.

20 Dugdale, ii, 207.

21 A G Dickens (ed), *Tudor Treatises*, Yorks Arch Record Series, 125 (1959), 125.

22 Felicity Heal and Clive Holmes, *The Gentry in England and Wales, 1500–1700* (1994), 326; W G Hoskins, *The Age of Plunder* (1976), 136–8.

23 *LP*, xv (2), 542.

24 *LP*, xix (1), 378.

25 *DNB*, v, 823–4.

26 *LP*, xiii (1), g 384 (47) (Hertford Priory); *LP*, xi, g 519 (12) (Cheshunt); *VCH*, iv, 453 (Hertford Friary).

27 *LP*, xiv (2), g 113 (16).

28 *DNB*, xix, 1099.

29 *Cal Pat R, Ed VI*, iii, 238.

30 Howard Colvin *et al* (eds), *The History of the King's Works, iii, 1485–1660*, pt 1 (1975), 13.

31 *LP*, xiii, 489.

32 HRO, IV A 1.

33 PRO, SC6/Hen VIII/1606; *LP*, xii (1) no 571; PRO, SC6/Hen VIII/1607.

34 *DNB*, ii, 920–2.

35 *LP*, xiv (1), 610.

36 Thomas Fuller, *The Worthies of England*, ed John Freeman (1952), 229.

37 Lionel Munby, *The Hertfordshire Landscape* (1977), 139–40.

38 Heal and Holmes, op cit, 312.

39 Dugdale, iv, 328.

40 Bodl, MS Willis p 40b, MS Top gen e 79, fols 8–11; D and S Lysons, *Magna Britannia*, i (1806), 492, 588; BL, Add MS 9460, fol 124.

41 Library Soc Antiquaries of London, MS 720, J Web-

ster, *Gleanings of Antiquity from Verolam and St Albans* (nd), 147.

42 *RCHM*, 104; BL, Add MS 36,366, fol 136.

43 Nikolaus Pevsner, *The Buildings of England: Hertford-shire* (2nd edn revised by Bridget Cherry, 1977), 201.

44 J Haythornthwaite, *The History of King's Langley* (1924), 46–7.

45 Ibid.

46 *VCH*, ii, 238.

47 BL, Add MS 32, 350, fols 121–4; Watford Central Library, photographic collection P 1462.

48 G G Scott (ed), *Personal and Professional Recollections by the late Sir George Gilbert Scott* (1879), 68; RIBA Drawings Collection, George Gilbert Scott Sketch-book, No 2 (1830–1).

49 Colin Platt, *Medieval England* (1978), 217–19.

50 Clement Spelman, Preface to Sir Henry Spelman's *Of the Rights and Respects Due unto the Church* printed in *The English Works of Sir Henry Spelman* (1723). Sir Henry, writing in the 1630s, was anxious to attribute the downfall of noble and gentry families to their acquisition of former monastic properties. See particularly his *The History and Fate of Sacrilege*, published posthumously in 1698.

51 *VCH*, ii, 368; J E Cussans, *The History of Hertfordshire*, iii, pt 2 (1881), 231; *Kelly's Directory for Essex, Herts and Middlesex, 1890*, 803.

52 Nicholas Doggett, *Patterns of Re-use: the transformation of Monastic Buildings in Post-Dissolution Hertfordshire, 1540–1600*, PhD thesis, Univ Southampton (1997). This is shortly to be published as a BAR.

53 Howard, op cit, 151–62.

54 J T Smith, *English Houses 1200–1800, the Hertfordshire Evidence* (1992), 46–60.

55 G W Copeland, 'Some Problems of Buckland Abbey', *Trans Devon Assoc*, 85 (1953), 41–52.

56 P M Christie and J G Croad, 'Excavations at Denny Abbey', *Arch J*, 137 (1980), 138–279; Howard, op cit, 149–50.

57 Doggett, op cit.

58 Pevsner, op cit, 243; Gilbert Burleigh *et al*, *Wymondley Priory, Hertfordshire* (unpublished evaluation report by North Herts District Council Museum, 1989).

59 Sir Henry Chauncy, *The Historical Antiquities of Hertfordshire*, i (1700, reprinted 1975), 110.

60 The original document is now apparently lost but the survey is printed in H J Todd, *The History of the College of Bonhommes of Ashridge* (1823), 83–8.

61 *VCH*, ii, 210.

62 *Cal Pat R, Ed VI*, iii, 238.

63 PRO, SP 12/12/38.

64 PRO, E 351/3202.

65 J Norden, *Speculi Britan(n)iae Pars, the Description of Hartfordshire* (1598), 11–12.

66 Bodl, MS Willis 102, fol 15v.

67 Todd, op cit, 88–9.

68 BL, Add MS 9063, fol 304, K Top viii 10 1 b; Bodl, Gough Maps 11, fol 62.

69 Portland MS II, *Historical Manuscripts Commission*, 13th Report App, pt ii (1893), 306.

70 Todd, op cit, 78–80.

71 *Med Arch*, 8 (1964), 242; 9 (1965), 179; 10 (1966), 177–80; 11 (1967), 274.

72 *Cal Pat Rolls, Ed VI*, iv, 5.

73 For a phased plan of the two conversions see Platt, op cit (1978), 216.

74 *VCH*, ii, 413.

75 Ibid.

76 Pevsner, op cit, 322–3, 337n.

77 Simon Thurley, *The Royal Palaces of Tudor England* (1993) 106–9.

78 Pevsner, op cit, 246.

79 J T Smith, *Hertfordshire Houses, Selective Inventory* (1993), 29–30.

80 BL, Harl MS 7389, p 34; *Cal Pat R, Ed VI*, i, 314–15.

81 W.H. Brigg (ed), *The Hertfordshire Genealogist*, iii (1897), 108–11; Toulmin Smith, op et loc cit.

82 BL, Add MS 32,349 fols 1–6; HRO, D/EX 55 Z 2/84; Oldfield Drawings, iv, 502

83 BL, Add MS 32,349, fol 5.

84 Thurley, op cit, 56–7.

85 PRO, E 314/20/3; *LP*, xix (1), 243–4, xx (1), 271.

86 Bodl, MS Rawl, A 195 C, fols 337–43; PRO, E 178/283.

87 *VCH*, ii, 510.

88 Dugdale, ii, 213.

89 Doggett, op cit.

90 W Stukeley, *Palaeographia Britannia... No 1, Origines Roystonianae* (1743), 51; BL, Add MS 5820, fols 20–6.

91 PRO, SP 12/125.

92 PRO, SC 12/8/29.

93 Robert Clutterbuck, *The History and Antiquities of Hertfordshire*, iii (1827), 20.

94 David King, *The Complete Works of Robert and James Adam* (1991), 386.

95 Pevsner, op cit, 204–5.

96 *VCH*, iii, 12.

97 Cussans, op cit, ii, pt 1 (1875), 21.

98 Doggett, op cit.

99 *VCH*, ii, 511.

100 Ibid, 58.

101 *Cal Pat R, Ed VI* v, 33.

102 Dugdale, ii, 207.

103 *Herts Mercury* (2 Dec 1893), unpublished R T Andrews' notebook, Hertford Museum; Hester Cooper-Reade, 'Jewson's Yard, Hertford, Excavations of St Mary's Priory and St John's Parish Church', *Herts Past*, 29 (1990), 29–37.

104 Chauncy, op cit, i, 506.

105 M W Beresford and J K St Joseph, *Medieval England, An Aerial Survey* (revd edn, 1979), 188–9.

106 *Statutes of the Realm*, iii (1817), 797.

107 *LP*, xvi, g 379 (60); Cussans, op cit, i, pt 3 (1873), 112.

108 Doggett, op cit.

109 Knowles, op cit, 387; A D Saunders, 'Blackfriars (Gloucester)', *Arch J*, 122 (1965), 217–19.

110 *Trans East Herts Arch Soc*, 5 (1912–14), 279; *VCH*, iii, 350.

111 Doggett, op cit.

112 *VCH*, ii, 196.

113 Howard Senar, *Little Gaddesden and Ashridge* (1983), 36.

114 Pevsner, op cit, 65; J. Bruce (ed), 'Letters and Papers of the Verney Family...to 1639', *Camden Soc*, 56 (1853), 80–5.

115 *VCH*, ii, 238.

11 Fountains Abbey: archaeological research directed by conservation and presentation

Glyn Coppack

Introduction: history and archaeology

Fountains Abbey is one of the best known and most heavily visited monastic ruins in Europe. The abbey is a World Heritage Site, owned by the National Trust and maintained by English Heritage. It is a flagship property to both organisations, on view to more than 300,000 visitors a year, where best practice and its development is a matter of course. To paraphrase Jane Austen, it is a truth universally acknowledged that a site which costs a good fortune to maintain must be in want of archaeological research and recording. The ruins have been in state guardianship since 1966 and are still undergoing first-time conservation, a process which will continue well into the first decade of the 21st century.

Fountains is not one monastery but three as we know from an early thirteenth century chronicle, the *Narratio de fundatione Fontanis monasterii*, or four if one includes the first settlement of December 1132 on a slightly different site (Gilyard-Beer and Coppack 1986, passim). It can be assumed that the three monasteries relate to the three phases in the normal development of a Cistercian monastery. The first was the temporary timber monastery that served while *stabilitas* was achieved. The second was a permanent stone monastery that served during the establishment of a *familia* when groups of monks and lay-brothers were detached to settle daughter-houses. The final stage was that of expanded mother-house that no longer sloughed off surplus personnel (Coppack 1993, 19–54). We also know the dates of these three stages. The first timber monastery was built in the late summer of 1133, building in stone began in 1136, and the rebuilding and enlargement of the monastery began after a fire in 1146. That much we know without even looking at the ruins, and it has provided a suitable framework that has placed Fountains in the forefront of monastic research.

Ideally, the study of a monastic ruin would begin with a thorough analysis of the standing buildings, followed by a carefully designed programme of excavation which would elucidate the site's development and reveal lost buildings. Fountains, however, was substantially excavated in the mid-nineteenth century by J R Walbran (1876, 107–58), while its masonry was recorded and analysed in detail in the later nineteenth century by J A Reeve (1892) and Sir William St John Hope (1900); its history is still hotly debated. The starting point for modern work came some way into the conservation of the building and was dictated by the immediate needs of an existing conservation programme that had only one aim: to complete the repair of the ruins and thus prevent further collapse. It is difficult to persuade administrators that it is important to spend large sums of money on researching a site which was widely thought to be well understood archaeologically and architecturally. Fountains also has immense problems of scale which only become apparent when one tries to understand the site.

The first modern archaeological examination of Fountains was in 1968 when the Minister of Public Works decided against professional advice to install floodlighting. This involved the digging of narrow trenches 1 m deep all over the site and Roger Mercer was dispatched to see what they revealed and to try and mitigate their damage. It is best to draw a veil over that exercise for the most part, but the opportunity was taken to dig a few trial trenches to check nineteenth century discoveries, and the result of that was a substantial re-interpretation of the standing fabric (Gilyard-Beer 1968). No further work was undertaken, largely because Mercer had not revealed anything new, and because the principal work was to standing fabric that required no clearance or excavation.

The Department of the Environment's and latterly

English Heritage's primary duty to the site is to ensure its survival as close as possible to the state it came into care in the first place, and leisurely archaeological research, though obviously highly desirable, remains a low priority. All the same, since 1977 there has been an ongoing programme of archaeological research at Fountains which is tied in to the conservation programme in such a way as to ensure the highest possible capture of information. Since 1984 there has been a permanent archaeological presence on site, recording the fabric as the first stage in preparing architects' drawings for the conservation programme. Since 1987 there has been a limited programme of excavation, confined to key areas where archaeological deposits were inevitably going to be damaged in the course of conservation work. Excavations have been designed to leave the greater part of the site's archaeology intact while providing the basic information needed to understand the physical development of the site. Working on the premise that it is essential to understand how a structure works before it can be satisfactorily conserved and displayed, Fountains is an incredible success story.

The Woolhouse

Archaeology came to Fountains not exactly by accident in 1977 but very nearly. A tree growing on the site of the supposed bakehouse blew down, exposing masonry that needed to be conserved, and thus finding work for a mason who could not work at heights. Before conservation could begin, an excavation was required to determine the extent of the masonry which was not recorded on nineteenth century excavation plans (Reeve 1892, pl 39). If I had not been excavating outer court buildings at

Thornholme Priory in the mid to late 1970s I probably would not have been asked to advise on the best course of action to follow at Fountains.

Naturally, I wanted to dig and the resulting excavation was carried out in four seasons over four years revealing a substantial twelfth and thirteenth century building that had served as the abbey's home woolhouse (Fig 11.1). Sufficient remained to enable its reconstruction on paper (Fig. 11.2), a new

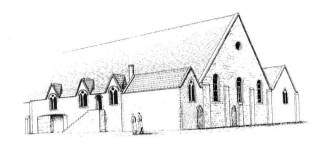

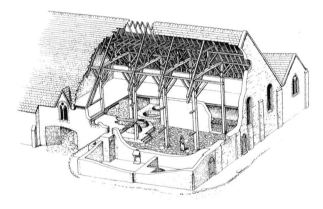

Fig 11.2 *Reconstructed on the basis of its plan and fallen architectural detail, the wool house was a major building whose phases of construction matched those of the central buildings of the abbey (Simon Hayfield)*

Fig 11.1 *The home wool house of Fountains Abbey seen from the north on the completion of excavation (G Coppack)*

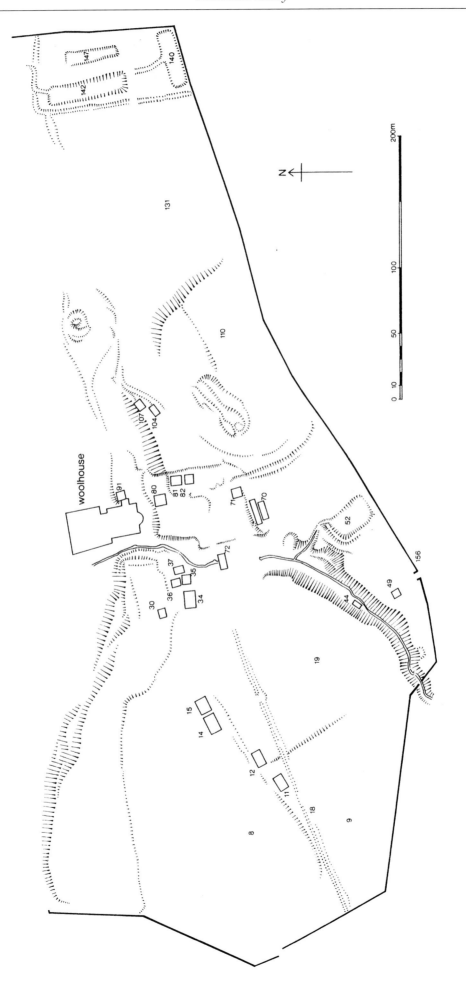

Fig 11.3 *The outer court of Fountains Abbey lay on the south side of the River Skell and was enclosed by a substantial precinct wall, much of which stands to full height. With the exception of the wool house and bakehouse none of this area has been excavated although at least 18 further buildings and their associated yards can be identified from a survey of their earthworks (after RCHME)*

major Cistercian building, and one which could be related directly to the abbey's economy – a growing area of research in the 1970s (Coppack 1986). The building had seven major phases of development between the 1150s and its demolition in the late fifteenth century, and it had been barely touched by earlier excavations.

As always, some conservation had started before excavation began (a very common occurrence in the 1970s) but the majority of this was confined to a stone spoil-heap revetment from Hope's excavation of the building in 1889. At least the site was shown to have remarkable archaeological potential. It could also be shown that the 40 acres of the Outer Court, then not even scheduled, was substantially intact and of equal if not greater potential. Its earthworks survive in remarkable condition, as does the enclosing precinct wall (Fig. 11.3; also see below).

Fig 11.4 *The south transept of the first stone church at Fountains as revealed by excavation. This building, begun in 1136, overlies the post pits of two earlier timber buildings, the church and a domestic range of the timber monastery built in 1133 (Glyn Coppack)*

The development of the Church and Cloister

Establishing an archaeological presence on site in the late 1970s had a remarkable effect on the way conservation and maintenance was planned. When it was decided that the only way to make the grass grow in the south transept of the abbey church was to put in drainage and a sump, it was decided to excavate first, and to excavate a larger and deeper hole than was really necessary. The excavation of the south transept in 1979–80 started out with reasonably minor aims: to record the floors of the standing church which was presumed to pre-date the fire of 1146 because a lot of the masonry of the crossing appeared to have been burned. Therefore, the story ran, you are not likely to find anything very exciting. The rest is history.

Excavation revealed a series of earlier excavation trenches, one of 1852, and two of 1968, dug by Roger Mercer for Roy Gilyard-Beer, as well as a series of very interesting floors untouched by nineteenth century excavation. Emptying Mercer's trenches, the existence of which had been suppressed in the finest tradition of the Civil Service, revealed an earlier building and substantial evidence of burning. In a morning we had effectively re-written the earliest history of Cistercian development and questioned the early dating of all the surviving twelfth century churches of the family of Clairvaux. We had to wait until the following spring to complete the excavation, when the south transept of an earlier church was finally uncovered, and beneath that the post-holes of an even earlier church and a domestic building (Fig 11.4). Even then, excavation was delayed by the use of Fountains as the set for the closing scene of *Omen III, the Final Conflict*, when the

early church had to disappear beneath stage dressing.

More worrying was the fact that the site was about to change hands and there was a suggestion that guardianship would be rescinded when the National Trust acquired the site. There was a very real risk that the excavation would be abandoned unfinished, a purely administrative decision. Fortunately wiser council prevailed and the excavation was completed as planned. Effectively, we had the full development of Fountains Abbey in a hole 10 m square (Gilyard-Beer and Coppack 1986). No more of the church has been excavated, but from a study of the fabric of the standing church which was built around its predecessor, it is possible to reconstruct the ground plan with some certainty, and to observe that the original short un-aisled nave was replaced before 1146 with a large aisled nave.

A short section of the south aisle wall of this new nave actually survives inside the west range, though it appears to have remained un-noticed by anyone until Stuart Harrison pointed it out to me, wondering what it might be as it did not seem to fit with my interpretation (Fig 11.5). If we presume for a moment that a new nave was added to our first masonry church in the 1140s, and we look at the church built at Vauclair by Henry Murdac immediately before he became abbot of Fountains in 1143 (Fig 11.6), it might come as no surprise that the Vauclair plan can be overlaid onto the plan of the early church (including the fragment of south aisle wall) at Fountains to provide an exact fit, to the inch. Because of the nature of our work at Fountains, it is unlikely that any part of this added nave will be seen in excavation and its precise form will have to remain a problem for the future, but at least its existence has been established. Work on the church, coupled with my spending a

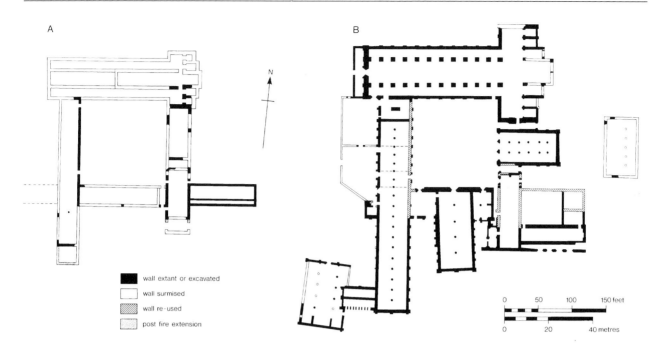

Fig 11.5 *A: the ground plan of the pre-fire monastery with an extended nave and cloister buildings added by Abbot Henry Murdac; B: the ground plan of the mother house developed between 1160 and 1180 by Abbots Richard of Clairvaux and Robert of Pipewell*

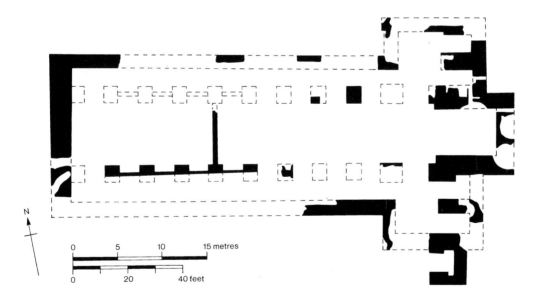

Fig 11.6 *The ground plan of Henry Murdac's church at Vauclair, built immediately before he came to Fountains (after Courtois and 'le groupe sources')*

lot of time at Fountains as a result of the works programme, led to more general consideration of the cloister buildings which were not yet being repaired. This enabled me to identify elements of the east, south, and west ranges that were demonstrably contemporary with the first stone church, the first piece of truly academic research funded by DoE and then English Heritage (Fig 11.5). By plotting

extant early masonry and walls encountered by Hope or during the laying of cables for floodlighting in 1968, it was possible to recover the 1140s ground plan. Limited excavation in 1986 within the west range before the repair of the tunnels which carry the 1170s range over the river located the south wall of the original range, evidence of its destruction by fire, presumably in 1146, and more important

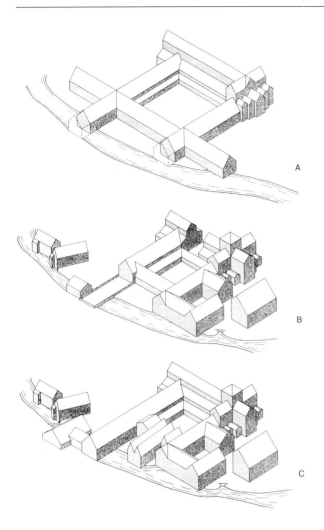

Fig 11.7 *A: The first stone monastery at Fountains, burned in 1146. Post-fire extensions to the west and east ranges are shown in broken line; B: The extent of rebuilding at Fountains on the death of Abbot Richard of Clairvaux in 1170; C: The extent of the expanded abbey buildings at the death of Abbot Robert of Pipewell in 1180 (not to scale; Karen Nichols after Glyn Coppack and Kate Morton)*

evidence for its reconstruction and extension. Later work by Judith Roebuck and Keith Emerick in the east range was to confirm the evidence of fire-damage there in the early chapter-house. From this work, we are able to reconstruct in outline the plan and elevation of the monastery at the height of its mission stage, the only fully understood Bernardine monastery in Europe (Fig 11.7A).

A similar exercise was undertaken simultaneously on the buildings of the post-fire reconstruction, and it is possible to take snap-shots of the development of the monastery in both 1170 when the church and cloister ranges were reaching completion (Fig 11.7B), and in 1180 when the development of the abbey as the mother-house of a substantial family was com-

pleted (Fig 11.7C). Most of this work was not strictly necessary for the immediate conservation of the monument, but it has done two things which were needed. It has provided a framework for the future recording of those elements as the works programme has developed (and in some cases has altered the priorities of conservation); and it has also provided critical information for the interpretation of a classic site to the public. When Gough Whitlam was considering the relevance of Fountains as a World Heritage Site he asked me why it should be included alongside Fontenay which had already been accepted. The answer was simple – Fountains was altogether a more important site. Moreover it was perhaps the best understood major monastery in Europe and had demonstrable potential for future research.

More prosaically, the work provided the basis for a handbook (Coppack and Gilyard-Beer 1993) and for informing the National Trust guides who ensure that visitors get the very best information about so fascinating a site. Lessons learned at Fountains of course also have a knock on effect in the understanding of other Cistercian sites, and if the work had not been done at Fountains, the American National Endowment for the Humanities would not have invested £200,000 in a parallel study of Rievaulx, an equally if not more important abbey (Coppack and Fergusson 1994; Fergusson, and Harrison 1999).

The Precinct Wall

In parallel with the cloister ranges, the works programme has dictated archaeological study elsewhere. The precinct wall has been a long-standing problem. Architecturally unexciting it was more or less ignored until the mid 1980s. Suddenly, its repair became urgent and to a certain extent political.

Fig 11.8 *Detail from the 1150s church reused in the precinct wall (Glyn Coppack)*

These were the days of the Measured Term Contract, when simple and repetitive work was put out to contract with the intention of concentrating our limited direct labour force on more specialist work. Academically, the gain was the dating of the wall, for it was found to contain elements of the 1150s church, the east end of which was demolished in the early years of the thirteenth century (Fig 11.8). The measured term work was extended to cover the walls that canalise the River Skell through the precinct, and that work is continuing.

The effect was the need for a permanent archaeological presence to ensure that full documentation was provided for the contract work, and that any problems encountered during conservation could be dealt with immediately. Although much of this work was repetitive, it has provided us with significant information about the development of the precinct, an area generally overlooked in the conservation of guardianship monuments. Again it has provided us with the necessary information to advise the National Trust on the broader problems of estate management and the Department for Culture Media and Sport on Scheduled Monument Consent applications that arise from them.

The Water Mill

One building at Fountains Abbey is not accessible to the public at present, and it is perhaps the most significant building on the site. Monastic water mills are rare, and intact ones are rarer still. I was asked to look at the Fountains example in 1984 to decide how important it really was. The reasons were political – the National Trust wanted to use the building but it lay at the centre of our works compound and contained our masons' banker shop and stores. Management considerations should be tempered by knowledge not expediency, and we simply did not have the knowledge. We did have a good and partially reworked photogrammetric survey, and it was a relatively simple job to com-

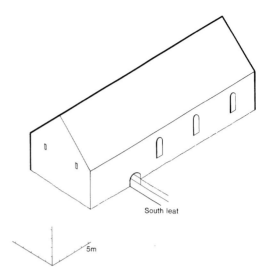

Fig 11.9 The 1140s water mill at Fountains Abbey (Glyn Coppack and Simon Hayfield)

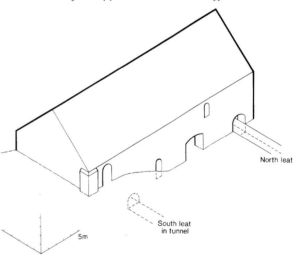

Fig 11.10 The 1160s water mill at Fountains Abbey (Glyn Coppack and Simon Hayfield)

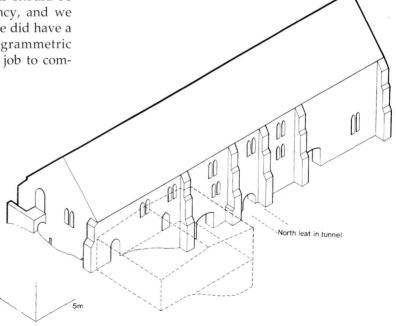

Fig 11.11 The thirteenth century water mill at Fountains Abbey, with its fourteenth century extension shown in broken line (Glyn Coppack and Simon Hayfield)

plete the recording of the structure. It took three days and was worked in with other time commitments. Analysis took a further two days.

The result was that we had not one mill but three – this should not be surprising considering the pattern of development seen in both the woolhouse and the cloister buildings. The earliest mill was a single storey building of the 1140s (Fig 11.9); it was buried within a mill-dam, and replaced by a larger building in the 1160s (Fig 11.10), and enlarged again in the 1230s when it was also re-windowed to confuse the poor archaeologist (Fig 11.11). It was further extended in the 14th century but that extension has gone apart from its roof scar and a door which has disappeared since 1900. Three phases of post-suppression alteration are not shown on Figures 11.9–11, but the mill remained in use until 1937–8. It is, in its first phase, the earliest surviving monastic mill in Europe, and the only industrial building to survive from the formative years of the Cistercian order. Its archaeological and architectural importance is unquestioned; its repair will be dictated by the data recovered from its archaeological analysis; and its future use will emphasise its importance.

Conclusion

Fountains Abbey has, in many ways, provided a case study for the development of archaeological research in the context of conservation and presentation. It began in a reactive way in the 1970s, rapidly came of age, and today is a critical component in the planning of conservation projects. Fountains has been a test-bed for developing new techniques, just as much as it has for developing archaeological models. Because it is a monument selected for

permanent preservation, the methods used are for the most part non-destructive. We will never know the full story, but we can prove that we know enough to ensure that its conservation is carried out to the highest standards, and we have recovered enough information to tell one of the most interesting stories of monastic development. The cost is high in cash terms but it is still no more than the architect's fees for conservation, which has to be a wise investment for the future. The work is also published, both in academic and popular form, to ensure that it is as widely available as the site is accessible (Coppack 1993; Coppack and Gilyard-Beer 1993).

Bibliography

Coppack G 1986, 'The excavation of an outer court building, perhaps the woolhouse, at Fountains Abbey, North Yorkshire', *Medieval Archaeology*, 30, 46–87.

Coppack G 1993, *Fountains Abbey*. London: Batsford/English Heritage.

Coppack G and Fergusson P J 1994, *Rievaulx Abbey*. London: English Heritage.

Coppack G and Gilyard-Beer R 1993, *Fountains Abbey*. London: English Heritage.

Fergusson P J and Harrison S 1999, *Rievaulx Abbey*, Yale

Gilyard-Beer R 1968, 'Fountains Abbey, the early buildings', *Archaeological Journal*, 125, 313–18.

Gilyard-Beer R and Coppack G 1986, 'Excavations at Fountains Abbey, North Yorkshire, 1979–80, the early development of the monastery', *Archaeologia*, 108, 147–88.

Hope W H St J 1900, 'Fountains Abbey', *Yorkshire Archaeological Journal*, 15, 269–402.

Reeve J A 1892, *A Monograph on the Abbey of St Mary of Fountains*. London

Walbran J R 1876, 'Memorials of the Abbey of St Mary of Fountains II', Pt 1. *Surtees Society*, 67.

12   The Hulton Abbey Project: research archaeology and public accountability

W Klemperer

Introduction

Hulton Abbey (SJ 9053 4916), founded by Henry of Audley and built between 1216 and 1223, completed the north Staffordshire and Cheshire plain group of Cistercian monasteries. Located at about 152.4 m (500') OD in the upper Trent valley (Fig 12.1) the abbey acquired substantial estates and established a mixed economy bearing modest wealth during the 13th century. The abbey, however, never acquired the wealth of some better known sister houses and as such is more representative of the mass of monastic institutions that characterise medieval England. The *Valor Ecclesiasticus* survey of 1535 lists only two Cistercian houses in England and Wales with a smaller income. Nevertheless Hulton escaped the closure of smaller houses, eventually surrendering on 23 September 1538 when Abbot Wilkins and eight choir monks signed the surrender document. Sixteen tons of lead were melted down on site and taken to Tutbury castle and the bells were taken down and sold for £19.16.0d. The abbey rapidly fell into ruin, and was entirely incorporated into agricultural land by the early 19th century.

Amateur excavations occurred sporadically following the site's rediscovery in 1885 and the results have been summarised (Wise 1985). A new project started in 1987 designed to excavate part of the site before undertaking consolidation and laying out within a parkland environment. A 2.63 ha (6.5 acre) area was evaluated and seasonal excavations undertaken between 1987 and 1995. Excavation has concentrated on the site of the church and chapter house (Fig 12.2). A dual approach was adopted from the outset combining detailed archaeological investigation of the church and chapter house with an active dissemination of information and promotion of the work. This paper summarises some of the archaeological results, and describes public aspects of the work which have been an integral and crucial element in the project's success.

Structural Evidence

The analysis of the architecture and worked stone has shown that the chancel and south transept were built first, with the crossing and remainder of the church following later in the 13th century. Bartraceried windows were added to the church in the 14th century (R K Morris, in Klemperer, forthcoming). The basic cruciform design of aisleless nave and transepts, with flat east ends to the chancel and transepts constitutes a late survival of the 'Bernardine plan', being better suited to the mid-12th century than the 1220s (Norton and Park 1986, 6). The relative poverty of the house probably explains this basic initial approach and lack of later elaboration. The church is 32 m wide across the transepts (105'), and 41.45 m long (136'). An unusual aspect of the design is that the church does not connect with the west range, the four-bay nave appearing rather short. Rather than this being the result of a shortening of the church the excavation has shown that the church never extended to the west range. In the absence of detailed excavation elsewhere in the inner court which may throw light on this, the most likely reason is that this was due to the demise of the lay brother system by the time of building which negated the need for a substantial nave (Coldstream 1986, 155 n 82).

A series of large postholes within the church indicate the positions of timber scaffolding dating from the construction. Over the 342 year occupation three major floors were laid inside the church represented by clay and crushed sandstone make up layers. Only a few disturbed tiles were found in the church although impressions noted in the north

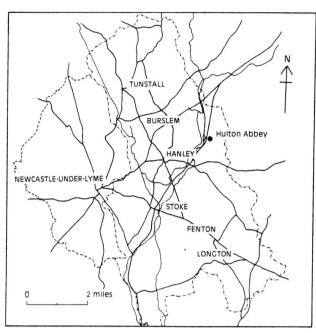

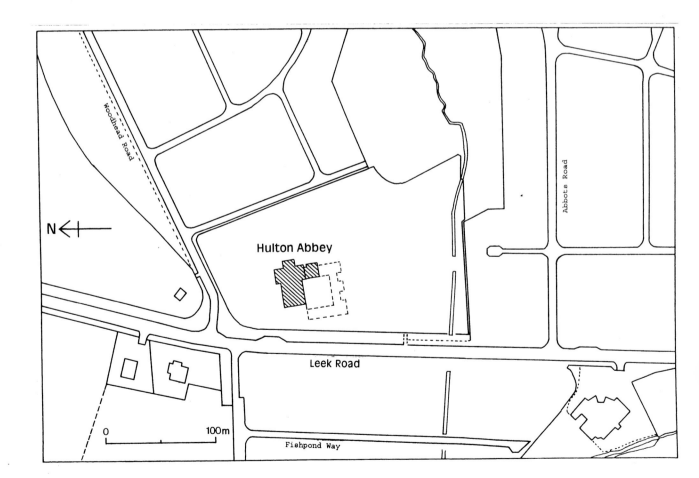

Fig 12.1 Hulton Abbey, location

Fig 12.2 *Aerial view of excavation of the church and chapter house at Hulton Abbey, 1989*

chapel of the south transept (Mountord 1966, 17) indicate decorative ceramic tiling to parts of the east end at least. Although the paucity of evidence for tile pavements in the church may result from the undoubted and extensive robbing of materials from the site, hundreds of decorated floor tiles were recovered from the chapter house overburden and a partially *in situ* late medieval tile floor was revealed in the north end of the west range. There is, however, very little evidence of ceramic or stone tiles in the church. Although parts of the east-end were tiled, it is likely that the majority of the church had a simple stone floor.

The arrangement of choir stalls relating to the earlier two floors is unknown. When the final floor was laid, however, choir stalls were located centrally within the crossing, partially overlying earlier burials. Although the north transept is badly damaged by the cellar of a 19th century farmhouse, vertical slots cut into piers for a blocking screen at the head of the north aisle, and a line of postholes separating the north transept from the crossing indicate that the transept was screened from the rest of the church in the latest phase. The density of burials is greater in the north transept than elsewhere in the eastern arm of the church, leading to the suggestion that it was used as a chantry chapel in the later period. This interpretation of a separated north transept presupposes that the nave was open. In fact there is no evidence that the nave and crossing were ever separated by a screen, again indicating that lay brothers may not have played an important role. Structural instability may have resulted in later modifications at the west end where a wall blocking the western arch of the north aisle was added as reinforcement.

The rectangular chapter house was built in the 1260s or 1270s, with four internal columns dividing the interior into nine rib-vaulted bays. The builders employed the fashionable new technique of bar tracery and Hulton can now be seen as an early and significant example of this technique applied to a new Cistercian chapter house. The mouldings were lavish compared to the earlier work in the church, and show a clear inspiration in the contemporary nave works at Lichfield Cathedral. A typically Cistercian tripartite arrangement of doorway with flanking windows with bar tracery was included in

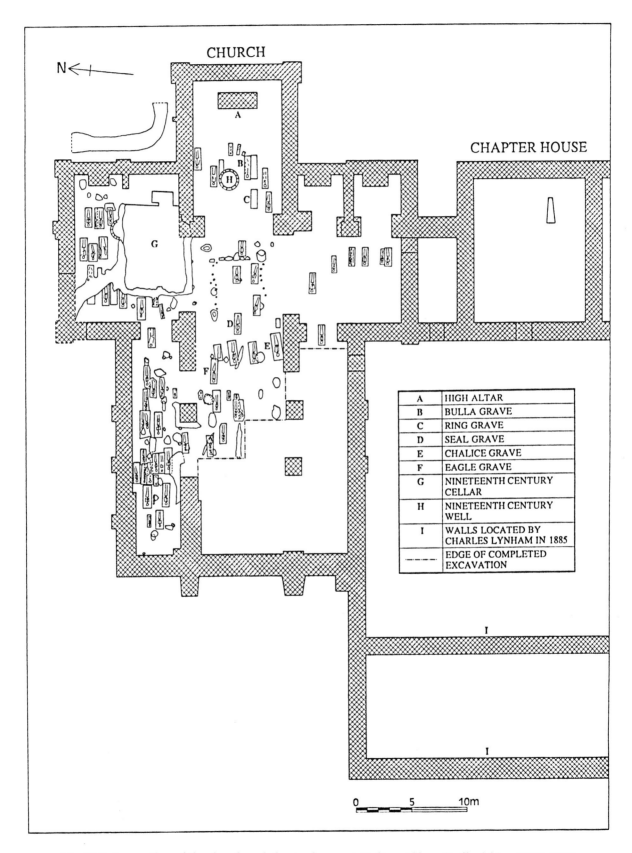

CHURCH

N

CHAPTER HOUSE

A	HIGH ALTAR
B	BULLA GRAVE
C	RING GRAVE
D	SEAL GRAVE
E	CHALICE GRAVE
F	EAGLE GRAVE
G	NINETEENTH CENTURY CELLAR
H	NINETEENTH CENTURY WELL
I	WALLS LOCATED BY CHARLES LYNHAM IN 1885
-------	EDGE OF COMPLETED EXCAVATION

0   5   10m

Fig 12.3 Excavation of the church and chapter house at Hulton Abbey, Staffordshire, 1987–1994

the west wall to the cloisters. A similar arrangement still survives at the nearby house of Croxden (R K Morris, in Klemperer, forthcoming).

Finds

Finds have included important assemblages of decorated floor tiles (predominantly bird and acorn and fleurs de lys designs), architectural stone and skeletons. Lesser assemblages include window glass, pottery, iron and copper alloy objects. Burials have been an important aspect of the work with a total assemblage of 82 recorded individuals. Pathology analysis by Sue Browne has produced a wealth of demographic data which has been supported by extensive pollen analysis from samples taken close to the bodies, analysis of wood, seeds, woven cloth, and leather.

Interesting burials

One skeleton had cut marks, probably caused by an axe and sword, on many bones (Fig 12.4). The body had been dismembered: the head had been cut off and the body split down the middle, and the remains buried in the chancel. The mutilation may have been motivated by a desire for personal revenge or by superstitions about the dead. The fate of the main benefacting family, the Audleys, is documented and if this was an Audley the most likely candidate is William Audley. Documentary research by Philip Morgan at Keele University has confirmed that William died on Anglesey on 6 November 1282, while with a 200 man unit of the English army cut off and massacred by the Welsh. William's brother Nicholas was also with Edward I's army, and would have had the opportunity of recovering the remains. Accelerated carbon dating has shown that the remains almost certainly are 13th century and although we cannot be sure that the remains are those of William, analysis of the bones, documentary research and carbon dating have combined to yield much information about this burial. Other interesting burials include a man who died aged about 35–45 years, with congenitally dislocated hips and extensive joint modifications. A number of burials were associated with artefacts illustrative of pilgrimage.

Interesting artefacts

Several interesting and unusual artefacts have been found within graves and elsewhere on the site. A burial in the east of the nave was accompanied by a silvered lead eagle about 45 mm tall, interpreted as a secular badge of office (Fig 12.5). A 13th-century gold and sapphire ring, a papal *bulla* of Innocent VI (1352–62), and two wooden coffins were recovered from graves in the chancel. Elsewhere coffins appear not to have been used. A wax seal impression and a wax chalice (Fig 12.6) were recovered from graves in the crossing. Gas chromatography analysis by the organic chemistry department at Keele University has identified the wax as pure beeswax. The seal is likely to be from the hospital of Santo-Spirito in Rome (Brian Spencer, pers comm) and accompanied a burial with leather shoes on the body. The seal would have been attached to a letter of indulgence to allow remission from purgatory, acquired as a sign of a completed pilgrimage. An unusual pilgrim badge (Fig 12.7) was recovered from dissolution deposits in the nave. This badge of 14th or 15th century date may represent the female Saint Wilgefort, (Brian Spencer, pers comm). Further evidence of the pilgrim tradition in burial is represented by staffs (some hazel) of varying size in at least nine graves (see Fig 12.5). Organic material survives reasonably well due to waterlogging, although the cell structure of the less substantial staffs has deteriorated making some identifications impossible.

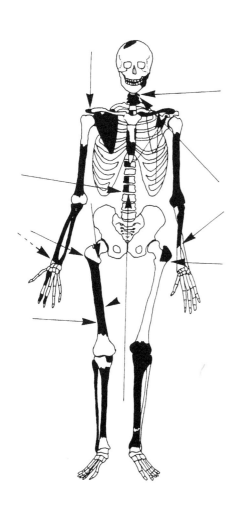

Fig 12.4 *Burial with cut marks HA 16*

Fig 12.5 Burial with silvered eagle and staff, HA41

Fig 12.7 Pilgrim badge

The wax chalice is a very unusual survival, a parallel being the wax chalice found in the burial of Bishop Thomas Tulloch in St Magnus Cathedral, Kirkwall (RCAHMS 1946, 126). In both cases the chalice was made as a funerary item specifically to accompany the burial. Chalices were normally of precious metal, but pewter or wax copies were made to accompany burials of priests.

Promotion of the work

The project is run by the Potteries Museum, Stoke-on-Trent. As with the vast majority of museums, this is an institution that collects, documents, interprets, preserves and displays things. The 1990s, however, have been a time of great emphasis on public accountability and customer care and we are increasingly asking and being asked: what are we to preserve?; and for whom? Archaeology can be justified in fundamental social and educational terms but the key to the success of this project was that the wider community perceived there to be a benefit. Archaeology which has a positive impact within and relevance to the wider community can help to develop a shared interest between the profession and the community in the continuation and success of archaeological work.

Fig 12.6 Wax Chalice

The site of Hulton Abbey is in the urban area of Stoke-on-Trent. From the outset it was realised that educational events could play an important part not only when the site work was finished but also while it was on-going. The Potteries Museum has an imposing city centre site and regularly attracts more than 200,000 visitors each year. Yet little outreach work was undertaken in the 1980s and it was clear that there were many local people who did not visit the museum or local historic sites. The excavation at Hulton Abbey gave an opportunity to reach a wide audience and interpret archaeology in a way that would not be possible in the classroom or museum gallery. Educational events at the site (Fig 12.8) have provided a showcase for on-going work, helped to develop suitable educational approaches and helped to maintain the project's profile and funding support. The events have also provided access within an exciting environment to aspects of local history and archaeology.

The National Curriculum Key Stage 3 core study unit 2, *Medieval Realms: 1066–1500* (see Fig 12.9), has been the inspiration for an annual series of events aimed at the main teaching areas in this topic. The educational events have been aimed specifically at schools, have been highly organised, and have been evaluated. Starting with the site itself schoolchildren are introduced to the physical remains and the notion of archaeology. Artefacts such as those described in the earlier summary are then viewed in a temporary on-site museum, either in low-level perspex cases in the case of more fragile finds, or passed around in the case of more robust pieces. Finally demonstrators make replica items and discuss the methods of production and role of the artefacts in an age before mass communication and transport systems. Detailed hand-outs allow active experimental follow-up work in the classroom.

Although museum education certainly has negative connections for some people (eg Addison 1986) evaluation has shown that the outdoor series of events have been a pleasurable learning experience for the overwhelming majority of students. The opportunity to see an archaeological site, then see finds in a temporary site museum, and to see virtually identical objects being made has given a knowledge of the historical and cultural context which enhanced the learning experience. The demonstrators role-played and wore costumes as they demonstrated and made items directly related to the site and its archaeology.

Many different interpretations are available during such events, from enactive interpretation through to much more detailed discussions around the topics undertaken as follow-up work using information sheets. The actual composition of information sheets therefore has to be carefully considered. One criticism of *Medieval Realms* is that the format required the demonstrators to be much more active than the children. This favoured imaginative and analytical

Fig 12.8 John Hudson demonstrates the art of the medieval potter with a kickwheel

learners at the expense of pragmatic and dynamic learners (McCarthy and Leflar 1983). Future events could have a greater impact by letting children try out more things for themselves. Children and adults, however, did warm to the created experiences and opportunities enabling integration of observations into concepts.

The benefits of direct sensory appreciation have been noted before (eg Hooper-Greenhill 1984) and this approach has allowed a wide audience of schoolchildren to connect with the archaeology and relate it to the modern world. *Medieval Realms* events have helped develop participants' sense of place and identity through pleasurable interpretation techniques undertaken on a site of archaeological and emotional importance to the community. One of the City's largest council estates is named Abbey Hulton and is built around the site. The *Medieval Realms* events are now well established, regularly attracting around 700 local schoolchildren in organised groups. More than any other single factor this has raised awareness of the work at the site amongst local people, the media and amongst local politicians.

A high profile proved useful in terms of developing a status within the local authority. Publicity does filter through to elected members who vote on

THE KEY STAGE FOCUS STATEMENTS FOR HISTORY

These provide a focus for teaching and learning across the key stage. They also identify the ways in which pupils' knowledge, understanding and skills are expected to develop in each stage. Although 'Medieval Realms' is a study unit of Key Stage 3, key stages 1,2 and 3 all place emphasis on the local context and all include 'Historical Enquiry' as a defined 'Key Element'. Clearly, presentation of archaeology has great potential in developing an awareness of the past for children of all ages.

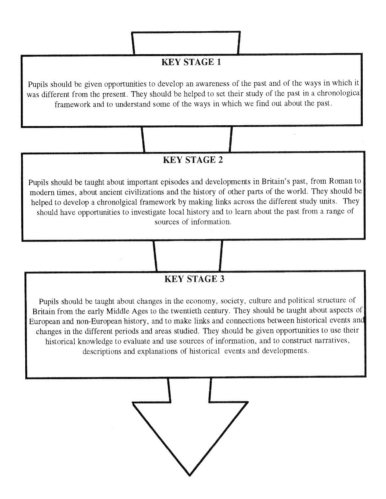

KEY STAGE 1

Pupils should be given opportunities to develop an awareness of the past and of the ways in which it was different from the present. They should be helped to set their study of the past in a chronological framework and to understand some of the ways in which we find out about the past.

KEY STAGE 2

Pupils should be taught about important episodes and developments in Britain's past, from Roman to modern times, about ancient civilizations and the history of other parts of the world. They should be helped to develop a chronolgical framework by making links across the different study units. They should have opportunities to investigate local history and to learn about the past from a range of sources of information.

KEY STAGE 3

Pupils should be taught about changes in the economy, society, culture and political structure of Britain from the early Middle Ages to the twentieth century. They should be taught about aspects of European and non-European history, and to make links and connections between historical events and changes in the different periods and areas studied. They should be given opportunities to use their historical knowledge to evaluate and use sources of information, and to construct narratives, descriptions and explanations of historical events and developments.

National Curriculum for History
Key Stage 3

Study Unit 1: Medieval realms: Britain 1066–1500

Building on their study in Key Stage 2 of the early history of Britain, pupils should be taught about some of the major features of Britain's medieval past, including the development of the medieval monarchy and the ways of life of the peoples of the British Isles:

The development of the English medieval monarchy	**a** the Norman conquest, including the Battle of Hastings (1066) and its impact, *eg changes in government and land holding, castle building, the Domesday survey*;
	b relations of the monarchy with the Church, barons and people, including Magna Carta (1215), *eg Thomas Becket and Henry II, changes in the law and the legal system, the Peasants' Revolt (1381), the Wars of the Roses*;
	c relations with other countries, *eg Richard I and the Crusade to the Holy Land, John in Ireland, Edward I in Wales, Edward III in Scotland, Henry V or Henry VI in France*;
Medieval society	**d** the structure of medieval society, including the role of the Church, *eg farming, crafts, towns and trade*;
	e health and disease, including the Black Death;
	f arts and architecture, *eg literature and the English language, castles, cathedrals, monastic buildings, parish churches, artefacts, paintings.*

Fig 12.9 This material from the National Curriculum is Crown copyright and is reproduced by permission of the Controller of HMSO

budgets for heritage work, and a good media profile was crucial in maintaining funding support during a period of increasing pressure on local authority budgets. Achieving status for the archaeological project was the key to transmuting political support into financial support. The educational events described above took place on a site which was officially derelict land. Increased awareness of the site resulted in widespread support for the development of a scheme to landscape the site. The City could not afford the necessary capital project and so an application was made to English Partnerships, a government body charged with bringing together the public, private and voluntary sectors to create economic growth, employment opportunities and environmental improvements throughout England. The response was a Derelict Land Grant of £158,000 awarded in 1995, equivalent to 100 % of landscaping works. Being able to demonstrate a use for the site in terms of leisure and education certainly helped in the procuring of the grant which has ensured the long-term preservation of the abbey site in an accessible public open space.

Conclusion

The excavation project at Hulton Abbey has resulted in detailed new information concerning the inner court of a lesser abbey, but has also shown how archaeology will be supported by the wider community if attempts are made to make it relevant to them. One of the paradoxes of modern archaeology is that we seek to preserve important archaeological sites which by definition are those which hold the greatest clues to developing our understanding of the past. The answer is not simply selective excavation but promotion and dissemination of results to as broad an audience as possible, as archaeology can and must be made accessible in an intellectually honest form to everyone.

Bibliography

Addison E 1986, Is marketing a threat, *Museums Bulletin*, summer

Coldstream N 1986, 'Cistercian architecture from Beaulieu to the Dissolution', in Norton and Park (eds) *Cistercian art and architecture in the British Isles*, Cambridge, 139–159

Hooper-Greenhill E 1984, *The Educational role of the Museum* Routledge

Klemperer W, *Excavations at Hulton Abbey, Staffordshire 1987–1994*, Forthcoming

Mountford, A R 1996, Hulton Abbey, Stoke-on-Trent, Excavation and Restoration 1959–1966, in *City of Stoke-on-Trent Museum Archaeological Society Reports No 2: 1966*

McCarthy B and Leflar S 1983, *4Mat in action: Creative lesson plans for teaching to learning styles with right/left mode techniques* Excel

Norton C and Park D (eds) 1986, *Cistercian Art and Architecture in the British Isles*, Cambridge University Press

Royal Commission on the Ancient (and Historical) Monuments of Scotland 1946, *Inventory of Ancient Monuments of Orkney and Shetland* Vol 2

Wise P 1985, *Hulton Abbey: A Century of Excavations*, Staffordshire Archaeological Studies 2

13   Education on Abbey Sites

Liz Hollinshead

Education is one of those elastic words which can stretch over many meanings. For the general visitor to an historic site it is represented by the information-giving aids that are available to them; the guide book, the audio or video tape, the museum or the panels situated at strategic points. To other groups, like schoolchildren, WEA classes or those engaged in tertiary education, the word signifies a more inter-active process, and the site is used to achieve a specified learning goal. For those responsible for running historic sites it helps to call the first of these functions interpretation, and the latter, education. It is this second branch of the definition with which this paper deals, in particular, with helping school-children come to an understanding of abbey sites.

There are lots of good reasons for teachers to use abbey sites with children. National Curriculum History includes study of the medieval period and also of the local environment. It requires children to assess the importance of three-dimensional evidence in building up a picture of the past, which they cannot do until they know how to 'read' and understand physical evidence. This brings into play the archaeological techniques of close observation, logical deduction and application of hypotheses, skills which need practising before children are brought anywhere near an historic site. But how are children who may have the Internet, Alton Towers, or the local football team heavy on their minds to be lured into curiosity about the living place of people who dressed in funny clothes and lived a very long time ago?

It is always easier to catch the imagination of children if their starting point is something with which they are familiar. They already know a good deal about community life, because they are part of it nearly every day. The school is an organisation which brings people together to achieve a common purpose, just as monasteries and convents did. It is

just the aims that are different. Getting children to make a list of the activities that go on in school, and adding to it those that might go on in a group of people brought together to worship God, gives the first point of contact. If this is followed up by looking, with the teacher, at how these different activities are accommodated in the buildings of both school and abbey, children begin to see that, although the terminolgy is strange and new, the abbey site is not some mysterious stone warren, but a working and living environment fulfilling similar human needs to their own.

Table 13.1 Comparing the working spaces for school and an abbey helps pupils recognise similarities and differences in the two types of buildings. Taken from 'A Teacher's Guide to Using Abbeys', Cooksey, C, English Heritage, 1992

Activity	School	Abbey
work	classroom	cloister
eating	dining room	refectory
cooking	kitchen	kitchen
assembly	hall	chapter house
church services	hall	church
going to the lavatory	lavatory	reredorter
illness	sick room	infirmary
reading	library	library
sleeping		dorter
walking	corridor	passage/slype
administration	head's room	abbot's lodgings

When children, or any of us for that matter, go on to a site, more satisfaction is derived from nosing out information by piecing together clues than by being lectured by someone paraphrasing the guide-book. By practising in school, children develop skills which they can apply on the visit to help them sort out the layout of the place for themselves. They can use the school buildings to look at how rooms reflect function and status. For example, if they are asked to pretend that they are strangers to their own school, and to ignore all furnishings and fittings, they can hypothesize from looking at the relative sizes of rooms as to what activity might go on there. The hall, for instance, is the largest room, so it follows that this may be the place where the school community gets together for meetings, presentations, religious services and the like. The classroom is large enough to accommodate thirty people, and as this is roughly the number of the usual working group it is a reasonable assumption that this may be where routine schoolwork goes on. The lavatory cubicle holds only one person, so this must be reserved for an activity that goes on alone.

Location of a room in relation to another room or feature also gives a clue to function. For example, it is likely that facilities for washing hands are likely to be found near lavatories, a kitchen will be next to a dining room, or a changing room situated near a gym.

Still in school, teachers can introduce a similar exercise using the furnishings and general level of decor to discover which are the most prestigious rooms, which again reflects function. The foyer, for example, through which most visitors pass, is likely to have a better standard of presentation than a back corridor, and the headteacher's office, where parents are received, will boast more luxurious wall and floor coverings than the boiler room. A survey of all the rooms comparing the provision of facilities helps in establishing the relationship between standard of decoration and status (Table 13.2).

Children can use similar indicators on the abbey site to discover the function of different parts of the buildings: the largest room with the most decoration, the huge ornate windows and highly carved doorways must be the most important building and could accommodate the whole community at one go, ergo it is probably the church. The plain, low-ceilinged, ground floor room with a few small windows could be a storage area. And so on.

Asking children to think about how their school community works is a good way of introducing the lifestyle of monks or nuns. Why, for example, is it necessary to have a strict timetable punctuated by bells? Or why is there a set of rules? This line of thought can be extended to the division of labour necessary in communities, particularly those aiming at self-sufficiency, and to the additional facilities which might be needed to sustain this. These areas of common experience provide stepping stones back into the past that teachers can build on with information about the period. This is the point at which it should be explained that although those who lived in the abbeys may have originally aimed to concern themselves purely with spiritual matters, it was impossible for them to remain aloof from the business of the world. In fact, their way of life often resulted in them being at the heart of it, either as landowners with political or personal power, or as benefactors, or as the leaders in the field in new ideas and discoveries in scholarship, agriculture and medicine.

Armed with information about lifestyle and the function of buildings, older children can be asked to design the layout of an abbey site. Extra hints will help: the church, for example, generally has an east-west axis, or the kitchen and the lavatories were ideally placed by a stream or culvert – which would be downstream? It is unlikely that a class will produce the typical abbey plan, but an exercise like this will make children think hard about the logistics of layout, and will help them to both recognise and appreciate the site when they visit (Fig 13.1).

Before the visit takes place teachers need to prepare pupils for the fact that what they are going to see will be a ruin, with parts that are entirely missing. One way of introducing the idea of decay is to get a volunteer to lie down on the floor, whilst the rest of the class imagines time travelling forward a couple of hundred years. What is left of the volunteer? After quite a lot of fun and some working out children will come up with the conclusion that the soft bits – the flesh, the textiles, the KitKat in the pocket, will all decay, and the hard bits, the bones, the metal zips and the coins will all remain.

The next step is to apply the same thought process to the likely fate of the classroom after two hundred

Table 13.2 The status of rooms can be graded by giving a score out of three

Room	Heat	Light	Space	Floor	Decor	Walls	Furniture	
Head	3	3	3	3	3	3	3	21
Staffroom	3	3	2	3	2	3	2	18
Classroom	3	3	1	1	2	1	1	12
Kitchen	1	3	3	1	0	0	0	8
Boiler House	1	1	1	1	0	0	0	4
Cloakroom	1	1	0	1	0	1	0	4
Corridor	1	1	0	0	0	1	0	3
Caretaker	1	1	0	0	0	1	0	3

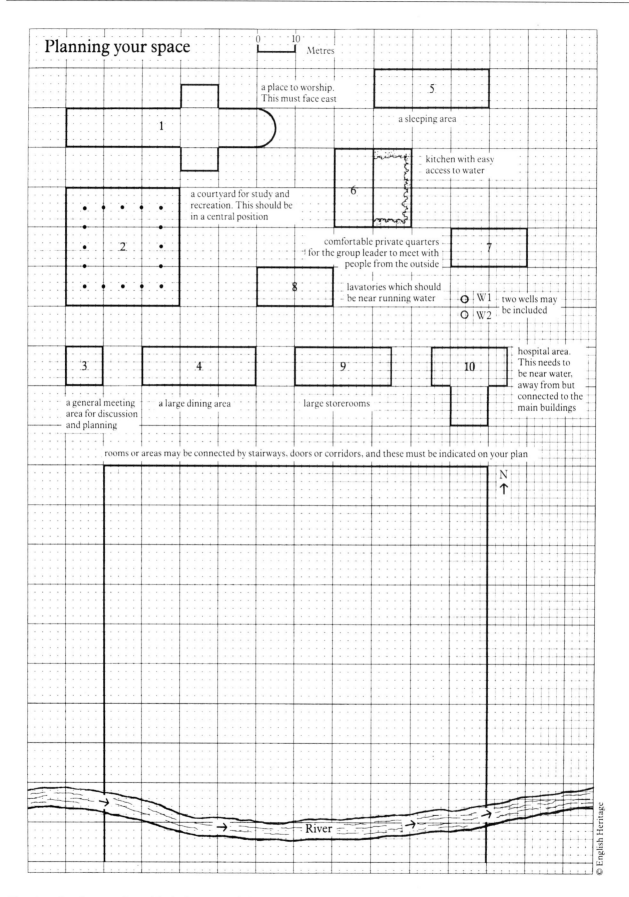

Fig 13.1 *Getting to grips with the logistics of planning a site (which buildings need running water, should the lavatories be up- or downstream of the kitchens?) will help understanding the physical remains. Taken from A Teacher's Handbook to Castle Acre Priory and Castle, Staszewska, L, and Cocksedge, H, English Heritage, 1994*

years' neglect. The answer is the same, the soft bits – the wooden door and fittings, the textile carpet, the books and general impedimenta of the room will rot, whilst the hard bits – the walls, the steel girders, the metal window frames will remain. In addition, from their own experience of life around them, they can suggest other agents which speed up decay; vandals who break the windows and roof tiles, thus letting damp in, or thieves who remove furniture or other materials for sale or use elsewhere. When children who have undergone this type of preparatory work are confronted with the abbey building that has genuinely decayed over several hundred years, they will be equipped to understand the fragments which are left. They can look for evidence of where the soft bits have been, and by working out what has disappeared, they may be able to make a tentative picture of the building as it was. Importantly the point will have been made that the place was not always ruinous, and that what they see now is an incomplete picture.

Take this view of Monk Bretton Priory (Fig 13.2), for example. What were the soft bits likely to have been? Textiles, like wall hangings, the furniture, the wooden doors and floor. There is no evidence of the first two, but it is easy to see where the door belonged. Children often go for the quick answer, so their first location for the floor may be over the two large recesses which resemble the resting places for supporting beams. If they test this theory, they can see that the floor would cut straight across the

fireplace, so they need to think again. Having noticed the fireplace, the application of common sense dictates that the floor must have been situated at the base of it. But there is more than one fireplace, so the location of a second floor can be mapped in. What about the opening on the right hand side of the wall – door or window? Again a quick answer, based on shape, suggests a door, but the position in relation to the floor confirms it is a window. Children will recognise that one fireplace is larger and more decorative than the other, which gives them a clue to status of the rooms, and can lead to an hypothesis about function. Perhaps the middle room was for entertaining, whilst the upper was for a more private purpose, like sleeping. They will also know from their preparatory work that the one building on an abbey site which is designed to be comfortable and prestigious is the abbot's lodging, the equivalent to the headteacher's accommodation in school. From this children may be able to picture the room in use; an abbot sitting near a warm fire with the sun coming in through an elegant window, perhaps reaching out for a scroll kept in one of those wall recesses.

Parts of many abbey sites were made into residences after the Dissolution, or were altered for other purposes. Teachers need to be aware of this, but they often feel deeply unsure about explaining the changes to their class, feeling that they should know precise dates, culled either from the guide book or from knowledge of architectural styles. This

Fig 13.2 *When pupils know what clues to look for, they can begin to build up a picture of what an incomplete building looked like when it was in use. Monk Bretton Priory, South Yorkshire*

Fig 13.3 *By using close observation and common sense, pupils can work out for themselves the order in which alterations took place*

is not necessary, as the evidence of deliberate alteration is often hard to miss, and usually the sequence of changes can be worked out by close inspection. In order to de-mystify this process teachers on courses run by English Heritage are asked to put the alterations made to this house into chronological order: it is an exercise relying on observation and deduction, precisely the skills that are needed on site.

After this amount of preparatory work, children are able to go on site and begin to make sense of what they see for themselves. Working in groups gets round the problem of overcrowding, and also promotes discussion, decision-making and patience in listening. A useful ploy for teachers is to make each group responsible for following different lines of enquiry and asking them to present their findings to the rest of the class. This not only concentrates the mind, but also ensures that more facets of the site are investigated than would be possible with a single class activity.

The actual tasks children are given on site depends on what it is the teacher wants them to learn. It may be that the aim is to use the skill of reading three-dimensional evidence that they have been practising in school. A simple exercise for this would be to give groups a labelled stereotype plan

of an abbey, and a blank plan of the site they are on, and ask them to find one room each, say the kitchen. When they locate the place, which will almost certainly be labelled, they should draw up a list of the clues that helped the original archaeologist decide what that room was. This will involve looking at what is left, and also trying to find indications of those things which have disappeared. Inside a kitchen area there may be fragments or evidence for hearths, stone sinks, drainage chutes, and decoration on doorways or windows. Outside, the clues may be drains, proximity to water, and relationship to other rooms, like the refectory (there may even be a hatch in the wall between the two) (Figs 13.1 and 13.4).

Some teachers may want to take this further and elicit an understanding of what it was like to live at the site. Role cards describing the work of different members of the abbey community may be given out, and children asked to find the place most associated with that person (Fig 13.5). How would their character have used that area? Can they work out the route to the church from there, entering by what is left of the doorways and not walking over wall footings? How long does it take? Can they work out, by consulting the timetable, how many times a day that journey would be made? How different is it from school?

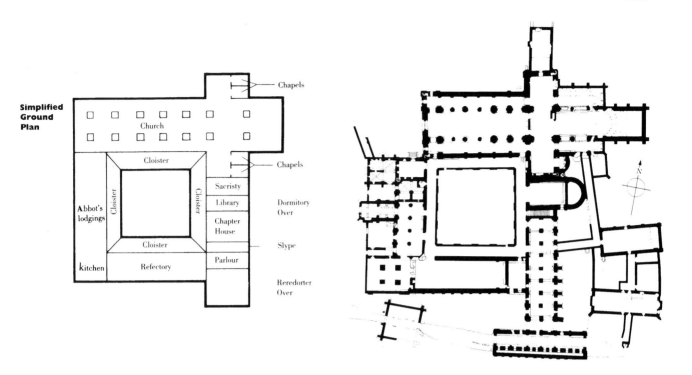

Fig 13.4 *Investigating the site using a stereotype plan and unlabelled site plan will help pupils to understand the clues archaeologists look for in ascribing function to place*

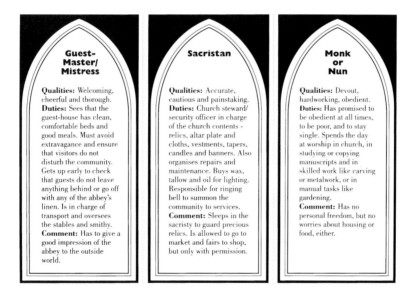

Fig 13.5 *Role cards help in re-creating what it was like to live at an abbey. Taken from A Teacher's Guide to Using Abbeys, Cooksey, C, English Heritage, 1992*

It may be that teachers want to combine study of the site with another subject area, like English, Maths, or Technology. An exercise like writing new interpretation panels that are suitable for six year-olds requires not only a good knowledge of the site, but also draws on skills specified in the English curriculum (writing for a specified audience, using appropriate language). Very few abbeys have com-plete floors of tiles, but there is often the odd tile dotted about. Children can be asked to work out, by measuring and calculation, how many would be needed to cover the refectory floor. They can study the patterns on individual tiles and record them, or make up their own, inspired by decorative details from elsewhere on site, and plan the design of the floor. If the tiles are not square, more demanding work on tesselation might follow. They can use their designs to make their own tiles back in class. The techniques may not be the same as the ones used in medieval times, but they will get an idea of the effort originally involved in beautifying the abbey.

The National Curriculum requires children to look at ways in which history has been interpreted, investigating sources such as documents, history books, television programmes, and drama, for unintentional bias or deliberate distortion of facts. The interpretation schemes at many of the abbeys in the care of English Heritage feature artists' impressions of the site as it was when lived in. These can be used by teachers as an accessible, child-friendly source for investigating one way in which historical information is passed to us. The first step is for children to look closely to see what is still left of the building on which the artist has based the picture. The next is to see what evidence has been used to create the rest of the picture. Is there another building, or a feature like a window, on site which is in a more complete state and has been used as a reference? Where might the rest of the information have come from – another similar site, an archaeologist or historian who has worked here, a document relating to the site, or a book about abbeys? Does this fall into the catagory of fact or educated guesswork? Lastly, how far does the artist's style influence us? A gloomy, mist-laden scene with a few lean and hungry-looking monks being particularly miserable will convey a very different message from a picture containing a chubby, red-cheeked monk tending a sun-drenched garden. Is it better never to include pictures of people, or does that deny visitors information about how people who lived on site looked? Would the absence of people make the picture less appealing, and therefore perhaps less closely studied by the general visitor? Children can understand the dilemma here and make their own judgements whilst being aware of the bias involved.

Sites and schools are symbiotic. Schoolchildren benefit from site visits because, with preparation and thoughtful teacher guidance, they can begin to understand not only what the half walls and ruined doorways represent, but also what the complete building might have been like. This is important because with a well-reasoned framework the imagination can do its part in bringing the site to life, accompanied by the thrill of knowing that parts of what can be seen and touched now were also seen and touched by some long-robed figure several hundred years ago. On the other side of the equation, sites benefit from welcoming schoolchildren because familiarity and understanding have a good chance of generating respect and a feeling of responsibility. And that is the attitude which will ensure the future care of our ancient abbeys and other historic sites.

Bibliography

Cooksey C 1992, *A Teacher's Guide to Using Abbeys*, English Heritage

Staszewska L and Cocksedge H 1994, *A Teacher's Handbook to Castle Acre Priory and Castle*, English Heritage

English Heritage Education aims to help teachers at all levels make use of the resource of the historic environment. Educational groups can make free visits to over 400 sites managed by English Heritage. The following booklets are free on request: *Free Educational Visits* contains details of how to book, a list of all English Heritage properties and a booking form. *Making Successful Visits to Historic Sites* has ideas and activities for National Curriculum study. A catalogue, Resources, lists books and audio-visual material. Please contact:

English Heritage Education
Freepost 22 (WD214)
London W1E 7EZ.
Tel: 020 7973 3442
Fax: 020 7973 3443
www. HeritageEducation.net

Index

Aachen 107
Abbotsbury 60, **61**, 102
Abingdon 41, 55, 62, 63, 64, 66, 67, 68, 69, 70, 71, 73, 74, 101, 102, 103, 111, 112, 114, 124, 138, 143, 147, 148, 149
Accona 17
Acre 21, 22, 25, 32, 33
Aix-en-Provence 108
Alcantara 32
Alciston 76
Aldbury 173
Alfama 33
Alnwick 91
Alton Priors 67
Amesbury 122
Anglesey 187
Aragon 32, 107
Arbroath 118
Arbroath 16
Ardchattan 15
Arrouaise 31
Ashleworth **61**
Ashridge 34, 165, 166, 167, 168, 169, 170, 173
Assisi 33
Athelney 73
Aubazine 16, 32
Auxerre 109
Avignon 46, 107
Aviz 33
Axholme 28
Bapaume 19
Barcelona 33
Bardney 26
Barking 69, 93, 122, 123, 131
Barlings 91, 103
Barnack 103
Barton by Guiting 114
Barton-on-Humber 101
Basingwerk 100
Bath 123–124, 129, 130
Battenhall 76, 83
Battle 58, 64, 65, 66, 67, 69, 70, 72, 75, 76, 77, 78, 79, 80, 82, 91, 95, 103, 114, 115, 122, 124,130
Beaulieu **61**, 62, 63, 64, 65, 67, 69, 70, 75, 76, 77, 79, 80, 81, 82, 95, 97, 114, 130
Beaulieu St Leonards 60

Beauly 15
Beaume Lès Messieurs 11
Beauvais 109
Beauvale 28
Bec 58, 64
Bedlam 24
Beechwood 169, 173
Berkeley 110
Berkhamsted 171
Bermondsey 121
Berwick-upon-Tweed 167
Bicester 63, 143
Binsey 100
Blandinium 111
Boigny 32
Bolingbroke 95
Bologna 10, 20, 25, 32
Bolton 26, 59, 62, 63, 64, 69, 70, 72, 75, 79, 80, 82
Bordesley 2, 4, 5, 59, 67, 81, 105, 114, 148
Boroughbury 81
Boston 70, 95, 99, 130
Boxley 105, 114
Bradford-on-Avon 60, **61**
Bradwell 62
Brescia 35, 107
Breslau 24
Bridgnorth 131
Bridlington 26
Brioude 11
Bristol 62, 63, 65, 66, 79, 82, **91**, 99, 127, 129, 130
Broadwas 68
Broxbourne Bury 169
Buckfast 70, 80
Buckland 169
Burnham 122
Burton 124, 130
Bury St Edmunds 58, 73, 82, 112, 124, 129
Byland 5, 74, **78**, 102, 105, 113
Caceres 32
Caen 25, 108, 109
Calatrava 21, 22, 32
Calder 91
Callington 100
Camaldoli 11, 31
Cambridge 130

Cams Head 74
Canons Ashby 91
Canterbury 1, 4, 5, 6, 55, 56, 58, 64, 68, 69, 70, 72, 78, 89, 91, **92**, 95, 96, **97**, 101, 102, 103, 104, 110, 111, 112, 113, 114, 122, 129, 171
Carlisle 110
Carlton 59
Cartagena 34
Castile 107
Castle Acre 121
Castro Marino 34
Catterick 106
Cerfroid 22, 33
Chaalis 51
Chaise Dieu 31
Chalais 31
Châlons-sur-Marne 109
Chamalières 11
Chart 110, 114
Chartres 109, 110
Cheddar 82
Chelmsford 97, 130
Chelsea 66
Cheshunt 166, 167, 168
Chester 91, 93, 94, 100, 130
Chichester 131
Chingley 114
Cholsey 60, **61**
Christleton 100
Church Enstone **61**
Cirencester 106, 126, 129, 130
Cîteaux 12, 13, **16**, 31, 52, 94
Clairvaux 12, 13, **17**, 52, 178
Clamecy 24
Clarlieu 20, 33
Cleeve **105**, **117**
Clementhorpe 26
Cluny 10, 11, 23, 31, 110, 119, 120
Cockersand 58
Cogges 144
Coimbra 19, 32
Colchester 20, 106, 127, 130
Cologne 25
Combley 83
Conishead 126, 131
Corbie 112
Cordoba 109
Coutances 107

Coventry 2, 66, 131, 161–164
Coxwell **61**, 64
Coyroux 51
Cracow 22, 34
Crowland 26
Crowle 73, 76, 83
Croxden 187
Cumnor 143
Cyprus 32, 33, 71
Dartford 166, 167, 168
Daventry 99, 130
Dean Court 66, 67, 68, 69, 73, 74
Dean Moor 80
Denny 56, 67, 72, 103, 121, 169
Deventer 19
Dieulacres 106
Dijon 108
Dobrin 22, 33
Doddenham 68
Dolaucothi 106
Doncaster 79
Dorchester 94, 95, 106
Dorchester on Thames 143
Doulting **61**, 100
Dover 167
Drohiczyn 22
Dublin 25
Dupath Well 100
Durham 65, 66, 67, 69, 70, 71, 72, 74,
    75, 76, 80, 83, 91, 105, 113, 115, 124,
    129
Earl's Colne 124, 129
East Brent 67
Eastoft 59
Edington **92**
El Escorial 35
Eling 150
Elstow 116, 121
Elvas 107
Ely 5, 55, 68, 69, 73, 112
Etampes 109
Evesham 55, 59, 60, 68, 76, 129
Evora 33, 107
Exeter 112, 115, 129, 130, 131
Eye 66
Eynsham 2, 4, 62, 65, 116, 143, 144–
    147, 148, 149
Faversham 91, 103, 116
Fenouillet 34
Fishbourne 6
Fladbury 68
Flamstead 166, 167
Flanders 25
Fleet 74
Fleury 111
Florence 17, 34, 108
Fonte Avellana 11
Fontenay 180
Fontevrault 23, 31
Fontfroide 37, 45–50, 51, 52, 53, 113
Forde **118**
Fountains 5, 6, 26, 67, 78, 91, 93, 97, 99,

101, 102, 105, 114, 117, 165, 175–182
Fregionaria 19
Fréjus 108
Frocester **61**
Fulda 109
Furness 5, 58, 102, **104**
Fyvie 16
Garendon 6
Garthorpe 59
Garway 82
Ghent 35
Glastonbury 55, **59**, 60, **61**, 62, 63, 64,
    65, 67, 68, 69, 72, 73, 74, 82, 98, 103,
    105, 112, 116, 124–125, 129, 165
Glenluce 97, **98**
Gloucester 91, **92**, 93, **98**, 99, 113, **116**,
    129, 130
Godstow 122, 125, 129, 138
Gorhambury 169
Gorze 11, 31
Gosek 110
Granada 109
Grande-Sauve 21
Grandmont 11, 31
Grantham 91, 130
Grimley 66, 68, 76
Grimsby 130
Grosmont 28
Grotta Ferrata 31
Grove 62
Guisborough 5, 26, 95
Hailes **117**, 118
Halesowen 100
Hallow 69, 76, 83
Hampton 68
Hampton Court 6, 171
Hartpury **61**
Hastings 69
Haughmond **92**
Haverfordwest 5, 6, 103
Haverholme 91
Hazleton 89
Hempstead **92**, 93
Henwick 83
Hereford 66
Hertford 165, 166, 171, 172
Hexham 111, 126, 129
Higham 121, 125, 130
Hippo 88
Hitchin 166, 168, 169, 171, 172
Hitchingbroke 169
Hoddom 100
Holm Cultram 58
Holywell 100
Housesteads 106
Hull 28, 69, 72
Hulne 1, 137
Hulton 2, 183–191
Huntingdon 130
Hurdwick 64, 81
Hyde 66, 99
Jarrow 111, 112

Jedburgh 69
Jerusalem 19, 21, 22, 31, 32
Jervaulx 105
Kelso 16
Kenilworth 129
Kettering 83
Keynsham 83
Kilwinning 16
Kings Langley 130, 165, 166, 167, 168,
    173
Kings Lynn 130
Kingswood 89, 125–126, 130
Kirby Hall 6
Kirkham 26, 95
Kirkstall 5, 26, 62, 78, 80, 81, 99, 101,
    104, 114
Kirkwall 188
Knaresborough 28, 126, 131
Knebworth 169
Lacock 95, **118**, 122, 129, 169
La Chaise Dieu 11
La Ferté 12, 13, **16**, 52
La Grande Chartreuse 11, 31
La Rieunette **39**
Las Huelgas 51
Lastingham 26
Leicester 73, 75, 81, 82, 83, 106
Leigh **61**
Leith 23
Le Mans 107
Le Monastier sur Gazeille 11, **12**, **13**,
    33
Lenton 26
Lérins 111
Lesmahagaw 16
Le Thoronet **39**
Lewes 101, 102, 104, 115, 120
Lichfield 96, 129, 130, 185
Liège 21, 25
Lillechurch 125, 130
Limassol 21, 32
Lincoln 5, 95, 106, 129, 130, 131
Lindisfarne 110, 111
Lindores 16
Little Gaddesden 173
Little Marlow 104, 122
Llanthony 82, **92**, 93
Llantwit **61**
Loches 109,
London 23, 24, 33, 34, 65, 66, 70, 71,
    72, 81, 93, 94, 96, 97, 99, 122, 129,
    130, 131, 166, 167, 172
Lorches **112**
Loubigny 15
Louth Park 126, 131
Loxwell 94
Lucca 31
Lüttich 110
Lyon 46, 108, 111
Lys 51
Majorca 25
Malham 80, 99, 128, 129

Malmesbury 76, 129
Malta 21, 32
Malton 58
Margam 58
Marienburg 22, 33
Markyate 166, 167, 169, 171
Marley 82
Marseilles 25
Massangis 43
Maubuisson 42, 51
Mdina Azahara 109
Meare 69, 74, **75**
Meaux 5, 103, 126, 129
Mechelen 35
Mellifont **115**
Melrose 69, 104, 117
Mendip 82, 113
Merevale 60, 63, 64, 66, 69, 70, 79
Michelmersh 65
Middle Littleton **60**, **61**
Milan 20, 25, 35, 107, 108
Milton Abbas 167
Minchery Farm 144
Molesme 11
Monfrague 33
Monk Bretton 26, 105, 121, **195**
Monknash 6, **61**
Monkton Farleigh **92**
Monreal del Campo 31
Montbard 43
Monte Cassino 75, 88, 110, 112
Monte Fano 17, 34
Monte Morone 16, 34
Monte Senario 17, 34
Montemer-en-Lyons 113
Montesa 35
Montier-en-Der 109
Montpellier 10, 25, 32
Morella 107
Morimond 12, 13, **17**, 21, 22, 52
Mottisfont 169
Mount Carmel 33
Mount Grace 28, 60, 62, 66, 91, **92**, 93, 97, 102, 105, 114, 161, **163**, 164
Mount Olivet 17
Much Wenlock 115
Muchelney 63, 65, 68, 69, 73, 76, 91, 97, 122
Muret 11, 31
Naples 20, 25, 35, 111
Narbonne 34, 46
Navarre 107
Netley 169
Nettleden 166, 168
Newcastle upon Tyne 69
Newhouse Grange 60
Newsam 114
Newsham 26
Newstead 26, 28, 114, 169
Noirlac **39**
Northampton 130, 157
Norton 2, 4, 5, 6, 75, 76, 81, 83, 105, 146

Norwich 65
Nottingham 127, 130
Noyon 109
Nuits St George 12
Nun Monkton 26
Nuneaton 63, 101, 121
Nursling 150
Old Warden 74
Old Windsor 114
Orléans 25
Oseney 59, 64, 125, 129, 130, 138, 139, **140**, 147
Ospringe 20
Owston 74
Oxford 10, 25, 66, 67, 68, 70, 73, 75, 76, 77, 81, 82, 83, 100, 112, 113, 125, 128, 129, 137, 138–139, **141**, **142**, 143, 144, 147, 148, 149
Panborough **68**
Paola 35
Paris 10, 19, 22, 25, 31, 33, 110
Parma 25
Patach 18, 34
Pavia 24, 107
Pedrosa 35
Pereiro 22, 32
Pershore 55, 129
Perugia 107
Peterborough 55, 56, 62, 68, 69, 70, 71, 72, 73, 74, 75, 76, 77, 78, 79, 81, 83, 116
Pilton **61**
Pinwall Grange 79
Pisa 108
Pisilia 18, 34
Pluscarden 15, 70
Poblet 45
Poitiers 25, 108
Polesworth 121
Polsloe 56, 91, 97
Pontefract 26, 79, 131
Pontigny 12, 13, **16**, 37, 40–45, 50, 51, 52, 53
Portchester 4
Portsmouth 73
Potterne 101
Prague 24, 34
Prémontré 32
Priors Barton 81
Prüm 109
Quarr 69, 83
Ramsey 55, 58, 63, 64, 73, 78, 81, 103, 111, 112
Ravenna 107, 108
Reading 95, 131, 159
Redbourn 165, 169
Regensburg 110
Reichenau 112
Reigate 20
Reims 25, 109
Rennes 69
Repton 101

Rewley 138, 139, 140, 147, 148
Rhodes 21, 32
Richmond 131
Rickmansworth 166
Rievaulx 2, 5, 6, 26, 60, 103, **117**, 137, 165, 180
Riga 33
Ripple 69
Roche 167
Rochester 76, 167
Rome 20, 21, 23, 25, 32, 35, 106, 110, 111, 112, 187
Romney Marsh 64
Romsey 122, 150–160
Rouen 69, 108
Rowney 165, 168
Royaumont 42, 51, 52
Royston 166, 167, 169, 171
Roystone Grange 6
St Agatha 21
St Albans 4, 56, 68, 78, 110, 112, 165, 166, 167, 170, 171, 172
St Amour 34
St Benoît-sur-Loire 109
St Bertin 109
St Denis 112
St Gall 1, 65, 101, 109
St Germain-des-Prés 109
St Germans 100
St Mary de Pré 165, 168
St Neot's 63
St Paul's 165
St Pierre-de-Lobbes 109
St Ruf 19, 31
Salvatierra 22, 32
San Frediano 18
Sandwell 2, 5
Sandwich 69
Santiago 22, 34
Savigny 16, 32
Sawley 73
Sawtry 103
Scarborough 99, 130
Scilly Isles 83
Sedlescombe 114
Segovia 107
Selby 26, 59, 62, 63, 64, 66, 69, 70, 71, 72, 73, 75, 76, 77, 79, 81, 83
Selkirk 16
Sempringham 19, 26, 32
Senlis 109
Sens 109
Seville 109
Shaftesbury 60, 122
Shap 105
Sheen 17, 130, 131
Sherborne 12, **116**
Shilton **61**
Shippon **61**
Shouldham 6
Sibton 58, 63, 64, 66, 70, 71, 72, 73, 75, 77, 79, 81, 82

Siena 107
Silkstead 67
Somascha 35
Sopwell 166, 167, 169, 170, 171
South Shields 106
South Witham 60, 63, 80
Southampton 73, 82, 91, 99, 130, 150
Southwick 73
Sowy 67
Spalding 26
Spoleto 107
Stafford 127–128, 130
Stallingborough 59
Stamford 129, 131
Standon 165, 169, 172
Stanley **94**, 129
Stoke Bishop 110
Stoke-on-Trent 188
Stourbridge 72
Stow 144
Strata Marcella 105
Strood 66
Sudbury 130
Sutton Courtenay 112
Swalcliffe 144
Tadmarton **61**, 112
Tamworth 114
Taunton 73, 93, 129, 130
Tavistock 55, 58, 64, 78, 81, 82, 83
Temple Dinsley 165
Terrassa 108
The Biggin 168,169
Thele 165
Thetford **83**, 95, 104, 120, 157
Thines 11
Thomar 34
Thorney 68, 73
Thornholme 26, 60, 62, 63, 95, 176
Thorpe Willoughby 83
Thurgarton 126, 129
Tintern 63, 82, **104**, **105**, **117**

Tiron 16, 31
Tisbury **61**
Titchfield 74, 82, 169
Toledo 109
Tonnerre 12
Torre **61**
Toul 11
Toulouse 33, 34
Tournai 25
Trier 11
Trujillo 32
Tupholme 103
Tutbury 183
Tyre 32
Ucles 22, 32
Uden 21
Ulcio 19, 31
Vadstena 35
Val Croissant 15
Val de Choux 10, 15, 33
Valencia 25
Valle Crucis **92**
Vallombrosa 11, 31
Valmagne **47**
Vauclair 178, **179**
Venasque 108
Venice 20, 22, 25, 33, 35
Vercelli 33
Verulamium 106
Vienne 31, 107
Villefranche 25
Villiers-la-Grange **41**, **42**
Vivarium 101, 109, 112
Viviers 108
Wallingford 144
Walmley 95
Waltham 63, 70, 76, 80, 91, 95, 96, 97, 99, 113, 126–127, 129
Ware 165, 166, 167, 172
Warter 129
Washford 74

Waterbeach 121
Watton 26
Waverley 63, 78, 95, 97, 117, 129
Wearmouth 111, 112
Wells 99, 129, 131
Werrington 81
West Bradley **61**
West Dereham 6
Westbury 69
Westminster 55, 56, 62, 65, 66, 67, 68, 71, 72, 73, 76, 77, 78, 80, 81, 83, 97, 99, 105,114, 129, 165
Whalley **117**
Whaplode 20
Wherwell 122
Whitby 26, 111
Whithorn 6, 110
Wigmore 89
Wilton 62, 64, 75, 76, 77, 79, 82, 122
Winchcombe 91, 129
Winchelsea 69
Winchester 33, 56, 65, 66, 67, 68, 69, 70, 71, 72, 73, 74, **77**, 78, 80, 81, 82, 112
Windesheim 19, 35
Windsor 166, 168
Wissembourg 109
Witham 82
Woodspring 91
Wookey 74
Worcester 55, 66, 67, 68, 74, 83, 93, 95, 113, 122, 130
Worksop 26
Wroxeter 106
Wroxton 144
Wye 64
Wymondley 165, 166, 167, 169, 172
York 7, 26, 66, 69, 71, 72, 73 106, 112, 113
Zaragoza 25
Zwettl 42